ILEC	incumbent local exchange carrier
IMAP	Internet Mail Access Protocol
INTERNIC	Internet Network Information Center
IP	Internetworking Protocol
IPng	Internetworking Protocol, next generation
IPSec	IP Security
IPv6	Internetworking Protocol, version 6
IRTF	Internet Research Task Force
ISO	International Organization for Standardization
ISOC	Internet Society
ISP	Internet service provider
ITU-T	International Telecommunications Union-Telecommunication Standardization Sector
IXC	interexchange carrier
LAN	local area network
LAN	mixed architecture
LANE	LAN emulation
LATA	Local Access and Transport Area
LEC	local exchange carrier
LF	low frequency
LLC	logical link control
LRC	longitudinal redundancy check
MA	multiple access
MAC	medium access control
MAN	metropolitan area network
MF	middle frequency
MIB	management information base
MIME	Multipurpose Internet Mail Extension
MTA	mail transfer agent
MTU	maximum transfer unit

NAK	negative acknowledgment
NAP	Network Access Point
NAT	network address translation
NDLC	network development life cycle
NIC	Network Information Center
NIC	network interface card
NOS	network operating system
NSP	national service provider
NVT	network virtual terminal
OSI	Open Systems Interconnection
OSPF	Open Shortest Path First
PCM	pulse code modulation
PGP	Pretty Good Privacy
POP	point of presence
POP3	Post Office Protocol, version 3
PSK	phase shift keying
RARP	Reverse Address Resolution Protocol
RF	radio frequency
RFC	Request for Comment
RIP	Routing Information Protocol
SDLC	system development life cycle
SHF	superhigh frequency
SMI	Structure of Management Information
SMTP	Simple Mail Transfer Protocol
SNMP	Simple Network Management Protocol
SONET	synchronous optical network
STP	shielded twisted-pair
TCP	Transmission Control Protocol
TCP/IP	Transmission Control Protocol/ Internetworking Protocol

IMPORTANT:

HERE IS YOUR REGISTRATION CODE TO ACCESS
YOUR PREMIUM McGRAW-HILL ONLINE RESOURCES.

Registering for McGraw-Hill Online Resources

TO gain access to your McGraw-Hill web resources simply follow the steps below:

1. USE YOUR WEB BROWSER TO GO TO: **http://highered.mcgraw-hill.com/sites/0072397020/**
2. CLICK ON **FIRST TIME USER**.
3. ENTER THE REGISTRATION CODE* PRINTED ON THE TEAR-OFF BOOKMARK ON THE RIGHT.
4. AFTER YOU HAVE ENTERED YOUR REGISTRATION CODE, CLICK **REGISTER**.
5. FOLLOW THE INSTRUCTIONS TO SET-UP YOUR PERSONAL UserID AND PASSWORD.
6. WRITE YOUR UserID AND PASSWORD DOWN FOR FUTURE REFERENCE.
   KEEP IT IN A SAFE PLACE.

TO GAIN ACCESS to the McGraw-Hill content in your instructor's **WebCT** or **Blackboard** course simply log in to the course with the UserID and Password provided by your instructor. Enter the registration code exactly as it appears in the box to the right when prompted by the system. You will only need to use the code the first time you click on McGraw-Hill content.

Thank you, and welcome to your McGraw-Hill online Resources!

Mc Graw Hill **Higher Education**

*YOUR REGISTRATION CODE CAN BE USED ONLY ONCE TO ESTABLISH ACCESS. IT IS NOT TRANSFERABLE.

0-07-239702-0 FOROUZAN, BUSINESS DATA COMMUNICATIONS

MCGRAW-HILL
ONLINE RESOURCES

REGISTRATION CODE

repression-38240356

Mc Graw Hill **Higher Education**

BUSINESS DATA COMMUNICATIONS

McGraw-Hill Forouzan Networking Series

Titles by Behrouz A. Forouzan:

Data Communications and Networking
TCP/IP Protocol Suite
Local Area Networks
Business Data Communications

BUSINESS DATA COMMUNICATIONS

Behrouz A. Forouzan
DeAnza College

with

Sophia Chung Fegan

Boston   Burr Ridge, IL   Dubuque, IA   Madison, WI   New York   San Francisco   St. Louis
Bangkok   Bogotá   Caracas   Kuala Lumpur   Lisbon   London   Madrid   Mexico City
Milan   Montreal   New Delhi   Santiago   Seoul   Singapore   Sydney   Taipei   Toronto

McGraw-Hill Higher Education

*A Division of The **McGraw-Hill** Companies*

BUSINESS DATA COMMUNICATIONS

Published by McGraw-Hill, a business unit of The McGraw-Hill Companies, Inc., 1221 Avenue of the Americas, New York, NY 10020. Copyright © 2003 by The McGraw-Hill Companies, Inc.

Some ancillaries, including electronic and print components, may not be available to customers outside the United States.

This book is printed on acid-free paper.

International   1 2 3 4 5 6 7 8 9 0 QPF/QPF 0 9 8 7 6 5 4 3 2
Domestic   1 2 3 4 5 6 7 8 9 0 QPF/QPF 0 9 8 7 6 5 4 3 2

ISBN 0–07–239702–0
ISBN 0–07–112194–3 (ISE)

Publisher: *Elizabeth A. Jones*
Senior developmental editor: *Emily J. Lupash*
Executive marketing manager: *John Wannemacher*
Project manager: *Sheila M. Frank*
Production supervisor: *Kara Kudronowicz*
Media project manager: *Jodi K. Banowetz*
Senior media technology producer: *Phillip Meek*
Coordinator of freelance design: *Rick D. Noel*
Cover designer: *Ellen Pettengell*
Cover image: *©Eyewire, Image #E09928, Charles River with rowing team, Boston beyond*
Compositor: *Interactive Composition Corporation*
Typeface: *10/12 Times Roman*
Printer: *Quebecor World Fairfield, PA*

Library of Congress Cataloging-in-Publication Data

Forouzan, Behrouz A.
   Business data communications / Behrouz A. Forouzan. — 1st ed.
     p. cm. — (McGraw-Hill Forouzan networking series)
   Includes bibliographical references and index.
   ISBN 0–07–239702–0 — ISBN 0–07–112194–3 (ISE)
   1. Business enterprises--Computer networks. I. Title. II. Series.

HD30.37 .F673   2003
004.6—dc21   2002026444
                                           CIP

www.mhhe.com

To Firouz and Elahe

———————————————

—Behrouz Forouzan

BRIEF TABLE OF CONTENTS

CONTENTS

Part IV   **Security and Management**

Chapter 14   **Network Security: Firewalls and VPNs   303**

Chapter 15   **Network Analysis, Design, and Implementation   321**

PREFACE

Data communications and networking may be the fastest growing fields in our culture today. One of the ramifications of this growth is a dramatic increase in the number of professions where an understanding of these technologies is essential for success—and a proportionate increase in the number and types of students taking courses to learn about them. In today's world, the business student needs to understand the concepts and mechanisms underlying data communications and networking.

STRUCTURE OF THE BOOK

This text is designed to make it particularly easy for students to understand data communications and networking. We have used the five-layer Internet model as the framework for the text. We have used a top-down approach, discussing the fifth layer first and the first layer last, to make it more relevant for business students who often look at the big picture before focusing on the physical details.

This text is designed for business students with little or no background in data communications. Again, the top-down approach is more appropriate. Students learn first about the applications before learning about the physical networks. The book is divided into four parts.

Part I: Data Communications Basics

The first eight chapters of the book introduce the basics of data communications. Chapter 1 is an introduction. Chapters 2 to 6 discuss the five layers of the Internet model. Chapter 7 is devoted to transmission media (traditionally called layer zero). Chapter 8 introduces telephone and cable networks, an essential part of data communications.

Part II: LAN and WAN Technology

The second part of the book takes the concepts and protocols defined in the first part to introduce the technologies used by local area and wide area networks. Chapters 9 and 10 are devoted to LANs and Chapter 11 is devoted to WANs.

Part III: Internetworking and Internet

The third part of the book discusses two important issues. Chapter 12 shows how to connect LANs and WANs to create backbone networks and internetworks. Chapter 13 explores three concepts: internets, intranets, and extranets.

Part IV: Security and Management

The last part of the book has three chapters that tie data communications and networking to management. Chapter 14 discusses network security and virtual private networks (VPNs), a method to provide security for an organization. Chapter 15 introduces network design, which is an ongoing process in today's networks. Chapter 16 discusses network management.

FEATURES OF THE BOOK

Several features of the book are designed with the business student in mind.

Start of Each Chapter

Each chapter begins with a short summary of the chapter contents. This is followed by a bulleted list of objectives that gives the students a preview of the important concepts to be learned.

Visual Approach

The book presents highly technical matter without complex formulas by using a balance of text and figures. The approximately 200 figures accompanying the text provide a visual and intuitive opportunity for understanding the material. Figures are particularly important in explaining networking concepts, which are based on connections and transmissions. They are both often more easily grasped visually than verbally.

Highlighted Points

We have repeated important concepts in boxes for quick reference and immediate attention.

Business Focus

Business focus sections are networking and data communications concepts that are particularly relevant to the business world. Some contain interesting bits of data communications and networking history.

Technical Focus

In the technical focus sections we provide further information about the concepts just discussed.

Examples and Applications

Whenever appropriate, we have included examples that illustrate the concepts introduced in the text.

Cumulative Case Study

A case study follows a fictional company and its data communications and networking problems and solutions.

Summary

Each chapter ends with a bulleted summary of the materials covered in the chapter. The summary is a brief overview of all the important points in the chapter.

Key Terms

Each chapter includes a list of key terms used throughout the chapter. The definition of each term is provided in the glossary at the end of the book.

Practice Set

Each chapter includes a practice set designed to reinforce salient concepts and to encourage students to apply them. It consists of two parts: review questions and multiple-choice questions. Review questions are intended to test students for their basic understanding of the materials presented in the chapter. Multiple-choice questions test students' grasp of concepts and terminology.

Appendixes

The appendixes are intended to provide quick reference material or a review of materials as needed to understand the concepts discussed in the book.

Glossary

The book contains an extensive glossary.

Acronyms

An alphabetical list of acronyms appears on the endpapers of the text.

Online Supplementary Materials

Online Learning Center at www.mhhe.com/forouzan

- ❑ PowerPoints: Four-color slides, including figures from the book and lecture notes, are a great resource for instructors and students alike.
- ❑ Solutions: A complete set of solutions is password protected and available only to instructors. The solutions to odd-numbered exercises are made available to students to promote self-study.
- ❑ Animations of selected figures from the book are available to help networking concepts come to life. You can watch as the diagrams actively demonstrate their concepts.

❏ Additional Online Case Studies are available, giving students additional opportunity to think about applying concepts in the real world.

❏ PageOut: PageOut is an exclusive McGraw-Hill product that makes it easy to create a website for your networking course. It requires no prior knowledge of HTML, no long hours, and no design skills on your part. Instead PageOut offers a series of templates. Simply fill them in with your course information and click on one of 16 designs. This short process leaves you with a professionally designed website.

Instructor Section

❏ Solutions to all questions
❏ PowerPoint presentations
❏ Animations
❏ Test banks

Student Section

❏ Solutions to all odd-numbered questions
❏ Quizzes

How To Use The Book

This text is for those individuals whose primary area of interest is business. The text is suitable for both an academic and a professional audience. The book can be used as a self-study guide for interested professionals. As a textbook, it can be used for a one-semester or one-quarter course.

Acknowledgement

It is obvious that the development of a book of this scope needs the support of many people. The most important contribution comes from peer reviews. We cannot express our gratitude in words for the many reviewers who spent numerous hours reading the manuscripts and providing us with helpful comments and ideas. We would especially like to acknowledge the contributions of the following reviewers:

Anthony Cantarella, *Murray State University*
Gregory Stefanelli, *Carroll Community College*
Judy Wynekoop, *Florida Gulf Coast University*
Jan L. Harrington, *Marist College*
Nilkantan Nagarajan, *University of Maryland, University College*
John Eatman, *University of North Carolina, Greensboro*
J. Stephanie College, *Southern New Hampshire University*
Joe Baxter, *Dalton State College*
Kenneth M. Griffin, *University of Central Arkansas*
Marcos S. Pinto, *Baruch College*
Don Chrusciel, *Iowa State University*
E. Sonny Butler, *Eastern Kentucky University*
Thomas P. Cavaiani, *Boise State University*

Special thanks go to the staff of McGraw-Hill. The idea for the book came from our publisher, Betsy Jones. Emily Lupash, our senior developmental editor, gave us help and guidance when needed; without her the project would never have materialized. Sheila Frank, our project manager, guided us through the production process with enormous enthusiasm and encouragement. We also thank Rick Noel in design, Sherry Kane in production, John Leland in photo research, and Barbara Somogyi the copy editor.

Trademark Notices

Throughout the text we have used several trademarks. Rather than insert a trademark symbol with each mention of the trademarked name, we acknowledge the trademarks here and state that they are used with no intention of infringement. Other product names, trademarks, and registered trademarks are the property of their respective owners.

- ❏ Apple, AppleTalk, EtherTalk, LocalTalk, TokenTalk, and Macintosh are registered trademarks of Apple Computer, Inc.
- ❏ Bell and StarLan are registered trademarks of AT&T.
- ❏ DEC, DECnet, VAX, and DNA are trademarks of Digital Equipment Corp.
- ❏ IBM, SDLC, SNA, and IBM PC are registered trademarks of International Business Machine Corp.
- ❏ Novell, Netware, IPX, and SPX are registered trademarks of Novell, Inc.
- ❏ Network File System and NFS are registered trademarks of Sun Microsystems, Inc.
- ❏ PostScript is a registered trademark of Adobe Systems, Inc.
- ❏ UNIX is a registered trademark of UNIX System Laboratories, Inc., a wholly owned subsidiary of Novell, Inc.
- ❏ Xerox is a trademark and Ethernet is a registered trademark of Xerox Corp.

PART I

Data Communications Basics

CHAPTER 1

Introduction

Data communications are changing the way we do business. Business decisions have to be made ever more quickly, and the decision makers require immediate access to accurate information. Why wait a week for that report from Germany to arrive by mail when it could appear almost instantaneously through computer networks? Businesses today rely on computer networks and internetworks. But before we ask how quickly we can get hooked up, we need to know how networks operate, what types of technologies are available, and which design best fills which set of needs.

This chapter addresses four issues: data communications, networks, protocols and standards, and standards organizations. First, we give a broad definition of data communications. We then define networks as a highway on which data can travel. We also discuss different types of protocols and the difference between protocols and standards. Then, we give a brief review of the standards organizations that we refer to throughout the book. Finally, we discuss network models.

OBJECTIVES

After reading this chapter, the reader should be able to:

- Understand the difference between telecommunications and data communications.
- List the components of a data communications system.
- Understand the need for a network and distinguish between different network types.
- Understand the difference between a protocol and a standard.

- Be familiar with standards organizations and their duties.
- Understand the duties of the layers in the OSI model.
- Understand the duties of the layers in the Internet model.
- Be able to compare the layers in the OSI and Internet model.

1.1 DATA COMMUNICATIONS

When we communicate, we are sharing information. This sharing can be local or remote. Between individuals, local communication usually occurs face to face, while remote communication takes place over distance. The term **telecommunication,** which includes telephony, telegraphy, and television, means communication at a distance (*tele* is Greek for far).

The word **data** refers to facts, concepts, and instructions presented in whatever form is agreed upon by the parties creating and using the data. In the context of computer information systems, data are represented by binary information units or bits (BInary digiT) produced and consumed in the form of 0s and 1s.

In computer information systems, data are represented by binary information units (or bits) produced and consumed in the form of 0s and 1s.

Data communications is the exchange of data (in the form of 0s and 1s) between two devices via some form of transmission medium such as a wire cable. Usually, the communication is considered local if the communicating devices are in the same building or a similarly restricted geographical area; the communication is remote if the devices are farther apart.

For data communication to occur, the communicating devices must be part of a communication system made up of a combination of hardware (physical equipment) and software (programs). The effectiveness of a data communications system depends on three fundamental characteristics:

1. **Delivery.** The system must deliver data to the correct destination. Data must be received by the intended device or user and only by that device or user.
2. **Accuracy.** The system must deliver the data accurately. Data that have been altered in transmission and left uncorrected are unusable.
3. **Timeliness.** The system must deliver data in a timely manner. Data delivered late are useless. In the case of video, audio, and voice data, timely delivery means delivering data as they are produced, in the same order that they are produced, and without significant delay. This kind of delivery is called *real-time* transmission.

COMPONENTS

A data communications system has five components (see Figure 1.1).

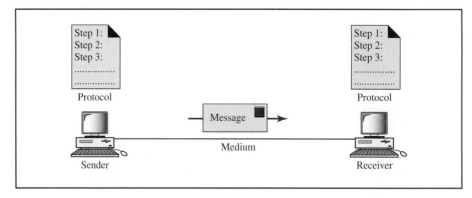

Figure 1.1   Data communications system components

1. **Message.** The **message** is the information (data) to be communicated. It can consist of text, numbers, pictures, sound, or video—or any combination of these.
2. **Sender.** The **sender** is the device that sends the data message. It can be a computer, workstation, telephone handset, video camera, and so on.
3. **Receiver.** The **receiver** is the device that receives the message. It can be a computer, workstation, telephone handset, television, and so on.
4. **Medium.** The **transmission medium** is the physical path by which a message travels from sender to receiver. It could be a twisted-pair wire, coaxial cable, fiber-optic cable, laser, or radio waves (terrestrial or satellite microwave).
5. **Protocol.** A **protocol** is a set of rules that governs data communications. It represents an agreement between the communicating devices. Without a protocol, two devices may be connected but not communicating, just as a person speaking French cannot be understood by a person who speaks only Japanese.

In data communications, a protocol is a set of rules (conventions) that governs all aspects of information communication.

1.2 NETWORKS

A **network** is a set of devices (often referred to as *nodes*) connected by media links. A node can be a computer, printer, or any other device capable of sending and/or receiving data generated by other nodes on the network. The links connecting the devices are often called communication *channels*.

DISTRIBUTED PROCESSING

Most networks use **distributed processing,** in which a task is divided among multiple computers. Instead of a single large machine being responsible for all aspects of a process, separate computers (usually a personal computer or workstation) handle a subset. Features of distributed processing include the following:

❏ **Security.** Access to the system is often controlled by a combination of specific codes such as account number and PIN (personal identification number).
❏ **Distributed databases.** No one system needs to provide storage capacity for the entire database. A distributed database is a database in which the data are stored and manipulated on more than one computer; the database itself is a union of all its parts.
❏ **Faster problem solving.** Multiple computers working on parts of a problem concurrently can often solve a problem faster than a single machine working alone. For example, networks of PCs have broken encryption codes that were previously assumed to be unbreakable (on a single computer).
❏ **Fault tolerance through redundancy.** Multiple computers running the same program at the same time can provide fault tolerance through redundancy. For example, in the space shuttle, three computers can run the same program so that a hardware error on one computer can be compensated by the other two.
❏ **Collaborative processing.** Both multiple computers and multiple users may interact on a task. For example, in multiuser network games the actions of each player are visible to and affect all the others.

NETWORK CRITERIA

A network must be able to meet a certain number of criteria. The most important of these are performance, reliability, and security (see Figure 1.2).

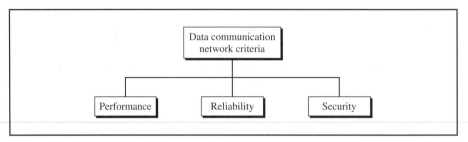

Figure 1.2   Network criteria

Performance

Performance can be measured in many ways, including transit time and response time. Transit time is the amount of time required for a message to travel from one device to another. Response time is the elapsed time between an inquiry and a response.

The performance of a network depends on a number of factors, including the number of users, the type of transmission medium, the capabilities of the connected hardware, and the efficiency of the software.

❏ **Number of users.** Having a large number of concurrent users can slow response time in a network not designed to handle heavy traffic loads. An assessment of the average number of users that will be communicating at any one time is a factor in network design. In peak load periods, the actual number of users can exceed the average and thereby decrease performance. How a network responds to loading is a measure of its performance.

❏ **Type of transmission medium.** The medium defines the speed (data rate) at which data can travel through a connection. Today's networks are moving to faster and faster transmission media. For example, 10BASE-T Ethernet has a data rate of 10 Mbps while the increasingly popular 100BASE-T network can move data 10 times faster. The upper bound on the data rate is the speed of light.

❏ **Hardware.** The types of hardware included in a network affect both the speed and capacity of transmission. For example, an Intel Pentium processor with a high speed can process data faster than the previous processor in the family.

❏ **Software.** The software used to process data at the sender, receiver, and intermediate nodes also affects network performance. Moving a message from node to node through a network requires processing to transform the raw data into transmittable signals, to route these signals to the proper destination, to ensure error-free delivery, and to recast the signals into a form the receiver can use. The software that provides these services affects both the speed and the reliability of a network link.

❏ **Throughput.** The throughput is the measurement of how fast data can pass through a point.

Reliability

In addition to accuracy of delivery, network **reliability** is measured by frequency of failure, the time it takes a link to recover from a failure, and the network's robustness in a catastrophe.

- ❑ **Frequency of failure.** This is defined as the number of times a network fails in a specified period of time.
- ❑ **Recovery time of a network after a failure.** This is defined as the time it takes to restore service.
- ❑ **Catastrophe.** Networks must be protected from catastrophic events such as fire, earthquake, or theft. One protection against unforeseen damage is a reliable system to back up network software.

Security

Network **security** issues include protecting data from unauthorized access and viruses.

- ❑ **Unauthorized access.** A network needs to protect sensitive data from unauthorized access. Protection can be accomplished at a number of levels. At the lowest level are user identification codes and passwords. At a higher level are encryption techniques in which data are systematically altered in such a way that they are unintelligible to an unauthorized user.
- ❑ **Viruses.** Because a network is accessible from many points, it can be susceptible to computer viruses. A virus is an illicitly introduced code that usually damages the system. A good network is protected from viruses by specially designed hardware and software.

TYPE OF NETWORKS

Today when we speak of networks, we are generally referring to three primary categories: local area networks (LANs), metropolitan area networks (MANs), and wide area networks (WANs). The category a network falls into is determined by its size, its ownership, the distance it covers, and its physical architecture. We discuss these networks in detail in later chapters and give just a brief discussion of each here.

Local Area Network (LAN)

A **local area network** is usually privately owned and links the devices in a single office, building, or campus (see Figure 1.3). Depending on the needs of an organization and the type of technology used, a LAN can be as simple as two PCs and a printer in someone's home office, or it can extend throughout a company and include voice, sound, and video peripherals. Currently, LAN size is limited to a couple of miles.

LANs are designed to allow resources to be shared between personal computers or workstations. The resources to be shared can include hardware (e.g., a printer), software (e.g., an application program), or data. A common example of a LAN, found in many business environments, links a work group of task-related computers, for example, engineering workstations or accounting PCs. One of the computers may be given a large-capacity disk drive and become a server to the other clients. Software can be stored on this central server and used as needed by the whole group. In this example, the size of the LAN may be determined by licensing restrictions on the number of users per copy of software, or by restrictions on the number of users licensed to access the operating system.

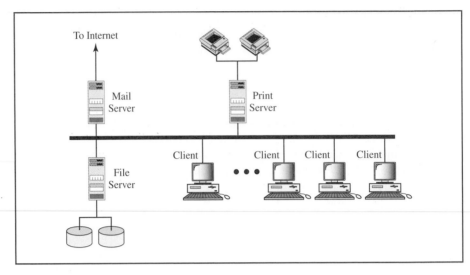

Figure 1.3   LAN

Metropolitan Area Network (MAN)

A **metropolitan area network** is designed to extend over an entire city. It may be a single network such as a cable television network, or it may be a means of connecting a number of LANs into a larger network so that resources may be shared LAN-to-LAN as well as device-to-device. For example, a company can use a MAN to connect the LANs in all of its offices throughout a city (see Figure 1.4).

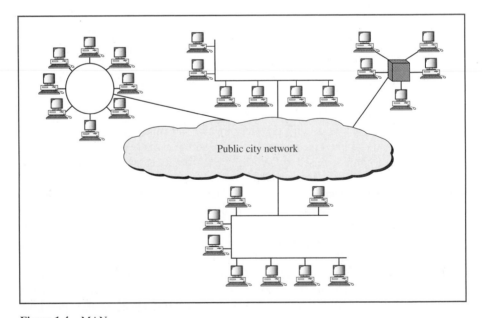

Figure 1.4   MAN

Wide Area Network (WAN)

A **wide area network** provides long-distance transmission of data, voice, image, and video information over large geographical areas that may comprise a country, a continent, or even the whole world (see Figure 1.5).

Figure 1.5   WAN

In contrast to LANs (which depend on their own hardware for transmission), WANs may utilize public, leased, or private communication devices, usually in combination, and can therefore span an unlimited number of miles.

Internetworks

When two or more networks are connected, they become an **internetwork,** or internet. Individual networks are joined into internetworks by the use of routers. We discuss routers in Chapter 12. The term *internet* (lowercase i) should not be confused with *the* **Internet** (uppercase I). The first is a generic term used to mean an interconnection of networks. The second is the name of a specific worldwide network. Figure 1.6 shows an internet. We discuss the Internet (the global internet) in Chapter 13.

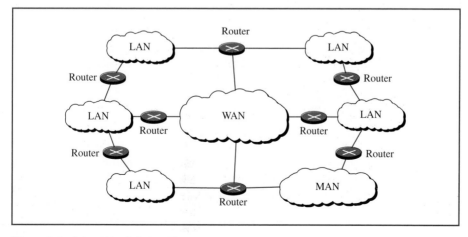

Figure 1.6   Internetwork (internet)

TECHNICAL FOCUS: REPRESENTING INFORMATION

ormation stored inside the computer consists of only two symbols: 0 and 1. This is cause the memory of the computer is made of electronic switches that are either on off. When the switch is off, it stores a 0; when the switch is on, it stores a 1.

This means that any type of information must be represented as a sequence of 0s ind 1s for storage inside the computer. Because data communications is the process of moving information from one computer to another, data communications also uses 0s and 1s to represent information.

In future chapters we show how different types of information such as text, numbers, audio, and video are represented using only these two symbols (0 and 1).

1.3 PROTOCOLS AND STANDARDS

Two terms are often heard in data communications and networking: protocols and standards.

PROTOCOLS

In computer networks, communication occurs between entities in different systems. We define an entity as anything capable of sending or receiving information. Examples include application programs, file transfer packages, browsers, database management systems, and electronic mail software. A system is a physical object that contains one or more entities. Examples include computers and terminals.

But two entities cannot just send bit streams (sequences of 0s and 1s) to each other and expect to be understood. For communication to occur, the entities must agree on a protocol. As defined on page 3, a protocol is a set of rules that governs data communications. A protocol defines what is communicated, how it is communicated, and when it is communicated. The key elements of a protocol are *syntax, semantics,* and *timing*.

Syntax

Syntax refers to the structure or format of the data, meaning the order in which they are presented. For example, a simple protocol might expect the first 8 bits of data to be the address of the sender, the second 8 bits to be the address of the receiver, and the rest of the stream to be the message itself.

Semantics

Semantics refers to the meaning of each section of bits. How is a particular pattern to be interpreted, and what action is to be taken based on that interpretation? For example, does an address identify the route to be taken or the final destination of the message?

Timing

Timing refers to two characteristics: when data should be sent and how fast they can be sent. For example, if a sender transmits data at 100 Mbps but the receiver can receive data at only 1 Mbps, the transmission will overload the receiver and data will be largely lost.

STANDARDS

With so many factors to synchronize, a great deal of coordination across the nodes of a network is necessary if communication is to occur at all, let alone accurately or efficiently. A single manufacturer can build all of its products to work well together, but what if some of the best components for your needs are not made by the same company? What good is a television that can pick up only one set of signals if local stations are broadcasting another? Where there are no **standards,** difficulties arise. Automobiles are an example of nonstandardized products. A steering wheel from one make or model of car will not fit into another model without modification. A standard provides a model for development that makes it possible for a product to work regardless of the individual manufacturer.

Standards are essential in creating and maintaining an open and competitive market for equipment manufacturers and in guaranteeing national and international interoperability of data and telecommunications technology and processes. They provide guidelines to manufacturers, vendors, government agencies, and other service providers to ensure the kind of interconnectivity necessary in today's marketplace and in international communications.

Poorly thought-out standards can slow development by forcing adherence to early, possibly inflexible, designs. But today pragmatism and consumer pressure have forced the industry to recognize the need for general models, and there is growing agreement as to what those models are. The intelligence and foresight of designers seem to be such that the standards now being adopted will encourage rather than hinder technical advancement.

Data communications standards fall into two categories: *de facto* (meaning by fact or by convention) and *de jure* (meaning by law or by regulation). See Figure 1.7.

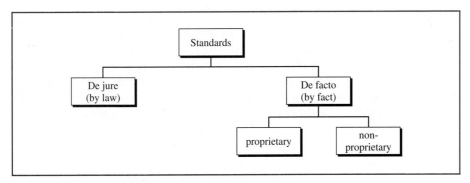

Figure 1.7 Categories of standards

De jure standards are those that have been legislated by an officially recognized body. Standards that have not been approved by an organized body but have been adopted as standards through widespread use are de facto standards. De facto standards are often established originally by manufacturers seeking to define the functionality of a new product or technology.

De facto standards can be further subdivided into two classes: *proprietary* and *nonproprietary*. Proprietary standards are those originally invented by a commercial organization as a basis for the operation of its products. They are called proprietary because they are wholly owned by the company that invented them. These standards are also called *closed* standards because they close off communications between systems produced by different vendors. Nonproprietary standards are those originally developed by groups or committees that have passed them into the public domain; they are also called *open* standards because they open communications between different systems.

1.4 STANDARDS ORGANIZATIONS

Standards are developed by cooperation among standards creation committees, forums, and government regulatory agencies.

STANDARDS CREATION COMMITTEES

While many organizations are dedicated to the establishment of standards, data and telecommunications in North America rely primarily on those published by the following:

- ❏ The International Organization for Standardization (ISO).
- ❏ The International Telecommunications Union–Telecommunication Standards Sector (ITU-T, formerly the CCITT).
- ❏ The American National Standards Institute (ANSI).
- ❏ The Institute of Electrical and Electronics Engineers (IEEE).
- ❏ The Electronic Industries Association (EIA).

FORUMS

Telecommunications technology development is moving faster than the ability of standards committees to ratify standards. Standards committees are procedural bodies and by nature slow moving. To accommodate the need for working models and agreements and to facilitate the standardization process, many special interest groups have developed **forums** made up of representatives from interested corporations. The forums work with universities and users to test, evaluate, and standardize new technologies. By concentrating their efforts on a particular technology, the forums are able to speed acceptance and use of those technologies in the telecommunications community. The forums present their conclusions to the standards bodies.

REGULATORY AGENCIES

All communications technologies are subject to regulation by government agencies such as the **Federal Communications Commission** (FCC) in the United States. The purpose of these agencies is to protect the public interest by regulating radio, television, and wire/cable communications.

BUSINESS FOCUS: STANDARDS ORGANIZATIONS

The following gives additional information about standard organizations mentioned in this chapter.

ISO

The **International Organization for Standardization** (ISO) is a multinational body whose membership is drawn mainly from the standards creation committees of various governments throughout the world.

ITU-T

By the early 1970s a number of countries were defining national standards for telecommunications, but there was still little international compatibility. The United Nations responded by forming, as part of its International Telecommunications Union (ITU), a committee called the **International Telecommunications Union–Telecommunication Standards Sector** (ITU-T).

ANSI

Despite its name, the **American National Standards Institute** (ANSI) is a completely private nonprofit corporation not affiliated with the U.S. federal government. Its expressed aims include serving as the national coordinating institution for voluntary standardization in the United States.

IEEE

The **Institute of Electrical and Electronics Engineers** (IEEE) is the largest professional engineering society in the world. International in scope, it aims to advance theory, creativity, and product quality in the fields of electrical engineering, electronics, and radio as well as in all related branches of engineering. As one of its goals, the IEEE oversees the development and adoption of international standards for computing and communication.

EIA

Aligned with ANSI, the **Electronic Industries Association** (EIA) is a nonprofit organization devoted to the promotion of electronics manufacturing concerns. Its activities include public awareness education and lobbying efforts in addition to standards development.

TECHNICAL FOCUS: FORUMS

The following gives additional information about forums mentioned in this chapter.

Frame Relay Forum

The Frame Relay Forum was formed by DEC, Northern Telecom, Cisco, and StrataCom to promote the acceptance and implementation of Frame Relay (a wide area network protocol described in Chapter 11).

ATM Forum and ATM Consortium

The ATM Forum and the ATM Consortium promote the acceptance and use of Asynchronous Transfer Mode (ATM) technology, a wide area network technology described in Chapter 11.

Internet Society (ISOC) and Internet Engineering Task Force (IETF)

The Internet Society (ISOC) and the Internet Engineering Task Force (IETF) are concerned with speeding the growth and evolution of Internet communications. The ISOC concentrates on user issues, including enhancements to the protocol suite used by the Internet. The IETF is the standards body for the Internet itself. It reviews Internet software and hardware.

BUSINESS FOCUS: FCC

The FCC has authority over interstate and international commerce as it relates to communications. Every piece of communications technology must have FCC approval before it may be marketed (check the bottom of your telephone for an FCC approval code). Specific FCC responsibilities include the following:

❏ Review rate and service-charge applications made by telegraph and telephone providers.
❏ Review the technical specifications of communications hardware.
❏ Establish reasonable common carrier rates of return.
❏ Divide and allocate radio frequencies.
❏ Assign carrier frequencies for radio and television broadcasts.

1.5 NETWORK MODELS

For two users to communicate from one point of the globe to another, there is a need to connect networks. Each network is made and maintained by different organizations. Each network's hardware and software are provided by different vendors. How can these networks communicate?

The solution is to concentrate on the service each entity provides rather than how it is provided. As a rough analogy, think of building a house. This is a very complex project with many tasks. How are these tasks related to each other? Some are unrelated, but others cannot start until another is finished; there is a sense of order or hierarchy. For example, the roof cannot be built before the walls are in place. And the walls cannot be constructed until the foundation is laid. There might be three different contractors for the foundation, walls, and roof. Does the roofing contractor care about the foundation or wall details? No, he is only concerned that the walls are in place to provide a base for his roof. Likewise, the wall contractor is only concerned that the foundation is able to provide a base for his walls. As long as the foundation can provide its service and the walls can provide its service, the roof can be installed.

In data communications, sending data from one place to another is also a complex undertaking that can be broken into several tasks, one built over the other. Each of the tasks is handled by an entity. As long as the lower entity provides services to the upper entity, it does not matter how the service is accomplished.

During the last few decades, several network models have been devised to break the complex job of data communications into tasks. Two of these models are dominant: the open systems interconnection (OSI) model and the Internet model.

The Internet model came first and with the growth of the Internet became the de facto model. The OSI model was developed later as a theoretical model. The OSI model defines seven layers of functionalities (tasks); the Internet model defines five levels of functionalities (tasks). The OSI model is better for understanding the tasks and their boundaries, but it has never been implemented; the Internet model has some vague boundaries between the tasks, but it has been implemented and is running. We understand the OSI model better but the Internet model is in use. Therefore, we briefly introduce the OSI model and use the Internet model elsewhere in the book.

THE OSI MODEL

The open systems interconnection (OSI) model is a layered framework for the design of network systems that allows communication across all types of computer systems. It consists of seven separate but related layers, each of which defines a step in the process of moving information across a network. Figure 1.8 shows the seven layers of the OSI model.

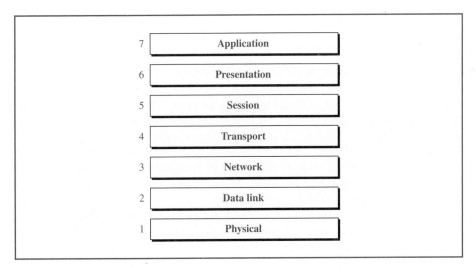

Figure 1.8 OSI model

Application Layer
The application layer is the service provider. It gives services to the user of the network. For example, the user may need to use the network to send electronic mail. The user may need to access the website of a company. The user may need to transfer files from a remote computer.

The application layer has a set of application programs that facilitates access to the network. Because the services needed by users fall into just a few categories, an application program has been written for each category. There is an application program for sending mail, an application program for transferring a file, an application program for surfing the Web, and so on. In addition, there is a general application program that allows a user access to a remote computer and the services available on that computer.

Figure 1.9 shows the application layer.

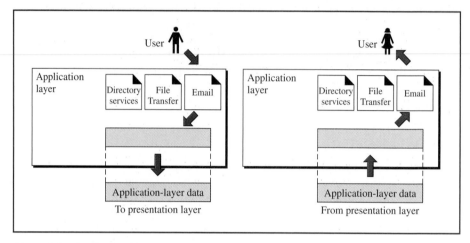

Figure 1.9   Application layer

PRESENTATION LAYER

Data created in the application layer may not be suitable for communication. For example, one computer may use ASCII code (see Appendix A) to encode data into a stream of 0s and 1s, while another computer may use another encoding system. If two computers use different encoding systems, they cannot understand each other. It's similar to someone writing a letter in English and sending it to someone who only knows French. Data must be encoded in a common encoding system if they are to be understood by any computer in the world. The presentation layer is responsible for **translation,** translating data from the computer's encoding system to some international code. The destination computer must, of course, do the reverse.

The sender and receiver of the data may need to have privacy. This is achieved through **encryption,** a second responsibility of the presentation layer. Encryption/decryption can be done at several layers and does not belong exclusively to the presentation layer.

The data to be sent may contain redundant information. **Data compression,** another presentation layer responsibility, can reduce the amount of data to be sent, thereby conserving the network capacity.

In summary, the presentation layer at the sender is responsible for translating data, encrypting data, and compressing data. At the receiver, the presentation layer decompresses data, decrypts data, and translates data.

Figure 1.10 shows the presentation layer.

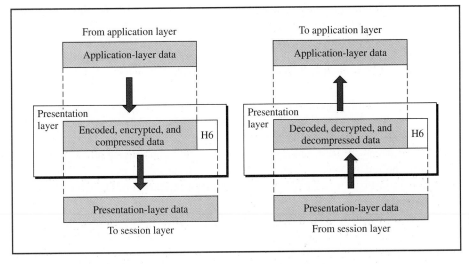

From application layer	To application layer
Application-layer data	Application-layer data

Presentation layer: Encoded, encrypted, and compressed data | H6

Presentation layer: Decoded, decrypted, and decompressed data | H6

Presentation-layer data	Presentation-layer data
To session layer	From session layer

Figure 1.10   Presentation layer

Session Layer

In some applications, such as electronic mail, communication is just one way. For example, a sender sends mail and does not expect the receiver to be sitting at the computer to respond immediately. However, some applications need a two-way interaction between sender and receiver. For example, a bank customer using the ATM machine to get some cash is involved in a dialog. The customer inserts the ATM card in the ATM machine, punches in a pin number, specifies a dollar amount, and waits for an answer from the other side. This is called a **session.** The session starts when the card is inserted

© Corbis/Vol. 12

Some network applications, such as ATM machines, require two-way interaction between sender and receiver.

in the machine and ends when the money is received if no further transactions are desired. The session layer provides two-way communication.

The session layer also provides synchronization between the sender and receiver. Suppose an author needs to send a 1000-page manuscript to a publisher electronically. Even with a high-speed connection, it may take hours before all the data are sent. What happens if after one hour, the communication is broken and then reestablished? Must the author's computer start sending from the first page even though the receiver may have received the first 432 pages? The session layer can help here by inserting marks, called synchronization points, in the data after every 100 pages. After the first 100 pages are sent, the session layer can wait and request an acknowledgement from the receiver before sending the next 100 pages. In this way, if there is a communication break after page 432, the sender can start sending from page 401 instead of page 1.

In summary, the session layer is responsible for creating a two-way session for the application program and providing synchronization points upon request. Figure 1.11 shows the session layer.

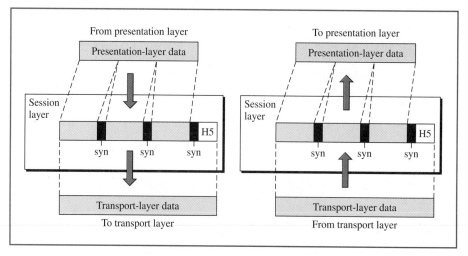

Figure 1.11   Session layer

Transport Layer

Data delivery through a network is the main responsibility of the transport layer. The data may have been created by the application layer. The data may have been translated, encrypted, and compressed by the presentation layer. A dialog may have been started between the two users, but the transport of data from one place to another is the responsibility of the transport layer. We must be aware, however, that the transport level does not do the actual physical delivery; it manages the delivery. It **packetizes** (packages) the data into manageable units; it labels the packets and makes sure that the packets arrive at the transport layer of the destination safe and sound. The physical delivery is done by the lower layers; management and control is handled by the transport layer.

In particular, the transport layer divides data into manageable packets; a large message such as 100 pages of data cannot be sent in one unit. The transport layer adds labels to each packet. One label is the address (identity) of the application program that is sending the data; another is the address of the application program that is receiving the data. Another label can define a packet sequence number. The physical delivery at the lower layers may cause packets belonging to the same message to arrive out of order; the sequence number allows the transport layer at the receiver to put the packets back in order. The transport layer also ensures that the data are exchanged between the intended applications since a computer may be running several applications at the same time. Another responsibility is error checking and error correction.

In summary, the transport layer is responsible for packetizing, address labeling, sequence labeling, and error control. Figure 1.12 shows the transport layer.

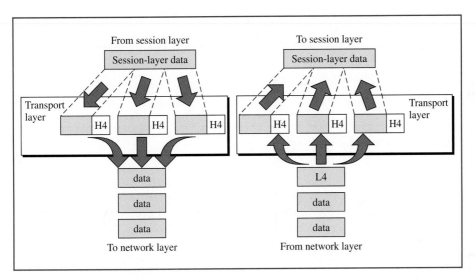

Figure 1.12   Transport layer

Network Layer

Although the ultimate delivery is from one specific application in one computer to another specific application in another computer, delivery must first be made to the destination computer. Consider the transport layer as a high-level manager responsible for delivery between the two applications; the network layer, then, is a low-level manager responsible for delivery between the two computers. The first is an application-to-application delivery, the second is a source-to-destination delivery.

To deliver the data unit from the source to destination, packetizing is again needed. The network layer adds a pair of addresses. The addresses are the unique global addresses that identify both the destination computer for delivery and the source computer for returning purposes.

As part of host-to-host delivery, the network layer makes decisions about the route of each packet. The transport layer just wants the packet delivered from one application to another; it does not care about the route. The network layer, however, must choose an optimal route for a packet. Since there is not just one network, a packet, from its source to its destination, may travel across several networks. At each boundary between networks, there may be several options. Here, the network layer makes a routing decision that is optimal for each packet. For example, if the packet needs to reach the destination very fast, a router with minimum delay is chosen; if a packet needs reliability, a more reliable network is chosen.

Figure 1.13 shows the network layer.

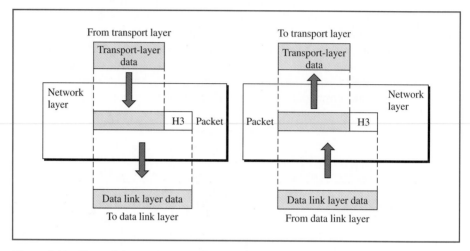

Figure 1.13   Network layer

Data Link Layer

As you have learned, a packet does not normally go directly from the source to the destination; instead, it passes through several networks. It goes from one connecting device to another one. Each connecting device must find the optimal route and direct the packet through one of the networks to which it is connected. The term to describe the movement from one connecting device to another is *hop-to-hop delivery*. The data link layer of one connecting device coordinates with the data link layer of the next connecting device. The connection between the two hops is a called a link; it is the responsibility of the data link layer to guide the packet through the link. In other words, the data link layer is another delivery manager, but only for part of the journey, between two hops. The data link layer is a hop-to-hop (or node-to-node) delivery manager.

To deliver data from one hop to the next again requires packetizing. In the data link layer the term is called *framing*. A packet coming from the network layer is inserted inside a frame with a new label. The label contains the address of the previous hop and the address of the next hop. These addresses are different from the addresses at the network layer. They are called *physical addresses*. They are necessary because networks in the path may be using different protocols and the equipment may be coming from different vendors. Each network type has its own addressing mechanism to define its devices. Until there is universal agreement among all manufacturers, we need to use physical addresses to define the hops. Note that the framing and labeling in the data link layer are temporary. When the frame arrives at a hop, the frame and the addresses are changed to reflect the new information.

Another responsibility of the data link layer, as the lowest level delivery manager, is to make sure that a frame arrives at the next hop safe and sound. The error checking, however, is hop-to-hop, not end-to-end.

We will see in Chapter 5 that the data link layer has yet another function, that of link access. It must decide which of several computers connected to the same link, can have control of the link to send data. The data link layers of the computers cooperate to determine the sender. Figure 1.14 shows the data link layer.

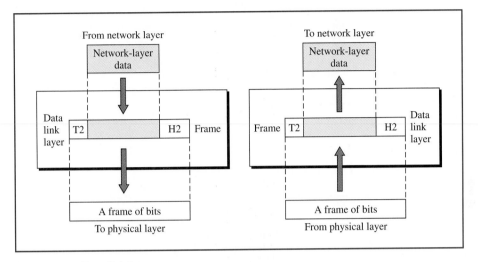

Figure 1.14   Data link layer

Physical Layer

The physical layer prepares the data for the actual movement over the transmission media (layer zero). The transport, network, and data link layers are managers; they supervise the delivery, but they do not do the actual delivery. Data, packed in the frames and coming from the data link layer cannot be put in motion. The frames are passive, not active.

As an analogy, consider a new home owner who has purchased furniture for a house. Everything is packaged and labeled. But the packages cannot move by themselves; they do not have moving capabilities. We cannot put them on the road and expect them to move. We need to load the packages on a truck and use the truck's moving capability to transport the packages.

In data communications, frames, as a sequence of 0s and 1s, have no moving capabilities. Electromagnetic signals, on the other hand, move and can propagate in air and wire cable. We can hear the broadcast from a radio station and see the video from a cable TV station. The frames must be represented by electromagnetic signals in order to go from one device to another. The physical layer is responsible for converting data to signals. We can consider it to be a loader that takes data and loads them on to signals to be sent on the transmission medium.

Although the physical layer is a loader, it also has some road management responsibilities. It manages the transmission media. It divides the medium (road) into channels (lanes) and makes sure that each packet travels in its assigned channel. It also decides if the transmission medium is a one-way or two-way link.

Figure 1.15 shows the physical layer.

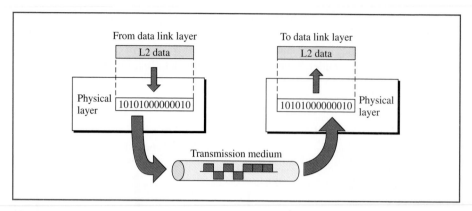

Figure 1.15 Physical layer

Summary of Layer Functions
The functions of the seven layers are summarized in Figure 1.16.

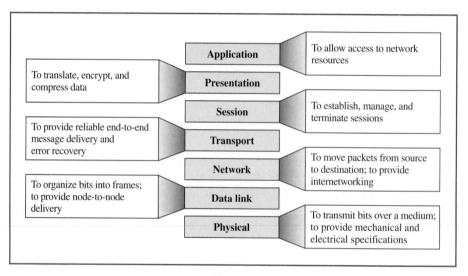

Figure 1.16 Summary of layer functions

THE INTERNET MODEL

The Internet model is made of five layers. The four lower layers roughly match the four lower layers of the OSI model. Most of the responsibilities of the three topmost layers of the OSI model are assigned to the Internet model's application layer, with some of the session layer duties going to the transport layer. Figure 1.17 shows the Internet model compared to the OSI model.

Application Layer
The application layer of the Internet model contains several protocols and programs used to access the resources of a remote system. These application programs are mostly self-contained; they provide services that are defined in the presentation and session layers.

We discuss the application layer of the Internet model in detail in Chapter 2.

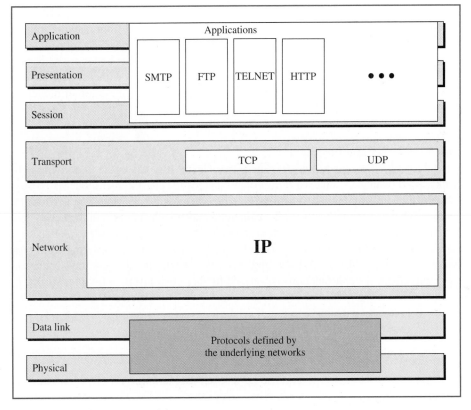

Figure 1.17   The Internet model

Transport Layer

The transport layer of the Internet model contains two protocols: TCP and UDP. The first, the Transmission Control Protocol (TCP), is a reliable protocol that allows two application layers to converse with each other. It delivers a stream of characters from a source to a destination and vice versa. At the source it divides the stream of bytes into manageable segments. At the destination, it creates a stream of bytes from the received segments for the use of the application layer. TCP performance goes beyond that of the OSI model transport layer; it performs some of the tasks defined for the session layer in the OSI model. For example, it creates a two-way connection (a dialog) between two application layers.

The second protocol, the User Datagram Protocol (UDP), is just a very simple transport layer protocol that ignores even some of the duties of the transport layer as defined in the OSI model. It is an unreliable protocol that is used by applications that need fast delivery of single packets without worrying about flow and error control. We discuss the transport layer of the Internet model in detail in Chapter 3.

Internet Layer

The layer corresponding to the OSI network layer in the Internet model is sometimes called the network layer or the internetwork layer; most often it is referred to as the Internet layer. Whatever its name, it contains few protocols. The main protocol, the

Internet Protocol (IP), is responsible for creating network-layer packets called IP datagrams and sending them to the destination. The datagrams travel from network to network (LAN or WAN) and may reach the destination in or out of order. The upper layers are responsible for ordering the received packets. The intermediate nodes are responsible for routing the datagrams through the most appropriate routes without changing the data portion of the datagram. We discuss the network layer of the Internet model in detail in Chapter 4.

Data Link Layer and Physical Layer

The Internet model does not discuss these two layers. It is left to the underlying networks to use whatever standard or protocol they desire. The Internet model is mostly concerned about source-to-destination delivery, where data goes from one network to another. What is done at the physical and data link layer is the concern of the LANs and WANs that make up the internetwork or internet. The data link layer for a LAN is usually different from that in a WAN. The physical layer is also very different from one protocol to another. Instead of discussing every data link layer and every physical layer, we discuss the tasks and functions performed by these two layers in Chapters 6 and 7. We then discuss the particular protocols when we discuss different LANs and WANs protocols in future chapters.

CASE STUDY

NEW AGE HOME PHARMACY

To better understand the role of data communications and networking in business, we have designed a set of case studies that spans the text. The case studies concentrate on a fictitious firm, called New Age Home Pharmacy, or NAHP, that provides pharmaceutical services for homebound patients.

In this chapter, we begin with a general introduction to the firm; in future chapters we explore how data communications and networking technologies are used by this firm.

NAHP was founded in 1982. Its purpose was to provide pharmaceutical services for elderly patients living at home or in home care centers. The business first operated out of a very small three-room office. Today, it occupies a six-story building (including a basement) in the city of Pasadena, California.

The first floor of the building is currently used for shipping and receiving (delivery of products and the receiving of raw materials).The second floor is occupied by administrative assistants who take orders via telephone or computer. The third floor is occupied by the insurance clerks and the accountants. The insurance clerks are responsible for billing the services to the insurance companies and for follow-up procedures. The accountants are responsible for keeping track of all monetary transactions.

The top three floors are used by the pharmacists and technicians to prepare the drugs. Each of these floors is supervised by a pharmacist, who is also a shareholder and a member of the board of directors. The chairperson of the board is Madeline Lindsey, the pharmacist who founded NAHP.

To manage the network administration and maintenance, NAHP hired a networking consulting firm, Modern Networking Corporation.

The orders for drugs arrive via email, the website, and the telephone from doctors, homebound patients, and home care centers. The orders include pre-packed drugs and IVs and are distributed daily by a fleet of 10 small vehicles owned by the firm.

Starting in the next chapter, we will see how data communications and networking technologies are used by this midsize company.

1.6 KEY TERMS

American National Standards Institute (ANSI)

application layer

ATM Forum

bit

compression

data

data link layer

de facto standard

de jure standard

destination address

distributed database

distributed processing

Electronic Industries Association (EIA)

encryption

error

Federal Communications Commission (FCC)

forum

frame

Frame Relay Forum

framing

hop-to-hop delivery

host-to-host delivery

Institute of Electrical and Electronics Engineers (IEEE)

International Organization for Standardization (ISO)

International Telecommunications Union–Telecommunication Standards Sector (ITU-T)

Internet

Internet Engineering Task Force (IETF)

Internet model

Internet Society (ISOC)

local area network (LAN)

message

metropolitan area network (MAN)

network

network layer

node-to-node delivery

open systems interconnection (OSI) model

packetizing

physical address

physical layer

presentation layer

protocol

receiver

reliability

security

semantics

sender

session layer

source address

source-to-destination delivery

standard

synchronization point

syntax

Telcordia

telecommunication

timing

translation

transport layer

1.7 SUMMARY

❏ Data communications is the transfer of data from one device to another via some form of transmission medium in an accurate and timely manner.

❏ The effectiveness of a data communications system depends on the delivery, accuracy, and timeliness.

❏ The five basic components of a data communications system are the message, the sender, the receiver, the medium, and the protocol.

❏ Most networks use distributed processing, in which a task is divided among multiple computers.

❏ Networks are judged by their performance, reliability, and security.

❑ A network is generally classified as a local area network, a metropolitan area network, or a wide area network.

❑ When two or more networks are connected, they become an internetwork, or internet.

❑ A protocol is a set of rules that governs data communications; the key elements of a protocol are syntax, semantics, and timing.

❑ Standards are necessary to ensure that products from different manufacturers can work together as expected.

❑ The ISO, ITU-T, ANSI, IEEE, EIA, and Telcordia (Bellcore) are some of the organizations involved in standards creation.

❑ Forums consist of representatives from corporations that test, evaluate, and standardize new technologies.

❑ Some important forums are the Frame Relay Forum, the ATM Forum, the Internet Society, and the Internet Engineering Task Force.

❑ The FCC is a regulatory agency that regulates radio, television, and wire/cable communications.

❑ In a layered data communications model, each layer provides services to its upper layer.

❑ A seven-layer theoretical model called the open systems interconnection (OSI) shows how diverse systems can communicate.

❑ The application layer gives services to users of the network.

❑ The sender's presentation layer translates, encrypts, and compresses data.

❑ The session layer creates two-way interactions and synchronization points.

❑ The transport layer is responsible for the delivery of the entire message from application program to application program.

❑ The network layer is responsible for the delivery of a packet from one host to another host.

❑ The data link layer is responsible for delivering frames from one hop to the next.

❑ The physical layer coordinates the functions required to transmit a bit stream over a transmission medium.

❑ The five-layer Internet model is the protocol suite used by the Internet.

 PRACTICE SET

Review Questions

1. Identify the five components of a data communications system.
2. What is the relationship between telecommunications and data communications? Is one a subset of the other? Give reasons for your answers.
3. What three fundamental characteristics determine the effectiveness of a data communications system?
4. Name some factors that can affect the performance of a network.
5. Name some factors that can affect the security of a network.
6. Why are protocols needed?
7. Why are standards needed?
8. What are the key elements of a protocol?
9. What is the difference between a de facto standard and a de jure standard?

10. What is the purpose of the ITU-T?

11. What is the purpose of ANSI?
12. What are some of the factors that determine whether a network is a LAN, MAN, or WAN?
13. How are forums involved in standards creation?
14. What is the difference between network-layer-delivery and transport-layer-delivery?
15. List the layers of the OSI model.
16. What are the responsibilities of the presentation layer?
17. What are the responsibilities of the session layer?
18. What are the responsibilities of the transport layer?
19. What are the responsibilities of the network layer?
20. What are the responsibilities of the data link layer?
21. How do the layers of the Internet model correlate to the layers of the OSI model?

Multiple-Choice Questions

22. The _____ is the physical path over which a message travels.
    a. protocol
    b. medium
    c. signal
    d. all of the above
23. Frequency of failure and network recovery time after a failure are measures of the _____ of a network.
    a. performance
    b. reliability
    c. security
    d. feasibility
24. The performance of a data communications network depends on _____ .
    a. the number of users
    b. the transmission media
    c. the hardware and software
    d. all of the above
25. Viruses are a network _____ issue.
    a. performance
    b. reliability
    c. security
    d. all of the above
26. Protection of data from a natural disaster such as a tornado is a network _____ issue.
    a. performance
    b. reliability
    c. security
    d. management
27. Which organization has authority over interstate and international commerce in the communications field?
    a. ITU-T
    b. IEEE
    c. FCC
    d. Internet Society

28. _____ are special-interest groups that quickly test, evaluate, and standardize new technologies.
   a. Forums
   b. Regulatory agencies
   c. Standards organizations
   d. all of the above

29. The information to be communicated in a data communications system is the

   _____.
   a. medium
   b. protocol
   c. message
   d. transmission

30. _____ is the division of one task among multiple computers.
   a. Distributed processing
   b. Distributed messaging
   c. Distributed telephony
   d. Electronic messaging

31. Which international agency is concerned with standards in science and technology?
   a. ISO
   b. OSI
   c. EIA
   d. ANSI

32. If a protocol specifies that data should be sent at 100 Mbps, this is a _____ issue.
   a. syntax
   b. semantics
   c. timing
   d. none of the above

33. When a protocol specifies that the address of the sender must occupy the first four bytes of a message, this is a _____ issue.
   a. syntax
   b. semantics
   c. timing
   d. none of the above

34. When a protocol specifies that the address of the sender means the most recent sender and not the original source, this is a _____ issue.
   a. syntax
   b. semantics
   c. timing
   d. none of the above

35. What is the main difference between a de facto standard and a de jure standard?
   a. A de facto standard has been legislated by an officially recognized body; a de jure standard has not.
   b. A de jure standard has been legislated by an officially recognized body; a de facto standard has not.
   c. The inventing company can wholly own a de jure standard and not a de facto standard.
   d. A de jure standard is proprietary; a de facto standard is not.

36. The _____ model shows how the network functions of a computer ought to be organized.
    a. ITU-T
    b. OSI
    c. ISO
    d. ANSI
37. The OSI model consists of _____ layers.
    a. three
    b. five
    c. seven
    d. eight
38. The OSI model's _____ layer decides the location of synchronization points.
    a. transport
    b. session
    c. presentation
    d. application
39. The end-to-end delivery of the entire message is the responsibility of the OSI model's _____ layer.
    a. network
    b. transport
    c. session
    d. presentation
40. The _____ layer is the layer closest to the transmission medium.
    a. physical
    b. data link
    c. network
    d. transport
41. In the _____ layer, the data unit is called a frame.
    a. physical
    b. data link
    c. network
    d. transport
42. Decryption and encryption of data are the responsibility of the OSI model's _____ layer.
    a. physical
    b. data link
    c. presentation
    d. session
43. Dialog control is a function of the OSI model's _____ layer.
    a. transport
    b. session
    c. presentation
    d. application
44. Mail services and directory services are available to network users through the OSI model's _____ layer.
    a. data link
    b. session
    c. transport
    d. application

45. Node-to-node delivery of the data unit is the responsibility of the OSI model's _____ layer.
    a. physical
    b. data link
    c. transport
    d. network

46. The OSI model's _____ layer lies between the network layer and the session layer.
    a. physical
    b. data link
    c. transport
    d. presentation

47. In the OSI model's _____ layer, translations from one character code to another occur.
    a. transport
    b. session
    c. presentation
    d. application

48. The _____ layer changes bits into electromagnetic signals.
    a. physical
    b. data link
    c. transport
    d. presentation

49. The physical layer is concerned with the transmission of _____ over the physical medium.
    a. programs
    b. dialogs
    c. protocols
    d. bits

50. What is the main function of the OSI model's transport layer?
    a. node-to-node delivery
    b. end-to-end message delivery
    c. synchronization
    d. updating and maintenance of routing tables

51. Which of the following is an application layer service?
    a. network virtual terminal
    b. file transfer, access, and management
    c. mail service
    d. all of the above

CHAPTER 2

Application Layer

This chapter explores the different application programs, or services, available at the topmost layer, layer five, of the Internet model.

The application layer allows people to use the Internet. We could say that the other four layers are created so that people can use these application programs. This is the reason that we start with this layer, and, in Chapters 3–7, we move downward through the other four layers to see how they provide services to the application layer.

In this chapter, we introduce the application layer and its relationships to the other layers. We discuss the client-server paradigm, the only one used today in the Internet. We also discuss addressing, a feature inseparable from the application layer. We then explore the most common application programs used in the Internet including electronic mail, file transfer, remote logging, World Wide Web, list servers, videoconferencing, and chatting.

The list of application programs does not end here. We introduce some less obvious applications throughout the book. For example, we show how network management is handled by an application program in Chapter 16.

OBJECTIVES

After reading this chapter, the reader should be able to understand:

- ❏ The client-server paradigm
- ❏ Electronic mail
- ❏ File transfer
- ❏ Remote login
- ❏ The World Wide Web
- ❏ Other applications such as videoconferencing and chatting

2.1 INTRODUCTION

Figure 2.1 shows the position of the application layer in the Internet model. For the typical end user, this is the only layer of interest. This user only needs to know how to use the application programs available in this layer. They need to know how to send and receive email; they need to know how to use a browser to surf the World Wide Web. Some may need to use file transfer programs to send and receive bulky files.

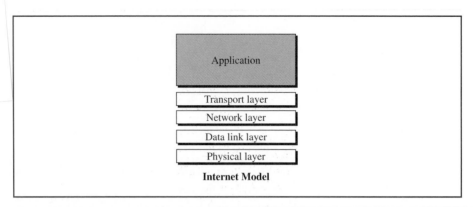

Figure 2.1 Position of application layer in the Internet model

A business manager, however, needs to be aware of the technologies available in each layer and how they can best be used. This knowledge enables a manager to make wise decisions concerning data communications and networking. This chapter, and Chapters 3–6, gives a manager insight into these layers.

2.2 CLIENT-SERVER PARADIGM

The application layer programs are based on the concept of clients and servers. The purpose of a network, and in particular, the global Internet, is to provide a service to a user. A user at a local site wants to receive a service from a computer at a remote site. For example, perhaps a user wants to retrieve a file from a remote computer. How can this be done? Both computers must run programs. The local computer runs a program that requests a service from another program on the remote computer. This means that both computers must run a program, one to request a service and one to provide a service.

At first glance, communication between two application programs—one running at the local site, the other running at the remote site—seems like a simple task. But many questions arise upon the actual implementation of the approach. Some questions that we may ask are:

❑ Should the application program be able to request as well as provide services or should the application program just do one or the other? One solution is to have an application program, called the **client,** running on the local machine, request a service from another application program, called the **server,** running on the remote machine. In other words, the tasks of requesting a service and providing a service are separate from each other. An application program is either a requester (a client) or a provider (a server). They come in pairs, client and server, both having the same name. Figure 2.2 illustrates this **client-server model.**

Application-layer programs in the Internet model communicate using the client-server paradigm.

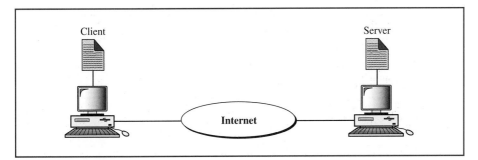

Figure 2.2   Client-server model

❏   Should an application program provide service for only one specific program installed elsewhere or should it provide service for any application program that requests this service? The most common solution is a server providing a service for any client, not just one particular client. In other words, the client-server relationship is many-to-one. Many clients can use the services of one server (see Figure 2.3).

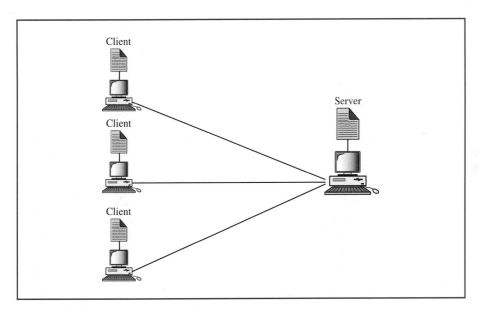

Figure 2.3   Client-server relationship

❏   When should an application program be running? All of the time or just when there is a need for the service? Generally, a client program, which requests a service, runs only when it is needed. The server program, which provides a service, runs all of the time because it does not know when its service will be needed.

❏   Should there be just one universal application program that can provide any type of service a user wants? Or should there be one application program for each type of service? Generally, a service needed frequently and by many users has a specific client-server application program. For example, one client-server application program allows users to access files; a different client-server application program allows users to send email, and so on. For services that are more customized, we have one generic application program that allows users to access the services available on a remote computer. For example, there is a client-server application program that allows the user to log onto a remote computer and then use the services provided by that computer.

In the client-server paradigm, many clients can be served by one server, either one at a time or concurrently.

In the client-server paradigm, a client runs for a specific period of time; the server runs continuously.

In the client-server paradigm, there are specific servers and normally one general-purpose server.

CLIENT

A **client** is a program running on the local machine requesting service from a server. A client program is started by the user when the service is needed and terminates when the service is complete. A client opens the communication channel, sends its request, receives the response, and closes the channel. Multiple requests and responses are allowed in one session.

SERVER

A **server** is a program running on the remote machine providing service to the clients. When it starts, it opens the door for incoming requests from clients, but it never initiates a service until it is requested to do so. A server program normally runs infinitely unless a problem arises. It waits for incoming requests from clients. When a request arrives, it responds to the request.

2.3   ADDRESSING

A client and a server communicate with each other through addresses. When a client requests a service from a server, it must include the address of the server as the destination address, as well as its own address as the source address. The source address is required so that the server knows where to send the response. When the server responds to the request, it reverses the addresses; it uses its own address as the source and the address of the client as the destination.

Each application has its own address format. For example, an email address may look like *forouzan@fhda.edu,* while an address to access a web page may look like *http://www.fhda.edu.*

The Internet uses an address to identify an entity. Each computer connected to the Internet needs to be uniquely identified. To prevent duplication, a **hierarchical** or **tree name space** was proposed in which each name has several parts. The first part can define the nature of the organization, the second part can define the name of an organization, the third part can define departments in the organization, and so on. In this way, assignment and control of the name space can be decentralized.

Each node in the tree has a label. A full **domain name** is a sequence of labels separated by dots. For example, *challenger.atc.fhda.edu* is a domain name that defines a computer at De Anza College. Each label in the domain may define an entity in the organization; the level of detail increases from right to left.

The domain names are divided into two categories: generic domain names and country domain names. In the generic domain name, the rightmost label defines the type of activity. Traditionally, the Internet has defined seven labels: **com** (commerce), **edu** (education), **gov** (government), **int** (international), **net** (Internet), and **org** (non-profit organization). Recently, seven more labels were added to the list: **aero** (airlines and aerospace), **biz** (business and firms), **coop** (cooperative organizations), **info** (information service providers), **museum** (museums and other similar organizations), **name** (personal names), and **pro** (professional organizations).

2.4 ELECTRONIC MAIL

The earliest and the most common application of the Internet is **electronic mail** or email. Email is a store-and-forward application. This means a message can be sent to someone not currently connected to the Internet. The message can remain in the system until the recipient retrieves it.

Email is a store-and-forward application on the Internet.

The email application allows a user to send messages over a private network or the global Internet. Email supports:

❏ Sending a single message to one or more recipients.
❏ Sending messages that include text, voice, video, or graphics.
❏ Organization of message-based criteria such as priority.

EMAIL AND SNAIL MAIL

Email can be compared and contrasted with regular mail, which is often referred to as *snail mail*.

Advantages
Email has several advantages over snail mail:

❏ It is faster. In normal traffic hours, an email message can only take a few seconds or minutes to reach the destination if the recipient is in the same country or region;

it may take a few hours to reach an overseas recipient. Snail mail usually takes a couple of days, if not a week or two, to reach its destination.

❏ It is easier to distribute to a group of recipients. The sender creates a *distribution list* that contains the email addresses of all recipients. The list is given a group name. The email is sent using the group name as the virtual recipient. The email is delivered to all recipients on the list. In other words, a group name can be used instead of a single recipient. For example, if your clients are categorized according to geographical location, you might have group names such as clients_east, clients_west and so on. With snail mail separate envelopes must be sent to each individual in the group.

❏ It is less expensive. Sending an email is essentially free today if we ignore the cost of being connected to the Internet, which can be justified for other purposes. Sending letters via post office or other couriers is actually more costly than just the price of postage. To find the true cost of sending a letter, we need to add the cost of office supplies (paper, etc.), the cost of typing the letter, and the cost of delivering the letter to the post office.

❏ It can be less time-consuming. The first emails were friendly, informal messages. This tradition has found its way into business today. Email exchanged between organizations tend to be less formal than letters. This means less time and effort on both sides to accomplish the same task.

Disadvantages

We must not ignore some problems associated with the sending of email.

❏ An email cannot be certified. Although the sender can check to see if the receiver has received the mail, it cannot be used as legal proof. If we need a signature from the recipient, we still need to use the services of snail mail or some other courier service.

❏ The privacy of email is still an open question. Although several software packages are on the market to make email confidential, it cannot be guaranteed unless everyone uses one of these packages.

❏ Email messaging is subject to abuse. Unwanted and unsolicited email is a nuisance and can fill mailboxes much like junk mail. In addition, there is the threat of viruses and other potentially damaging code attached to email.

COMPONENTS

The sending of electronic mail in the Internet requires these components: user agents (UAs), mail transfer agents (MTAs), and the protocol that controls mail delivery— **Simple Mail Transfer Protocol** (SMTP).

User Agent (UA)

The **user agent** is software installed on the user computer that reads, replies, forwards, saves, and composes messages. In the beginning of the electronic mail era, the popular user agents such as Berkeley Mail, Pine, and Elm were text-based. Today, user agents such as Eudora, Microsoft's Outlook, and Netscape's Messenger use a GUI (graphic user interface) to provide the users with a menu or window environment and allow the sending of text and multimedia.

A user agent controls the composing, reading, forwarding, replying, and saving of email messages. The user agent is not responsible for sending or receiving email.

Mail Transfer Agent (MTA)

The actual mail transfer requires a **mail transfer agent** (MTA). To send mail, a system must have a client MTA, and to receive mail, a system must have a server MTA. The client MTA is installed on the user's computer. The client and the server MTA are installed on a computer that is used as the mail server.

The task of sending and receiving email is done by a mail transfer agent (MTA).

Simple Mail Transfer Protocol

Simple mail transfer protocol (SMTP) is the protocol that defines the relationship between the UAs and MTAs, defines the format of the message to be transferred, and defines the type of the characters to be used.

The formal protocol for electronic mail in the Internet is Simple Mail Transfer Protocol or SMTP.

MAIL DELIVERY

Now that we know the components of electronic mail, let us show how mail is delivered from the sender to the receiver. The delivery of email from the sender to the receiver takes place in three stages (see Figure 2.4).

First Stage

In the first stage, the email goes from the user agent to the local server. The mail is stored here until the remote server is available. The user agent uses SMTP client software and the local server uses SMTP server software. The message is stored in a queue to be sent when the remote mail server is ready for receiving.

Second Stage

In the second stage, the email is relayed by the local server, which now acts as the SMTP client, to the remote server, which is now the SMTP server. The email is delivered to the remote server, not to the remote user agent. The reason is that SMTP messages must be received by a server that is always running since mail can arrive at any time. However, people often turn off their computers at the end of the day, and those with laptops or mobile computers do not normally have them on all the time. So usually an organization (or an ISP) assigns a computer to be the email server and runs the SMTP server program. The email is received by this mail server and stored in the mailbox of the user for later retrieval.

Third Stage

In the third stage, the remote user agent uses a mail access protocol such as POP3 or IMAP4 (both discussed in the next section) to access the mailbox and retrieve the mail.

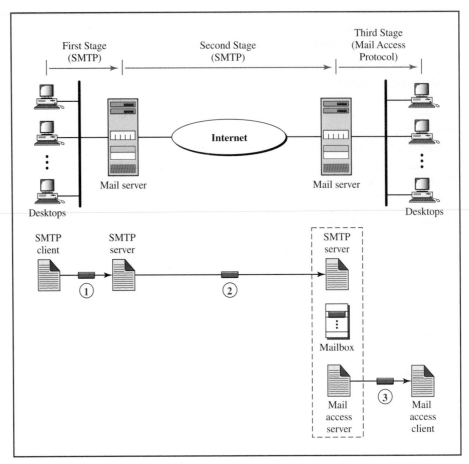

Figure 2.4 Email delivery

MAIL ACCESS PROTOCOLS

The stored mail remains in the mail server until it is retrieved by the recipient through an access protocol. Currently two mail access protocols are available: Post Office Protocol, version 3 (POP3) and Internet Mail Access Protocol (IMAP).

POP

Post Office Protocol (POP) is simple but limited in functionality. The client POP software is installed on the recipient computer; the server POP software is installed on the mail server.

Mail access starts with the client when the user needs to download the received email from the mailbox on the mail server. The client (user agent) sends the user name and password to access the mailbox. The user can then list and retrieve the mail messages, one by one. Figure 2.5 shows an example of downloading using POP.

IMAP

POP has several deficiencies. It does not allow the user to organize mail on the server. The user cannot have different folders on the server. (Of course, the user can create

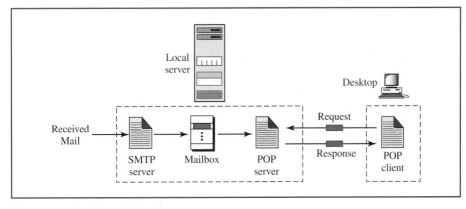

Figure 2.5 POP

folders on her own computer.) In addition, POP does not allow the user to check the contents of the mail before downloading.

A second popular mail access protocol, Internet Mail Access Protocol (IMAP), can handle these deficiencies. IMAP, though similar to POP, has more features and is more powerful and complex.

IMAP provides the following extra functions:

❏   A user can check the email header prior to downloading.
❏   A user can search the contents of the email prior to downloading.
❏   A user can partially download email. This is especially useful if the user has limited capacity and the email is long.
❏   A user can create, delete, or rename mailboxes on the mail server.
❏   A user can create a hierarchy of mailboxes in a folder for email storage.

The version of IMAP in use today is version 4.

ADDRESSES

A mail handling system must have a unique addressing system to deliver mail. The addressing system used by SMTP consists of two parts: a *local part* and a *domain name,* separated by an @ sign (see Figure 2.6).

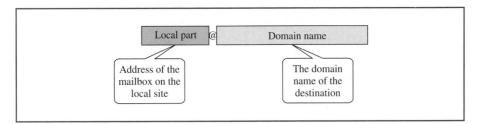

Figure 2.6 Email address

Local Part

The local part defines the name of a special file, called the user mailbox, where all of the mail received for a user is stored for retrieval by the user agent.

Domain Name

The second part of the address is the name of a computer. An organization usually selects one or more hosts to receive and send email. The computer name assigned to each mail server, the **domain name,** comes from a universal naming system called the domain name system (DNS).

TECHNICAL FOCUS: INSIDE AN EMAIL MESSAGE

An email is made of an envelope and a letter. The letter itself is made of a header and a body as shown in the following figure:

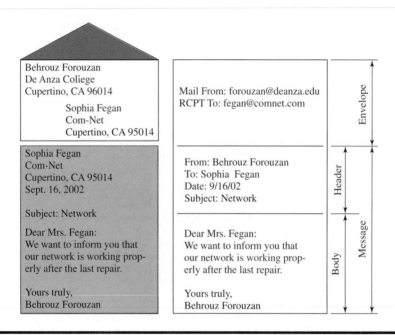

MULTIPURPOSE INTERNET MAIL EXTENSION (MIME)

SMTP is a simple mail transfer protocol. Its simplicity, however, comes with a price. SMTP can send messages only in NVT 7-bit ASCII format. It cannot be used for languages that are not supported by 7-bit ASCII characters (such as French, German, Hebrew, Russian, Chinese, and Japanese). Also, it cannot be used to send binary files or video or audio data.

Multipurpose Internet Mail Extension (MIME) is a supplementary protocol that allows non-ASCII data to be sent through SMTP. MIME is not a mail protocol and cannot replace SMTP; it is only an extension to SMTP.

MIME transforms non-ASCII data at the sender site to NVT ASCII data and delivers it to the client SMTP to be sent through the Internet. The server SMTP at the receiving side receives the NVT ASCII data and delivers it to MIME to be transformed back to the original data.

We can think of MIME as a set of software functions that transforms non-ASCII data to ASCII data and vice versa (see Figure 2.7).

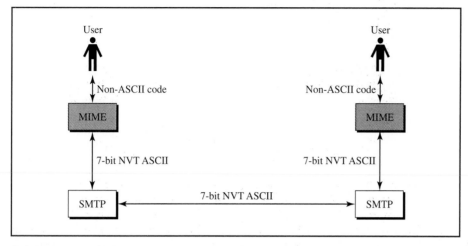

Figure 2.7 MIME

***TECHNICAL FOCUS:* HOW MIME WORKS**

MIME has five header types that can be added to the original SMTP header section to define the transformation parameters:

1. MIME-Version
2. Content-Type
3. Content-Transfer-Encoding
4. Content-Id
5. Content-Description

Each header defines one feature of the transformation.

2.5 FILE TRANSFER

Another common user application is file transfer. We often need to electronically transfer files from one computer to another. Although email can be used for this purpose (as an attached document), there are some drawbacks. One problem is that the user who wants the remote file must first contact someone at the remote site to ask that the file be sent. This creates one extra communication and is inconvenient. The second problem is that the bandwidth assigned for email does not allow for quick transferral of a large file. Bandwidth is discussed in the future chapters; for the moment, think of bandwidth as the number of characters allowed on a connection. Transferring a large file needs a lot of bandwidth if we need it sent quickly.

Two applications are currently available for transferring files over the Internet: File Transfer Protocol (FTP) and Trivial File Transfer Protocol (TFTP).

FILE TRANSFER PROTOCOL (FTP)

File Transfer Protocol (FTP) is the standard mechanism for one of the most common tasks on the Internet, copying a file from one computer to another.

Although file transfer from one system to another seems simple and straightforward, some problems must be dealt with first. For example, two systems may use different file name conventions. Two systems may have different ways to represent text and data. Two systems may have different directory structures. All of these problems have been solved by FTP in a very simple and elegant approach.

FTP differs from other client-server applications in that it establishes two connections between the hosts. One connection is used for data transfer, the other for control information (commands and responses). Separation of commands and data transfer makes FTP more efficient. The control connection uses very simple rules of communication. We need to transfer only a line of command or a line of response at a time. The data connection, on the other hand, needs more complex rules due to the variety of data types transferred.

Figure 2.8 shows the basic model of FTP. The client has three components: the user interface, the client control process, and the client data transfer process. The server has two components: the server control process and the server data transfer process. The control connection is made between the control processes. The data connection is made between the data transfer processes.

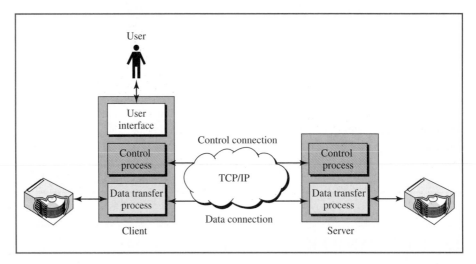

Figure 2.8   FTP

The control connection remains open during the entire interactive FTP session. The data connection is opened and then closed for each file transferred. It opens each time commands that involve transferring files are used, and it closes after the file is transferred. The two FTP connections, control and data, use different strategies and different port numbers.

Closed and Open FTP

The sites that run the FTP server to allow the user to access files on the site use one of two strategies. A site is either closed or open to the public. A closed FTP site allows only specific users to access files. The access is controlled by the user account and password. The public is not allowed to access files at these sites.

An open FTP site allows the public to access files. These sites offer what is called **anonymous FTP.** The user can use *anonymous* as the user name and *guest* as the password. User participation in this system is very limited. Some sites allow anonymous users only a subset of commands. For example, most sites allow the user to copy some files, but do not allow navigation through the file system. We show an example of anonymous FTP. We connect to internic.net and we assume there are public data available for transfer.

```
% ftp internic.net
Connected to internic.net
220 Server ready
Name: anonymous
331 Guest login OK, send "guest" as password
Password: guest
ftp > pwd
257 '/' is current directory
ftp > ls
200 OK
150 Opening ASCII mode
bin
...
ftp > close
221 Goodbye
ftp > quit
```

TRIVIAL FILE TRANSFER PROTOCOL (TFTP)

There are occasions when we need to simply copy a file without the need for all of the functionalities of FTP. **Trivial File Transfer Protocol** (TFTP) is designed for these types of file transfer. It makes one single connection and transfers a small file quickly. However, this application is not universally available.

2.6 GENERAL-PURPOSE APPLICATION: TELNET

The main task of the application layer is to provide services for users. For example, users want to be able to run different application programs at a remote site and create results that can be transferred to their local site. One way to satisfy these demands is to create different client-server application programs for each desired service. Programs such as file transfer programs (FTP and TFTP), email (SMTP), and so on are already available. But it would be impossible to write a specific client-server program for each demand.

TELNET is a general-purpose client-server program that lets a user access any application program on a remote computer; in other words, it allows the user to log onto a remote computer. After logging on, a user can use the services available on the remote computer and transfer the results back to the local computer.

TELNET is an abbreviation for terminal network. TELNET enables the establishment of a connection to a remote system in such a way that the local terminal appears to be a terminal at the remote system.

TELNET is a general-purpose client-server application program.

Local Login   When a user logs onto a local time-sharing system, it is called **local login.** As a user types at a terminal or at a workstation running a terminal emulator, the keystrokes are accepted by the terminal driver. The terminal driver passes the characters to the operating system. The operating system, in turn, interprets the combination of characters and invokes the desired application program or utility (see Figure 2.9).

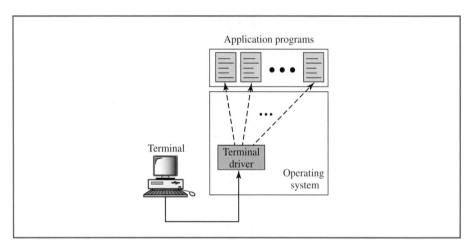

Figure 2.9   Local login

The mechanism, however, is not as simple as it seems because the operating system may assign special meanings to special characters. For example, in UNIX some combinations of characters have special meanings, such as the combination of the control character with the character z means suspend; the combination of the control character with the character c means abort; and so on. Whereas these special situations do not create any problem in local login because the terminal emulator and the terminal driver know the exact meaning of each character or combination of characters, they may create problems in remote login. Which process should interpret special characters? The client or the server? We will clarify this situation later in this section.

Remote Login   When a user wants to access an application program or utility located on a remote machine, he or she performs remote login. Here the TELNET client and server programs come into use. The user sends the keystrokes to the terminal driver where the local operating system accepts the characters but does not interpret them. The characters are sent to the TELNET client, which transforms the characters to a universal character set called *network virtual terminal characters* and delivers them to the local TCP/IP stack (see Figure 2.10).

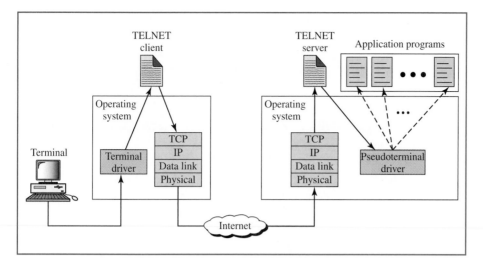

Figure 2.10 Remote login

2.7 WORLD WIDE WEB (WWW)

The World Wide Web (WWW), or the Web, is a repository of information spread all over the world and linked together. The WWW has a unique combination of flexibility, portability, and user-friendly features that distinguish it from other services provided by the Internet.

© Corbis/Vol. 147

The world wide web has revolutionized the way we access information, shop, conduct business.

The WWW today is a distributed client-server service, in which a client using a browser can access a service using a server. However, the service provided is distributed over many locations called *websites* (see Figure 2.11).

HYPERTEXT AND HYPERMEDIA

The WWW uses the concept of hypertext and hypermedia. In a hypertext environment, information is stored in a set of documents that are linked together using the concept of pointers. An item can be associated with another document using a pointer. The reader who

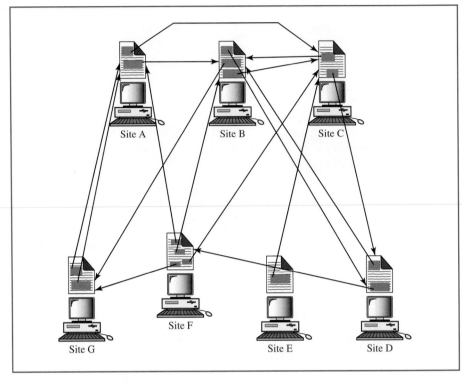

Figure 2.11 Distributed services

is browsing through the document can move to other documents by choosing (clicking) the items that are linked to other documents. Figure 2.12 shows the concept of hypertext.

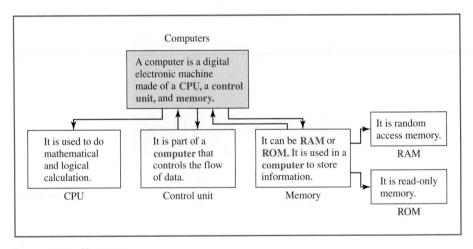

Figure 2.12 Hypertext

Whereas hypertext documents contain only text, hypermedia documents can contain pictures, graphics, and sound.

A unit of hypertext or hypermedia available on the Web is called a *page*. The main page for an organization or an individual is known as a *homepage*.

To use WWW, we need three components: a browser, a web server, and a protocol called the Hypertext Transfer Protocol (HTTP).

Browser

A variety of vendors offer commercial browsers that interpret and display a web document, and all of them use nearly the same architecture. Each browser usually consists of three parts: a controller, client programs, and interpreters. The controller receives input from the keyboard or the mouse and uses the client programs to access the document. After the document has been accessed, the controller uses one of the interpreters to display the document on the screen. The client program can be one of the protocols described previously such as FTP, or TELNET, but it is usually HTTP. The interpreter is a language used today on the Internet such as HTML or Java (see Figure 2.13).

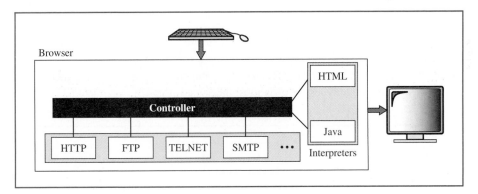

Figure 2.13   Browser architecture

Server

The server stores all pages belonging to the site.

HYPERTEXT TRANSFER PROTOCOL (HTTP)

The **Hypertext Transfer Protocol** (HTTP) is a protocol used mainly to access data on the World Wide Web. The protocol transfers data in the form of plain text, hypertext, audio, video, and so on. It is called the Hypertext Transfer Protocol because its efficiency allows its use in a hypertext environment where there are rapid jumps from one document to another.

The idea of HTTP is very simple. A client sends a request, which looks like mail, to the server. The server sends the response, which looks like a mail reply, to the client. The request and response messages carry data in the form of a letter with MIME-like format.

The commands from the client to the server are embedded in a letterlike request message. The contents of the requested file or other information are embedded in a letterlike response message.

HTTP Transaction

Figure 2.14 illustrates an HTTP transaction between the client and server. The client initializes the transaction by sending a request message. The server replies by sending a response.

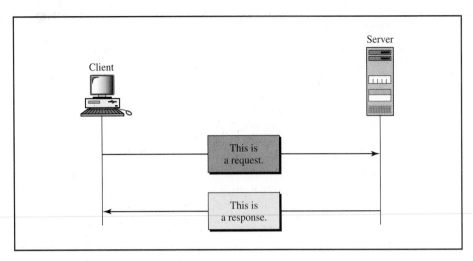

Figure 2.14 HTTP transaction

Messages

There are two general types of HTTP messages, shown in Figure 2.15: a request and a response. Both message types follow almost the same format.

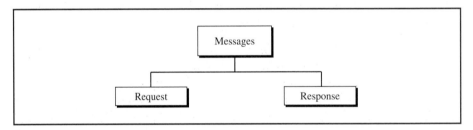

Figure 2.15 Message categories

Request Message A request message consists of a request line, headers, and sometimes a body (see Figure 2.16).

Response Message A response message consists of a status line, headers, and sometimes a body (see Figure 2.16).

ADDRESSES

A client that wants to access a document needs an address. To facilitate the access of documents distributed throughout the world, HTTP uses the concept of locators. The uniform resource locator (URL) is a standard for specifying any kind of information on the Internet. The URL defines four things: method, host computer, port, and path (see Figure 2.17).

The *method* is the protocol used to retrieve the document, for example, HTTP. The *host* is the computer on which the information is located, although the name of the computer can be an alias. Web pages are usually stored in computers, and computers are given alias names that usually begin with the characters "www." This is not mandatory, however, as the host can be any name given to the computer that hosts the web page.

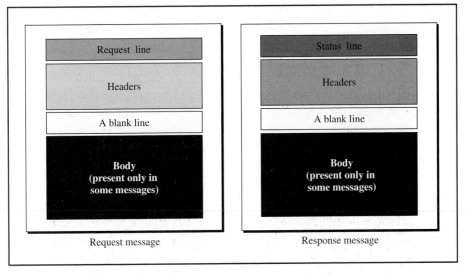

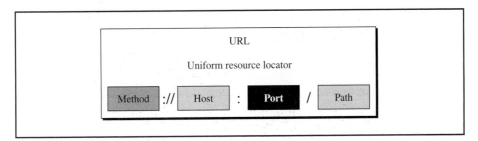

Figure 2.16 Request and response messages

Figure 2.17 URL

The URL optionally can contain the port number of the server. If the *port* is included, it should be inserted between the host and the path, and it should be separated from the host by a colon.

The *path* is the pathname of the file where the information is located. Note that the path can itself contain slashes that, in the UNIX operating system, separate the directories from the subdirectories and files.

BUSINESS FOCUS: HISTORY OF WWW

The idea of the World Wide Web started in 1989 at the European Particle Physics Laboratory, CERN, in Geneva, Switzerland. Tim Bernes-Lee needed to create a large database for physics research, which he found impossible to do using one single computer. The obvious solution was to let each piece of information be stored on an appropriate computer and let the computers be linked together through hypertext.

In 1993, the University of Illinois, under the supervision of Anderson, created the first graphical browser called Mosaic.

In 1994, Anderson and some colleagues started Netscape, one of the most popular browsers today. Another widely used browser is Microsoft Explorer.

TECHNICAL FOCUS: HTML

Hypertext Markup Language (HTML) is a language for creating web pages. The term *markup language* comes from the book publishing industry. Before a book is typeset and printed, a copy editor reads the manuscript and corrects it with marks. These marks tell the designer how to format the text. For example, if the copy editor wants part of a line to be printed in boldface, a wavy line is drawn under that part. In the same way, data for a web page are formatted for interpretation by a browser.

Let us explain the idea with an example. To make part of a text displayed in boldface with HTML, we must include the beginning and ending boldface tags (marks) in the text, as shown below:

<B> This is the text to be bold </B>

The two tags <B> and </B> are instructions for the browser. When the browser sees these two marks, it knows that the text must be boldfaced.

HTML lets us use ASCII characters (see Appendix A) for both the main text and formatting instructions. In this way, every computer can receive the whole document as an ASCII document. The main text is the data, and the formatting instructions can be used by the browser to format the data.

A tag is enclosed in two brackets (< and >) and usually comes in pairs. The beginning tag starts with the name of the tag, and the ending tag starts with a slash followed by the name of the tag.

2.8   VIDEOCONFERENCING

Another popular application is **videoconferencing.** Videoconferencing can eliminate the cost of traveling, and save time and energy. Videoconferencing can provide communication between two or more groups of participants or a set of individual participants (sometimes called desktop videoconferencing).

© Corbis/Vol. 147

Videoconferencing can eliminate the cost of traveling and save time and energy.

Each participant or group of participants uses a videoconferencing client program. The video and audio data are sent from the clients to the videoconferencing server program, which then distributes data to all clients as shown in Figure 2.18.

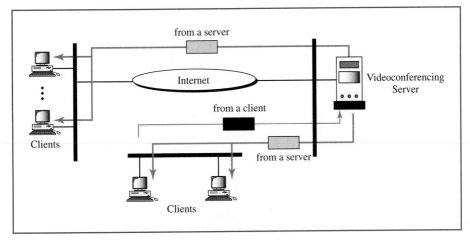

Figure 2.18 Videoconferencing

COMPRESSION

Video and audio communication requires the exchange of a large volume of data in a short period of time. As we know from the motion picture industry, a video is made of tens of picture frames sent each second to simulate a moving picture. This means that we send tens of picture frames per second with each picture frame containing thousands of picture elements (dots). Each picture element is encoded to represent the color of the dot. Video and audio data require the user to send a large amount of data to the network. In data communications parlance, this means that the user must be allocated a large bandwidth. The data road from the network to the user must be a freeway, not a one-lane street. To alleviate the situation, data can be compressed.

2.9   GROUP DISCUSSION: LISTSERV

Another popular application is **listserv,** which allows a group of users to discuss a common topic of interest. For example, there could be a group for those interested in seventeenth century Flemish tapestries or a group for San Francisco Seals fans. One popular use of listserv is the creation of discussion groups for students at colleges and universities, especially for those enrolled in distance learning classes. This is an excellent way for students unable to attend a traditional class to communicate with each other.

This application, like the others we have discussed, is also a client-server application. However, there are two server programs running on the server: the subscriber server and the mailer server. Figure 2.19 shows the situation.

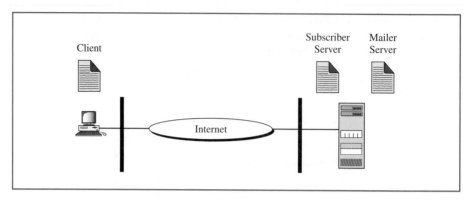

Figure 2.19   Listserv

SUBSCRIBING

The subscriber server accepts membership in a group. A user who wants to be a member of the group sends an email addressed to this server. The email contains the SUBSCRIBE command that is scanned by the subscriber server. The user is then registered if the user has permission to be part of the group. The subscriber server informs the user of the registration by a return email. A typical subscribe command is shown below:

SUBSCRIBE **mailer-server-email-address** *user-email-address*

To subscribe, the user sends the request to the subscriber server, not the mailer server.

SENDING EMAIL

After subscribing, a user can send email to the group. This time, the user sends an email addressed to the mailer server. The mailer server automatically relays the email to every member of the group if the email is from a registered user.

To send an email to every member of the group, the user sends it to the mailer server, which then automatically relays it to every subscriber.

UNSUBSCRIBING

To cancel a subscription, a user sends an UNSUBSCRIBE command to the subscriber server. A typical unsubscribe command is shown below:

UNSUBSCRIBE **mailer-server-email-address** *user-email-address*

The use of listserv in business is gaining in popularity. First, an organization can set up a group for each department for interdepartmental communication. Second, a group can be created between different organizations interested in a particular topic.

2.10 CHATTING

Another application in this layer is **chatting.** This is a real-time application like video-conferencing, in which two parties are involved in a real-time exchange of text, audio, and video. The two parties can send text to each other, talk to each other (the same way they talk on the phone), and even see each other.

Chatting works the same way as videoconferencing but on a smaller scale. The two parties each use a client program to send text, audio, or video information to a server. The server receives the information and relays the data, with a small delay.

Chatting has not found a place in the business world as yet. Currently, it is mostly used for personal purposes, but vendors hope that this will change.

CASE STUDY

NEW AGE HOME PHARMACY

NAHP uses standard application-layer programs: SMTP, POP, FTP, and HTTP. The most widely-used application program is electronic mail (email). An SMTP server program is installed on the main server computer in the basement. All incoming email are received by this server program and stored in mailboxes. Each employee has a mailbox (a file) in this computer. A copy of the SMTP client is installed on each desktop or laptop. The SMTP clients are responsible for sending mail. A copy of the POP client program is also installed on each user computer. The POP client periodically contacts the POP server, installed on the server in the basement, to retrieve any new email in the corresponding mailbox. The user interface, which is also installed on each user computer, is Eudora. This program creates, edits, formats, saves, and deletes email. It calls the POP client to get the received email and calls the SMTP client to send outgoing email. Because NAHP uses non-ASCII characters in email communication, the management has agreed to use MIME.

The addresses adopted for email communication have the domain name *nahp.com,* which is appended to the mailbox name. The mailbox name is the last name of the employee followed by the first name. For example, the email address of Madeline Lindsey is *lindseymadeline@nahp.com.*

Two years ago management hired a web page programmer to create a website for NAHP. The site, called *http://www.nahp.com,* advertises the services offered by NAHP to its target customer, the medical doctor. The website is maintained on the general server in the basement. The protocol used to retrieve web pages is HTTP.

NAHP also uses FTP. However, at present, this protocol is strictly for internal use. As we will see in the Chapter 14 case study, a firewall prevents FTP packets from leaving or entering the organization. FTP is used internally to transfer files (such as customer files) inside the organization.

2.11   KEY TERMS

anonymous FTP

browser

chatting

client

client-server model

electronic mail (email)

File Transfer Protocol (FTP)

Hypertext Markup Language (HTML)

Hypertext Transfer Protocol (HTTP)

Internet mail access protocol (IMAP)

listserv

local login

mail transfer agent (MTA)

multipurpose Internet mail extension
   (MIME)

network virtual terminal (NVT)

Post Office Protocol, version 3 (POP3)

remote login

server

Simple Mail Transfer Protocol
   (SMTP)

Simple Network Management Protocol
   (SNMP)

terminal network (TELNET)

Trivial File Transfer Protocol
   (TFTP)

uniform resource locator (URL)

user agent (UA)

videoconferencing

World Wide Web (WWW)

2.12   SUMMARY

❏   In the client-server model, the client runs a program to request a service and the
    server runs a program to provide the service. These two programs communicate
    with each other.

❏   One server program can provide services for many client programs.

❏   The server program is on at all times while the client program is run only when
    needed.

❏   The TCP/IP protocol that supports email on the Internet is called Simple Mail
    Transfer Protocol (SMTP).

❏   Both SMTP client and server require a user agent (UA) and a mail transfer
    agent (MTA).

❏   Post Office Protocol (POP) is a protocol used by a mail server in conjunction with
    SMTP to receive and hold mail for hosts.

❏   Multipurpose Internet mail extension (MIME) is an extension of SMTP that allows
    the transfer of multimedia messages.

❏   TELNET is a client-server application that allows a user to logon to a remote
    machine, giving the user access to the remote system.

❏   The World Wide Web (WWW) is a repository of information spread all over the
    world and linked together.

❏   Hypertext and hypermedia are documents linked to one another through the
    concept of pointers.

❏   The Hypertext Transfer Protocol (HTTP) is the main protocol used to access data
    on the World Wide Web (WWW).

❏   File Transfer Protocol (FTP) is a TCP/IP client-server application for copying files
    from one host to another.

❏   Trivial File Transfer Protocol (TFTP) is a simple file transfer protocol without the
    complexities and sophistication of FTP.

❏   Hypertext Markup Language (HTML) is a language used to create static web
    pages.

□ Videoconferencing allows people at different sites to participate in a conference.
□ Listserv is an application that allows a group of users to discuss a common topic of interest.
□ Chatting is a real-time application in which two parties are involved in a real-time exchange of text, audio, and video.

PRACTICE SET

Review Questions

1. In the client-server model, what is the role of the client program? What is the role of the server program?
2. What application program allows connection to a remote system in such a way that the local terminal appears to be a terminal at the remote system?
3. How is TFTP different from FTP?
4. What is the function of SMTP?
5. What is the difference between a user agent (UA) and a mail transfer agent (MTA)?
6. How does MIME enhance SMTP?
7. Why is an application such as POP needed for electronic messaging?
8. How are HTTP and the WWW related to the Internet?
9. What is the purpose of HTML?
10. Why should the server always be running whereas the client program should not?
11. Name three advantages of email over snail mail.
12. What is the purpose of an email server?
13. How is IMAP superior to POP?
14. What is the purpose of anonymous FTP?
15. Why is TELNET needed?
16. What are the components of the World Wide Web?
17. How is listserv different from chatting?

Multiple-Choice Questions

18. _____ can request a service.
    a. A socket interface
    b. A port
    c. A client
    d. A server
19. The UA is responsible for _____.
    a. message preparation
    b. message forwarding
    c. sending messages across the Internet
    d. a and b
20. The purpose of the MTA is _____.
    a. message preparation
    b. envelope creation
    c. sending messages across the Internet
    d. a and b

21. When a message is sent using SMTP, the local mail server has SMTP _____ software.
    a. client
    b. server
    c. a and b
    d. none of the above

22. MIME allows _____ data to be sent through SMTP.
    a. audio
    b. non-ASCII data
    c. image
    d. all of the above

23. Which of the following is a browser client program?
    a. HTTP
    b. FTP
    c. TELNET
    d. all of the above

24. Hypertext documents are linked through _____.
    a. DNS
    b. TELNET
    c. pointers
    d. homepages

25. What are the components of a browser?
    a. retrieval method, host computer, pathname
    b. controller, client program, interpreter
    c. hypertext, hypermedia, HTML
    d. all of the above

26. A server provides a _____ to a client.
    a. service
    b. paradigm
    c. browser
    d. none of the above

27. One server can service _____.
    a. one client
    b. two clients
    c. many clients
    d. one paradigm

28. A client runs _____; a server runs _____.
    a. continuously; continuously
    b. for a limited amount of time; for a limited amount of time
    c. continuously; for a limited amount of time
    d. for a limited amount of time; continuously

29. Email goes from the user agent to the _____.
    a. local server
    b. remote server
    c. remote user agent
    d. mailbox

30. _____ is a popular mail access protocol.
    a. SMTP
    b. POP
    c. MIME
    d. HTTP
31. IMAP has more sophisticated features for mail retrieval than _____.
    a. SMTP
    b. POP
    c. MIME
    d. HTTP
32. To transfer large files from one computer to another, _____ is the better choice.
    a. HTTP
    b. FTP
    c. TFTP
    d. SMTP
33. An open _____ site allows the public to access a limited set of files.
    a. OSI
    b. TELNET
    c. HTTP
    d. FTP
34. _____ is a general-purpose client-server program that lets a user access any application program on a remote computer.
    a. OSI
    b. TELNET
    c. HTTP
    d. FTP
35. A _____ interprets and displays a web document.
    a. controller
    b. port
    c. MIME
    d. browser
36. What does the URL need to access a document?
    a. pathname
    b. host computer
    c. retrieval method
    d. all of the above

CHAPTER 3

Transport Layer

The **transport layer** is the core of the Internet (and OSI) model. Protocols at this layer oversee the delivery of data from an application program on one computer to an application program on another computer. More importantly, they act as a liaison between the application-layer protocols and the services provided by the lower layers (network, data link, and physical). The application layer programs interact with each other, using the services of the transport layer without even being aware of the existence of the lower layers. In other words, the application layer programs are oblivious to the intricacies of the physical network and are not dependent on the physical network type. Only one set of upper layer software needs to be developed. To the application layer program, the physical networks are simply a homogeneous cloud that somehow takes data and delivers it to its destination safe and sound.

OBJECTIVES

After reading this chapter, the reader should be able to:

❏ Understand the position of the transport layer in the Internet model.

❏ Understand the rationale for the existence of the transport layer.

❏ Understand the concept of application-to-application delivery.

❏ Understand the duties of the transport layer: packetizing, addressing,

connection creation, and reliable delivery.

❏ Distinguish between the two transport-layer protocols used in the Internet: UDP and TCP.

❏ Know which application layer program can use UDP and which can use TCP.

3.1 APPLICATION-TO-APPLICATION DELIVERY

Figure 3.1 shows the position of the transport layer in the Internet model. The transport layer provides **application-to-application delivery** (sometimes called *process-to-process delivery* because when a program is running it is called a process) in the Internet. By application-to-application we mean from one application program to another application program. Later, we will see that delivery to the network or data link layers is different. A transport-layer protocol takes a message from an application program, such as a client, running on a computer, and delivers it to another application program, such as

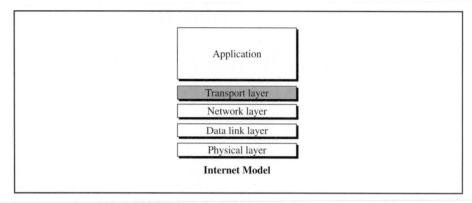

Figure 3.1   Transport layer in the Internet model

a server, running on another computer. The application program is aware of only one layer (the transport layer) involved in this delivery. Consider our own postal system. We are not aware, and we do not care, how our letter reaches its destination; we think of the post office only as a transport facility that delivers our letter. Figure 3.2 shows application-to-application delivery.

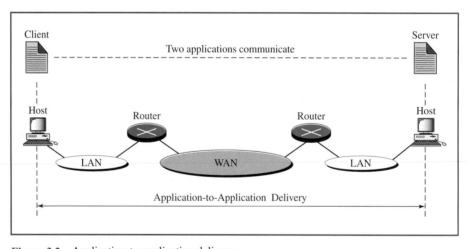

Figure 3.2   Application-to-application delivery

3.2   DUTIES

Application-to-application delivery is achieved through a set of functions performed by the transport layer. The most important are packetizing, creating a connection, addressing, and providing reliability as shown in Figure 3.3.

PACKETIZING

The transport layer creates packets out of the message received from the application layer. **Packetizing** divides a long message into smaller ones; these smaller units are encapsulated into the data field of the transport-layer packet and headers are added.

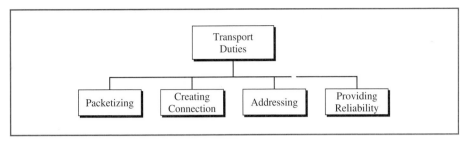

Figure 3.3   Duties of the transport layer

Dividing Large Messages
The message an application program sends can vary in length. For example, an SMTP client (email protocol) may send a short message (several lines) or a long message with several attachments and multimedia documents. A long message may be larger than the maximum size that can be handled by the lower-layer protocols. For example, some network layers can only handle packets with a few thousand characters or less. This means that long messages from the application layer must be divided into sections with each section inserted (encapsulated) into a separate packet. This is similar to what happens using snail mail. If we have a letter with many pages and we only have standard size envelopes, we need to separate the letter and send multiple envelopes addressed to the same destination.

Adding a Header
Even if the message arriving from the application layer is small enough to be handled by the network layer, the transport layer still inserts (encapsulates) the data into a transport-layer packet. A **header** is added to allow the transport layer to perform its other functions.

CREATING CONNECTION

Transport-layer protocols today are divided into two categories: **connection-oriented** and **connectionless.**

Connection-Oriented Delivery
A connection-oriented protocol first establishes a connection (a virtual path) between the sender and receiver. The connection is virtual; that is, the application layer thinks that a single path has been created; in reality, the packets may travel through different physical paths. We can say that a session exists between the sender and the receiver. The session remains intact until it is broken by one of the parties. In the meantime, the two parties can send multiple packets related to each other, traveling one after another through the virtual path. Of course, the packets may travel out of order, but the transport layer ensures that this is transparent to the application program. The packets are numbered consecutively and communication can take place in both directions.

The connection-oriented protocol has three phases: connection establishment, data transfer, and connection termination. The process is much like a telephone call. First, a connection is made: The caller dials and the receiver answers. Then voice transfer occurs in both directions. Finally, the parties terminate the communication by hanging up.

Connection Establishment   Before either communicating device can send data to the other, the initiating device must first determine the availability of the other to exchange data and a pathway must be found through the network so that data can be sent. This is called **connection establishment.** Connection establishment requires three steps in what is called a **three-way handshake** as shown in Figure 3.4.

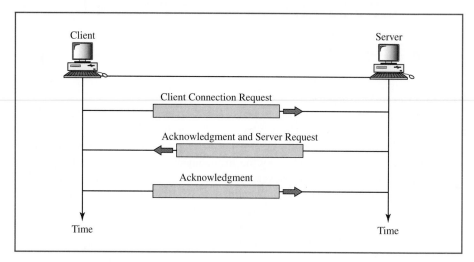

Figure 3.4   Connection establishment

1. The computer requesting the connection sends a connection request packet to the intended receiver.
2. The responding computer returns a confirmation packet to the requesting computer.
3. The requesting computer returns a packet acknowledging the confirmation.

Data Transfer   After connection establishment, the parties can send data back and forth. As mentioned earlier, the packets are numbered to preserve the ordered relationship between the packets.

Connection Termination   At any moment, either party can terminate the connection. Termination requires four (or sometimes three) steps as shown in Figure 3.5.

1. The party that wants to terminate the connection sends a termination request packet to the other party.
2. The second party acknowledges the receipt of the termination. The connection is terminated in one direction.
3. The second party sends its own termination request to terminate the connection in the opposite direction. If the connection is terminated by one party, and the second party has no more data to send, this step can be combined with the second step.
4. The first party acknowledges the receipt of the termination request from the second party. Steps 2 and 3 can be done simultaneously if the two parties finish at the same time.

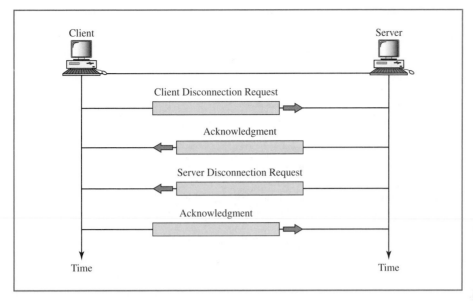

Figure 3.5   Connection termination

Connectionless Delivery

Connectionless delivery means that there is no virtual connection (no session) between two application programs. A connectionless transport-layer protocol is used when when an application needs to send one packet quickly without the overhead of connection establishment and termination.

Connection is closely related to reliability: A connectionless protocol cannot be reliable because the relationship between packets provides reliability.

ADDRESSING

Imagine an HTTP client (a browser) on a local computer needs to send a request to an HTTP server on a remote computer. First, the client needs the address of the remote computer, which must be unique to distinguish it from all the computers in the world. This addressing is implemented in the network layer, which we discuss in the next chapter. For the moment, let us assume that the client knows the address of this remote computer.

There is, however, another problem that must be solved. The remote computer may be running several server programs, such as HTTP, SMTP, and TELNET, at the same time. When the request arrives at the remote computer, the computer must deliver the request to the HTTP server program, not to any other server program. In other words, the packet carrying the request must specify to which server program the request must be delivered.

The request packet must also specify the client program that sent the packet. The server uses this when it responds to the request. The reason is that the local computer may also be running several clients. People normally open several client programs at the same time (using different windows, for example). In this way, the local computer can match the response to the client.

Figure 3.6 shows application programs running on two computers.

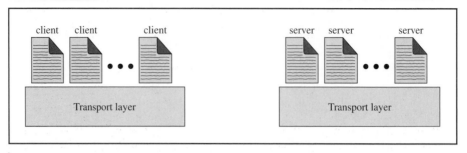

Figure 3.6 Application programs

Local Addresses

It is obvious that, at the transport layer, we need two addresses in each communication, one for the client and one for the server. However, these addresses need not be universal. In other words, we do not need to assign a unique address to every client and server program in the world. The addresses can be local to the computer that is running the application program. That is, a computer running an HTTP client on a computer can have the same client address as another computer somewhere else in the world using an HTTP or an SMTP or some other client program. There is no ambiguity, because the computer address (discussed in the next chapter) first defines the computer and then the application address defines the client or server running on the computer.

Let us give an analogy. The apartment number of two people may be the same as long as they live in different buildings. The first person lives in apartment 47 on 1200 MacKenzie Boulevard; the other person lives in apartment 47 on 2000 Gregory Drive. The mailman never mistakes these two addresses; the apartment numbers are the same, but the street addresses are different.

The addresses of client and server programs are defined at the transport layer. These addresses are local to the computer running the programs. The addresses must be unique locally but not universally.

Port Numbers

In the Internet model, the addresses at the transport layer are called **port numbers.** In other words, when a client communicates with a server, two port numbers are involved: the client port number and the server port number. A port number is a number between 0 and 65,535; this range is large enough to allow thousands of clients or servers to run at the same time on a computer.

Client Port Number When a client wants to send a message to a server, the transport layer chooses a client port number. The transport layer follows these rules in this selection:

1. The number must be within a predefined range.
2. The number must be unique and not given to any other client or server.
3. The transport layer locks the number until the communication is over; the number is recycled after that.

Server Port Number The port number for a server program requires more attention. If the computer running a server program chooses a port number for each server program it is running, how can this information be conveyed to a computer that is running a client program? For example, suppose an HTTP client wants to send a request to an HTTP server. It knows the computer address, but it does not know the port number of the HTTP server. To solve this dilemma, the Internet authorities have decided to use *well-known* port numbers for servers. In other words, for each type of server program, a port number is assigned that is known to every computer connected to the Internet. For example, for an HTTP server, the well-known port number is 80. So when a computer running an HTTP client wants to send a message to an HTTP server, it chooses an arbitrary client port number, but it uses 80 as the server port number. Figure 3.7 shows the idea.

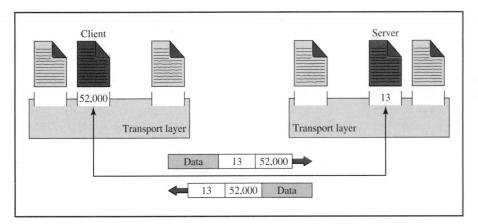

Figure 3.7 Port numbers

TECHNICAL FOCUS:
RANGE OF PORT NUMBERS

The port numbers defined in the Internet range from 0 to 65,535. These port numbers are divided into three ranges by the Internet Assigned Numbers Authority (IANA).

1. The numbers from 0 to 1023 are well-known port numbers; they can only be assigned to server programs that are, or will become, standard in the Internet.
2. The numbers from 1024 to 49,151 are assigned to registered server programs. An organization may write a server program and assign a number in this range as the server port number. However, the organization must register it with Internet authorities if it does not want this number to be used by another organization.
3. The numbers from 49,152 to 65,535 are temporary port numbers that can be used as client port numbers.

Some well-known port numbers are shown below:

FTP: 20 (for data connection) and 21 (for control connection)
TELNET: 23
SMTP: 25
TFTP: 69
HTTP: 80

A client uses a temporary port number; a server uses a well-known port number.

RELIABILITY

A transport-layer protocol must deliver packets from a client program running on one computer to a server program running on another computer and vice versa. The service can be reliable or unreliable.

Unreliable Service

Some transport-layer protocols (such as UDP, discussed later) are designed for speed, not reliability. They quickly deliver packets from the client to the server and vice versa; they do not guarantee reliability. In this service, a packet can be damaged (contents changed), a packet can be lost, a packet can arrive out of order, or a packet can be duplicated. This unreliable service provided by the transport layer does not accept responsibility for the packets. Reliability is sacrificed for quick service. The TFTP protocol discussed in Chapter 2 uses this type of service. It is designed for quick delivery of a small file. If the file is lost or damaged, the user requests it again. Some management protocols (see Chapter 16) also use this service. A manager often wants to quickly send a message to a computer or a connecting device. Speed is more important than accuracy; if the message is corrupted, it is simply discarded.

A good example of an unreliable service is snail mail. If we send a series of letters to the same destination, there is no guarantee of perfect delivery. Some may be lost; some may be delivered out of order. The post office tries its best (best-effort delivery), but there is no guarantee. If we need a guarantee, we use a higher level, more expensive service such as registered mail.

Reliable Service

Some transport-layer protocols (such as TCP, discussed later) are designed for reliability. This reliable delivery comes with a cost: The delivery is slower and more complicated. In networking, reliability means **damage control, loss control, order control,** and **duplicate control.** To achieve these four goals, a reliable transport layer inserts a **sequence number** in a packet. For example, if a client sends 10 packets to a server in one connection, the

Snail mail is an example of unreliable service. The post office
tries its best (best-effort delivery), but there are no guarantees.

packets must be numbered sequentially. The numbering does not need to start from 1; it
can start from any number as long as the numbers are consecutive. In our example, the first
packet can be numbered 100, the next 101, the next 102, and the last 109. The rationale
behind numbering is discussed later.

**For reliable service, the transport layer needs to number packets belonging to a
connection using sequence numbers.**

Damage Control   The first goal of reliability is damage control. A packet may be damaged during transmission. In Chapter 5, we will show how this happens and discuss the
types of errors created. Errors are inevitable even when we use sophisticated devices and
the best transmission medium. Now the reader may ask, how can damage be controlled in
the transport layer if the underlying network is unreliable? There are three procedures:

1. The sender includes extra information in the packet that is generated by
   manipulation of the data. The sender also sets a timer when it sends a packet and
   keeps a copy of the packet. As a very simple example, if we want to send a
   series of numbers, we can also send their sum. If a number has changed during
   transmission, the sum is no longer valid. When the receiver receives the packet
   there will be a mismatch between the two sums and the receiver will know that
   the packet is damaged. This is called **error detection.** The example we gave is
   very primitive and does not cover many cases. For example, what happens if
   two numbers are changed simultaneously, one incremented by 5 and the other
   decremented by 5? The error cannot be detected because the sum is the same.
   What happens if the sum itself is corrupted? We learn about more sophisticated
   error detection methods in Chapter 5.
2. If the packet is received error-free, the receiver accepts the packet and sends
   a note (called an **acknowledgment** or **ACK**) to let the sender know. In the
   acknowledgment, the receiver specifies which packet was received. Most
   transport-layer protocols use cumulative acknowledgment; they wait until a
   series of packets have arrived and then send an acknowledgment with a number
   one more than the sequence number of the last packet received. For example, if

packets with sequence numbers 101, 102, 103, and 104 have arrived without error, the receiver sends an acknowledgment with number 105. This means "I have received all packets up to 104, safe and sound, and I am expecting packet 105." When the sender receives an acknowledgment, it destroys its copy of the packets and cancels the timers.

3. If a packet is received corrupted, the receiver does not send an acknowledgment for that packet. The sender, after its timer has expired, knows that something is wrong and sends the packet again. A packet may be sent several times before a safe and sound packet is received by the receiver.

Figure 3.8 shows the idea of damage control. Note that by holding a copy, using a timer, and resending the packet if it is damaged, we can create a reliable, logical connection between two transport-layer protocols even though the underlying (physical) network is unreliable.

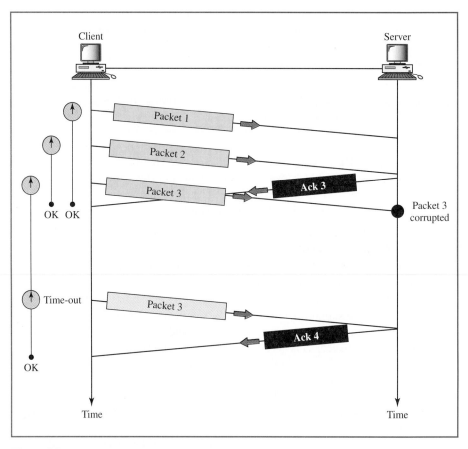

Figure 3.8   Damage control

As an analogy, suppose that we (the authors) need to send a manuscript to our publisher; we can use any carrier. We keep a copy of the manuscript and request the publisher to call us when the package has arrived. If the call does not came through, we can send another copy.

Loss Control   The provision for damage control can also take care of the lost packet situation. If the packet is lost, it is never received and no acknowledgment is sent. The timer of the sender expires and the sender sends that packet again. Again, the underlying network may lose a packet, but the reliable transport protocol will resend it. A packet may be lost for many reasons. One of the most important is **congestion.** For example, one of the connecting devices may receive so many packets from different sources that it is overwhelmed and has to discard some of the packets.

It may happen that the packet arrives safe and sound, but the acknowledgment sent by the receiver is lost. Again, the timer set by the sender will cause the resending of the packet. For the sender, it does not matter what is lost: the original packet or the acknowledgment; it just sends the packet again. It may happen that the receiver ends up with two copies of the same packet. Duplicate control, discussed later, will take care of this situation.

Order Control   For the underlying network, each packet is an entity, independent from another packet. The underlying network makes routing decisions about each packet. For example, six packets belonging to the same connection may arrive at a connecting device (a router) that decides to send the first three via a slow transmission medium (the only one available at the moment) and the next three through a newly available fast transmission medium. Packets 4, 5, and 6 arrive before packets 1, 2, and 3. The packets cannot be delivered to the application program in the order they were received; for example, we do not want to receive an email in which the second page precedes the first page. The reliable transport-layer protocol takes care of this situation. The transport-layer delivers the packets to the application layer based on the sequence number. It waits until all packets arrive, puts the packet in order, and delivers them to the application layer.

Duplicate Control   A duplicate packet is undesirable. For example, if we sent a message to a bank to transfer money from one account to another, we do not want this packet to be duplicated. Duplication can be avoided through the transport-layer protocol's use of sequence numbers. If, during a connection, the transport layer receives two packets with the same sequence number, it just discards one packet. Duplication may occur, as we said before, because an acknowledgment is lost or if a device is faulty.

A reliable transport protocol provides damage control, loss control, order control, and duplicate control even if the underlying networking technology and lower-level protocols are not reliable.

This is done through sequence numbers, timers, error detection, and retransmission.

3.3   INTERNET PROTOCOLS

The Internet specifies two protocols for the transport layer: **User Datagram Protocol** (UDP) and **Transmission Control Protocol** (TCP). Figure 3.9 shows the position of these two protocols in the Internet model.

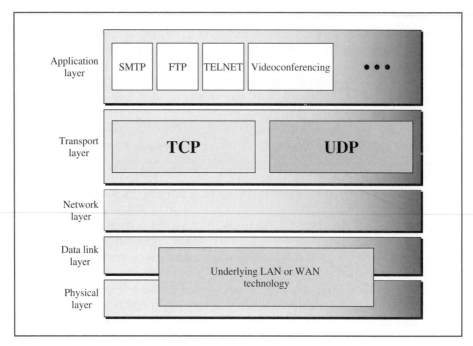

Figure 3.9   UDP and TCP in the Internet model

USER DATAGRAM PROTOCOL (UDP)

UDP is a *connectionless, unreliable* transport protocol. It receives a message from the application program, adds a small header to the message, and sends the message. Of the four duties described for a transport layer, it does only two and a little bit of the third. It does packetizing by adding a header to the message received from the application program. It provides addressing by adding sender and receiver port numbers. It is connectionless and unreliable. However, it does add extra information, called a checksum, to allow the receiver to detect errors. If an error is detected, the packet is simply discarded with no notification to the sender.

UDP performs the bare-bone functions of a transport-layer protocol. However, it eliminates the overhead needed for a fully loaded protocol. UDP is used when an application needs quick action. For example, TFTP and SNMP (a management protocol discussed in Chapter 16) use the services of UDP because TFTP needs to send the contents of a small file quickly and SNMP needs to send a message to a device as fast as possible. They prefer speed to the advantages of a connection-oriented and reliable protocol.

User Datagram

UDP packets are called **user datagrams.** A user datagram consists of a header of 8 bytes (64 bits) in the form of four separate fields as well as the message received from the application program. Figure 3.10 shows a user datagram.

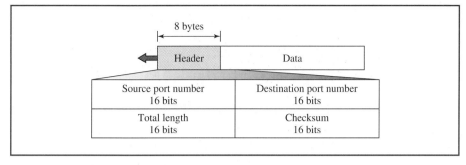

Figure 3.10 User datagram

TECHNICAL FOCUS: USER DATAGRAM

The fields in a user datagram are as follows:

❑ **Source port number.** The port number used by the sender of the user datagram.
❑ **Destination port number.** The port number used by the destination of the user datagram.
❑ **Length.** A number that defines the total length of the user datagram in bytes. Because the length of a packet is variable, a field inside the packet must define the length so that the receiver knows when the whole packet has arrived.
❑ **Checksum.** This field is used to detect errors over the entire user datagram (header plus data). The checksum is discussed in a future chapter.

TRANSMISSION CONTROL PROTOCOL (TCP)

TCP is a *connection-oriented, reliable* transport protocol. It receives a message from the application program, adds a header to the message, and sends the message. It performs all four duties defined for a transport-layer protocol. It does packetizing by adding a header to the message received from the application program. It provides addressing by adding sender and receiver port numbers. It establishes a connection before data transfer and terminates the connection after data transfer. It provides damage control, loss control, order control, and duplicate control.

Most of the application protocols, SMTP, HTTP, FTP, and TELNET, use the services of TCP.

Segment

TCP packets are called **segments.** A message received from the application is divided into segments and a header of 20 to 60 bytes is added as shown in Figure 3.11.

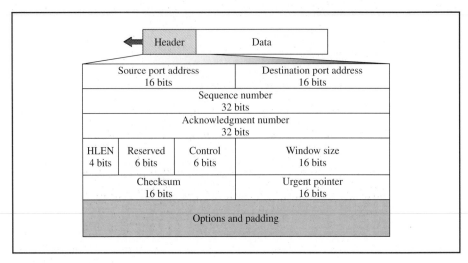

Figure 3.11   Segment

TECHNICAL FOCUS: SEGMENT

The fields in a segment are as follows:

❏ **Source port number.** The port number used by the sender of the segment.
❏ **Destination port number.** The port number used by the destination of the segment.
❏ **Sequence number.** This sequence number is used for ordering the segments.
❏ **Header length.** The header length is a number that must be multiplied by four to find the length of the header. This field is needed because the header is of variable size.
❏ **Control flags.** Six 1-bit flags define the purpose of the segment (connection establishment, connection termination, acknowledgment, and so on).
❏ **Checksum.** This field is used for error detection.
❏ **Urgent pointer.** This field is a pointer that indicates the end of urgent data should the segment be carrying any.
❏ **Option.** This field contains optional (up to 40 bytes) information used by the sender and the receiver.

CASE STUDY

NEW AGE HOME PHARMACY

N AHP decided on a PC platform for all computers, desktops, and laptops. The original operating system was Windows 98; it was upgraded to Windows 2000 in 2001. The TCP/IP protocol is part of the Windows 2000 operating system. Although Windows 2000 is a network operating system and is capable of handling networking, all LANs use the TCP/IP protocol suite for internal and external communications.

The transport-layer protocol is primarily TCP. However, UDP is also needed for some application programs, such as SNMP (see Chapter 16).

The use of the transport layers is transparent to most users. However, management is aware that the system uses TCP and UDP for application-to-application communication.

The transport-layer protocols are more visible at the server site. TCP and UDP are monitored by the network management program. The program has issued several warnings concerning TCP in the last few months. The number of TCP clients, both internal and external, has increased tremendously. Modern Networking has contacted NAHP management to warn that overloads (number of segments received and sent) may create problems in the future. For example, TCP might drop some of the packets received. The consulting firm has proposed two solutions:

1. Upgrade the server to a faster computer with more memory and more disk space.
2. Add a new server and distribute the application programs over these two servers. One server is to be used for email communication (SMTP and POP); the other for HTTP and FTP.

Management has requested a feasibility study for these two proposals; the cost and the downtime are the two main issues that must be included. The decision on this issue is postponed until the completion of the study.

3.4   KEY TERMS

acknowledgment (ACK)
application-to-application delivery
congestion
connection-oriented delivery
connectionless delivery
connection establishment
connection termination
damage control
duplicate control
error detection
header
loss control
order control

packetizing
port number
reliable service
segment
sequence number
three-way handshake
transmission control protocol
   (TCP)
transport layer
unreliable service
user datagram
user datagram protocol (UDP)
well-known port number

3.5 SUMMARY

❏ The transport-layer protocols oversee the application-to-application delivery of data from an application program on one computer to an application program on another computer.

❏ The transport-layer protocol functions include packetizing a message, creating a connection, addressing, and providing reliability.

❏ Packetizing can involve the division of an application-layer message into smaller units. Each unit is encapsulated into a transport-layer packet and a header is added.

❏ A transport-layer protocol is either connection-oriented or connectionless.

❏ A connection-oriented protocol first establishes a connection (a virtual path) between the sender and receiver. After data transfer is complete, the connection is formally terminated.

❏ The addresses at the transport layer are called port numbers. The server port number is called a well-known port.

❏ A transport-layer protocol can be reliable or unreliable. Reliability means damage control, loss control, order control, and duplicate control.

❏ UDP is a connectionless, unreliable transport protocol.

❏ TCP is a connection-oriented, reliable transport protocol.

 PRACTICE SET

Review Questions

1. What do we mean when we say that the transport layer makes data transmission transparent to the upper layers?
2. What is application-to-application delivery?
3. Why must large messages be divided into smaller units?
4. What are the phases in a connection-oriented delivery?
5. What is a three-way handshake and when is it used?
6. What is a four-way handshake and when is it used?
7. How is a port number related to an application program?
8. How does the port number for a client program differ from a port number for a server program?
9. What does the term reliable service mean?
10. What is the function of a sequence number of a packet?
11. What are the two transport-layer protocols defined by the Internet model?
12. Which specific applications use UDP?
13. Which specific applications use TCP?

14. The delivery of a message from one application program to another application program is called _____ delivery.
    a. transport-to-transport
    b. network-to-network
    c. station-to-station
    d. application-to-application

15. The transport layer is responsible for _____.
    a. packetizing
    b. creating a connection
    c. addressing
    d. all of the above

16. The division of a long message into smaller units is called _____.
    a. packetizing
    b. addressing
    c. concatenation
    d. multiplexing

17. A _____ handshake is needed for connection establishment.
    a. one-way
    b. two-way
    c. three-way
    d. four-way

18. Connection establishment, data transfer, and connection termination are steps in a _____ delivery.
    a. connectionless
    b. connection-oriented
    c. control
    d. client-server

19. A program has a port number of 23. This is _____.
    a. a client program
    b. a server program
    c. connection establishment
    d. a temporary port

20. A TELNET client can use a port number of _____.
    a. 20
    b. 23
    c. 49152
    d. any of the above

21. A transport protocol is reliable if it has _____.
    a. loss control
    b. damage control
    c. duplication control
    d. all of the above

22. In a reliable transport service, if a packet is lost, _____.
    a. the sender resends the packet
    b. the receiver sends a negative acknowledgment
    c. the sender sends an acknowledgment
    d. the receiver's timer goes off
23. In a reliable transport service, if a packet is duplicated, _____.
    a. the receiver notifies the sender
    b. the sender sends an acknowledgment
    c. the sender's timer goes off
    d. one of the duplicates is discarded
24. UDP is a _____ transport protocol.
    a. connectionless, reliable
    b. connectionless, unreliable
    c. connection-oriented, reliable
    d. connection-oriented, unreliable
25. TCP is a _____ transport protocol.
    a. connectionless, reliable
    b. connectionless, unreliable
    c. connection-oriented, reliable
    d. connection-oriented, unreliable
26. The UDP packet is called a _____.
    a. datagram
    b. user datagram
    c. segment
    d. user segment
27. The TCP packet is called a _____.
    a. datagram
    b. user datagram
    c. segment
    d. user segment

CHAPTER 4

Network Layer

The **network layer** in the Internet model is responsible for carrying a packet from one computer to another; it is responsible for *computer-to-computer* or *host-to-host* delivery. In other words, when we send a packet from San Francisco to Miami, the two network-layer protocols in the two computers cooperate to supervise the delivery of a message.

A packet traveling from a source to a destination needs two addresses. The addresses in the network layer must be unique to avoid any ambiguity. If two computers, one in Miami, and one in Paris (France) have the same network-layer address, a packet intended for Miami may end up in Paris. The network layer is responsible for defining and handling addresses.

Due to the complex structure of the Internet, several routes may be available for the delivery of a packet from the source to the destination. However, one of these routes is the best (optimal) route for the packet. The route determination and actual routing of the packet from the source to the destination is another responsibility of the network layer.

Finally, a packet in the network layer must adhere to the format as defined by its protocol. The user datagram or segment received from the transport layer may need to be packaged into smaller units before a header is added. The network layer, like other layers, is responsible for packetizing.

OBJECTIVES

After reading this chapter, the reader should be able to:

- ❑ Understand the position of the network layer in the Internet model.
- ❑ Understand the rationale for the existence of the network layer.
- ❑ Understand the concept of host-to-host delivery.

- ❑ Understand the duties of the network layer: packetizing, addressing, routing.
- ❑ Understand the network-layer protocol, IP, used in the Internet.
- ❑ Know which upper-layer protocol can use the services of IP.

4.1   INTRODUCTION

Figure 4.1 shows the position of the network layer in the Internet model. The network layer provides **host-to-host delivery.** By host-to-host we mean from the source computer to the destination computer. A network-layer protocol takes a message from a computer and delivers it to another computer.

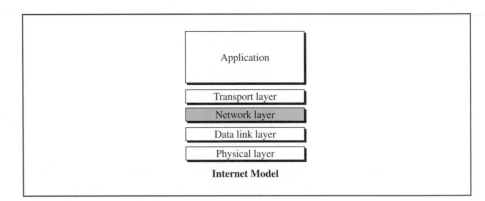

Figure 4.1 Network layer in the Internet model

The network layer has a defined set of duties. The most important are addressing, routing, packetizing, and fragmenting as shown in Figure 4.2.

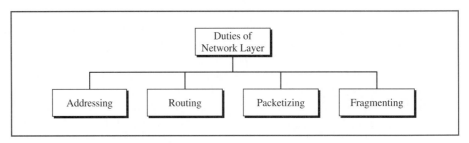

Figure 4.2 Duties of the network layer

4.2 ADDRESSING

At the network layer, we need to uniquely identify each device on the Internet to allow global communication between all devices. This is analogous to the telephone system, where each telephone subscriber has a unique telephone number if we consider the country code and the area code as part of the identifying scheme. For example, the telephone number 011 86 731 220 8098 uniquely identifies a number in the city of Changsha in Hunan Province in China.

The addresses used in the network layer must *uniquely* and *universally* define the connection of a host (computer) or a router to the Internet. The addresses at the network layer must be unique in the sense that each address defines one, and only one, connection to the Internet. Two devices on the Internet can never have the same address. However, if a device has two connections to the Internet, it has two addresses.

The network addresses must be unique.

The network addresses are universal in the sense that the addressing system must be accepted by any host that wants to be connected to the Internet.

IP Addresses

Addresses used in the Internet are called **IP addresses.** An IP address is made of 4 byt (32 bits), where each byte can have a value between 0 and 255. The bytes are separate a dot (.) when used by people and programs. For example, the following is an IP addr

10.34.234.8

The notation is referred to as **dotted-decimal notation.**

TECHNICAL FOCUS:
BINARY NOTATION OF IP ADDRESSES

An IP address is stored as a binary number in the computer. A 4-part dotted-decimal address can be converted to binary if we replace each part by its binary equivalent. The following shows the IP address 10.34.234.8 in dotted-decimal and binary notation:

10.34.224.8

00001010 00100010 11100000 00001000

TECHNICAL FOCUS:
ADDRESS SPACE

A protocol such as IP that defines addresses has an address space. An address space is the total number of addresses available to the protocol. If a protocol uses N bits to define an address, the address space is 2^N because each bit can have two different values (0 and 1); N bits can have 2^N values.

The Internet uses 32-bit addresses, which means that the address space is 2^{32} or 4,294,967,296 (more than 4 billion). This means that theoretically, if there were no restrictions, more than 4 billion devices could be connected to the Internet.

ADDRESS HIERARCHY

To make network-layer addressing more functional, the Internet has an addressing hierarchy. This is similar to snail-mail addressing and telephone numbering. In snail mail, a person's address consists of a country, state, city, street, and street number. For example, the address *123 Main Street, New City, CA, USA* contains these five levels of hierarchy. Every household on Main Street has four of the same identifiers; only the street number (123) changes. The telephone number system uses the same strategy. A telephone number has four levels of hierarchy: country code, area code, exchange, and number. For example, the telephone number [01]-(408)-864-8902 defines [01] as the country code, (408) as the area code, 864 as the exchange code, and 8902 as the number. Every telephone in the same exchange area (telephone company switching station) has the same first three identifiers; the only identifier that differs is the last part, the number.

The Internet has two or three levels of hierarchy in addressing (some Internet service providers, ISPs, may have more).

Two-Level Address: Network and Host

If an organization has only one single network (which is improbable), two levels of addressing is adequate. In this case, the first part of an address defines the organization's network and the second part defines a host on that network. The first part of the address is the same for each host; the second part differs to define each host. For example, Figure 4.3 shows a hypothetical network in an organization. The organization is granted 65,536 addresses from the Internet authorities. The addresses range from 181.74.0.0 to 181.74.255.255. Note that this range contains 65,536 addresses because the third and the fourth bytes can have values of 0 to 255 and 256 × 256 is 65,536. The first address, 181.74.0.0 is a reserved address and represents the entire network (organization); the last address 181.74.255.255 is also a reserved address and represents a limited broadcast address (used in case a host wants to send a message to every host). The remaining addresses belong to the organization and can be assigned to hosts. Note that all hosts always have the first two parts of the address (181.74) in common; the last 2 bytes change from host to host. This doesn't preclude hosts having the first 3 bytes in common.

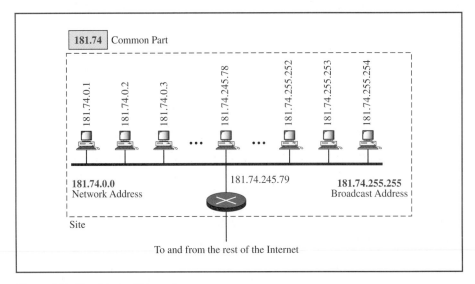

Figure 4.3　Two levels of hierarchy

The common part of the address is called the netid (or prefix); the variable part is called the hostid. The first address in the group, which always has a hostid of zero, is called the **network address.**

When using two levels of address hierarchy, the common part is referred to as the netid or prefix and the variable part is referred to as the hostid, or suffix.

Three-Level Address: Network, Subnetwork, and Host

It is often difficult to connect all of the computers in an organization to the same network. For example, on a college campus, each department usually has its own building. All computers in the engineering department can be connected to one LAN; all computers in the business department can be connected to another LAN; and so on. A backbone can connect all of these LANs together. The benefits are many. The cabling costs are less. Troubleshooting is easier on a smaller network. A problem on one LAN does not usually affect the other LANs. And traffic is reduced since the packets exchanged between people in one department do not have to go through other LANs. Finally, security is easier to handle on smaller LANs.

In this three-level addressing scheme, the individual LANs are referred to as subnetworks (or subnets) while the whole system is referred to as a network (or site).

The addresses can reflect this hierarchy in the physical network. Using the previous example, if the campus is granted 65,536 addresses, the first 2 bytes can define the whole network (site); the third byte can define the **subnet;** and the fourth byte can define a host on a subnet. The first 2 bytes, as before, are the same for all computers. The third byte is the same for those computers connected to the same subnet, and the fourth byte is unique for each computer.

Some addresses have special meanings. The first address defines the entire site (campus). The first address of each subnet defines the **subnet address.** The last address of each subnet is used for broadcasting to all computers in the same subnet. Figure 4.4 shows this situation.

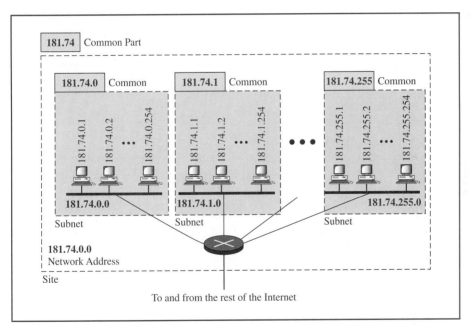

Figure 4.4   Three levels of hierarchy

ADDRESS RESOLUTION

We have introduced three types of addresses: the application-layer address, the transport-layer address, and the network-layer address. Let us clarify the differences between them and show when they are used. The following are examples of these three types of addresses.

The user is aware of only the first one. When an organization or a school advertises its services, it gives its **application-layer address.** For example, a potential student may use a browser to access a college website such as *www.fhda.edu*. However, to send a request for information to the college, the computer must use the network-layer and the transport-layer addresses. The network-layer address is needed to reach the computer; the transport-layer address is needed to reach the application program (HTTP in this case).

With three levels of address hierarchy, the common part is referred to as the netid. The part common to all computers connected to the same subnet is referred to as the subnetid. The unique part is referred to as the hostid.

Application-layer address ➡ www.fhda.edu

Transport-layer address ➡ 46017, 80 (client and server port number)

Network-layer address ➡ 201.23.56.8, 181.17.43.56 (source and destination IP addresses)

The packet going from the HTTP browser to the HTTP server needs four addresses: source and destination port numbers and source and destination IP addresses.

A packet traveling from the source to the destination needs at least four addresses: source and destination port numbers and source and destination IP addresses.

The question is: How is the application-layer address translated to the other address pairs?

Source and Destination Port Addresses

The first two, the source and destination **port addresses,** are easy to determine. The transport layer assigns a temporary address to the client port and it has a table that maps the client program to the well-known port address. For example, if the packet is going from a client HTTP to a server HTTP, the transport layer assigns the following:

client port address ➡ 46017

well-known port address ➡ 80

Source and Destination IP Address

Determination of the source IP address is simple. Each computer knows its IP address. The difficulty is finding the IP address of the destination. In other words, we have the following situation:

source IP address ➡ 201.23.56.8

destination IP address ➡ ????????????

One solution is for every computer to have a table with two columns: one column holding the application-layer address (such as www.fhda.edu) and the other column holding the corresponding IP address (such as 201.23.56.8). This is just a theoretical solution and is highly impractical. The table would be so large that it would not even fit into the memory of a computer. In addition, updating would be a huge problem since every computer has a copy of the table.

We present a feasible solution consisting of two features: a distribution system and an application program called the Domain Name System.

Distribution System The file holding all the application-layer addresses is broken into several files to be handled by multiple computers located throughout the world. Some computers store information for addresses ending with *com;* others store information for those addresses ending with *edu,* and so on. In addition, some computers store information for local application-layer addresses; others store information for remote application-layer addresses. The application-layer addresses are distributed to many computers; there is no one computer with all the data.

Domain Name System To obtain the IP addresses from these computers, another application-layer protocol called the **Domain Name System** (DNS) is needed. A computer that needs to obtain an IP destination address uses the client DNS; a computer that stores the mapping between the application-layer address and the IP address uses the server DNS. Every computer knows the address of at least one DNS server. It sends its request to that server. Either the server knows the IP address corresponding to the application-layer address, or it knows another server that does.

AN EXAMPLE

A user is sitting at a computer with IP address 200.31.45.8 and wants to send a message to the company with web (application-layer) address *www.goodproduct.com.* Figure 4.5 shows the four steps involved to reach the company *GoodProduct*.

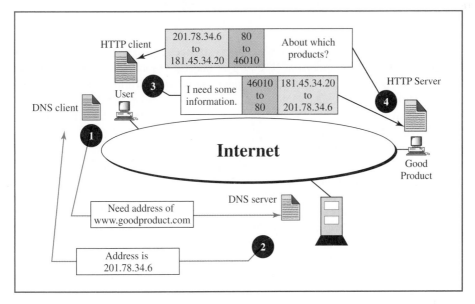

Figure 4.5   DNS example

4.3 ROUTING

Have you ever been faced with this dilemma? You want to reach a destination, but there are several routes from which you can choose. One route is shorter, but the road is in bad condition. Another route is longer, but safer. One route, which is normally congested during rush hour, connects you to the destination for a fee. Another route goes through a mountainous road that may be icy.

Whenever there are multiple routes to a destination, we must make a decision and choose one route. Our decision is usually based on some criteria that are important for us. If we have a car that is not so reliable, we might choose the longer road to avoid the danger associated with an icy road. If time is of the essence we might choose the shortest route. The Internet too is a combination of roads through which the IP packets travel to reach their destinations. Each IP packet can normally reach its destination via several routes. The difference is that the packet cannot choose the route; the router connecting the LANs and WANs makes this decision.

© Corbis/Vol. 163

Network cables are plugged into routers or hubs, which help direct information transfer across the network.

As we discussed in Chapter 1, computers that need to communicate with each other are connected to LANs and WANs. The Internet is made of LANs and WANs connected together to make global communication possible. Think of WANs as freeways and highways that connect cities, states, or countries. Think of LANs as roads and streets. In our rough analogy, the routers can be thought of as connectors that connect two WANs (a freeway-to-freeway ramp), one WAN to a LAN (a freeway exit) or two LANs (an intersection). Figure 4.6 shows a hypothetical part of the Internet.

Host A, somewhere in California, sends a packet to host B, somewhere in Florida. In this hypothetical section, computers on the West Coast are connected to computers on the East Coast by two WANs. WAN 1 uses fiber-optic cable as the transmission media. The packet travels 5000 miles with minimum delay. However, this WAN is very crowded; it is popular because of the low delay. There is a good possibility of packets being dropped. WAN 2, on the other hand, is a satellite wide area network; the messages must travel more than 40,000 miles (20,000 miles to and from the satellite). The messages traveling on this WAN experience an inevitable delay. WAN 2, however, is not very crowded and there is little possibility of a packet being dropped due to congestion in the network.

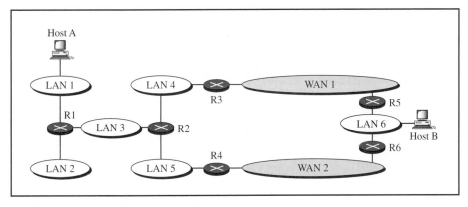

Figure 4.6 Example of portion of the Internet

A packet starting from host A can follow two different routes to reach host B. It can go through LAN 1, R1 (a router), LAN 3, R2, LAN 4, R3, WAN 1, R5, and LAN 6. Or it can go through LAN 1, R1, LAN 3, R2, LAN 5, R4, WAN 2, R6, and LAN 6. There are two questions here:

1. Which of the above routes must the packet take?
2. When a choice is made, how is the packet routed to reach the final destination?

WHICH ROUTE?

The answer to the first question depends on the **type of service** (TOS) required by the packet. If the packet is carrying multimedia information for a videoconference between two companies, minimum delay is of utmost importance. The people in a videoconference cannot wait for their voice or picture to ascend to the satellite and then descend and reach the other party. Here it is not important that some packets are lost due to congestion;

© Corbis/Vol. 38

Different types of applications require different routing choices. Videoconferencing cannot wait for data to ascend to a satellite and then come back down, nor is it important that some packets are lost due to congestion; whereas a large data transfer would rather have the delay and no data lost.

tens of frames are being sent every second. If a small part of the frame is lost, the video is still of good quality. In other words, for this application, delay is not acceptable, but the loss of a few packets is. Packets for this application should travel through WAN 1.

If, however, host A is sending a very large amount of data such as the entire customer accounts comprising hundreds of pages, delay is not so important. The data can arrive a few seconds later. What is important is the accuracy. The company does not want to lose part of the data due to congestion in WAN 1. The choice is definitely WAN 2.

Figure 4.7 shows the two routes; one suitable for videoconferencing and one suitable for transferring bulk data. If the packet comes from a videoconference application, route 1 is the better choice. If the packet comes from a file transfer application, such as FTP, route 2 is the better choice. The quality of service or type of service desired can determine the route choice. Videoconferencing requires *minimum delay;* file transfer requires *reliability.*

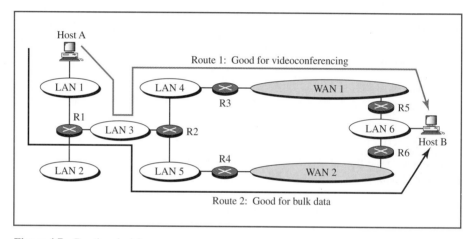

Figure 4.7   Routing decisions

Host A can include a field in the packet that specifies that the packet is to travel through a minimum delay route or a reliable route. The routers can use the value in this field to make a decision.

HOW TO ROUTE?

The second question, how to route the packet, is more difficult to answer. Suppose the packet belongs to a videoconferencing application program. The chosen route goes through the optical fiber WAN. But how does each router route the packet to the final destination? The answer is routing tables. Each router must have (at least) two tables: one table to route packets that need minimum delay and another for packets that need reliability.

Examine the situation of router R1. This router has three interfaces (connections). When it receives a packet from interface 1, it makes a decision on how to route the packet, that is, from which interface the packet should be sent. For router R1, the table is simple. For a packet for destination B with a minimum delay service type, the packet goes out from interface 2 as shown in Figure 4.8.

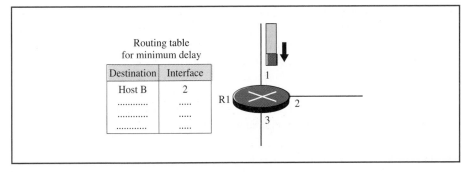

Figure 4.8   Routing table for router R1

The other routers have their own routing tables for minimum delay. For example, the routing tables for routers R2, R3, and R5 are shown in Figure 4.9.

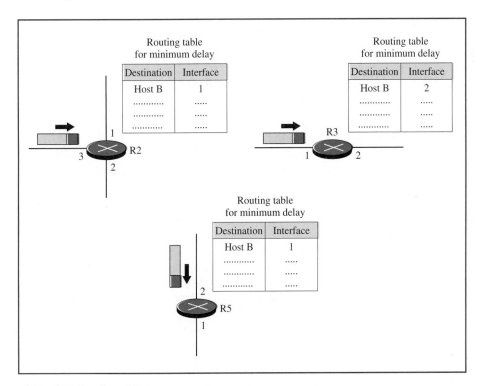

Figure 4.9   Routing tables

ROUTING TABLES

It is obvious that we need **routing tables** in the Internet to route the packets from the source to destination. However, the term *routing table* is perhaps somewhat misleading. The tables in the two previous figures do not show the route; they just gave an outgoing interface. The packet can still reach its destination; the key is consistency. If the routing tables are consistent, they can lead the packet to its final destination. Let us give an analogy. Suppose a person wants to drive from San Diego, California to Seattle,

Washington. There are probably no highway signs in San Diego that say Seattle. Instead, the driver just follows the signs that lead him to Los Angeles; in Los Angeles, he follows the signs to San Francisco, and so on up to Portland, Oregon, and then to Seattle. The signs lead the driver to his final destination.

Similarly, the routing tables in the previous figures show how to get to the next router (or hop). These tables are sometimes called **next-hop routing** tables. When a packet gets to a router, a decision about the next hop is made. If the routing tables are consistent, they take the packet to its final destination.

Routing tables can be based on next-hop routing.

In reality, routing tables have more columns than we showed; one column is the address of the next hop (a router).

SIZE OF ROUTING TABLE

The way we have shown the routing tables, it might appear that each router must have a routing table with the number of rows equal to the number of computers connected to the Internet (hundreds of millions if not a billion). This is not true. A routing table is nowhere near that size. This is because the Internet normally has two strategies to reduce the table size: network-specific routing and hierarchical routing.

Network-Specific Versus Host-Specific

The routing tables we showed in Figure 4.9 are for host-specific routing. Each row is based on the address of a host. Although this type of routing is sometimes used for specific needs, the routing table is normally based on the address of the network, not the host. Once the packet is delivered to the destination LAN, it can easily reach the host. Most of the LANs today are broadcast LANs; when they receive a packet, it is broadcast and received by every host, including the destination. The other hosts look at the destination address and discard the packet.

Network-specific routing tremendously reduces the size of routing tables. If we consider that a LAN normally hosts hundreds or thousands of hosts, the size of each routing table can be reduced by a factor of 100 or 1000 (2 or 3 orders of magnitude). As an analogy, consider that a city map usually does not display house addresses. Instead, it shows street names. A traveler usually finds the street and then finds the target house.

Routing tables for the Internet are usually network-specific rather than host-specific. The router routes the packet to the final network; it is then broadcast to reach the final destination.

Network-based routing reduces the size of routing tables.

Hierarchical Routing: Autonomous Systems

Another way to reduce the size of a routing table is to divide the Internet into smaller sections called autonomous systems. An **autonomous system** (AS) is a group of networks and routers under the authority of a single administration. Routing inside an autonomous system is referred to as **interior routing.** Routing between autonomous systems is referred to as **exterior routing.** Autonomous systems reduce the size of tables considerably. The size of the table for each interior router is the number of networks inside the autonomous system plus one (or perhaps two or three) entry that shows the outgoing interface for a packet leaving the autonomous system. In other words, each network inside the router has an entry; for all other networks, there is only one entry. Figure 4.10 shows several connected autonomous systems. The black ovals are networks. The small routers are interior routers and the large routers are exterior routers.

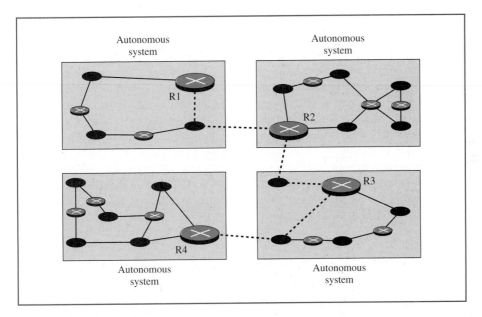

Figure 4.10 Autonomous systems

This is also called **hierarchical routing** because a packet first arrives at the autonomous system; then it is delivered to the appropriate network, and then to the final host.

Routing in the Internet is hierarchical. Delivery is first made to the autonomous system, then to the network, and finally to the host. Hierarchical routing reduces the size of the routing tables.

Static Versus Dynamic Routing

A host or a router has a routing table, with an entry for each destination, to route IP packets. The routing table can be either static or dynamic.

Static Routing Table
A **static routing table** contains information entered manually. The administrator enters the route for each destination into the table. Such a table cannot be updated automatically when there is a change in the Internet. The table must be manually altered by the administrator.

A static routing table is a good choice for a small internet that does not change very often, or in an experimental internet for troubleshooting. It is not good strategy to use a static routing table in a big internet such as the Internet.

Dynamic Routing Table

A **dynamic routing table** is updated periodically using a dynamic routing protocol. Whenever there is a change in the Internet, such as a shutdown of a router or a breaking of a link, the dynamic routing protocols update all of the tables in the routers (and eventually in the host). The routers in a big internet such as the Internet need to be updated dynamically for efficient delivery of IP packets.

ROUTING PROTOCOLS

Routing protocols have been created in response to the demand for dynamic routing tables. A routing protocol is a combination of rules and procedures that lets routers in an internet inform each other of changes. It allows routers to share whatever they know about the internet or their neighborhood. The sharing of information allows a router in San Francisco to know about the failure of a network in Texas. The routing protocols also include procedures for combining information received from other routers.

We briefly discuss two interior routing protocols, RIP and OSPF, that are used for routing inside autonomous systems; we discuss one exterior routing protocol BGP that is used for routing between autonomous systems.

RIP

The **Routing Information Protocol** (RIP) is an interior routing protocol used inside an autonomous system. It is a very simple protocol based on distance vector routing. In **distance vector routing,** each router periodically shares its knowledge about the entire internet with its neighbors. The three keys to understanding how this algorithm works are as follows:

1. **Sharing knowledge about the entire autonomous system.** Each router shares its knowledge about the entire autonomous system with its neighbors. At the outset, a router's knowledge may be sparse. How much it knows, however, is unimportant; it sends whatever it has.
2. **Sharing only with neighbors.** Each router sends its knowledge only to neighbors. It sends whatever knowledge it has through all of its interfaces.
3. **Sharing at regular intervals.** Each router sends its knowledge to its neighbors at fixed intervals, for example, every 30 seconds.

OSPF

The **Open Shortest Path First** (OSPF) protocol is another interior routing protocol that is gaining in popularity. Its domain is also an autonomous system. OSPF uses link state routing to update the routing tables in an area. **Link state routing** is a process in which each router shares its knowledge about its neighborhood with every router in the area. The three keys to understanding how this method works are as follows:

1. **Sharing knowledge about the neighborhood.** Each router sends the *state of its neighborhood* to every other router in the area.

2. **Sharing with every other router.** Each router sends the state of its neighborhood to *every other router in the area*. It does so by **flooding,** a process whereby a router sends its information to all of its neighbors (through all of its output ports). Each neighbor sends the packet to all of its neighbors, and so on. Every router that receives the packet sends copies to each of its neighbors. Eventually, every router (without exception) has received a copy of the same information.

3. **Sharing when there is a change.** Each router shares the state of its neighborhood only when there is a change. This rule contrasts with distance vector routing, where information is sent out at regular intervals regardless of change. This characteristic results in lower internet traffic than that required by distance vector routing.

BGP

Border Gateway Protocol (BGP) is an inter-autonomous system routing protocol. It first appeared in 1989 and has gone through four versions. BGP is based on a routing method called *path vector routing*. Path vector routing is different from both distance vector routing and link state routing. Each entry in the routing table contains the destination network, the next router, and the path to reach the destination. The path is usually defined as an ordered list of autonomous systems through which a packet must travel to reach the destination. Table 4.1 shows an example of a path vector routing table.

Table 4.1 *Path vector routing table*

Network	Next Router	Path
N01	R01	AS14, AS23, AS67
N02	R05	AS22, AS67, AS05, AS89
N03	R06	AS67, AS89, AS09, AS34
N04	R12	AS62, AS02, AS09

4.4 PACKETIZING: IP PROTOCOL

The network layer encapsulates packets received from upper-layer protocols and makes new packets out of them. In particular, the network layer adds a new header defined by the IP protocol.

IP PROTOCOL

The **Internet Protocol** (IP) is the transmission mechanism used by the TCP/IP protocols. Figure 4.11 shows the position of IP in the Internet model.

IP is an unreliable and connectionless datagram protocol—a best-effort delivery service. The term *best-effort* means that IP provides no error checking or tracking. IP assumes the unreliability of the underlying layers and does its best to get a transmission through to its destination, but with no guarantees. If reliability is important, IP must be paired with a reliable protocol such as TCP.

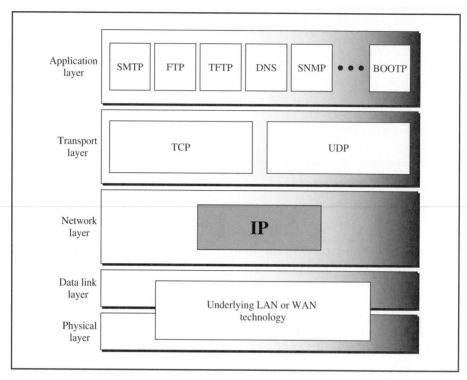

Figure 4.11 Position of IP in Internet

IP is also a connectionless protocol. This means that each packet is handled independently, and each packet can follow a different route to the destination. This implies that packets sent by the same source to the same destination could arrive out of order. Also, some could be lost or corrupted during transition. Again, IP relies on a higher-level protocol, such as TCP discussed in Chapter 3 to take care of all these problems.

DATAGRAM

Packets in the IP layer are called **datagrams.** Figure 4.12 shows the IP datagram format. A datagram is a variable-length packet consisting of two parts: header and data. The header is 20 to 60 bytes in length and contains information essential to routing and delivery.

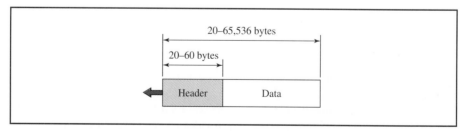

Figure 4.12 IP datagram format

❏ **Version (VER).** Defines the version of the protocol (currently 4).
❏ **Header length (HLEN).** Defines the length of header.
❏ **Differentiated services (formerly service type).** Defines the type of service.
❏ **Total length.** Defines the total length (header plus data) of the IP datagram.
❏ **Identification, flags, fragmentation offset.** Used in fragmentation.
❏ **Time to live.** Defines when the packet is to be discarded.
❏ **Protocol.** Defines the upper-layer protocol that uses the services of IP.
❏ **Checksum.** Used for error detection.
❏ **Source address.** The IP address of the source.
❏ **Destination address.** The IP address of the destination.

4.5 FRAGMENTING

A datagram can travel through different networks. Each router decapsulates the IP datagram from the received frame, processes it, and then encapsulates it in another frame. The format and size of the received frame depend on the protocol used by the physical network from which the frame has just arrived. The format and size of the departing frame depend on the protocol used by the physical network to which the frame is going.

Maximum Transfer Unit (MTU)

Each physical network has its own frame format. One of the fields defined in the format is the maximum size of the data field. In other words, when a datagram is encapsulated in a frame, the total size of the datagram must be less than this maximum size, which is defined by the restrictions imposed by the hardware and software used in the network. When a packet is passing through a network, the datagram must fit into the frame defined by that network; if it is larger, it must be divided. This is called **fragmentation.**

When a datagram is fragmented, each fragment has its own header with most of the fields repeated, and some of the fields changed. A fragmented datagram may itself be fragmented if it encounters a network with an even smaller **maximum transfer unit** (MTU). In other words, a datagram can be fragmented several times before it reaches the final destination.

A datagram can be fragmented by the source host or any router in the path. The reassembly of the datagram, however, is done only by the destination host because each fragment becomes an independent datagram.

Defining a Fragment

Defining a fragment requires three fields. First, each datagram has an identification number. When a datagram is fragmented, this number is preserved for each fragment. In this way, all fragments belonging to the original datagram can be identified. Second, each datagram (fragment or not) has a flag that indicates whether or not it is the last fragment. And third, each datagram has a unique number that shows its position (called the offset) with respect to the original datagram.

CASE STUDY

NEW AGE HOME PHARMACY

N AHP uses the IP protocol as well as the other three protocols at this layer: ICMP, IGMP, and ARP. The NAHP network is a site registered with the Internet authorities. NAHP was granted a class C address block. The block includes 256 addresses ranging from 201.14.56.0 to 201.14.56.255. NAHP uses only a portion of these addresses; the rest are reserved for future use. The Modern Networking consultants have divided the NAHP network into six subnetworks. Each subnetwork spans one floor. The switch, installed in a closet on each floor, acts as a router and separates each subnetwork from the others. The logical network is shown in the figure below:

The range of addresses (256) is divided into 8 blocks, with 32 addresses each. Six of these blocks are allocated, one for each floor; the remaining two blocks are reserved for future expansion. Thirty addresses are available for use on each floor. The first address is the subnet address and the last is the broadcast address.

NAHP uses the OSPF routing protocol, which is installed on each router. A router receives a packet and uses its routing table to direct the packet. IP packets destined for the same floor are routed through the corresponding switch installed on that floor. IP packets destined for other floors are first routed through the main switch in the basement and then sent through the appropriate switch installed in the floor. The packets destined for the outside are routed through the floor switch and then the main switch.

Incoming packets are first routed through the main switch in the basement, and then sent to the appropriate floor switch.

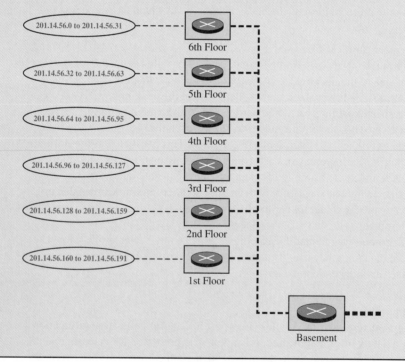

4.6 KEY TERMS

application layer
border gateway protocol (BGP)
datagram
distance vector routing
domain name system (DNS)
dotted-decimal notation
dynamic routing table
exterior routing
flooding
fragmentation
hierarchical routing
hostid
host-to-host-delivery
interior routing
Internet protocol (IP)
IP address
link state routing

maximum transfer unit (MTU)
netid
network address
network layer
network-specific routing
next-hop routing
open shortest path first (OSPF)
port address
prefix
routing information protocol (RIP)
routing table
static routing table
subnet
subnet address
subnetid
suffix
type of service (TOS)

4.7 SUMMARY

❏ The network layer in the Internet model is responsible for host-to-host delivery.
❏ The most important network layer duties are packetizing, addressing, fragmentation, and routing.
❏ The 4-byte hierarchical addresses used in the Internet are called IP addresses. An IP address can define a network, a subnetwork, and a host on the network.
❏ Address resolution involves a distributed file system and the domain name systerm.
❏ The choice of a route taken by a packet often depends on the type of service required by the packet.
❏ Routing tables are involved in routing the packets. The tables are usually network-specific.
❏ Dynamic routing tables are updated periodically through a dynamic routing protocol.
❏ Two popular interior routing protocols are RIP and OSPF.
❏ BGP is a popular exterior routing protocol.
❏ The best-effort, unreliable Internet Protocol is the transmission mechanism used by the TCP/IP protocol suite.
❏ A packet in the IP layer is called a datagram.
❏ The procedure to divide one datagram into several smaller ones is called fragmenation.

 PRACTICE SET

Review Questions

1. How is host-to-host delivery different from application-to-application delivery?
2. What is the position of the network layer in the Internet model?
3. What are the three main functions of the network layer?

4. What does the netid identify? What does the hostid identify?
5. Why are subnets needed in large organizations?
6. What is the difference between a port number and an IP address?
7. What is the function of the Domain Name System?
8. Where are the application-layer addresses stored?
9. How is network-specific routing different from host-specific routing.
10. What is an autonomous system?
11. How is a static routing table different from a dynamic routing table?
12. Name two interior routing protocols. Name an exterior routing protocol.
13. What are IP packets called?
14. When is a datagram fragmented?

Multiple-Choice Questions

15. The network layer is responsible for _____ delivery.
    a. host-to-host
    b. application-to-application
    c. port-to-port
    d. all of the above
16. The network layer uniquely identifies each device on the Internet to allow global communication through _____.
    a. addressing
    b. packetizing
    c. routing
    d. fragmenting
17. An IP address has _____ bytes.
    a. 2
    b. 4
    c. 16
    d. 32
18. A 32-bit address means that, theoretically, approximately _____ devices could be connected to the Internet.
    a. 32 million
    b. 32 billion
    c. 8 billion
    d. 4 billion
19. A small Ethernet LAN has only four PCs. How many netids and hostids on this network?
    a. 1 netid and 1 hostid
    b. 1 netid and 4 hostids
    c. 4 netids and 1 hostid
    d. 5 netids and 5 hostids
20. All hosts on a network share the same _____.
    a. netid
    b. hostid
    c. suffix
    d. a and b

21. The destination address 198.123.46.201 is _____ layer address.

   a. an application-

   b. a transport-

   c. a network-

   d. a data link

22. The route of a packet often depends on _____.

   a. its source port number

   b. its fragment number

   c. the type of service required by the packet

   d. the number of router interfaces

23. Routing between autonomous systems is called _____ routing.

   a. interior

   b. exterior

   c. posterior

   d. anterior

24. Routing inside an autonomous system is called _____ routing.

   a. interior

   b. exterior

   c. posterior

   d. anterior

25. _____ is an interior routing protocol based on distance vector routing.

   a. RIP

   b. OSPF

   c. BGP

   d. MTU

26. _____ is an interior routing protocol that uses link state routing to update routing tables.

   a. RIP

   b. OSPF

   c. BGP

   d. MTU

27. _____ is an exterior routing protocol based on path vector routing.

   a. RIP

   b. OSPF

   c. BGP

   d. MTU

28. The _____ is the maximum size of a data unit of a specific network.

   a. MTA

   b. MBA

   c. MTU

   d. BGP

29. The network layer encapsulates packets received from _____.

   a. lower-layer protocols

   b. upper-layer protocols

   c. the physical medium

   d. autonomous protocols

30. _____ is a process in which a router sends information from all of its ports to all of its neighbors.
    a. Fragmentation
    b. Flooding
    c. Routing
    d. Packetizing

31. An example of an application-layer address is _____.
    a. 34.34.56.23
    b. 34566
    c. www.gobears.com
    d. all of the above

CHAPTER 5

Data Link Layer

The **data link layer** is responsible for carrying a packet from one hop (computer or router) to the next hop. Unlike the network layer which has a global responsibility, the data link layer has a local responsibility. Its responsibility lies between two hops. In other words, because LANs and WANs in the Internet are delimited by hops, we can say that the responsibility of the data link layer is to carry a packet through a LAN or WAN.

The journey through a LAN or a WAN (between two hops) must preserve the integrity of the packet; the data link layer must make sure that the packet arrives safe and sound. If the packet is corrupted during the transmission, it must either be corrected or retransmitted. The data link layer must also make sure that the next hop is not over-whelmed with data by the previous hop; the flow of data must be controlled.

Access to a LAN or a WAN for the sending of data is also an issue. If several computers or routers are connected to one common medium (link), and more than one want to send data at the same time, which has the right to send? What is the access method?

Several data link protocols have been designed to provide all of these functions; only a few are in use today.

OBJECTIVES

After reading this chapter, the reader should be able to:

❏ Understand the functions of the data link layer.

❏ Understand the concept of hop-to-hop delivery compared to host-to-host delivery and application-to-application delivery.

❏ Understand the concept of access method and define different access methods used in LANs and WANs

❏ Understand how error control is handled at the data link layer.

❏ Understand the addressing mechanism used in the data link layer and how network layer addresses are mapped to data link layer addresses.

5.1 DUTIES OF THE DATA LINK LAYER

Figure 5.1 shows the position of the data link layer in the Internet model. The data link layer lies under the network layer in the Internet model. It provides services to the network layer. These services include hop-to-hop delivery, packetizing, addressing, error control, flow control, and medium access control as shown in Figure 5.2.

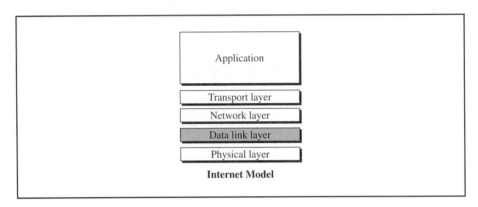

Figure 5.1   Data link layer in the Internet model

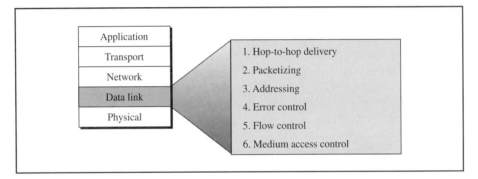

Figure 5.2   Data-link layer duties

❏ Hop-to-hop delivery is local delivery from one hop to the next. The network layer uses this service to accomplish its global delivery, from the source to the destination.

❏ Packetizing makes frames or cells out of the packets arriving from the network layer.

❏ Addressing enables the data link layer to choose between several hops, connected to a LAN or a WAN, as the next hop to bring the packet closer to its destination.

❏ Error control means error detection and correction. It allows the receiver to inform the sender of any frames lost or damaged in transmission and coordinates the retransmission of those frames by the sender.

❏ Flow control ensures that the next hop is not overwhelmed with data. It ensures that there is enough time for the next hop to process the data it has received before receiving the next packet.

❏ Access control coordinates the systems on the link. It determines which device can send and when it can send.

5.2   HOP-TO-HOP DELIVERY

Recall from Chapter 3 that a transport-layer protocol, such as UDP or TCP, is responsible for delivering a message from an application program to another application program.

From Chapter 4 recall that a network-layer protocol is responsible for host-to-host delivery, from a source computer to a destination computer. However, for a packet to reach its destination, it must pass through several LANs and WANs and the routers that connect them. A packet must be delivered from one hop (computer or router) to another hop (computer or router). In other words, a packet must travel hop to hop, passing through a LAN or a WAN, to reach its destination. This **hop-to-hop delivery** is the responsibility of the data link layer. The two data link layers, installed at adjoining hops, control the transmission of data through the LAN or the WAN. Figure 5.3 shows hop-to-hop delivery.

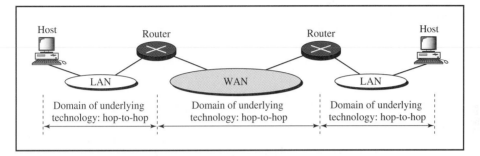

Figure 5.3   Hop-to-hop delivery

5.3   PACKETIZING

The data link layer is responsible for moving data from one hop to the next. To get to the next hop, the data must pass through a LAN or a WAN, each of which has its own protocols. Each LAN or WAN defines its own type of packet. Some protocols allow small packets; some allow large packets. The packet coming from the IP layer must therefore be encapsulated in the appropriate packet defined by the data link layer of the underlying LAN or WAN.

Different protocols have different names for the packet at the data link layer. However, most LANs refer to the packet as **frames.** The ATM WAN (see Chapter 11) refers to a packet as a cell. *Framing* is the common terminology for **packetizing** at the data link layer.

A **header** and a **trailer** are usually added to a packet received from the network layer. The header contains the length of the data coming from upper layer, addressing information, and information about the upper-layer protocol using the data link service. The trailer is used mostly for error detection. Extra data are added to detect errors during the transmission.

5.4   ADDRESSING

Recall from Chapter 2 that an application-layer address is needed to identify a remote application program (an email address, for example).

From Chapter 3 recall that a transport-layer address (port number) is needed to identify one of the many application programs running on one computer. Servers use the well-known ports and clients use temporary ports. The end user does not need to know these addresses.

In Chapter 4 on the network layer recall that a unique network-layer address (IP address) is needed to reach a computer. Here, also, the user need not know the IP address; an application program called DNS dynamically maps a computer name to an IP address.

Despite all these addresses, we still need one more **addressing** mechanism: data link layer addresses. The data-link layer addresses are called physical addresses (or sometimes MAC addresses) and are used to find the address of the next hop in hop-to-hop delivery.

The physical address used by a LAN is totally different from that used by a WAN. A LAN address is 6 bytes (48 bits) long. A WAN address is usually longer.

TECHNICAL FOCUS: ADDRESSES IN LOCAL AREA NETWORKS

The physical address for most computers on local area networks is imprinted on the network card that is installed in the computer. If the user or network manager changes the network card (because of a failure, for example), the physical address of the computer is changed. In most cases, changing the network card requires reconfiguration of the computer.

ADDRESS RESOLUTION

How does a computer or a router that has received a frame know the address of the next hop? The packet encapsulated in the frame carries only the IP addresses of the source and destination computers. Using a routing table, as discussed in Chapter 4, we can find the IP address of the next hop. But the data link layer does not need the IP address, it needs the physical address of the next hop.

The association between logical and physical addresses can be statically stored in a table. The sender can look in this table and find the physical address corresponding to a logical address. But this is not a good solution. Every time a physical address is changed, the table must be updated. Updating tables on all machines at frequent intervals is a very demanding task.

The mapping, however, can be done dynamically, which means that the sender asks the receiver to announce its physical address when needed. The Address Resolution Protocol (ARP) is designed for this purpose.

Anytime a host, or a router, needs to find the physical address of another host or router on its network, it sends an ARP query packet. The packet includes the physical and IP addresses of the sender and the IP address of the receiver. Because the sender does not know the physical address of the receiver, the query is broadcast over the network (see Figure 5.4).

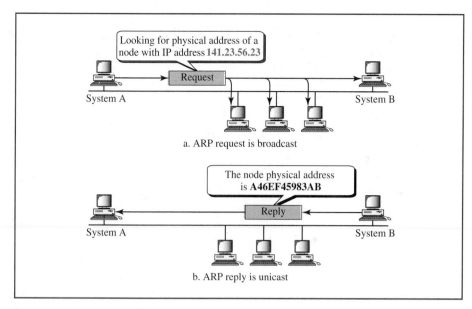

Figure 5.4   ARP operation

5.5   ERROR CONTROL

In data communication, errors are inevitable. Using better equipment and more reliable transmission media may reduce the severity or the frequency of occurrence, but it can never eliminate errors. In this section, we first discuss the sources and types of errors. We then discuss how we can prevent errors. Since prevention is not possible all of the time, we show how we can detect errors and how we can correct them.

Networks must be able to transfer data from one device to another with complete accuracy. A system that cannot guarantee that the data received by one device are identical to the data transmitted by another device is essentially useless. Yet anytime data are transmitted from source to destination, they can become corrupted in passage. In fact, it is more likely that some part of a message will be altered in transit than the entire contents will arrive intact.

Data can be corrupted during transmission. For reliable communication, errors must be prevented, or detected and corrected.

SOURCE OF ERRORS

Many situations can cause errors. We can better understand the nature of errors after the discussion on signals in Chapter 6. Here, we briefly mention error sources just to get a feeling for prevention.

White Noise

White noise, or thermal noise, or Gaussian noise, is an unwanted signal due to the heat created by the movement of electrons. This can be the hissing noise that we sometimes hear in the background when we talk on the phone. This type of noise is constant by nature; its intensity is the same whether or not the medium is transmitting data. For this reason, it is controllable. We can reduce its effect by using equipment that creates less heat or by cooling the media or equipment.

Impulse Noise

An **impulse noise,** or spike noise, is a surprise signal that suddenly affects the medium. The difficulty with this type of signal is that we never know when it comes; we cannot predict it. An example of spike noise is a scratch on a CD surface. The effect of impulse noise depends on the speed of data transmission. If we are sending at a high data rate, more bits are affected during the hit of the impulse noise; if we are sending at a low rate, less data are affected. As an analogy, consider an automobile accident; the higher the driving speed, the more serious the accident.

Crosstalk

Crosstalk is the effect of one medium on another. Each transmission medium acts as an antenna (sending and receiving). When we talk on a telephone line, we sometimes hear a conversation between two other people. They probably hear our conversation too. Each line acts as a sending and receiving antenna. Crosstalk can be prevented, as we see in Chapter 7, by shielding the cables to protect the signals.

Echo

We have **echo** when a sending device receives some of the energy it has sent. Echo can be a problem if the devices and medium are not correctly designed. A cable that does not have a cable end (terminator) to remove the signal that reaches the end of the cable may bounce back part of the signal; every device will then receive the data a second time, but weaker and delayed. This creates errors. Echo can be prevented with good design and appropriate devices.

Jitter

Jitter is the result of a change in the signal when it passes through an electronic device. The device (such as an amplifier) may create extra harmonics in the signal. Jitter is not a problem if it is weak.

Attenuation

A signal may become too weak if it travels a long distance. Some of the energy of the signal may be transformed to heat to overcome the resistance of the medium. If the signal becomes too weak, data cannot be recognized at the destination. **Attenuation** can be easily prevented if we install a repeater (a device to regenerate the signal) at regular intervals if the signal is to travel a long distance.

Distortion

The velocity with which the electrical or optical energy is traveling through transmission media depends on the frequency (pitch) of each individual harmonic in a signal.

A digital signal is made of several harmonics. This means that each harmonic travels at a different speed and reaches the destination at different times (different delays). When these harmonics are combined at the receiver, the signal is not the one sent by the sender. This may cause the receiver to misinterpret the signal. **Distortion** is not usually a severe problem.

TYPES OF ERRORS

Data are sent from one device to another in the form of binary data (0s and 1s). Two types of errors may happen: single-bit errors and burst errors.

Single-Bit Error

The term **single-bit error** means that only 1 bit of a given data unit (such as a byte, character, data unit, or packet) is changed from 1 to 0 or from 0 to 1.

In a single-bit error, only 1 bit in the data unit has changed.

Figure 5.5 shows the effect of a single-bit error on a data unit. To understand the impact of the change, imagine that each group of 8 bits is an ASCII character with a 0 bit added to the left. In the figure, 00000010 (ASCII *STX*) was sent, meaning *start of text,* but 00001010 (ASCII *LF*) was received, meaning *line feed.* (For more information about ASCII code, see Appendix A.)

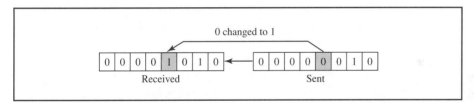

Figure 5.5   Single-bit error

Burst Error

The term **burst error** means that two or more bits in the data unit have changed from 1 to 0 or from 0 to 1.

A burst error means that two or more bits in the data unit have changed.

Figure 5.6 shows the effect of a burst error on a data unit. In this case, 0100010001000011 was sent, but 0101110101000011 was received. Note that a burst error does not necessarily mean that the errors occur in consecutive bits. The length of the burst is measured from the first corrupted bit to the last corrupted bit. Some bits in between may not have been corrupted.

ERROR PREVENTION

We mentioned several ways to prevent errors when we discussed the error sources. Error prevention requires finding the error source. If the error is due to white noise, we

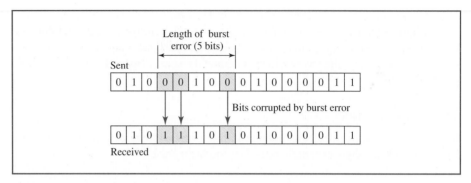

Figure 5.6 Burst error of length five

need to reduce the ambient temperature. If the error is due to crosstalk, we need to twist or shield the cable. If the error is due to attenuation, we need to use repeaters.

We may need to request better service from the service provider. Or, we may even need to move to a better or more sophisticated technology. In general, digital technology is superior to analog technology (see Chapter 6).

Error prevention methods can help to some extent. Errors, however, are inevitable. For accuracy we need to detect and correct errors.

ERROR DETECTION

Even if we know what types of errors can occur, will we recognize one when we see it? If we have a copy of the intended transmission for comparison, of course we will. But what if we don't have a copy of the original? Then we will have no way of knowing we have received an error until we have decoded the transmission and failed to make sense of it. For a machine to check for errors this way would be slow, costly, and of questionable value. We don't need a system where computers decode whatever comes in, then sit around trying to decide if the sender really meant to use the word *glbrshnif* in the middle of an array of weather statistics. What we need is a mechanism that is simple and completely objective.

Redundancy

The key to error detection is **redundancy,** a short group of bits appended to or inserted to each unit of data. This technique is called redundancy because the extra bits are redundant to the information; they are discarded as soon as the accuracy of the transmission has been determined.

Error detection uses the concept of redundancy, which means adding extra bits for detecting errors at the destination.

Figure 5.7 shows the process of using redundant bits to check the accuracy of a data unit. Once the data stream has been generated, it passes through a device that analyzes it and adds on an appropriately coded redundancy check. The data unit, now enlarged by several bits (in this illustration, seven), travels over the link to the receiver. The receiver puts the entire stream through a checking function. If the received bit stream passes the checking criteria, the data portion of the data unit is accepted and the redundant bits are discarded.

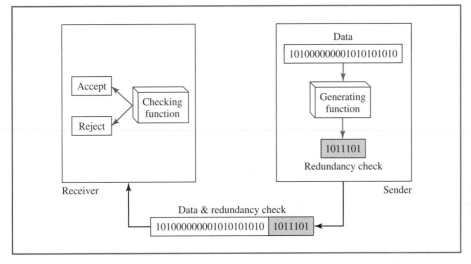

Figure 5.7   Redundancy

Three types of redundancy checks are used in the data link layer: vertical redundancy check (VRC), longitudinal redundancy check (LRC), and cyclic redundancy check (CRC) as shown in Figure 5.8.

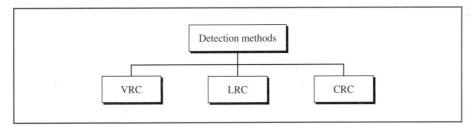

Figure 5.8   Detection methods

Vertical Redundancy Check (VRC)
The most common and least expensive mechanism for error detection is the **vertical redundancy check** (VRC), often called a **parity check.** In this technique, a redundant bit, called a parity bit, is appended to every data unit so that the total number of 1s in the unit (including the parity bit) becomes even as shown in Figure 5.9.

In vertical redundancy check (VRC), a parity bit is added to every data unit so that the total number of 1s becomes even.

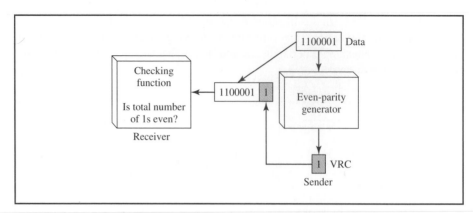

Figure 5.9　Even parity VRC concept

Longitudinal Redundancy Check (LRC)

In **longitudinal redundancy check** (LRC), a block of bits is organized in a table (rows and columns). For example, instead of sending a block of 32 bits, we organize them in a table made of four rows and eight columns, as shown in Figure 5.10. We then calculate the parity bit for each column and create a new row of 8 bits, which are the parity bits for the whole block. Note that the first parity bit in the fifth row is calculated based on all first bits. The second parity bit is calculated based on all second bits, and so on. We then attach the 8 parity bits to the original data and send them to the receiver.

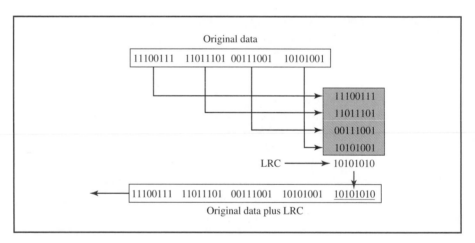

Figure 5.10　LRC

In longitudinal redundancy check (LRC), a block of bits is divided into rows and a redundant row of bits is added to the whole block.

Cyclic Redundancy Check (CRC)

The third and most powerful of the redundancy checking techniques is the **cyclic redundancy check** (CRC). Unlike VRC and LRC, which are based on addition, CRC is based on binary division. In CRC, instead of adding bits together to achieve a desired parity, a sequence of redundant bits, called the CRC or the CRC remainder, is appended to the end of a data unit so that the resulting data unit becomes exactly divisible by a second, predetermined binary number. At its destination, the incoming data unit is divided by the same number. If at this step there is no remainder, the data unit is assumed to be intact and is therefore accepted. A remainder indicates that the data unit has been damaged in transit and therefore must be rejected. Figure 5.11 shows the idea of CRC.

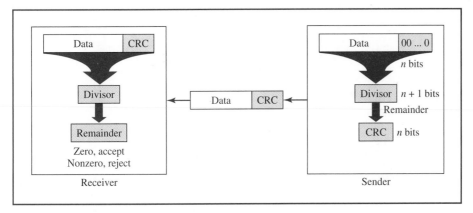

Figure 5.11   CRC

ERROR CORRECTION

It is crucial that the error be detected at the receiver because we do not want erroneous data delivered to the application program. You can imagine what would happen if a number is changed from one thousand to one million. Once the data are detected, the receiver has three choices: simply discard the data, discard the data but request a retransmission, or correct the data. The first choice, simply discarding the data happens often in real-time video or audio. In this application, TV broadcasting, for example, there is no time to wait for a retransmission and there is no way we can correct a frame. However, if a frame or two is lost (in 30 or 60 frames received), this is normally not apparent to the user. The second choice, requesting retransmission, is selected when we need absolute accuracy in all the data and cannot afford to discard part of the data. The third choice, data correction, is very difficult to achieve if there are more than a few bits in error. Data correction is selected when the data packet is very small and we need the accuracy but cannot wait for retransmission.

Error Correction Using Retransmission

Error correction using retransmission follows a very simple rule. If the sender has not received positive news in due time, the frame is retransmitted. Frames are retransmitted in three cases: the frame is damaged (the receiver sends a negative acknowledgment or no acknowledgment), the frame is lost, or the acknowledgment is lost. In all three cases, the sender does not receive positive news and the frame is resent. There are two protocols for retransmission: stop-and-wait automatic repeat request and sliding-window automatic repeat request.

Stop-and-Wait ARQ   In **stop-and-wait automatic repeat request** (stop-and-wait ARQ), only the fate of one frame at any moment is unknown. The sender sends one frame and waits until the fate of this frame is determined. If the sender has received a positive acknowledgment (ACK) in a predetermined amount of time, the sender sends the next frame. Otherwise, the sender resends the frame. This is called stop-and-wait ARQ because the sender, after sending a frame, stops and waits before the next frame is sent. Figure 5.12 shows stop-and-wait ARQ.

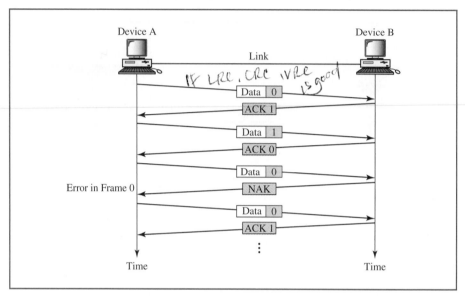

Figure 5.12   Stop and wait ARQ

TECHNICAL FOCUS: PROCEDURE FOR STOP-AND-WAIT ARQ

❑   The sending device keeps a copy of the last frame transmitted until it receives an acknowledgment for that frame.

❑   For identification purposes, both data frames and ACK frames are numbered 0 and 1 alternately. A data 0 frame is acknowledged by an ACK 1 frame, indicating that the receiver has gotten data 0 and is now expecting data 1.

❑   If an error is discovered in a data frame, a negative acknowledgment (NAK) frame is returned. A NAK frame tells the sender to retransmit the last frame sent.

❑   The sending device is equipped with a timer. If an expected acknowledgment is not received within an allotted time period, the sender assumes that the last data frame was lost in transit and sends it again.

Sliding-Window ARQ   Stop-and-wait ARQ is very slow. The sender stops sending until it hears about the fate of the one frame sent. A better solution is **sliding-window ARQ.** In this strategy, the sender can send several frames. There are several frames in transition at any given moment. The sender, for example, can send six frames one after the other. If during this time, an ACK arrives from the receiver, the sender continues to send. If, however, a NAK is received or a timer expires, it stops sending. This method is called *sliding window* because an imaginary window slides over a buffer of frames. Figure 5.13 shows an example of sliding-window ARQ.

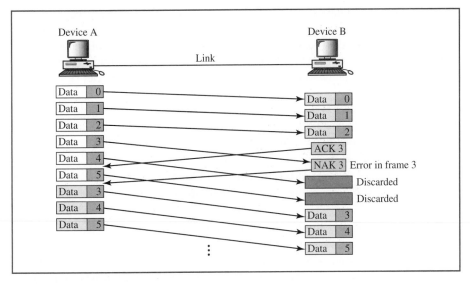

Figure 5.13   Sliding-window ARQ

TECHNICAL FOCUS: **PROCEDURE FOR SLIDING-WINDOW ARQ**

❏   The sending device keeps copies of all transmitted frames until they have been acknowledged.

❏   In addition to ACK frames, a receiver can return a NAK frame if the data have been received damaged. The NAK frame tells the sender to retransmit a damaged frame.

❏   Like stop-and-wait ARQ, the sending device in sliding-window ARQ is equipped with a timer to enable it to handle lost acknowledgments.

Forward Error Correction

Because data in communications is transmitted using bits (0 and 1), it is possible for the receiver to correct errors without asking for retransmission. When a bit is corrupted, a 0 becomes a 1 and vice versa. For example, if only 1 bit is corrupted during transmission, the receiver can automatically correct it if it knows the position of the bit in the data unit. The receiver changes that bit, from a 0 to a 1 or from a 1 to a 0. To find the position of the corrupted bit, however, we need to send redundant bits (much more than needed to detect a single bit).

The number of required redundant bits increases when we need to correct more than a 1-bit error. For this reason, forward error correction is normally used when retransmission is not possible or requires a long delay. For example, there is a relatively long delay time in satellite communications; retransmission to correct errors is unacceptable.

5.6   FLOW CONTROL

Another responsibility of the data link layer is **flow control.** In most protocols, flow control is a set of procedures that tells the sender how much data it can transmit before it must wait for an acknowledgment from the receiver. The flow of data must not be allowed to overwhelm the receiver. Any receiving device has a limited speed at which it can process incoming data and a limited amount of memory in which to store incoming data. The receiving device must be able to inform the sending device before those limits are reached and to request that the transmitting device send fewer frames or stop temporarily. Incoming data must be checked and processed before they can be used. The rate of such processing is often slower than the rate of transmission. For this reason, each receiving device has a block of memory, called a buffer, reserved for storing incoming data until they are processed. If the buffer begins to fill up, the receiver must be able to tell the sender to halt transmission until it is once again able to receive.

Flow control refers to a set of procedures used to restrict the amount of data the sender can send before waiting for acknowledgment.

The two methods we discussed for error control can actually provide flow control at the same time. Stop-and-wait ARQ provides flow control because the frames are sent one by one. Sliding-window ARQ provides flow control because the size of the sending window can be matched to the size of the receiver buffer; the sender can always send as many frames as the receiver can handle.

5.7 MEDIUM ACCESS CONTROL

When computers use a shared medium (cable or air), there must be a method to control access to the medium at any moment. This is analogous to a situation in which two vehicles traveling on two perpendicular roads arrive at an intersection at the same time. The intersection, not the roads, is to be shared. If there is no rule to specify which vehicle has the right-of-way, there may be a conflict or even a collision.

To prevent this conflict or collision on a network, there is a need for a **medium access control** (MAC) method. This method defines the procedure a computer follows when it needs to send a frame or frames. The use of a regulated method ensures that there is no conflict among the stations.

The problem of controlling the access to the medium can also be compared to the rules of speaking in an assembly. Different procedures guarantee that the right to speak is upheld and that two people do not speak at the same time.

Several methods for access control have been devised in the past; they can be divided into two broad categories as shown in Figure 5.14: controlled access and random access. We discuss two popular methods in each category.

CONTROLLED ACCESS

In **controlled access** methods, there is a need for a *permit* to send a frame or a set of frames. A computer that wants to send data must first acquire the permit. The permit can be obtained in several ways. We discuss two of them here: poll/select and token passing.

Poll/Select

In the **poll/select** method, the permit to send data is issued from a central authority. One computer (the most powerful one), called the primary, controls the other computers, called the secondaries. The **primary computer** sends and receive frames from the

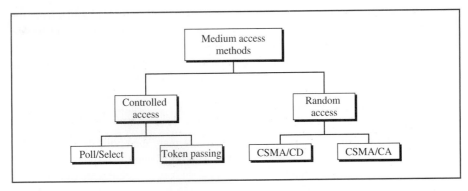

Figure 5.14 Medium access methods

secondaries and controls which computer can send data at any moment. In other words, the permit for sending and receiving data is issued by the primary computer. In this method, the **secondary computers** are not allowed to communicate with each other. The communication must always go through the primary. In other words, if computer A (a secondary) needs to send data to computer B (another secondary), A sends the data to the primary and the primary sends it to B. This means that the primary either has data to send to a secondary or needs to check if a secondary has data to send. Two procedures are needed for this purpose: select and poll.

Select The **select** procedure is used whenever the primary has something to send. Because the primary controls the link, it knows when the link is idle. In the poll/select method, the select procedure has priority over the poll procedure; if the primary has data to send to a secondary, it does not accept data from the secondaries.

   Figure 5.15 illustrates this procedure. Although the primary is the controller, before sending data to the secondary, it needs to know if the secondary is ready to accept the data. It sends a SEL frame (for select) to the secondary. If it receives an ACK frame (for acknowledgment), it knows that the secondary is ready and it sends the data frame.

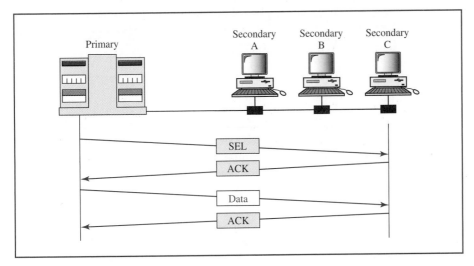

Figure 5.15 Select

Poll   The polling procedure is used by the primary to solicit transmissions from the secondary devices. As noted above, the secondaries are not allowed to send frames unless asked (don't call us—we'll call you). By keeping all control with the primary, the system guarantees that only one transmission can occur at a time, thereby ensuring that there are no collisions. When the primary is ready to receive data, it must ask (poll) each device in turn if it has anything to send. When the first secondary is approached, it responds either with a NAK frame if it has nothing to send or with data (in the form of a data frame) if it does.

If the response is negative (a NAK frame), the primary then polls the next secondary in the same way until it finds one with data to send. When the response is positive (a data frame), the primary reads the frame and returns an acknowledgment (ACK frame) verifying its receipt. The secondary may send several data frames one after the other, or it may be required to wait for an ACK before sending each one, depending on the protocol being used. Figure 5.16 shows the procedure.

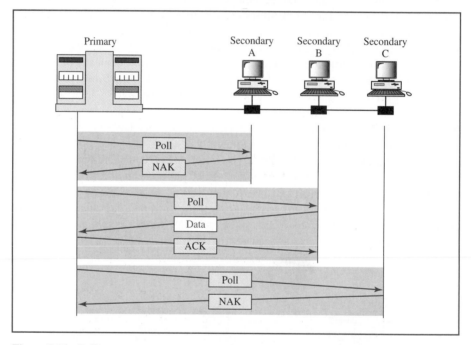

Figure 5.16   Poll

The poll/select method is mostly used in time-sharing systems when a central computer is used to control other computers.

Token Passing

In the **token passing** method, the permit is passed from one computer to another. In this method, stations are arranged around a physical or logical ring. In a physical ring implementation each station is physically connected to its predecessor and successor. In a logical ring implementation a station is logically connected to its predecessor or successor. In both cases, frames are coming from the predecessor and going to the successor.

When no data are being sent, the permit, in the form of a small frame, called a **token,** circulates around the ring. If a station needs to send data, it waits for the token. The station captures the token, sends one or more frames (as long as it has frames to send or the allocated time has not expired), and finally it releases the token to be used by the successor station (the next station on the physical or logical ring). Figure 5.17 shows the idea.

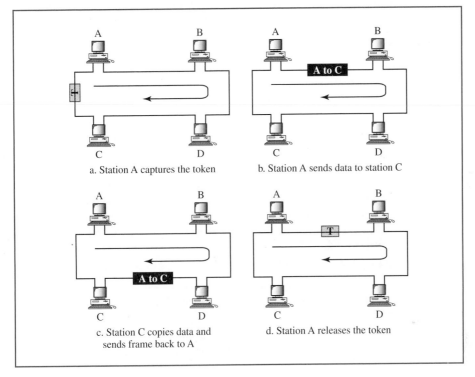

a. Station A captures the token

b. Station A sends data to station C

c. Station C copies data and
sends frame back to A

d. Station A releases the token

Figure 5.17   Token passing network

Token passing is used mostly by local area networks (LANs). We discuss LANs in Chapter 9.

RANDOM ACCESS

In **random access** or **contention** methods, there is no permit. Each computer contends for access to the medium. In these methods, no station is superior to another station and none has control over another. A station with data to send tries to get access to the medium.

Two features give this method its name. First, there is no scheduled time for a station to transmit. Transmission is random among the stations. Hence the term *random access*. Second, no rules specify which station should send. Stations compete with each other to access the medium. Hence the term *contention*.

In a random access method, if more than one station tries to send at the same time, there is an access conflict (collision) and the frames will either be destroyed or modified.

To avoid access conflict or to resolve it when it does happen, each station follows certain steps to access the medium.

1. The station checks to make sure the medium is idle. This is called carrier sense. This is analogous to the rules in an assembly. If a person wants to speak, he must first listen to make sure no one else is talking.
2. If the medium is idle, the station can send data.
3. Even though steps 1 and 2 are followed, there is still a potential for collision. For example, two stations may be checking the medium at the same time; neither senses that the medium is in use and both send at the same time. Collisions need to be either avoided or detected. To avoid collision the sending stations can make a reservation for use of the medium. To detect collision (and send the data again), the station needs to continue monitoring the medium.

CSMA/CD

In **carrier sense multiple access with collision detection** (CSMA/CD), the station first checks the idleness of the medium (by checking the level of energy in the medium). If the medium is idle, the station sends its frame. However, it may happen that a distant station has already sent a frame on the line that is not yet detectable by other stations. In this case, collision is unavoidable. The procedure dictates that the sending stations continue to check the medium after a frame has been sent; if they discover a collision (a very high level of energy), they know that their frames have been destroyed. To minimize the risk of another collision, the two stations each wait a random amount of time before sending again.

CSMA/CD is used in the Ethernet LAN discussed in Chapter 9.

CSMA/CA

In this method, the collision is avoided. A station still checks the idleness of the line. However, before sending data, it sends a special frame to tell every other station how long it is using the medium. If it receives no objection from any station, it means it can send data. The other stations refrain from sending data during the reserved time slot.

The CSMA/CA is used in the wireless LANs discussed in Chapter 10.

5.8   DATA LINK PROTOCOLS

Data link protocols are sets of specifications used to implement the data link layer. To this end, they contain rules for framing, addressing, and error and flow control.

A data link protocol is a set of specifications used to implement the data link layer.

Data link protocols can be divided into two subgroups: asynchronous protocols and synchronous protocols. Asynchronous protocols treat each character in a bit stream independently. Synchronous protocols take the whole bit stream and chop it into characters of equal size.

ASYNCHRONOUS PROTOCOLS

A number of **asynchronous data link protocols** have been developed over the last several decades. Today, these protocols are mostly outdated. Due to its inherent slowness, asynchronous transmission at this level is being replaced by higher-speed synchronous mechanisms.

SYNCHRONOUS PROTOCOLS

The speed of synchronous transmission makes it the better choice over asynchronous transmission for LAN, MAN, and WAN technology. Protocols governing synchronous transmission can be divided into two classes: character-oriented protocols and bit-oriented protocols.

Character-oriented protocols (also called byte-oriented protocols) interpret a transmission frame or packet as a succession of characters, each usually composed of 1 byte (8 bits). All control information is in the form of an existing character encoding system (e.g., ASCII characters).

Bit-oriented protocols interpret a transmission frame or packet as a succession of individual bits, made meaningful by their placement in the frame and by their juxtaposition with other bits. Control information in a bit-oriented protocol can be one or multiple bits depending on the information embodied in the pattern.

In a character-oriented protocol, the frame is interpreted as a series of characters. In a bit-oriented protocol, the frame or packet is interpreted as a series of bits.

Character-Oriented Protocols

Character-oriented protocols are not as efficient as bit-oriented protocols and therefore are now seldom used. They are, however, easy to comprehend and employ the same logic and organization as the bit-oriented protocols.

In all data link protocols, control information is inserted into the data stream either as separate control frames or as additions to existing data frames. In character-oriented protocols, this information is in the form of code words taken from existing character sets such as ASCII or EBCDIC. These multibit characters carry information about line discipline, flow control, and error control. Of the several existing character-oriented protocols, the best known is IBM's binary synchronous communication (BSC).

Bit-Oriented Protocols

In character-oriented protocols, bits are grouped into predefined patterns forming characters. By comparison, bit-oriented protocols can pack more information into shorter frames.

Given the advantages of bit-oriented protocols and the lack of any preexisting coding system (like ASCII) to tie them to, it is no wonder that over the last two decades many different bit-oriented protocols have been developed, all vying to become the standard. Most of these offerings have been proprietary, designed by manufacturers to support their own products. One of them, HDLC, is the design of the ISO and has become the basis for all bit-oriented protocols in use today.

In 1975, IBM pioneered the development of bit-oriented protocols with synchronous data link control (SDLC) and lobbied the ISO to make SDLC the standard. In 1979, the ISO answered with high-level data link control (HDLC), which was based on

SDLC. Adoption of HDLC by the ISO committees led to its adoption and extension by other organizations. The ITU-T was one of the first organizations to embrace HDLC. Since 1981, ITU-T has developed a series of protocols called link access protocols (LAPs: LAPB, LAPD, LAPM, LAPX, etc.), all based on HDLC. Other protocols (such as Frame Relay, PPP, etc.) developed by both ITU-T and ANSI also derive from HDLC, as do most LANs' access control protocols. In short, all bit-oriented protocols in use today either derive from or are sources for HDLC.

All bit-oriented protocols are related to **high-level data link control (HDLC)**, a bit-oriented protocol published by ISO.

HDLC   HDLC is a bit-oriented data link protocol designed to support both half-duplex and full-duplex communication over point-to-point and multipoint links. Systems using HDLC can be characterized by their station types, their configurations, and their response modes.

CASE STUDY

NEW AGE HOME PHARMACY

At NAHP, the hop-to-hop delivery at the data-link layer is accomplished by the software installed at each station and at each switch. When a station sends a frame to another station on the same floor, only two hops are involved: from the sending station to the switch, and from the switch to the receiving station. On the other hand, when a station sends a frame to a station on a different floor, four hops are involved: from the sending station to the floor switch, from the floor switch to the main switch in the basement, from the main switch to the destination floor switch, and from the destination floor switch to the receiving station. When a frame is sent outside the company, or when a frame is received from the outside, many hops are involved, some from inside the company and some from outside.

NAHP uses two protocols at the data-link layer: Ethernet and Fast Ethernet (see Chapter 9). The Ethernet protocol controls the movement of frames in the floor network that connects each station to the switch in the closet. Each computer is connected to the switch by four pairs of cables. In this case, although the CSMA/CD software is installed in each station and in the switch, it is not really needed because each station has a two-way (full-duplex) connection to the switch. Each station can send and receive frames at the same time (the connection is like a two-way street in which cars can travel in both directions). In other words, the medium is dedicated for communication between the switch and the station and no sharing is involved. CSMA/CD, which handles contention, is actually useless here. The protocol, however, is part of the data-link layer software which handles other duties such as hop-to-hop delivery, framing, and addressing.

The Fast Ethernet protocol, which creates a backbone network between the floors, also uses two-way communication between the main switch and the switches on each floor. Here again there is no need for any access control method.

Recently, a pharmacist became apprehensive about the accuracy of the data in transmission. Specifically, she was concerned that dosage values would be corrupted during transmission. The concern was relayed to the Modern Networking Corporation. The consultant assured the board members that the CRC protocol used at the data-link layer and the checksum protocol used at the transport layer are very reliable. He recommended an additional method of error checking to be used on top of the other two: Data can be sent two times. After an order is received, a copy of the order is sent back to the sender and confirmation is requested. The pharmacists approved this process.

5.9   KEY TERMS

acknowledgment (ACK)

addressing

asynchronous protocol

attenuation

bit-oriented protocol

buffer

burst error

carrier sense multiple access with
   collision detection (CSMA/CD)

character-oriented protocol

contention

controlled access

crosstalk

cyclic redundancy check (CRC)

data link layer

distortion

echo

error control

error correction

error detection

flow control

forward error correction

frame

header

high-level data link control (HDLC)

hop-to-hop delivery

impulse noise

jitter

longitudinal redundancy check (LRC)

medium access control (MAC)

negative acknowledgment (NAK)

packetizing

parity check

poll

poll/select

primary computer

random access

redundancy

secondary computer

select

single-bit error

sliding-window ARQ

stop-and-wait ARQ

token

token passing

trailer

vertical redundancy check (VRC)

white noise

5.10   SUMMARY

❏   The main functions of the data link layer are hop-to-hop delivery, packetizing, addressing, error control, flow control, and medium access control.

❏   Hop-to-hop delivery is the delivery of a packet from one computer or router to the next computer or router.

❏   Packetizing is the encapsulation of the packet coming from the IP layer. The new packet is called a frame.

❏   The data-link layer addresses are called physical addresses (or sometimes MAC addresses).

❏   The Address Resolution Protocol finds the physical address given the IP address.

❏   Errors can be caused by white noise, impulse noise, crosstalk, echo, jitter, attenuation, and distortion.

❏   Errors can be categorized as single-bit errors or burst errors.

❏   Redundancy is the concept of sending extra bits for use in error detection.

❏   Four common methods of error detection are the following:

   a. Vertical redundancy check (VRC).

   b. Longitudinal redundancy check (LRC).

   c. Cyclic redundancy check (CRC).

❏   In VRC an extra bit (parity bit) is added to the data unit.

❏ In LRC a redundant data unit follows *n* data units.

❏ CRC, the most powerful of the redundancy checking techniques, is based on binary division.

❏ Error correction may involve retransmission. There are two protocols for retransmission: stop-and-wait automatic repeat request and sliding-window automatic repeat request.

❏ Forward error correction is normally used if retransmission is not possible or takes too long.

❏ Flow control is regulation of data transmission so that the receiver buffer does not become overwhelmed by data.

❏ The two main methods of flow control are stop-and-wait flow control and sliding-window flow control.

❏ Medium access control defines methods (controlled or random) to determine a computer's access to the medium.

❏ Two controlled access methods are poll/select and token passing.

❏ Two random access methods are CSMA/CD and CSMA/CA.

❏ Data link protocols, a set of specifications used to implement the data link layer, can be classified as synchronous or asynchronous.

❏ Synchronous protocols can be classified as character-oriented protocols or bit-oriented protocols.

❏ All bit-oriented protocols are related to a protocol called high-level data link control (HDLC).

 PRACTICE SET

Review Questions

1. What are the main functions of the data link layer?
2. Compare hop-to-hop delivery with host-to-host delivery.
3. Compare hop-to-hop delivery with application-to-application delivery.
4. What is a frame? How is a frame formed?
5. What is the purpose of the header added to the data coming from an upper layer?
6. What is the purpose of the trailer added to the data coming from an upper layer?
7. What is a MAC address?
8. Why is ARP needed?
9. Name five sources of errors.
10. How does a single-bit error differ from a burst error?
11. Discuss the concept of redundancy in error detection.
12. How is VRC related to LRC?
13. What does the CRC generator append to the data unit?
14. How does the CRC checker know that the received data unit is undamaged?
15. What are the two protocols for retransmission?
16. Define flow control.
17. Why is medium access control needed?
18. What is the difference between polling and selecting?
19. Why is token passing considered a controlled access method?

20. Why is CSMA/CD a random access method?
21. How are synchronous protocols classified? What is the basis of the classification?

Multiple-Choice Questions

22. Which of the following is a data link layer function?
    a. packetizing
    b. error and flow control
    c. medium access control
    d. all of the above
23. The data link layer is responsible for _____ delivery.
    a. port-to-port
    b. source-to-destination
    c. hop-to-hop
    d. all of the above
24. The data packet at the data link layer is usually called a _____.
    a. frame
    b. datagram
    c. user datagram
    d. segment
25. The protocol for obtaining the physical address of a node when the IP address is known is called _____.
    a. TCP/IP
    b. TCP
    c. ARP
    d. ARQ
26. A signal can lose energy due to the resistance of the medium. This is called _____.
    a. crosstalk
    b. jitter
    c. impulse noise
    d. attenuation
27. _____ can cause errors during data transmission.
    a. White noise
    b. Impulse noise
    c. Echo
    d. All of the above
28. Which of the following best describes a single-bit error?
    a. A single bit is inverted.
    b. A single bit is inverted per data unit.
    c. A single bit is inverted per transmission.
    d. Any of the above
29. If the ASCII character G is sent and the character D is received, what type of error is this?
    a. single-bit
    b. multiple-bit
    c. burst
    d. recoverable

30. If the ASCII character H is sent and the character I is received, what type of error is this?
    a. single-bit
    b. multiple-bit
    c. burst
    d. recoverable

31. _____ in error detection involves the addition of extra bits to the data unit.
    a. Redundancy
    b. Flow control
    c. Stop-and-wait ARQ
    d. Random access

32. Which error detection method consists of a parity bit for each data unit as well as an entire data unit of parity bits?
    a. VRC
    b. LRC
    c. CRC
    d. ARQ

33. Which error detection method consists of just one redundant bit per data unit?
    a. VRC
    b. LRC
    c. CRC
    d. ARQ

34. Which error detection method involves the use of parity bits?
    a. VRC
    b. LRC
    c. CRC
    d. a and b

35. The protocol to correct errors by retransmitting the data is known as _____.
    a. stop-and-wait ARQ
    b. sliding-window ARQ
    c. redundancy
    d. a and b

36. Regulation of the rate of transmission of data frames is known as _____.
    a. line discipline
    b. flow control
    c. data rate control
    d. switch control

37. _____ methods prevent collisions between two or more computers that want to send data at the same time.
    a. Flow control
    b. Error control
    c. Medium access control
    d. Addressing

38. _____ is a controlled access method.
    a. Token passing
    b. Poll/select
    c. CSMA/CD
    d. a and b

39. When a primary device wants to send data to a secondary device, it needs to first send _____ frame.
    a. an ACK
    b. a poll
    c. a SEL
    d. an ENQ

40. When a secondary device is ready to send data, it must wait for _____ frame.
    a. an ACK
    b. a poll
    c. a SEL
    d. an ENQ

41. _____ is a random access (or contention) method.
    a. Token passing
    b. Poll/select
    c. CSMA/CD
    d. a and b

42. Ethernet LANs use _____ for medium access control.
    a. token passing
    b. poll/select
    c. CSMA/CD
    d. CSMA/CA

43. Wireless LANs use _____ for medium access control.
    a. token passing
    b. poll/select
    c. CSMA/CD
    d. CSMA/CA

44. Flow control is needed to prevent _____.
    a. bit errors
    b. overflow of the sender buffer
    c. overflow of the receiver buffer
    d. collision between sender and receiver

45. ARQ stands for _____.
    a. automatic repeat quantization
    b. automatic repeat request
    c. automatic retransmission request
    d. acknowledge repeat request

46. A timer is set when _____ is sent out.
    a. a packet
    b. an ACK
    c. a NAK
    d. all of the above

47. HDLC is a _____ protocol.
    a. character-oriented
    b. bit-oriented
    c. byte-oriented
    d. count-oriented

CHAPTER 6

Physical Layer

The physical layer, positioned between the data link layer and the transmission medium, has very complex tasks to perform. One major task is to provide services for the data link layer. Recall that the data in the data link layer consists of frames of 0s and 1s that are ready to be sent across the transmission medium. This stream of 0s and 1s must first be converted into another entity: signals. One of the services provided by the physical layer is to create a signal that represents this stream of bits.

The physical layer must also take care of the physical network, the transmission medium. The transmission medium is a passive entity; it has no internal program or logic for control like other layers. The transmission medium must be controlled by the physical layer. The physical layer decides on the directions of data flow. The physical layer decides on the number of logical channels for transporting data coming from different sources.

In this chapter, we study the duties of the physical layer, first as a converter that converts data to signals, then as a manager that controls the medium.

OBJECTIVES

After reading this chapter, the reader should be able to:

- Distinguish between analog and digital data.
- Distinguish between analog and digital signals.
- Understand the concept of bandwidth and the relationship between bandwidth and data transmission speed.
- Understand digital-to-digital, digital-to-analog, and analog-to-digital encoding.
- Understand multiplexing and the difference between a link and a channel.

6.1 DIGITAL AND ANALOG

We encounter analog and digital entities in our daily life, but we usually do not distinguish between the two. Digital entities are made of separate parts; they can easily be divided into countable parts. For example, we can say how many oranges we have in a basket; we can count them. Each orange has an existence separate from the other oranges. The oranges in a basket are a digital (discrete) entity.

On the other hand, we cannot count the oil contained in a tank. We could use a unit such as gallon and measure the amount of oil in the tank, but this is not real counting. Each molecule of oil is part of the whole and its boundary is not visibly defined. The oil in the tank is an analog (continuous) entity.

Figure 6.1 shows the idea of analog and digital entities.

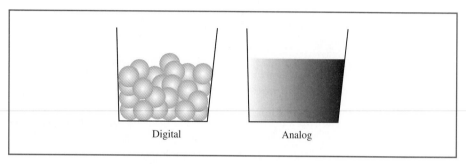

Figure 6.1   Analog and digital entities

When it comes to the transportation of entities from one point to another, we can also see the difference between digital and analog entities. Water, when being transported on a river bed or in a pipe, is a good example of something with an analog nature; the flow of the water is continuous. On the other hand, the movement of cars on a highway clearly shows the nature of something that is digital; the cars are moving one by one with each car being totally distinguishable from another car.

DIGITAL AND ANALOG DATA

The data we use in data communications can also be analog or digital.

Digital Data

Digital data uses a combination of symbols, selected from a predetermined list of symbols, to convey information. For example, a word uses a limited set of symbols (characters) to represent a concept. A novel uses a limited set of symbols (uppercase letters, lowercase letters, and punctuation marks) to tell a story. The type of information is digital because we can always tell how many characters are in a certain novel; we can count them (with a computer program, for example). The whole is made of small separable parts (characters). The information contained in a book can be compared to the basket of oranges; the characters are of different types and the oranges of different sizes, but both are countable.

The computer also stores data in the form of symbols. However, the type of symbols used is different. Each symbol must be stored in the memory of the computer. Each unit of memory is a switch; it can be on or off. This means that we can have only two symbols; one to represent the *off* position and one to represent the *on* position. The computer uses two symbols 0 and 1 (each is called a bit). In other words, a unit of information is stored in the memory of the computer as a combination (series of) 0s and 1s. The data are in digital format, because they are made of separate symbols. We can always count how many bits are stored in the memory of a computer.

Note that everything stored in the computer must be digital and the only two symbols used are 0 and 1. The contents of a book, although digital in nature, cannot be stored in the computer directly; it must be encoded into bits (as we discussed in Chapter 1) before being stored. Audio and video information, both analog entities, must be converted to digital format (digitized) before being stored in the memory of a computer. Figure 6.2 is an example of digital data.

0000111010 10101010

Figure 6.2   Digital data

Analog Data ⟋ *first*

Analog data is information that is continuous. Continuous is a mathematical concept. It means that the data can be drawn on paper without interruption, without lifting your pencil from the paper. This would be impossible to do if your data values are just 0s and 1s. Audio and video are two examples of analog data. Before the popularity of the digital disc (compact disc), analog disks were used to store audio information (music and songs) that could be played back using a head that moved over the surface of the disk to reproduce the original audio. Figure 6.3 shows an example of analog data.

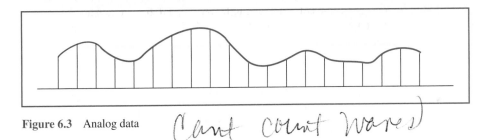

Figure 6.3   Analog data   *Cant count waves*

DIGITAL AND ANALOG SIGNALS

In data communications we need to transfer data from one computer to another using transmission media. The transmission media must move the data and the data have to be in a form that is acceptable to the transmission media. Data must be transformed to electromagnetic energy.

Cars as digital entities can be parked in a parking lot. If they are to be used to move people from one place to another, they need to be put in motion and they need a road (transmission medium). Water as an analog entity can be stored in a tank. If we need to move water from one place to another, we need to have a river bed or a pipe (transmission medium) and somehow put the water in motion (using a pump, for example).

Unfortunately, data are not cars or water and cannot be put in motion directly. They must be represented by electromagnetic energy (signals). Just like data, signals can be either analog or digital.

Digital Signals

Data (digital or analog) can be represented by a digital signal. For example, a 1 can be encoded as a positive voltage and a 0 as zero level of energy as shown in Figure 6.4.

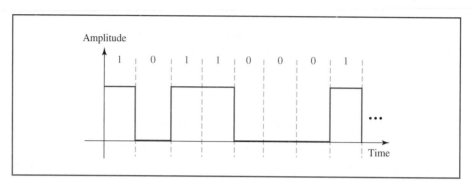

Figure 6.4 Digital signal

Think of the above signal as an instance of traffic on a one-lane road. The positive level shows the existence of a car, the zero level shows the lack of a car.

Bit Interval and Bit Rate   When dealing with digital signals, we need to understand two terms, *bit interval* and *bit rate*. The bit interval is the time required to send one single bit. The bit rate is the number of bit intervals per second. This means that the bit rate is the number of bits sent in one second, usually expressed in bits per second (bps) (see Figure 6.5).

(amount of time to send a bit)

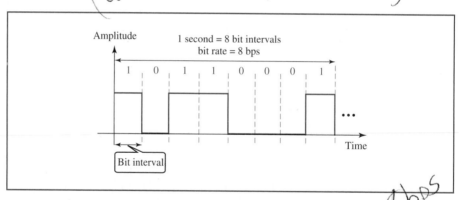

Figure 6.5 Bit rate and bit interval

8bps

TECHNICAL FOCUS: UNITS OF BIT RATE

One bit per second (bps): 1 bps
Kilobits per second (kbps): 1000 bps
Megabits per second (Mbps): 1,000,000 bps
Gigabits per second (Gbps): 1,000,000,000 bps
Terabits per second (Tbps): 1,000,000,000,000 bps   *1 trillion bps*

the higher the bits, the faster the equipment cost more

Analog Signals

An analog signal can be simple or composite. A complex (or composite) signal is a combination of more than one simple signal.

Simple Signal: A Sine Wave   The sine wave is the most fundamental form of an analog signal. Visualized as a simple oscillating curve, its change over the course of a cycle is smooth and consistent, a continuous, rolling flow. Figure 6.6 shows a sine wave. Each cycle consists of a single arc above the time axis followed by a single arc below it. Sine waves can be fully described by three characteristics: *amplitude, period* or *frequency,* and *phase*.

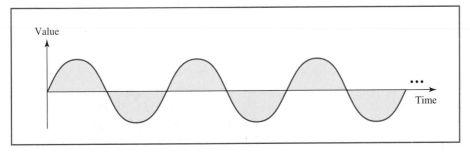

Figure 6.6   A sine wave

Amplitude   The amplitude of a signal is the value of the signal at any point on the wave. It is equal to the vertical distance from a given point on the wave form to the horizontal axis. The maximum amplitude of a sine wave is equal to the highest value it reaches on the vertical axis (see Figure 6.7).

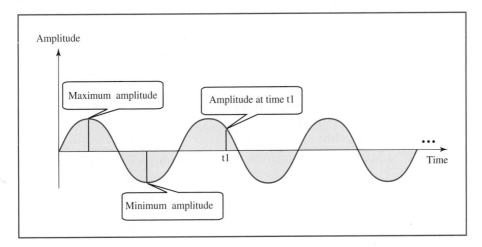

Figure 6.7   Amplitude

Period and Frequency   *Period* refers to the amount of time, in seconds, a signal needs to complete one cycle. Frequency refers to the number of periods in one second. The frequency of a signal is its number of cycles per second. Figure 6.8 shows the concept of period and frequency.

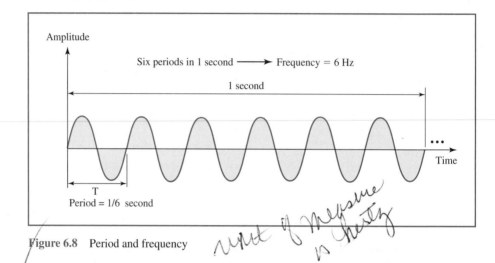

Figure 6.8   Period and frequency

unit of measure is hertz

TECHNICAL FOCUS:
UNITS OF FREQUENCY

Hertz (Hz): 1 Hz
Kilohertz (kHz): 10^3 Hz
Megahertz (MHz): 10^6 Hz
Gigahertz (GHz): 10^9 Hz
Terahertz (THz): 10^{12} Hz

TECHNICAL FOCUS:
FREQUENCY AND CHANGE

The concept of frequency is similar to the concept of change. If a signal (or data) is changing rapidly, its frequency is higher. If it changes slowly, its frequency is lower. When a signal changes 10 times per second, its frequency is 10 Hz; when a signal changes 1000 times per second, its frequency is 1000 Hz.

Phase   The term *phase* describes the position of the waveform relative to time zero. If we think of the wave as something that can be shifted backward or forward along the time axis, phase describes the amount of that shift. It indicates the status of the first cycle.

Phase is measured in degrees or radians (360 degrees is 2π radians). A phase shift of 360 degrees corresponds to a shift of a complete period; a phase shift of 180 degrees corresponds to a shift of half a period; and a phase shift of 90 degrees corresponds to a shift of a quarter of a period (see Figure 6.9).

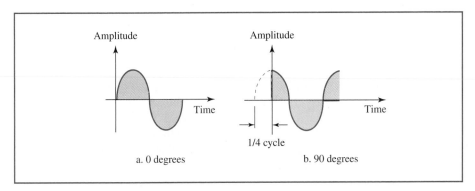

Figure 6.9   Phase

COMPLEX SIGNAL

In real life, complex signals are much more prevalent than simple signals; a signal is usually composed of multiple simple signals. For example, a complex signal can have frequencies between 1 kHz to 4 kHz or between 10 MHz and 70 MHz. To understand a complex signal, think about its components, the simple frequencies. If a signal has sharp changes (sudden changes in a very short period of time), the signal contains high frequencies. If the signal has smooth changes with time, the signal contains low frequencies.

At one extreme, a signal that does not change has zero frequency. A vertical spike representing a sudden change (theoretically in no time) contains a signal of infinite frequency. Figure 6.10 shows the concepts.

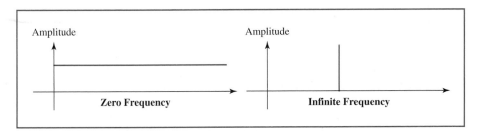

Figure 6.10   Zero frequency and infinite frequency

BANDWIDTH

In a complex signal, the **bandwidth** of a signal is the difference between the highest frequency and the lowest frequency. For example, a signal that carries frequencies between 10 kHz and 50 kHz has a bandwidth of 40 kHz.

Bandwidth is a very important concept in data communications. If a signal has a wide bandwidth, it means it is very complex. It can contain all of the frequencies from the highest frequency to the lowest frequency. To send this complex signal from one place to another, we need a medium (a cable for example) that can respond to these many changes. Each transmission medium also has its own bandwidth, that is, the range of frequencies that it can carry (be responsive to). To be able to send a complex signal through a medium, the bandwidth of the signal must match the bandwidth of the media. Otherwise, some of the frequencies cannot pass through the medium and cannot be received by the receiver.

As an example, suppose we have a signal with a bandwidth of 10 kHz. It contains frequencies between 0 and 10 kHz. We have a cable with a bandwidth of 6 kHz; it can pass frequencies between 2 and 8 kHz. If we try to send this complex signal through this cable, we lose some of the frequencies contained in the complex signal. The lowest frequencies (between 0 and 2 kHz) cannot be sent. The highest frequencies (between 8 and 10 kHz) also cannot be sent. The result at the receiver is a distorted form of the original signal. The low frequencies that represent the smooth (more horizontal) part are missing as are the high frequencies that represent sudden changes. The signal is totally distorted.

DIGITAL SIGNAL AS A COMPLEX SIGNAL

A digital signal is actually a complex signal. Consider the horizontal part of a digital signal as a component with 0 frequency and the vertical part of the signal as a component with infinite frequency. Also, consider the change from the horizontal to vertical as all the frequencies. Then we can claim that a digital signal is a complex signal with frequencies from 0 to infinity.

The reader may have guessed that it is more difficult to send a digital signal than an analog signal. The latter may have a limited bandwidth; the former has a (theoretically) infinite bandwidth. We need a better medium to send digital signals.

A digital signal has a much higher bandwidth than an analog signal. There is a need for a better media to send a digital signal.

BUSINESS FOCUS:
TWO FAMILIAR SIGNALS

A familiar signal in our daily lives is the electrical energy we use at home and at work. The signal we receive from the power company has an amplitude of 120 V and a frequency of 60 Hz (a simple analog signal). Another signal familiar to us is the power we get from a battery. It is an analog signal with an amplitude 6 V (or 12 or 24) and a frequency of zero.

One signal that is an integral part of our daily lives is the electrical energy that we use at home and at work.

The bandwidth of telephone lines was designed to carry human voice; a digital signal needs a higher bandwith, so you can run into trouble sending digital signals over telephone lines.

BUSINESS FOCUS:
THE BANDWIDTH OF TELEPHONE LINES

The conventional line that connects a home or business to the telephone office has a bandwidth of 4 kHz. These lines were designed for carrying human voice, which normally has a bandwidth in this range. Human voice has a frequency that is normally between 0 and 4 kHz. The telephone lines are perfect for this purpose. However, if we try to send a digital signal, we are in trouble. A digital signal needs a very high bandwidth (theoretically infinite); it cannot be sent using these lines. We must either improve the quality of these lines or change our digital signal to a complex signal that needs only 4 kHz.

6.2 TRANSFORMING DATA TO SIGNALS

If we consider our two categories of data, digital and analog, and the signals that can represent them, also digital and analog, we conclude that there are four situations: sending digital data using digital signals, sending digital data using analog signals, sending analog data using digital signals, and finally, sending analog data using analog signals. Figure 6.11 show these four situations.

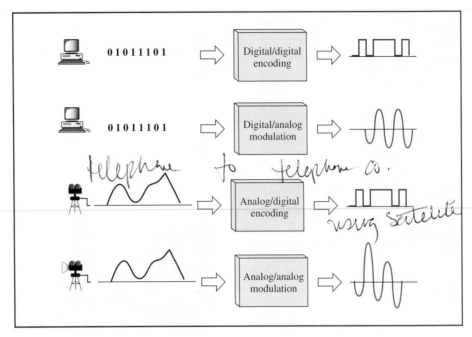

Figure 6.11 Transforming data to signals

The fourth method, sending analog data using analog signals is used primarily in audio and video communication (telephone, radio, and television) and is not discussed here.

DIGITAL ENCODING: DIGITAL-TO-DIGITAL CONVERSION

If the data to be sent are digital (in the form of 0s and 1s), and the transmission medium is capable of handling digital signals (has a high bandwidth), then the physical layer can encode the digital data into a digital signal suitable for transmission.

This is the case, for example, when we connect several computers to create a LAN (see Chapter 9). Here, the data produced by each computer are digital. The cable that connects the computers also has a high bandwidth and is of good quality. The best solution is digital-to-digital encoding; the information in the form of a digital signal is carried between the two computers.

Figure 6.12 shows this concept. The data, in the form of 0s and 1s, are represented by digital signals and sent through the media.

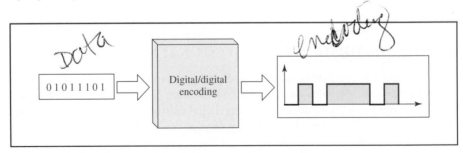

Figure 6.12 Digital-to-digital encoding

Most LANs use digital-to-digital encoding because the data stored in the computers are digital and the cable connecting them is capable of carrying digital signals.

But how are digital data encoded into digital signals? An ever-increasing need for higher and higher data rates (sending more data in less time) has resulted in many schemes. All of these methods can be categorized as **unipolar, polar,** or **bipolar.** Figure 6.13 names a few methods in each category.

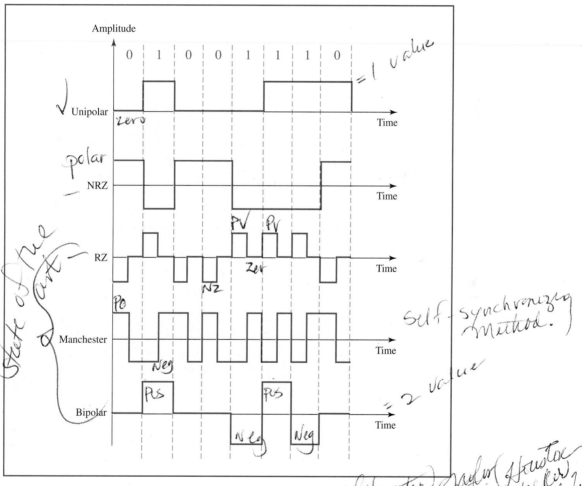

Figure 6.13 Digital encoding methods

Unipolar

In this method, 1s are encoded as a positive value and 0s are encoded as a zero value (or vice versa). Unipolar encoding is very simple and easy to implement. However it cannot be used for high-speed data transfer.

Polar

Polar encoding has two levels: one positive and one negative. For example, 1 can be represented by a positive value, 0 can be represented by a negative value. Polar encoding can transfer data at a higher rate than unipolar encoding. Of the many existing variations of polar encoding, the most familiar are nonreturn to zero (NRZ), return to zero (RZ), Manchester (used in Ethernet LANs), and Differential Manchester (used in Token Ring LANs).

Bipolar

Bipolar encoding has three levels: positive, negative, and zero. Here, the zero level represents 0, while the positive and negative levels alternately represent 1. That is, if 1 is represented by the positive level, the next 1 is represented by the negative level, and the next by a positive level. The simplest type of bipolar encoding, is called alternate mark inversion (AMI).

TECHNICAL FOCUS:
AVERAGE VALUES IN DIGITAL SIGNALS

With one exception, all of the signals in Figure 6.13 have an average value of zero (the positive and negative values cancel each other in the long run). The first signal, unipolar, has a positive average value. This average value, sometimes called the residual value, cannot pass through some devices (such as a transformer). In this case, the receiver receives a signal that can be totally different from the one sent and results in an erroneous interpretation of data.

TECHNICAL FOCUS:
SYNCHRONIZATION IN DIGITAL SIGNALS

To correctly interpret the signals received from the sender, the receiver's bit intervals must correspond exactly to the sender's bit intervals. If the receiver clock is faster or slower, the bit intervals are not matched and the receiver will interpret the signals differently than the sender intended. A **self-synchronizing** digital signal includes timing information in the data being transmitted. This can be achieved if there are transitions in the signal that alert the receiver to the beginning, middle, or end of the bit interval. If the receiver's clock is out of synchronization, these alerting points can reset the clock. The last three signals in Figure 6.13, RZ, Manchester, and bipolar, are self-synchronizing signals because there is a transition (from high value to low value and vice versa) in each bit interval.

MODULATION OF DIGITAL DATA:
DIGITAL-TO-ANALOG CONVERSION

Sometimes the physical layer needs to convert digital data to analog signals. Although this is not as desirable as conversion to digital signals, this happens, for example, when we use the existing telephone lines to send digital data from our computer to the Internet. We use a line that was designed for analog communication (voice) to send a signal from our residence to the telephone company. This line has a very narrow bandwidth (4 kHz) that does not allow a digital signal to be passed without totally losing its shape and rendering it unreadable at the destination. The low bandwidth of the medium is inadequate for a digital signal. In this case, the solution is digital-to-analog conversion, called **modulation.** A device called a **modem** (modulator/demodulator) is installed inside or outside the computer. It becomes part of the physical layer and modulates and demodulates the data. Figure 6.14 shows the concept.

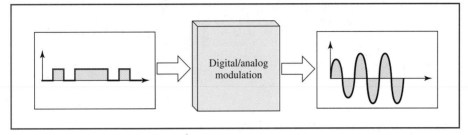

Figure 6.14   Digital-to-analog modulation

Of the many mechanisms for digital-to-analog modulation, we discuss only those most useful for data communications.

As discussed before, a sine wave is defined by three characteristics: amplitude, frequency, and phase. Any of these three characteristics can be altered, giving us at least three mechanisms: *amplitude shift keying* (ASK), *frequency shift keying* (FSK), and *phase shift keying* (PSK).

Amplitude Shift Keying (ASK)

In **amplitude shift keying** (ASK), the amplitude of the carrier signal is varied to represent binary 1 or 0. Both frequency and phase remain constant while the amplitude changes. A bit interval is the period of time that defines 1 bit. The peak amplitude of the signal during each bit interval is constant and its value depends on the bit (0 or 1). The speed of transmission using ASK is limited by the physical characteristics of the transmission medium. Figure 6.15 gives a conceptual view of ASK.

Unfortunately, ASK transmission is highly susceptible to noise interference. A 0 may be changed to a 1, and a 1 to 0. Noise usually affects amplitude.

Frequency Shift Keying (FSK)

In **frequency shift keying** (FSK), the frequency of the carrier signal is varied to represent binary 1 or 0. The frequency of the signal during each bit interval is constant and its value depends on the bit (0 or 1); both peak amplitude and phase remain constant. Figure 6.16 gives a conceptual view of FSK.

FSK avoids most of the noise problems of ASK. Because the receiving device is looking for specific frequency changes over a given number of periods, it can ignore amplitude spikes.

Phase Shift Keying (PSK)

In **phase shift keying** (PSK), the phase of the carrier is varied to represent binary 1 or 0. Both peak amplitude and frequency remain constant as the phase changes. For example, if

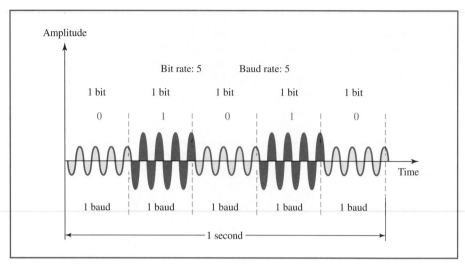

Figure 6.15   ASK

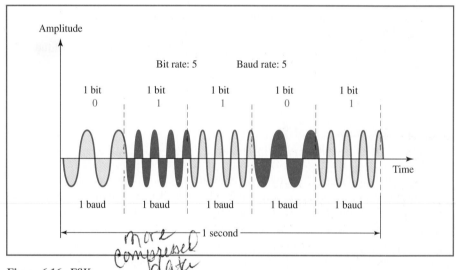

Figure 6.16   FSK

we start with a phase of 0 degrees to represent binary 0, then we can change the phase to 180 degrees to send binary 1. The phase of the signal during each bit interval is constant and its value depends on the bit (0 or 1). Figure 6.17 gives a conceptual view of PSK.

Multiple-Bit Modulation

In the three methods discussed so far (ASK, FSK, and PSK), we sent 1 bit for each change of signal characteristic. We can improve the rate of transmission if we send more than 1 bit for each change. For example, if we have four different amplitudes instead of two, we can send 2 bits at a time because 2 bits can be represented by four levels of amplitude. Level 1 can be 00, level 2 can be 01, level 3 can be 10, and level 4 can be 11.

FSK + PSK more efficient using band width

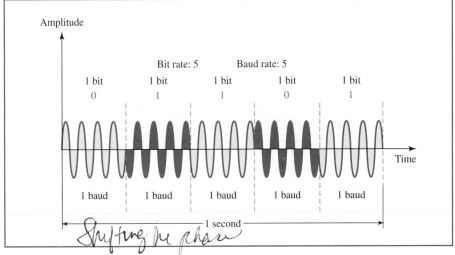

Shifting the phase

Figure 6.17 PSK

Similarly, if we have eight amplitude levels, we can send 3 bits at a time because 3 bits can be represented by eight levels (000, 001, 010, 011, 100, 101, 110, and 111).

The same is true for FSK and PSK. In FSK, we can use four different frequencies to represent the transmission of 2 bits at a time. In PSK, we can use, for example, eight different phases to represent 3 bits at a time.

Bit Rate and Baud Rate

Two terms used frequently in data communication are *bit rate* and *baud rate*. Bit rate is the number of bits transmitted during one second. Baud rate refers to the number of elements per second that are required to represent those bits. In discussions of computer efficiency, the bit rate is the more important—we want to know how long it takes to process each piece of information. In data transmission, however, we are more concerned with how efficiently we can move those data from place to place, whether singly (1 bit—bit rate) or in blocks (multiple bits—baud rate). The fewer changes required, the more efficient the system and the less bandwidth required to transmit more bits; so we are more concerned with baud rate. The baud rate determines the bandwidth required to send the signal.

TECHNICAL FOCUS:
UNDERSTANDING BIT RATE AND BAUD RATE

A transportation analogy can clarify the concept of bauds and bits. A baud is analogous to a car; a bit is analogous to a passenger. A car can carry one or more passengers. If 1000 cars go from one point to another each carrying only one passenger (the driver), then 1000 passengers are transported. However, if each car carries four passengers (car pooling), then 4000 passengers are transported. Note that the number of cars, not the number of passengers, determines the traffic and, therefore, the need for wider highways. Similarly, the number of bauds determines the required bandwidth, not the number of bits.

SAMPLING ANALOG DATA: ANALOG-TO-DIGITAL CONVERSION

Another type of conversion is necessary when the data is analog and we need to send it as a digital signal. This is the case when long distance telephone companies send voice over a digital network. Voice is transmitted as an analog signal from the subscriber telephone to the telephone office, but for long distances, it needs to be sent over a digital network to reach the other telephone office at the receiver's site. There are two major reasons for using digital signals in long distance telephony. First, digital signals are more noise resistant; some of us can remember when overseas telephone calls were analog and not noise free. Second, digital networks (such as the Internet) can be used for voice as well as data.

In situations such as the above, there is a need for analog-to-digital conversion, Figure 6.18 shows the analog-to-digital converter, called a codec (coder-decoder).

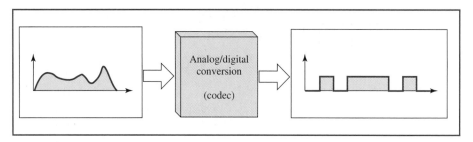

Figure 6.18   Analog-to-digital conversion

PCM

One of the common methods to convert an analog signal into a digital signal is called pulse code modulation (PCM). Figure 6.19 shows the steps to convert an analog signal to a digital signal.

Sampling   The first step in analog-to-digital conversion is sampling. The term **sampling** means measuring the amplitude of the signal at equal intervals. This technique takes an analog signal, measures it, and generates a series of pulses based on the results of the sampling.

Quantization   The second step is **quantization.** Each sample is assigned a value from a limited set. For example, telephone companies, after sampling the human voice on the phone, assign an integer between 0 to 127 to each sample.

Binary Transformation   The third step is to change the quantities assigned to each sample to binary numbers (see Appendix B).

Digital-to-Digital Encoding   The last step is the digital-to-digital encoding of the data obtained in the previous step. Any of the techniques we previously discussed can be used.

Number of Bits Per Second   To digitize voice, we need at least 8000 samples per second (see Technical Focus box). For a good replica of the voice, we need 256 levels for each sample. A number between 0 and 255 can be represented by 8 bits ($2^8 = 256$). Therefore, to represent voice with a digital signal, we need $8000 \times 8 = 64{,}000$ bps or 64 kbps.

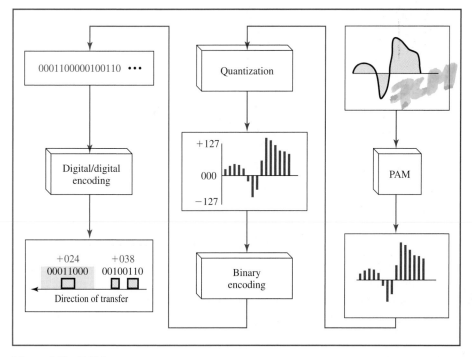

Figure 6.19   PCM

TECHNICAL FOCUS:
SAMPLING RATE AND NYQUIST THEOREM

As you can see from the preceding figures, the accuracy of any digital reproduction of an analog signal depends on the number of samples taken. So the question is, how many samples are sufficient? This question was answered by Nyquist. His theorem states that the sampling rate must be at least twice the highest frequency of the original signal to ensure the accurate reproduction of the original analog signal. So if we want to sample a telephone voice with a maximum frequency of 4000 Hz, we need a sampling rate of 8000 samples per second.

TECHNICAL FOCUS:
CAPACITY OF A CHANNEL

We often need to know the capacity of a channel; that is, how fast can we send data over a specific medium? The answer was given by Shannon. Shannon proved that the number of bits that we can send through a channel depends on two factors: the bandwidth of the channel and the noise in the channel. Shannon came up with the following formula:

$$C = B \log_2 (1 + \text{signal-to-noise ratio})$$

C is the capacity in bits per second; *B* is the bandwidth. For example, let us calculate the capacity of a standard telephone line. The bandwidth of a telephone line is 4000 Hz, but only 3000 Hz is suitable for data communication. The signal to noise ratio (the measure of the data signal to the noise) is close to 3162. Using the above formula, we can send only 34,860 bps or 34.86 kbps.

In Chapter 7 we will see that some modems using special techniques can achieve a rate higher than this.

6.3 TRANSMISSION MODES

Of primary concern when considering digital transmission of data from one device to another is the wiring, and of primary concern when considering the wiring is the data stream. Do we send 1 bit at a time, or do we group bits into larger groups and, if so, how? The transmission of binary data across a link can be accomplished either in parallel mode or serial mode. In parallel mode, multiple bits are sent with each clock pulse. In serial mode, 1 bit is sent with each clock pulse. While there is only one way to send parallel data, there are two subclasses of serial transmission: synchronous and asynchronous (see Figure 6.20).

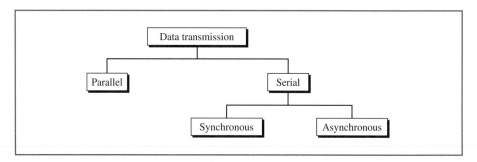

Figure 6.20 Data transmission

Parallel Transmission

Binary data, consisting of 1s and 0s, may be organized into groups of *n* bits each. Computers produce and consume data in groups of bits much as we conceive of and use spoken language in the form of words rather than letters. By grouping, we can send data *n* bits at a time instead of 1. This is called parallel transmission.

The mechanism for parallel transmission is a conceptually simple one: use *n* wires to send *n* bits at one time. That way each bit has its own wire, and all *n* bits of one group can be transmitted with each clock pulse from one device to another. Figure 6.21 shows how parallel transmission works for *n* = 8. Typically, the eight wires are bundled in a cable with a connector at each end.

The advantage of parallel transmission is speed. All else being equal, parallel transmission can increase the transfer speed by a factor of *n* over serial transmission. But there is a significant disadvantage: cost. Parallel transmission requires *n* communication lines

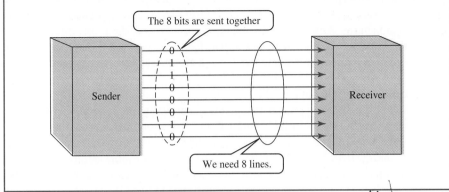

Figure 6.21 Parallel transmission *(8 bits concurrently) need a line for each bit. more expensive*

(wires in the example) just to transmit the data stream. Because this is expensive, parallel transmission is usually limited to short distances. *Cpu to HD = 32, 64 parallel inside cpu But not from one device to device*

Serial Transmission

In serial transmission 1 bit follows another, so we need only one communication channel rather than *n* to transmit data between two communicating devices (see Figure 6.22).

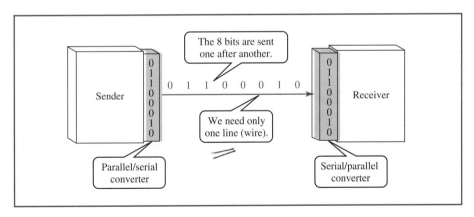

Figure 6.22 Serial transmission

The advantage of serial over parallel transmission is that with only one communication channel, serial transmission reduces the cost of transmission over parallel by roughly a factor of *n*.

Since communication within devices is parallel, conversion devices are required at the interface between the sender and the line (parallel-to-serial) and between the line and the receiver (serial-to-parallel).

Serial transmission occurs in one of two ways: asynchronous or synchronous.

Asynchronous Transmission Asynchronous transmission is so named because the timing of a signal is unimportant. Instead, information is received and translated by agreed-upon patterns. As long as those patterns are followed, the receiving device can retrieve the information without regard to the rhythm in which it is sent. Patterns are based on grouping the bit stream into bytes. Each group, usually 8 bits, is sent along the link as a unit. The sending system handles each group independently, relaying it to the link whenever ready, without regard to a timer.

Without a synchronizing pulse, the receiver cannot use timing to predict when the next group will arrive. To alert the receiver to the arrival of a new group, therefore, an extra bit is added to the beginning of each byte. This bit, usually a 0, is called the start bit. To let the receiver know that the byte is finished, 1 or more additional bits are appended to the end of the byte. These bits, usually 1s, are called stop bits. By this method, each byte is increased in size to at least 10 bits, of which 8 are information and 2 or more are signals to the receiver. In addition, the transmission of each byte may then be followed by a gap of varying duration. This gap can be represented either by an idle channel or by a stream of additional stop bits.

In asynchronous transmission, we send 1 start bit (0) at the beginning and 1 or more stop bits (1s) at the end of each byte. There may be a gap between each byte. *Gaps)*

The start and stop bits and the gap alert the receiver to the beginning and end of each byte and allow it to synchronize with the data stream. This mechanism is called asynchronous because, at the byte level, sender and receiver do not have to be synchronized. But within each byte, the receiver must still be synchronized with the incoming bit stream. That is, some synchronization is required, but only for the duration of a single byte. The receiving device resynchronizes at the onset of each new byte. When the receiver detects a start bit, it sets a timer and begins counting bits as they come in. After n bits, the receiver looks for a stop bit. As soon as it detects the stop bit, it ignores any received pulses until it detects the next start bit.

Asynchronous here means "asynchronous at the byte level," but the bits are still synchronized; their durations are the same.

Figure 6.23 is a schematic illustration of asynchronous transmission. In this example, the start bits are 0s, the stop bits are 1s, and the gap is represented by an idle line rather than by additional stop bits.

The addition of stop and start bits and the insertion of gaps into the bit stream make asynchronous transmission slower than forms of transmission that can operate without the addition of control information. But it is cheap and effective, two advantages that make it an attractive choice for situations like low-speed communication. For example, the connection of a terminal to a computer is a natural application for asynchronous transmission. A user types only one character at a time, types extremely slowly in data processing terms, and leaves unpredictable gaps of time between each character.

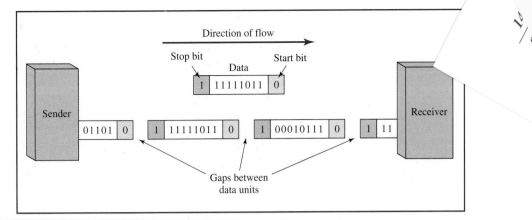

Figure 6.23 Asynchronous transmission

Synchronous Transmission   In synchronous transmission, the bit stream is combined into longer "frames," which may contain multiple bytes. Each byte, however, is introduced onto the transmission link without a gap between it and the next one. It is left to the receiver to separate the bit stream into bytes for decoding purposes. In other words, data are transmitted as an unbroken string of 1s and 0s, and the receiver separates that string into the bytes, or characters, it needs to reconstruct the information.

In synchronous transmission, we send bits one after another without start/stop bits or gaps. It is the responsibility of the receiver to group the bits.

Figure 6.24 gives a schematic illustration of synchronous transmission. We have drawn in the divisions between bytes. In reality, those divisions do not exist; the sender puts its data onto the line as one long string. If the sender wishes to send data in separate bursts, the gaps between bursts must be filled with a special sequence of 0s and 1s that means *idle*. The receiver counts the bits as they arrive and groups them in 8-bit units.

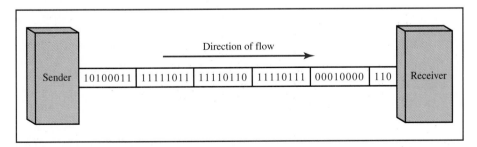

Figure 6.24 Synchronous transmission

Without gaps and start/stop bits, there is no built-in mechanism to help the receiving device adjust its bit synchronization in midstream. Timing becomes very important, therefore, because the accuracy of the received information is completely dependent on the ability of the receiving device to keep an accurate count of the bits as they come in.

The advantage of synchronous transmission is speed. With no extra bits or gaps to introduce at the sending end and remove at the receiving end and, by extension, with fewer bits to move across the link, synchronous transmission is faster than asynchronous transmission. For this reason, it is more useful for high-speed applications like the transmission of data from one computer to another. Byte synchronization is accomplished in the data link layer.

6.4 LINE CONFIGURATION

Line configuration refers to the way two or more communication devices attach to a *link*. A link is the physical communication pathway that transfers data from one device to another. For the purposes of visualization, it is simplest to imagine any link as a line drawn between two points. For communication to occur, two devices must be connected in some way to the same link at the same time. There are two possible line configurations: point-to-point and multipoint.

Line configuration defines the attachment of communication devices to a link.

POINT-TO-POINT

A point-to-point line configuration provides a dedicated link between two devices. The entire capacity of the channel is reserved for transmission between those two devices. Most point-to-point line configurations use an actual length of wire or cable to connect the two ends, but other options, such as microwave or satellite links, are also possible (see Figure 6.25). When you change television channels by infrared remote control, you are establishing a point-to-point line configuration between the remote control and the television's control system.

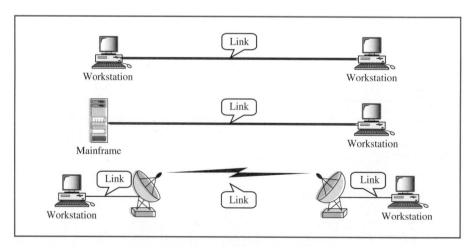

Figure 6.25   Point-to-point line configuration

A multipoint (also called multidrop) line configuration is one in which more than two specific devices share a single link (see Figure 6.26).

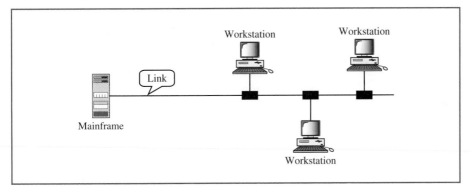

Figure 6.26   Multipoint line configuration

In a multipoint environment, the capacity of the channel is shared, either spatially or temporally. If several devices can use the link simultaneously, it is a *spatially shared* line configuration. If users must take turns, it is a *time-shared* line configuration.

6.5   DUPLEXITY

The term duplexity defines the direction of signal flow between two linked devices. There are two types of transmission modes: *half-duplex* and *full-duplex*.

HALF-DUPLEX

In **half-duplex mode,** each device can both transmit and receive but not at the same time. When one device is sending, the other can only receive, and vice versa (see Figure 6.27).

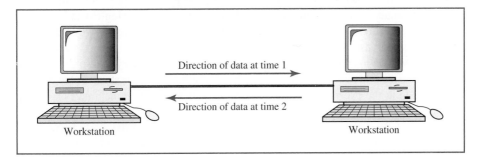

Figure 6.27   Half-duplex mode

The half-duplex mode is like a one-lane road with two-directional traffic. While cars are traveling one direction, cars going the other way must wait. In a half-duplex transmission, the entire capacity of a channel is taken over by whichever of the two devices is transmitting at the time. Walkie-talkies and CB (citizen's band) radios are both half-duplex systems.

FULL-DUPLEX

In **full-duplex mode** (also called duplex), both stations can transmit and receive simultaneously (see Figure 6.28).

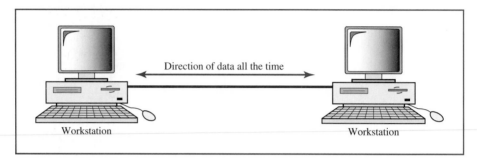

Figure 6.28   Full-duplex mode

The full-duplex mode is like a two-way street with traffic flowing in both directions at the same time. In full-duplex mode, signals going in either direction share the capacity of the link. This sharing can occur in two ways: either the link must contain two physically separate transmission paths, one for sending and the other for receiving, or the capacity of the channel is divided between signals traveling in opposite directions.

One common example of full-duplex communication is the telephone network. When two people are communicating by a telephone line, both can talk and listen at the same time.

6.6   MULTIPLEXING: SHARING THE MEDIA

Whenever the transmission capacity (the bandwidth or the number of bits that can be sent per second) of a medium linking two devices is greater than the transmission needs of each individual device, the link can be shared, much as a large water pipe can carry water to several separate houses at once. Multiplexing is the set of techniques that allows the simultaneous transmission of multiple signals across a single data link.

As data- and telecommunications usage increases, so does traffic. We can accommodate this increase by continuing to add individual lines each time a new link is needed, or we can install higher capacity links and use each to carry multiple signals. If the transmission capacity of a link is greater than the transmission needs of the devices connected to it, the excess capacity is wasted. An efficient system maximizes the utilization of all facilities.

Figure 6.29 shows two possible ways of linking four pairs of devices. In Figure 6.29*a*, each pair has its own link. If the full capacity of each link is not being utilized, a portion of that capacity is being wasted. In Figure 6.29*b*, transmissions between the pairs are multiplexed; the same four pairs share the capacity of a single link.

CHANNEL VERSUS LINK

In a multiplexed system, several devices share the capacity of one link. Figure 6.29*b* shows the basic format of a multiplexed system. The four devices on the left direct their transmission streams to a **multiplexer** (MUX), which combines them into a single

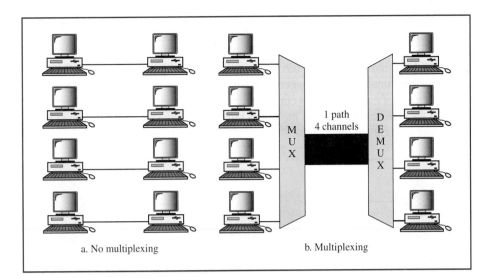

a. No multiplexing

b. Multiplexing

Figure 6.29   Multiplexing versus no multiplexing

stream (many to one). At the receiving end, that stream is fed into a demultiplexer (DEMUX), which separates the stream back into its component transmissions (one to many) and directs them to their intended receiving devices.

In Figure 6.29*b* the word **path** refers to the physical link. The word **channel** refers to a portion of a path that carries a transmission between a given pair of devices. One path can have several channels.

Signals are multiplexed using one of three basic techniques: frequency-division multiplexing (FDM), time-division multiplexing (TDM), and wave-division multiplexing (WDM). TDM is further subdivided into synchronous TDM (usually just called TDM) and asynchronous TDM, also called statistical TDM or concentrator (see Figure 6.30).

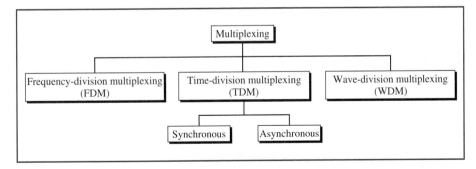

Figure 6.30   Categories of multiplexing

FREQUENCY-DIVISION MULTIPLEXING (FDM)

Frequency-division multiplexing (FDM) is an analog technique that can be applied when the bandwidth of a link is greater than the combined bandwidths of the signals to be transmitted. In FDM, signals generated by each sending device modulate different carrier frequencies. These modulated signals are then combined into a single complex signal that can be transported by the link. These bandwidth ranges are the channels

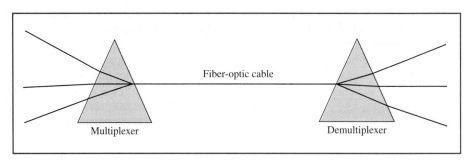

Figure 6.32 Prisms in WDM multiplexing and demultiplexing

TIME-DIVISION MULTIPLEXING (TDM)

Time-division multiplexing (TDM) is a digital process that can be applied when the data rate capacity of the transmission medium is greater than the data rate required by the sending and receiving devices. In such a case, multiple transmissions can occupy a single link by interleaving the signals.

Figure 6.33 gives a conceptual view of TDM. Note that the same link is used as in FDM; here, however, the link is shown sectioned by time rather than frequency.

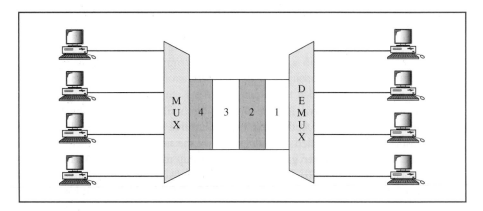

Figure 6.33   TDM

In other words, the usage of a high-capacity link is divided into time slots. Each device has a time slot.

In the TDM figure, portions of links 1, 2, 3, and 4 occupy the link sequentially. As an analogy, suppose a long bridge allows fast traffic (60 mph.) but has only one lane. Cars from four streets, each with a speed limit of 15 mph. can easily merge into this one-lane bridge without any congestion. The first car from the first street goes first, followed by the first car from the second street, and so on. After one car from each street enters the bridge, the second car from the first street can go, followed by the second car from the second street, and so on.

Note that TDM can be used only with a digital signal. If we want to use TDM with devices that send analog signals, we first need to convert the analog signal to digital.

TDM can be used only with digital signals.

TDM can be implemented through synchronous TDM or asynchronous TDM.

Synchronous TDM

In synchronous time-division multiplexing, the term *synchronous* has a different meaning from that used previously. Here synchronous means that the multiplexer allocates exactly a time slot to each device at all times, whether or not a device has anything to transmit. Time slot A, for example, is assigned to device A alone and cannot be used by any other device. When its allocated time slot comes up, a device has the opportunity to send a portion of its data. If a device is unable to transmit or does not have data to send, its time slot remains empty. Figure 6.34 shows the idea of synchronous TDM.

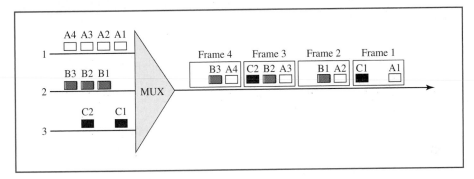

Figure 6.34 Synchronous TDM

BUSINESS FOCUS:
USE OF SYNCHRONOUS TDM IN TELEPHONE SYSTEMS

The telephone companies have developed a hierarchy of digital services much like that used for analog services. The following figure shows this hierarchy.

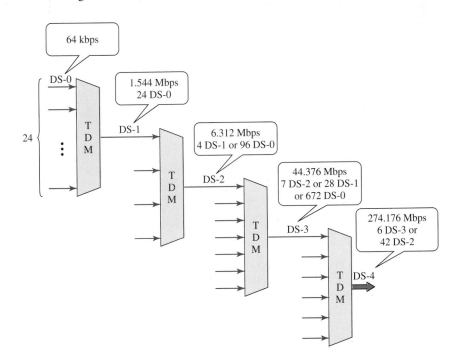

DS-0 is a 64 kbps channel. DS-1 is a 1.544-Mbps channel, made by multiplexing 24 DS-0 channels. DS-2 is a 6.312-Mbps channel, made by multiplexing four DS-1 channels. DS-3 is a 44.376-Mbps channel made by multiplexing seven DS-2 channels. DS-4 is a 274.176-Mbps channel, made by multiplexing six DS-3 channels.

Asynchronous TDM

As we saw in the previous section, synchronous TDM does not guarantee that the full capacity of a link is used. In fact, it is more likely that only a portion of the time slots is in use at a given instant. Because the time slots are preassigned and fixed, whenever a connected device is not transmitting, the corresponding slot is empty and that much of the path is wasted. For example, imagine that we have multiplexed the output of 20 identical computers onto a single line. Using synchronous TDM, the speed of that line must be at least 20 times the speed of each input line. But what if only 10 computers are in use at a time? Half of the capacity of the line is wasted.

Asynchronous time-division multiplexing, or statistical time-division multiplexing, is designed to avoid this type of waste. Like synchronous TDM, asynchronous TDM allows a number of lower-speed input lines to be multiplexed to a single higher-speed line. Unlike synchronous TDM, however, in asynchronous TDM the total speed of the input lines can be greater than the capacity of the path.

The number of time slots in an asynchronous TDM frame is based on a statistical analysis of the number of input lines that are likely to be transmitting at any given time. Rather than being preassigned, each slot is available to any of the attached input lines that have data to send. The multiplexer scans the input lines, accepts portions of data until a frame is filled, and then sends the frame across the link. Figure 6.35 shows asynchronous TDM.

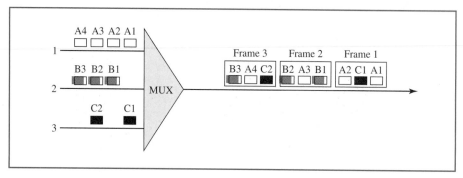

Figure 6.35   Asynchronous TDM

INVERSE MULTIPLEXING

As its name implies, inverse multiplexing is the opposite of multiplexing. Inverse multiplexing takes the data stream from one high-speed line and breaks it into portions that can be sent across several lower-speed lines simultaneously, with no loss in the collective data rate (see Figure 6.36).

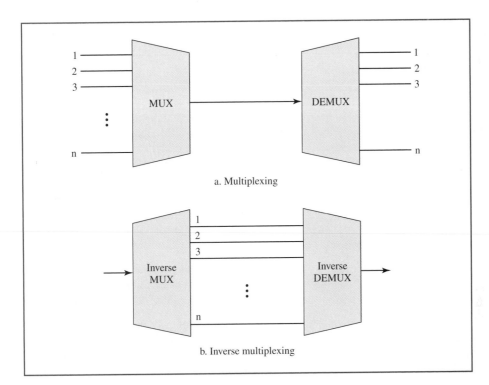

Figure 6.36 Multiplexing and inverse multiplexing

Why do we need inverse multiplexing? Think of an organization that wants to send data, voice, and video, each of which requires a different data rate. To send voice, it may need a 64 kbps link. To send data, it may need a 128 kbps link. And to send video, it may need a 1.544 Mbps link. To accommodate all of these needs, the organization has two options. It can lease a 1.544 Mbps channel from a common carrier (the telephone company) and use the full capacity only sometimes, which is not an efficient use of the facility. Or it can lease several separate channels of lower data rates. Using an agreement called bandwidth on demand, the organization can use any of these channels whenever and however it needs them. Voice transmissions can be sent intact over any of the channels. Data or video signals can be broken up and sent over two or more lines. In other words, the data and video signals can be inversely multiplexed over multiple lines.

BUSINESS FOCUS:
USE OF ASYNCHRONOUS TDM IN ATM NETWORKS

Asynchronous TDM is used today in the ATM network, a wide area network that we will study in Chapter 11. ATM is a cell network; the packets traveling through the network are small packets called cells.

CASE STUDY

NEW AGE HOME PHARMACY

N AHP has an Ethernet network on each floor. Ethernet, as we will see in Chapter 9, uses Manchester encoding with a data rate of 10 Mbps. Manchester encoding is a type of digital-to-digital conversion, in which each bit is half positive and half negative as shown in the following figure.

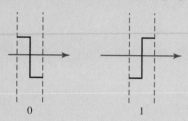

Manchester encoding has a self-synchronization feature. The signal level at the middle of the bit interval inverts and provides a way for the receiver to synchronize its clock.

The encoding for the backbone network (the network that connects the floor networks) is more complex. The backbone is Fast Ethernet with a data rate of 100 Mbps. To be able to transfer 100 Mbps, Fast Ethernet uses a more sophisticated encoding.

This year, NAHP management raised a question about the data rate of the floor networks. If the backbone transmits at 100 Mbps, why can't we have the same data rate for each floor network? The issue was relayed to Modern Networking. The consultant spent a few days at the company to check and measure the traffic on each floor to see if raising the data rate was justifiable. The following is a summary of the testing results for the connections on one floor.

Average number of packets per second: 345
Average size of a packet in bits: 12,140
Average data rate: 345 × 12140 = 4,188,300 bps

The data rates for other floors were similar. The results showed that the network transmits at approximately 4.2 Mbps, which is far below the capacity of the network (10 Mbps); this means there is no need for upgrading in the near future. In addition, some of this load (on average 20%) remains on the floor. This means that the backbone transmits at an average of 6 × 80% × 4.2 = 20.6 Mbps, which is below the capacity of Fast Ethernet (100 Mbps).

6.7   KEY TERMS

amplitude
amplitude shift keying (ASK)
analog data
analog signal
analog-to-digital encoding
asynchronous TDM
asynchronous transmission
bandwidth
baud rate
bipolar encoding
bit interval
bit rate
bits per second (bps)

carrier signal
channel
complex signal
digital data
digital signal
digital-to-analog modulation
digital-to-digital encoding
frequency
frequency-division multiplexing
   (FDM)
frequency modulation (FM)
frequency shift keying (FSK)
full-duplex transmission

half-duplex transmission
inverse multiplexing
line configuration
link
modulation
multipoint configuration
parallel transmission
path
period
phase
phase shift
phase shift keying (PSK)
physical layer

point-to-point configuration
polar encoding
pulse code modulation (PCM)
quantization
sampling
serial transmission
signal
sine wave
synchronous TDM
synchronous transmission
time-division multiplexing
unipolar encoding
wave-division modulation (WDM)

6.8   SUMMARY

❑   The physical layer provides services to the data link layer and controls the
   transmission medium.
❑   Information and signals can be either analog (continuous values) or digital
   (discrete values).
❑   Information must be transformed into an electromagnetic signal prior to
   transmission across a network.
❑   A sine wave can be characterized by its amplitude, frequency, and phase.
❑   A complex signal is composed of multiple sine waves. A digital signal is a
   complex signal.
❑   The bandwidth of a signal is the difference between the highest frequency and
   the lowest frequency.
❑   Conversion of data to signals can be digital-to-digital, analog-to-digital,
   digital-to-analog, or analog-to-analog.
❑   Digital data are converted to digital signals using unipolar, polar, or bipolar
   encoding methods.
❑   Digital data are converted to analog signals through ASK, FSK, or PSK
   modulation of a carrier signal.
❑   PCM is an analog-to-digital conversion method.
❑   Digital data can be transmitted either in parallel or serially.
❑   In parallel transmission, a group of bits is sent simultaneously, with each bit
   on a separate line.
❑   In serial transmission, which can be either synchronous or asynchronous, there
   is only one line and the bits are sent sequentially.
❑   In asynchronous serial transmission, each byte (group of 8 bits) is framed
   with a start bit and a stop bit. There may be a variable-length gap between
   each byte.
❑   In synchronous serial transmission, bits are sent in a continuous stream without
   start and stop bits and without gaps between bytes.
❑   Line configuration defines the attachment of communication devices to a link.
   The configuration can be point-to-point or multipoint.

❑ Duplexity defines the direction of signal flow between two linked devices.
❑ Multiplexing is the simultaneous transmission of multiple signals across a single data link.
❑ Signals can be multiplexed using FDM, TDM, or WDM.

 PRACTICE SET

Review Questions

1. What is the relationship between the physical layer and the data-link layer?
2. What is the relationship between the physical layer and the transmission medium?
3. Give your own examples of analog data and digital data.
4. Compare bit interval to bit rate.
5. What are the three characteristics that describe a sine wave?
6. What is the relationship between frequency and period?
7. Why is the bandwidth of a digital signal considered to be infinite?
8. Name three categories of digital-to-digital encoding.
9. What is the function of the carrier signal in modulation?
10. List the steps that take an analog signal to PCM digital code.
11. How does the sampling rate affect the transmitted digital signal?
12. How does the number of bits allotted for each sample affect the transmitted digital signal?
13. What are the advantages and disadvantages of parallel transmission?
14. Compare the two methods of serial transmission. Discuss the advantages and disadvantages of each.
15. Name two types of line configurations.
16. What is the difference between half-duplex and full-duplex transmission?
17. Compare the terms *path, channel,* and *link.*
18. Name three multiplexing techniques.

Multiple-Choice Questions

19. The physical layer is responsible for _____.
    a. controlling the transmission medium
    b. controlling the network layer
    c. controlling the data link layer
    d. a and c
20. Before information can be transmitted, it must be transformed into _____.
    a. periodic signals
    b. electromagnetic signals
    c. aperiodic signals
    d. low-frequency sine waves

21. The bit _____ is the number of bits sent in one second.
    a. interval
    b. rate
    c. bandwidth
    d. sample

22. A bit interval of 0.1 s means a bit rate of _____ bps.
    a. 0.1
    b. 1.0
    c. 10
    d. 100

23. A bit rate of 1 Mbps means that one bit has a duration of _____ seconds.
    a. 1,000,000
    b. 10
    c. 0.001
    d. 0.000001

24. A frequency of 100 Hz means that each cycle takes _____ seconds.
    a. 100
    b. 0.01
    c. 0.001
    d. 0.0001

25. A phase shift of 270 degrees corresponds to a shift of _____ of a period.
    a. one-quarter
    b. one-half
    c. three-quarters
    d. two-thirds

26. The lowest frequency of a signal is 10 kHz; the highest frequency is 1 MHz; the bandwidth is _____ MHz.
    a. 0.99
    b. 0.9
    c. 0.099
    d. 0.0099

27. A signal has a bandwidth of 250 MHz. The highest frequency component is 300 MHz. The lowest frequency component is _____ MHz.
    a. 250
    b. 550
    c. 50
    d. 100

28. ASK, PSK, and FSK are examples of _____ modulation.
    a. digital-to-digital
    b. digital-to-analog
    c. analog-to-analog
    d. analog-to-digital

29. Unipolar, bipolar, and polar encoding are types of _____ encoding.
    a. digital-to-digital
    b. digital-to-analog
    c. analog-to-analog
    d. analog-to-digital

30. PCM is an example of _____ conversion.
   a. digital-to-digital
   b. digital-to-analog
   c. analog-to-analog
   d. analog-to-digital
31. Which conversion type involves modulation of a signal?
   a. digital-to-digital conversion
   b. analog-to-digital conversion
   c. digital-to-analog conversion
   d. all of the above
32. Which conversion type involves sampling of a signal?
   a. digital-to-digital conversion
   b. analog-to-digital conversion
   c. digital-to-analog conversion
   d. all of the above
33. In _____, the frequency of a carrier signal is modulated.
   a. ASK
   b. FSK
   c. PSK
   d. all of the above
34. In _____, the signal is especially susceptible to corruption from noise.
   a. ASK
   b. FSK
   c. PSK
   d. all of the above
35. When a value (from a limited set of values) is assigned to a sample of a signal, this is called _____.
   a. sampling
   b. modulation
   c. multiplexing
   d. quantization
36. In _____ transmission, bits of a group are sent simultaneously, each on its own link.
   a. parallel
   b. synchronous
   c. asynchronous
   d. serial
37. A _____ line configuration provides a dedicated link between two devices.
   a. point-to-point
   b. multipoint
   c. half-duplex
   d. full-duplex
38. In the _____ mode, only one device can transmit at a time.
   a. half-duplex
   b. full-duplex
   c. one-duplex
   d. none of the above

39. The sharing of a medium by two or more devices is called _____.
    a. modulation
    b. encoding
    c. line discipline
    d. multiplexing
40. Which multiplexing technique transmits analog signals?
    a. FDM
    b. synchronous TDM
    c. asynchronous TDM
    d. b and c
41. Which multiplexing technique transmits digital signals?
    a. FDM
    b. synchronous TDM
    c. asynchronous TDM
    d. b and c

CHAPTER 7

Transmission Media

Although the physical layer of a particular protocol may define the specifications for the media, the transmission media itself is not physically part of the physical layer. It is below the physical layer. The transmission media is the path for signals that are created by the physical layer. Understanding the media, their capabilities, noise and error vulnerabilities is crucial for a manager.

Renovation or upgrading of a network often involves changing the transmission media, replacing old media technologies with new ones. The cost of transmission media renovation can be high, especially if little attention was paid to the previous installation. Media that are exposed and accessible to intruders do not create a safe, secure, and reliable data communication environment.

In this chapter we discuss different kinds of transmission media, their use, and their advantages and disadvantages.

OBJECTIVES

After reading this chapter, the reader should:

❑ Understand the difference between guided and unguided media.

❑ Be familiar with twisted-pair cable and the rationale for twisting.

❑ Be familiar with shielded twisted-pair cable and the rationale for shielding.

❑ Be familiar with coaxial cable.

❑ Understand how the air (or vacuum) can be a transmission medium for signals.

7.1 GUIDED MEDIA

Guided media, which are those that provide a physically limited path for the signal, include twisted-pair cable, coaxial cable, and fiber-optic cable (see Figure 7.1). A signal traveling along any of these media is directed and contained by the physical limits of the medium. Twisted-pair and coaxial cable use metallic (copper) conductors that accept and transport signals in the form of electrical current. Optical fiber is a glass or plastic cable that accepts and transports signals in the form of light.

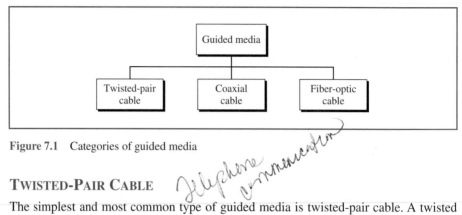

Figure 7.1 Categories of guided media

TWISTED-PAIR CABLE

The simplest and most common type of guided media is twisted-pair cable. A twisted pair is made of two insulated copper wires twisted together to reduce the effect of electrical interference of other electrical devices and other nearby cables.

Twisted-pair cable comes in two forms: unshielded and shielded.

Unshielded Twisted-Pair (UTP) Cable

Unshielded twisted-pair (UTP) cable is the most common type of telecommunication medium in use today. Although most familiar from its use in telephone systems, it is suitable for transmitting both data and voice. A twisted pair consists of two conductors (usually copper), each with its own colored plastic insulation. The plastic insulation is color-banded for identification (see Figure 7.2). Colors are used both to identify the specific conductors in a cable and to indicate which wires belong in pairs and how they relate to other pairs in a larger bundle.

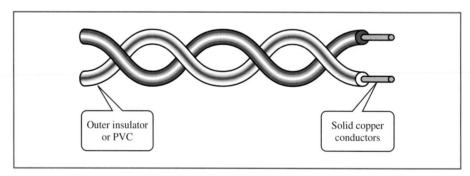

Figure 7.2 Twisted-pair cable

A twisted pair consists of two conductors each surrounded by an insulating material.

The two wires are twisted around each other at regular intervals (between 2 and 12 twists per foot). Twisting decreases the effect of noise on the signal being carried by the cable by creating two equal effects that cancel each other out when they arrive at the destination.

Advantages of UTP are its cost and ease of use. UTP is cheap, flexible, and easy to install. Higher grades of UTP are used in many LAN technologies, including Ethernet and Token Ring.

TECHNICAL FOCUS:
WHY TWISTED-PAIR CABLE REDUCES NOISE

Interference from devices such as a motor can create unequal noise over two parallel lines. The line that is closer to the device receives more interference than the one that is farther. If however, the wires are twisted around each other at regular intervals, each wire is closer to the noise source for half of the time and farther for the other half. Both receive the same amount of noise. The noise from two wires cancel each other out at the receiver.

TECHNICAL FOCUS:
CATEGORIES OF TWISTED-PAIR CABLES

The Electronic Industries Association (EIA) has developed standards to grade UTP cables by quality. Categories are determined by cable quality, with 1 as the lowest and 5 as the highest. Each EIA category is suitable for certain uses and not for others:

❏ **Category 1.** The basic twisted-pair cabling used in telephone systems. This level of quality is fine for voice but inadequate for all but low-speed data communication.
❏ **Category 2.** The next higher grade, suitable for voice and for data transmission of up to 4 Mbps.
❏ **Category 3.** Required to have at least three twists per foot and can be used for data transmission of up to 10 Mbps. It is now the standard cable for most telephone systems.
❏ **Category 4.** Must also have at least three twists per foot as well as other conditions to bring the possible transmission rate to 16 Mbps.
❏ **Category 5.** Used for data transmission up to 100 Mbps.

Cat VI.   100,000 Gbps   p ka taen

BUSINESS FOCUS:
USE OF TWISTED-PAIR CABLES IN TELEPHONE NETWORK

In the early days of the telephone network, the local loop, the two wires that connected a resident to the telephone office, was made of two parallel wires. The telephone companies later changed the local loop to a pair of twisted-pair wires, which is less prone to noise than the previous parallel wires.

Shielded Twisted-Pair (STP) Cable

Shielded twisted-pair (STP) cable has a metal foil or braided-mesh covering that encases each pair of insulated conductors (see Figure 7.3). The metal casing prevents the penetration of electromagnetic noise. It also can eliminate a phenomenon called crosstalk. This effect can be experienced during telephone conversations when one can hear other conversations in the background. Shielding each pair of a twisted-pair cable can eliminate most crosstalk.

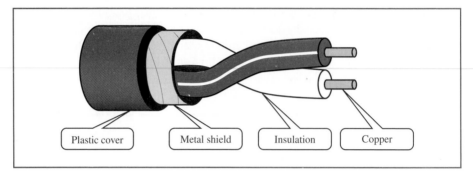

| Plastic cover | Metal shield | Insulation | Copper |

Figure 7.3   Shielded twisted-pair cable

STP has the same quality considerations and uses the same connectors as UTP, but the shield must be connected to a ground. Materials and manufacturing requirements make STP more expensive than UTP but less susceptible to noise.

TECHNICAL FOCUS: SHIELDING AND LIGHTNING

We can be immune from lightning in a desert if we are surrounded by a metallic cover (inside a car, for example). The reason is that electromagnetic energy (lightning) can penetrate the insulators, but not metals. Lightning on a metallic shell creates a current on the outside surface, which can be dangerous; the inside is protected. Note that this phenomenon is opposite from what happens with electricity. The electrical current passes through a metal, but it is stopped by an insulator. Electromagnetic energy passes through an insulator, but is stopped by a metal. The same idea is used in shielded twisted-pair cable. The shield is a metal that protects the cable from outside noise, electromagnetic interference.

COAXIAL CABLE

Coaxial cable (or *coax*) carries signals of higher-frequency ranges than twisted-pair cable. Instead of having two wires, coax has a central core conductor of solid or stranded wire (usually copper) enclosed in an insulating sheath, which is, in turn, encased in an outer conductor of metal foil, braid, or a combination of the two (also usually copper). The outer metallic wrapping serves both as a shield against noise and as the second conductor, which completes the circuit. This outer conductor is also enclosed in an insulating sheath, and the whole cable is protected by a plastic cover (see Figure 7.4).

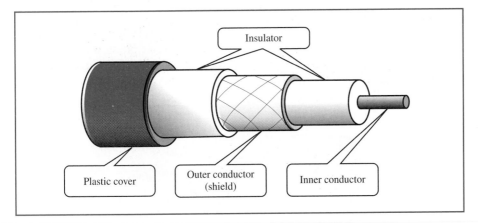

Figure 7.4 Coaxial cable

OPTICAL FIBER

Up until this point, we have discussed conductive (metal) cables that transmit signals in the form of current. Optical fiber, on the other hand, is made of glass or plastic and transmits signals in the form of light. To understand optical fiber, we first need to understand light refraction and reflection.

When a beam of light reaches an interface between two media with different densities, the beam is either refracted or reflected. If the angle of incidence (the angle the light makes with the line perpendicular to the interface) is less than the critical angle (determined by the relative density of the two media), the light is refracted. If the angle of incidence is greater than the critical angle, the light is reflected. Figure 7.5 shows refraction and reflection.

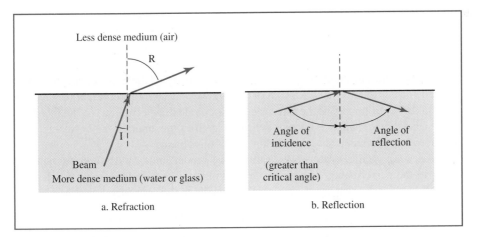

Figure 7.5 Refraction and reflection

Fiber-optic cables take advantage of this phenomenon. A fiber is made of two different plastic or glass concentric cylinders. The outer cylinder is called the cladding (lower density) and the inner cylinder is called the core.

Propagation Modes

Current technology supports two modes, multimode and single mode, for propagating light along optical channels. Each requires fiber with specific physical characteristics. Multimode can be implemented in two forms: step-index or graded-index. Figure 7.6 shows the three types of fiber-optic cables. The light source is composed of multiple beams (or rays), shown in Figure 7.6a.

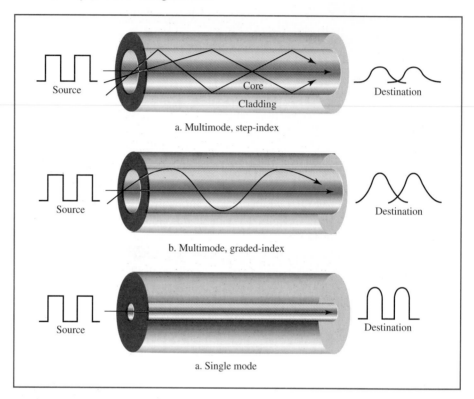

Figure 7.6   Propagation modes

Multimode   In multimode step-index fiber, the density of the core remains constant from the center to the edges. A beam of light moves through this constant density in a straight line until it reaches the interface of the core and the cladding. At the interface, there is an abrupt change to a lower density that alters the angle of the beam's motion. The term *step-index* refers to the suddenness of this change.

A second type of fiber, called multimode graded-index fiber, was designed to improve the performance of multimode step-index fiber. The core varies in density, being highest at the center and decreasing gradually to the core edge.

Single Mode   Single mode uses step-index fiber and a highly focused source of light that limits beams to a small range of angles, all close to the horizontal. The single-mode fiber itself is manufactured with a much smaller diameter than that of multimode fibers, and with substantially lower density. The decrease in density results in a critical angle that is close enough to 90 degrees to make the propagation of beams almost horizontal. In this case, propagation of different beams is almost identical and delays are negligible. All of the beams arrive at the destination "together" and can be recombined to look like the original signal.

Fiber Sizes

Optical fibers are defined by the ratio of the diameter of their core to the diameter of their cladding, both expressed in microns (micrometers). The common sizes are shown in Table 7.1. The last size listed is used only for single mode.

Table 7.1 *Fiber types*

Fiber Type	Core (microns)	Cladding (microns)
62.5/125	62.5	125
50/125	50.0	125
100/140	100.0	140
8.3/125	8.3	125

Advantages of Optical Fiber

The major advantages offered by fiber-optic cable over twisted-pair and coaxial cable are noise resistance, less signal attenuation, and higher bandwidth.

© Corbis/Vol. 110

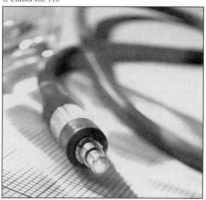

Fiber optic cables have the advantages of noise resistance, less signal attenuation, and higher bandwidth. The disadvantages are cost, more difficult maintenance, and fragility.

❑ **Noise resistance.** Because fiber-optic transmission uses light rather than electricity, noise is not a factor. External light, the only possible interference, is blocked from the channel by the outer jacket.

❑ **Less signal attenuation.** Fiber-optic transmission distance is significantly greater than that of other guided media. A signal can run for miles without requiring regeneration.

❑ **Higher bandwidth.** Fiber-optic cable can support dramatically higher bandwidths (and hence data rates) than either twisted-pair or coaxial cable. Currently, data rates and bandwidth utilization over fiber-optic cable are limited not by the medium but by the signal generation and reception technology available.

Disadvantages of Optical Fiber

The main disadvantages of fiber optic cable are cost, installation/maintenance, and fragility.

❑ **Cost.** Fiber-optic cable is expensive. Because any impurities or imperfections in the core can throw off the signal, manufacturing must be painstakingly precise.

Also, the light source (laser) can cost thousands of dollars, compared to hundreds of dollars for electrical signal generators.

❑ **Installation/maintenance.** Any roughness or cracking in the core of an optical cable diffuses light and alters the signal. All splices must be polished and precisely fused. All connections must be perfectly aligned and matched for core size and must provide a completely light-tight seal. Metallic media connections, on the other hand, can be made by cutting and crimping using relatively unsophisticated tools.

❑ **Fragility.** Glass fiber is more easily broken than wire, making it less useful for applications where hardware portability is required.

As manufacturing techniques have improved and costs have come down, high data rates and immunity to noise have made fiber optic cable increasingly popular.

UNGUIDED MEDIA

Unguided media, or wireless communication, transport electromagnetic waves without using a physical conductor. Instead, signals are broadcast through air (or, in some cases, water), and thus are available to anyone who has a device capable of receiving them.

Radio Frequency Allocation

The section of the electromagnetic spectrum defined as radio communication is divided into eight ranges, called bands, each regulated by government authorities. These bands are rated from very low frequency (VLF) to extremely high frequency (EHF).

VLF and LF

These types of signals are propagated very close to the surface of the earth; they cannot pass through solid objects. The signals are used in long-range radio navigation.

MF and HF

These signals travel to the upper layers that surround the air and then reflect back to the earth. They are commonly used for long-distance communication.

VHF and UHF

These signals are usually transmitted using line-of-sight. Uses include terrestrial and satellite microwave and radar communication.

EHF and SHF

These signals use space propagation to communicate with objects beyond the atmosphere.

TERRESTRIAL MICROWAVE

Microwaves do not follow the curvature of the earth and therefore require line-of-sight transmission and reception equipment. The distance coverable by a line-of-sight signal depends to a large extent on the height of the antennas: the taller the antennas, the longer the sight distance. Height allows the signal to travel farther without being stopped by the curvature of the planet and raises the signal above many surface obstacles, such as low hills and tall buildings that would otherwise block transmission. Typically, antennas are mounted on towers that are in turn often mounted on hills or mountains.

Microwave signals propagate in one direction at a time, which means that two frequencies are necessary for two-way communication such as a telephone conversation. One frequency is reserved for microwave transmission in one direction and the other for transmission in the other. Each frequency requires its own transmitter and receiver. Today, both pieces of equipment usually are combined in a single piece of equipment called a transceiver, which allows a single antenna to serve both frequencies and functions.

Repeaters

To increase the distance served by terrestrial microwave, a system of repeaters can be installed with each antenna. A signal received by one antenna is relayed to the next antenna (see Figure 7.7). The distance required between repeaters varies with the frequency of the signal and the environment in which the antennas are found. A repeater may broadcast the regenerated signal either at the original frequency or at a new frequency, depending on the system.

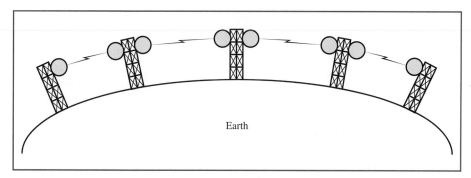

Figure 7.7   Terrestrial microwave

© Corbis/Vol. 123

Terrestrial microwave with repeaters provides the basis for most of today's telephone systems.

Terrestrial microwave with repeaters provides the basis for most contemporary telephone systems worldwide.

Satellite Communication

Satellite transmission is much like line-of-sight microwave transmission with one of the stations, a satellite, orbiting the earth. The principle is the same as terrestrial microwave, with a satellite acting as a supertall antenna and repeater (see Figure 7.8). Although in satellite transmission signals must still travel in straight lines, the limitations imposed on distance by the curvature of the earth are reduced. In this way, satellite relays allow microwave signals to span continents and oceans with a single bounce.

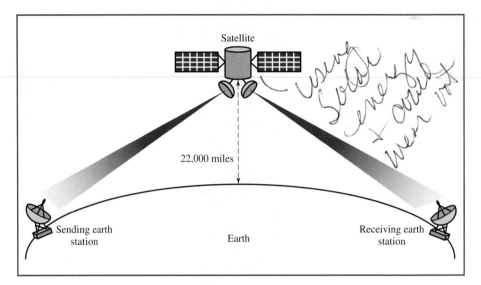

Figure 7.8 Satellite communication

Satellite microwave can provide transmission capability to and from any location on earth, no matter how remote. This advantage makes high-quality communication available to undeveloped parts of the world without requiring a huge investment in ground-based infrastructure. Satellites themselves are extremely expensive, of course, but leasing time or frequencies on one can be relatively cheap.

Geosynchronous Satellites   Line-of-sight propagation requires that the sending and receiving antennas be locked onto each other's location at all times (one antenna must have the other in sight). For this reason, a satellite that moves faster or slower than the earth's rotation is useful only for short periods of time (just as a stopped clock is accurate twice a day). To ensure constant communication, the satellite must move at the same speed as the earth so that it seems to remain fixed above a certain spot. Such satellites are called geosynchronous.

Because orbital speed is based on distance from the planet, only one orbit can be geosynchronous. This orbit occurs at the equatorial plane and is approximately 22,000 miles from the surface of the earth.

But one geosynchronous satellite cannot cover the whole earth. One satellite in orbit has line-of-sight contact with a vast number of stations, but the curvature of the earth still keeps much of the planet out of sight. It takes a minimum of three satellites equidistant from each other in geosynchronous orbit to provide full global transmission. Figure 7.9 shows three satellites, each 120 degrees from another in geosynchronous orbit around the equator. The view is from the North Pole.

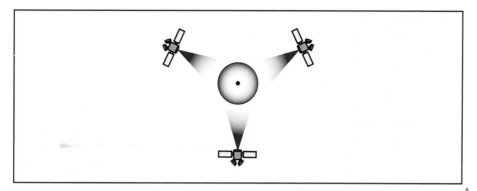

Figure 7.9 Satellites in geosynchronous orbit

MEDIA COMPARISON

When evaluating the suitability of a particular medium to a specific application, five factors should be kept in mind: cost, speed, attenuation, electromagnetic interference, and security.

❏ **Cost.** This is the cost of the materials, plus installation and maintenance.
❏ **Speed.** The speed is the maximum number of bits per second that a medium can transmit reliably. Among other factors, speed varies with frequency (higher frequencies can transport more bits per second), with the physical size of the medium and/or transmission equipment, and with the conditioning of the conductor.
❏ **Attenuation.** Attenuation is the tendency of an electromagnetic signal to become weak or distorted over distance. During transmission, the signal's energy can become absorbed or dissipated by the medium itself. For example, a wire's resistance can leach energy from a signal and emit it in the form of heat.
❏ **Electromagnetic interference (EMI).** Electromagnetic interference (EMI) is the susceptibility of the medium to external electromagnetic energy inadvertently introduced onto a link that interferes with the intelligibility of a signal. Familiar effects of EMI are static (audio) and snow (visual).
❏ **Security.** This is protection against eavesdropping. How easy is it for an unauthorized device to listen in on the link? Some media, like broadcast radio and unshielded twisted-pair cable, are easily intercepted. Others, like fiber-optic cable, are more secure.

Table 7.2 compares the various media based on the qualities listed above.

Table 7.2 *Transmission media performance*

Medium	Cost	Speed	Attenuation	EMI	Security
UTP	Low	1–100 Mbps	High	High	Low
STP	Moderate	1–150 Mbps	High	Moderate	Low
Coax	Moderate	1 Mbps–1 Gbps	Moderate	Moderate	Low
Optical fiber	High	10 Mbps–2 Gbps	Low	Low	High
Radio	Moderate	1–10 Mbps	Low–high	High	Low
Microwave	High	1 Mbps–10 Gbps	Variable	High	Moderate
Satellite	High	1 Mbps–10 Gbps	Variable	High	Moderate

CASE STUDY

NEW AGE HOME PHARMACY

NAHP uses two types of transmission media: twisted-pair and fiber-optic cable. Twisted pair cable, category 5, connects all of the computers on a floor to an Ethernet switch. The fiber-optic cable is used as a backbone to connect the switches on each floor.

When NAHP moved into its current site, each floor was wired with twisted-pair cable. The network consulting firm recommended an upgrade to UTP category 5. The conduits under the false floor remained in place; just the cables were changed. Four pairs of cables, bundled together, run from each computer to the closet. In the closet, a rack has been installed which holds the switch. The cables are connected to the switch. Additional information about this configuration is discussed in the Chapter 9 case study.

The figure below shows how transmission media connects the six floors occupied by NAHP.

When NAHP bought the building, there was no communication between floors since each floor was occupied by a different company. After rewiring each floor, the network consulting firm recommended the use of a backbone to connect the switches on each floor to a central switch in the basement. The new backbone network uses fiber-optic cable as the transmission medium.

NAHP does not use unguided media (air) for internal communication as yet, but management is considering buying another building across the street. The main networking concern is how to connect the first building to the second. The consulting firm has proposed wireless communication. The idea is to install an antenna on the roof of each of the two buildings for communication. Management is not fully satisfied with this scheme and has asked for more details in addition to a feasibility study.

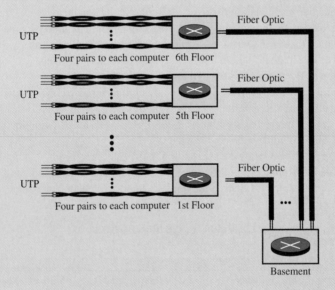

7.2 KEY TERMS

coaxial cable	optical fiber
critical angle	radio wave
crosstalk	reflection
electromagnetic interference (EMI)	refraction
electromagnetic spectrum	shielded twisted-pair (STP)
extremely high frequency (EHF)	single-mode fiber
geosynchronous orbit	space propagation
line-of-sight propagation	superhigh frequency (SHF)
low frequency (LF)	transmission medium
microwave	twisted-pair cable
microwave transmission	ultrahigh frequency (UHF)
middle frequency (MF)	unguided medium
multimode graded-index fiber	unshielded twisted-pair (UTP)
multimode step-index fiber	wireless communication

7.3 SUMMARY

❏ Signals travel from transmitter to receiver via a path. This path, called the medium, can be guided or unguided.

❏ A guided medium is contained within physical boundaries, while an unguided medium is boundless.

❏ The most popular types of guided media are twisted-pair cable (metallic), coaxial cable (metallic), and optical fiber (glass or plastic).

❏ Twisted-pair cable consists of two insulated copper wires twisted together.

❏ Shielded twisted-pair cable consists of insulated twisted pairs encased in a metal foil or braided-mesh covering.

❏ Coaxial cable consists of the following layers (starting from the center): a metallic rod-shaped inner conductor, an insulator covering the rod, a metallic outer conductor (shield), an insulator covering the shield, and a plastic cover.

❏ Both twisted-pair cable and coaxial cable transmit data in the form of an electric current.

❏ Fiber-optic cables are composed of a glass or plastic inner core surrounded by cladding, all encased in an outside jacket.

❏ Fiber-optic cables carry data signals in the form of light. The signal is propagated along the inner core by reflection.

❏ In fiber optics, signal propagation can be multimode or single mode.

❏ Radio waves can be used to transmit data. These waves use unguided media and are usually propagated through the air.

❏ Terrestrial microwaves use line-of-sight propagation for data transmission.

❏ Satellite microwaves can provide communication to and from any location on earth, no matter how remote.

PRACTICE SET

Review Questions

1. Name the two major categories of transmission media.
2. How do guided media differ from unguided media?
3. What are the three major classes of guided media?
4. What is the major advantage of shielded twisted-pair over unshielded twisted-pair?
5. Why is coaxial cable superior to twisted-pair cable?
6. Name the advantages of optical fiber over twisted-pair and coaxial cable.
7. Describe the components of a fiber-optic cable. Draw a picture.
8. What are the disadvantages of optical fiber as a transmission medium?
9. Name the bands classified as radio communication.
10. What hardware is needed to send terrestrial microwave signals?
11. What is the function of a repeater in terrestrial microwave transmission?
12. Why are communication satellites in geosynchronous orbit?

Multiple-Choice Questions

13. Transmission media are usually categorized as _____.
    a. fixed or unfixed
    b. guided or unguided
    c. determinate or indeterminate
    d. metallic or nonmetallic
14. _____ cable consists of an inner copper core and a second conducting outer sheath.
    a. Twisted-pair
    b. Coaxial
    c. Fiber-optic
    d. Shielded twisted-pair
15. In fiber optics, the signal source is _____ waves.
    a. light
    b. radio
    c. very low frequency
    d. none of the above
16. Smoke signals are an example of communication through _____.
    a. a guided medium
    b. an unguided medium
    c. a refractive medium
    d. a small or large medium
17. Which of the following primarily uses guided media?
    a. cellular telephone system
    b. local telephone system
    c. satellite communications
    d. radio broadcasting

18. Which of the following is not a guided medium?
    a. twisted-pair cable
    b. coaxial cable
    c. fiber-optic cable
    d. atmosphere
19. In an environment with many high-voltage devices, the best transmission medium would be _____.
    a. twisted-pair cable
    b. coaxial cable
    c. optical fiber
    d. the atmosphere
20. What is the major factor that makes coaxial cable less susceptible to noise than twisted-pair cable?
    a. inner conductor
    b. diameter of cable
    c. outer conductor
    d. insulating material
21. In an optical fiber, the inner core is _____ the cladding.
    a. more dense than
    b. less dense than
    c. the same density as
    d. another name for
22. The inner core of an optical fiber is _____ in composition.
    a. glass or plastic
    b. copper
    c. bimetallic
    d. liquid
23. When making connections in fiber optics, which of the following could contribute to signal distortion?
    a. inner cores of connecting fibers angularly or laterally misaligned
    b. a gap between connecting inner cores
    c. roughness of connecting fiber faces
    d. all of the above
24. The radio communication spectrum is divided into bands based on _____.
    a. amplitude
    b. frequency
    c. cost and hardware
    d. transmission medium
25. Space propagation uses _____ waves to communicate with objects beyond the atmosphere.
    a. VLF
    b. LF
    c. HF
    d. SHF

26. If a satellite is in geosynchronous orbit, it completes one orbit in _____.
   a. one hour
   b. 24 hours
   c. one month
   d. one year

27. If a satellite is in geosynchronous orbit, its distance from the sending station _____.
   a. is constant
   b. varies according to the time of day
   c. varies according to the radius of the orbit
   d. none of the above

28. When a beam of light travels through media of two different densities (from more dense to less dense), if the angle of incidence is greater than the critical angle, _____ occurs.
   a. reflection
   b. refraction
   c. incidence
   d. criticism

29. In _____ propagation, the beam of propagated light is almost horizontal and the low-density core has a small diameter compared to the cores of the other propagation modes.
   a. multimode step-index
   b. multimode graded-index
   c. multimode single-index
   d. single mode

30. In _____ propagation, the core is of varying densities.
   a. multimode step-index
   b. multimode graded-index
   c. multimode single-index
   d. single mode

31. When we talk about unguided media, usually we are referring to _____.
   a. metallic wires
   b. nonmetallic wires
   c. the atmosphere
   d. none of the above

32. Optical fibers, unlike wire media, are highly resistant to _____.
   a. high-frequency transmission
   b. low-frequency transmission
   c. electromagnetic interference
   d. refraction

33. _____ can increase the distance served in terrestrial microwave communication.
   a. Shields
   b. Repeaters
   c. Optical fibers
   d. All of the above

CHAPTER 8

Telephone and Cable TV Netv
Residential Connection to the Int

After having discussed the five layers of the Internet model and the transmission media that physically carries signals from a source to a destination, we are now ready to explore an important aspect of data communications: how many ways a resident can be connected to the Internet. Connecting to the Internet is a major requirement for most people who have a computer at home. Usually, an **Internet service provider** (ISP), through a point-to-point link, connects a residential customer to the Internet.

Connecting to the Internet from home requires the services provided by a telephone company or a cable TV company. Before we discuss the principles of connection, we need to be familiar with the technology behind a telephone network and a cable TV network.

Further knowledge about LANs and WANs is needed to connect an organization's network to the Internet. We also need to know more about connecting devices, the devices that join LANs and WANs together. These topics we leave for discussion in the coming chapters.

OBJECTIVES

After reading this chapter, the reader should:

❏ Understand the structure of the telephone network.

❏ Understand the services provided by the telephone network and how these services allow us to connect to the Internet.

❏ Understand the structure of the cable TV network.

❏ Understand the services provided by the cable TV network and how these services allow us to connect to the Internet.

8.1 TELEPHONE SYSTEM

The telephone network had its beginnings in the late 1800s. The entire network, which is referred to as the plain old telephone system (POTS), was originally an analog system using analog signals to transmit voice. With the advent of the computer era, the network, in the 1980s, began to carry data in addition to voice. During the last decade, the telephone network has undergone many technical changes. The network is now digital as well as analog.

© Corbis/Vol. 68

The telephone network started in the late 1800s and only used analog systems to transmit voice.

MAJOR COMPONENTS

The telephone system, as shown in Figure 8.1, is made of three major components: local loops, trunks, and switching offices. The telephone network has several levels of switching offices such as end offices, tandem offices, and regional offices.

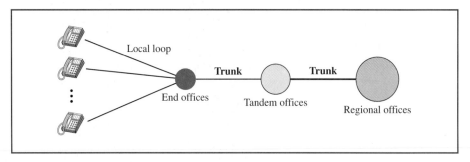

Figure 8.1   A telephone system

Local Loops

One component of the telephone network is the **local loop,** a twisted-pair cable that connects the subscriber telephone to the nearest **end office** or local central office. The local loop, when used for voice, has a bandwidth of 4000 Hz (4 kHz). It is interesting to note that each local loop is associated with a telephone number. The first three digits of a local telephone number define the office and the next four digits define the local loop number.

Trunks

Trunks are transmission media that handle the communication between offices. A trunk normally handles hundreds or thousands of connections through multiplexing. Transmission is usually through optical fibers or satellite links.

Switching Offices

To avoid having a permanent physical link between any two subscribers, the telephone company has switches located in a **switching office.** A switch connects several local loops or trunks and allows a connection between different subscribers.

After the divestiture of 1984, the United States of America was divided into more than 200 **local access transport areas** (LATAs). The number of LATAs has increased since then. A LATA can be a small or large metropolitan area. A small state may have one single LATA; a large state may have several LATAs. A LATA boundary may overlap the boundary of a state; part of a LATA can be in one state, part in another state.

Intra-LATA Services

The services offered by the **common carriers** (telephone companies) inside a LATA are called intra-LATA services. The carrier that handles these services is called a **local exchange carrier** (LEC). Before the Telecommunications Act of 1996 (see the focus box on page 184), the intra-LATA services were granted to one single carrier. This was a monopoly. After 1996, more than one carrier could provide services inside a LATA. The carrier that provided services before 1996 owns the cabling system (local loops) and is called the **incumbent local exchange carrier** (ILEC). The new carriers that can provide services are called **competitive local exchange carriers** (CLEC). To avoid the costs of new cabling, it was agreed that the ILEC would continue to provide the main services, and the CLECs would provide other services such as mobile telephone service, toll calls inside a LATA, and so on. Figure 8.2 shows a LATA and switching offices.

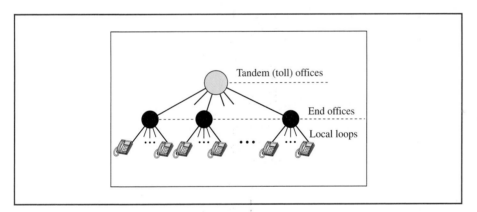

Figure 8.2   Switching offices in a LATA

Intra-LATA services are provided by local exchange carriers (LECs). Since 1996, there are two types of LECs: incumbent local exchange carriers (ILECs) and competitive local exchange carriers (CLECs).

Communication inside a LATA is handled by end switches and tandem switches. A call that can be completed by using only end offices is considered toll free. A call that has to go through a tandem office (intra-LATA toll office) is charged.

Inter-LATA Services

The services between LATAs are handled by **interexchange carriers** (IXCs). These carriers, sometimes called **long-distance companies,** provide communication services between two customers in different LATAs. After the Act of 1996, these services can be provided by any carrier, including those involved in intra-LATA services. The field is wide open. Carriers providing inter-LATA services include AT&T, MCI, WorldCom, Spirit, and Verizon.

The IXCs are long-distance carriers that provide general data communication services including telephone service. A telephone call going through an IXC is normally digitized with the carriers using several types of networks to provide service.

Points of Presence (POPs)

As we discussed, intra-LATA services can be provided by several LECs (one ILEC and possibly more than one CLEC). We also said that inter-LATA services can be provided by several IXCs. How do these carriers interact with each other? The answer is a switching office called a **point of presence** (POP). Each IXC that wants to provide inter-LATA services in a LATA must have a POP in that LATA. The LECs that provide services inside the LATA must provide connections so that every subscriber can have access to all POPs. Figure 8.3 illustrates the concept.

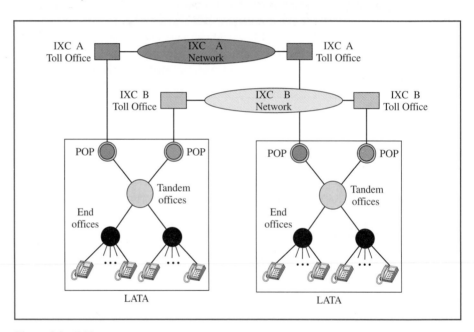

Figure 8.3   POPs

A subscriber who needs to make a connection with another subscriber is first connected to an end switch, and then, either directly or through a tandem switch, to a POP. The call now goes from the POP of an IXC (the one the subscriber has chosen) in the source LATA, to the POP of the same IXC in the destination LATA. The call will be passed through the toll office of the IXC and is carried through the network provided by the IXC.

MAKING A CONNECTION

Subscriber telephones are connected, through local loops, to end offices (or central offices).

Accessing the switching station at the end offices is accomplished through dialing. In the past, telephones featured rotary or pulse dialing, in which a digital signal was sent

A rotary phone and a touch-tone phone.

to the end office for each number dialed. This type of dialing was prone to errors due to the inconsistency of humans during the dialing process.

Today, dialing is accomplished through the touch-tone technique. In this method, instead of sending a digital signal, the user sends two small bursts of analog signals, called *dual tone*. The frequency of the signals sent depends on the row and column of the pressed pad.

Figure 8.4 shows a **rotary** and a **touch-tone** dialing system.

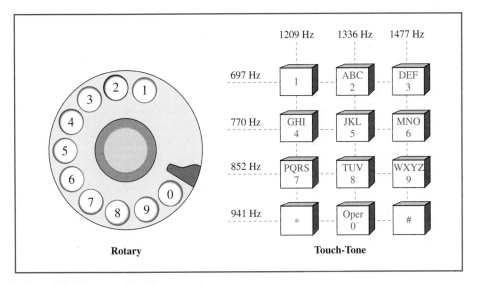

Figure 8.4   Rotary and touch-tone dialing

In Figure 8.4, if a user has a rotary telephone, the number 8 is represented by a digital signal. On the other hand, if a user has a touch-tone telephone, two bursts of analog signals with frequencies 852 and 1336 Hz are sent to the end office.

Voice communication used analog signals in the past, but is now moving to digital signals.

On the other hand, dialing started with digital signals (rotary) and is now moving to analog signals (touch-tone).

BUSINESS FOCUS: HISTORY OF COMMON CARRIERS IN U.S.A.

The history of common carriers in the United States can be divided into three eras: before 1984, between 1984 and 1996, and after 1996.

Before 1984

Before 1984, almost all local and long-distance services were provided by the AT&T Bell System. In 1970, the U.S. government, believing that the Bell System was monopolizing the telephone service industry, sued the company. The verdict was in favor of the government and, based on a document called the Modified Final Judgment (MFJ), from January 1, 1984, AT&T was broken into AT&T Long Lines, 23 Bell Operating Companies (BOCs), and others. The 23 BOCs were grouped together to make several Regional Bell Operating Systems (RBOCs). This landmark event, the AT&T divestiture of 1984, was beneficial to customers of telephone services. Telephone rates decreased.

Between 1984 and 1996

The divestiture divided the country into more than 200 LATAs; some companies were allowed to provide services inside a LATA (LECs) and some were allowed to provide services between LATAs (IXCs). Competition, particularly between long-distance carriers increased as new companies were formed. However, no LEC could provide long-distance services and no IXCs could provide local services.

After 1996

Another major change in telecommunications occurred in 1996. The Telecommunications Act of 1996 combined the different services provided by different companies under the umbrella of telecommunication services; this included local services, long-distance voice and data services, video services, and so on. In addition, the Act allowed any company to provide any of these services at the local and long-distance level. In other words, a common carrier company provides services both inside the LATA and between the LATAs. However, to prevent the recabling of residents, the carrier that was given intra-LATA services (ILEC) continues to provide the main services; the new competitors (CLECs) provide other services.

BUSINESS FOCUS: ANALOG VOICE SERVICES

The LECs and IXCs provide several services; the most common are listed below:

Local Call Services   A local call service is normally provided for a flat monthly rate, although in some LATAs, the carrier charges for each call or a set of calls. The rationale for a non-flat-rate charge is to provide cheaper service for those customers who do not make many calls.

Toll Calls   A toll call can be intra-LATA or inter-LATA. If the LATA is geographically large, a call may go through a tandem office (toll office) and the subscriber will pay a fee for the call. The inter-LATA calls are long-distance calls and are charged as such.

800/888 Services   If a subscriber (normally an organization) needs to provide free connections for other subscribers (normally customers), it can request an 800/888 (800 in the past, now 888 because 800 numbers are almost exhausted) service. In this case, the call is free for the caller, but it is paid by the callee. An organization uses this service to encourage customers to call. The rate is less expensive than a normal long-distance call.

WATS   The wide area telephone service (WATS) is the opposite of 800/888 service. The latter are inbound calls paid by the organization; the former are outbound calls paid by the organization. This service is a less expensive alternative to regular toll calls; charges are based on the number of calls. The service can be specified as outbound calls to the same state, several states, or the whole country, with rates charged accordingly.

900 Services   The 900 services are like 800/888 services, in that they are inbound calls to a subscriber. However, unlike 800/888 service, the call is paid by the caller and is normally much more expensive than a normal long-distance call. The reason is that the carrier charges two fees; the first is the long-distance toll, the second is the fee paid to the callee for each call. This service is used by an organization that needs to charge customers for its services. For example, a company may need to charge a customer for technical support.

8.2   INTERNET ACCESS VIA TELEPHONE

With the advent of the Internet, people wanted home access to the Internet to send and receive email, to surf the web, and so on. This access requires a physical connection to an ISP. Instead of laying new cable to connect a residential user to the local ISP, the existing cables (local loops) that connect each residence to the telephone switching office can be used. Now the problem is how to connect the switching offices to the local ISPs. This was accomplished using high-bandwidth trunks. Figure 8.5 shows how residential users can be connected to the Internet using the local loop, which was formerly used only for voice communication.

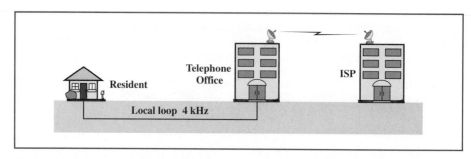

Figure 8.5   Internet access via the local loop

However, there is still another problem: A local loop is an analog line, but the data to be sent and received from the Internet is digital. The line, designed in the past for an analog signal, has a bandwidth of 4 kHz, which cannot handle a digital signal. Somehow, digital data must be sent through these analog lines.

During the past few decades, several solutions were proposed for this problem: conventional modems, 56K modems, and DSL modems.

CONVENTIONAL MODEMS

The term *modem* is a composite word that refers to the two functional entities that make up the device: a signal *mo*dulator and a signal *dem*odulator.

Modem **stands for modulator/demodulator.**

A **modulator** converts a digital signal into an analog signal using ASK, FSK, PSK, or a combination. A demodulator converts an analog signal into a digital signal. While a demodulator resembles an analog-to-digital converter, it is not in fact a converter of any kind. It does not sample a signal to create a digital facsimile; it merely reverses the process of modulation—that is, it performs demodulation.

A modulator converts a digital signal to an analog signal. A demodulator converts an analog signal to a digital signal.

Figure 8.6 shows the relationship of modems to a communication link. The computer creates a digital signal and relays it to the modem. The modulated signal is received by the demodulation function of the second modem. The demodulator takes the signal and decodes it into whatever format its computer can accept. It then relays the resulting digital signal to the receiving computer.

Traditional telephone lines can effectively carry frequencies between 300 Hz and 3300 Hz, resulting in a bandwidth of 3000 Hz. All of this range is used for transmitting voice, where a great deal of interference and distortion can be accepted without loss of intelligibility. However, data signals require a higher degree of accuracy to ensure integrity. For safety's sake, therefore, the boundaries of this range are not used for data communication.

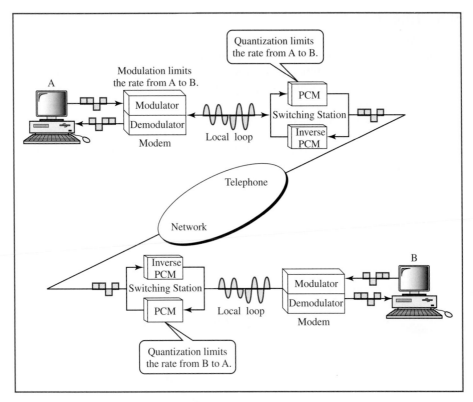

Figure 8.6   Modem concept

Modem Standards

Today, many of the most popular modems available are based on standards published by the ITU-T. Table 8.1 shows some of the common modem standards.

Table 8.1   *ITU-T modems*

ITU-T	Bit Rate
V.32bis	14,400
V.33	14,400
V.34	28,800

V.32bis   The V.32bis modem was the first of the ITU-T standards to support 14,400 bps transmission. The V.32bis (bis means second version) uses FDM (6 bits per baud) at a rate of 2400 baud ($2400 \times 6 = 14{,}400$ bps).

V.33   The V.33 is also based on the V.32. This modem, however, uses 7 bits per baud. Each signal change represents a pattern of 7 bits: 6 data bits and 1 redundant bit (for error detection). Six bits of data per change (baud) give it a speed of $6 \times 2400 = 14{,}400$ bps.

V.34   The V.34 modem, sometimes called V.fast, provides a bit rate of 28,800 or 33,600 bps. In addition, the V.34 provides data compression, which allows data rates as fast as two to three times its normal speed.

56K MODEMS (V.90)

Traditional modems have a limitation on the data rate (maximum of 33.6 kbps), as determined by the noisiness of the telephone line. Modems with a bit rate of 56,000 bps, called **56K modems** (or V.90), are now popular. These modems may be used only if one party is using digital signaling (such as an Internet provider). They are asymmetrical since the downloading (flow of data from the Internet provider to the resident) is a maximum of 56 kbps, while uploading (flow of data from the residence to the Internet provider) is a maximum of 33.6 kbps.

These modems use PCM and inverse PCM to accomplish the theoretical data rate of 33.6 in the downloading direction. Figure 8.7 shows the concept.

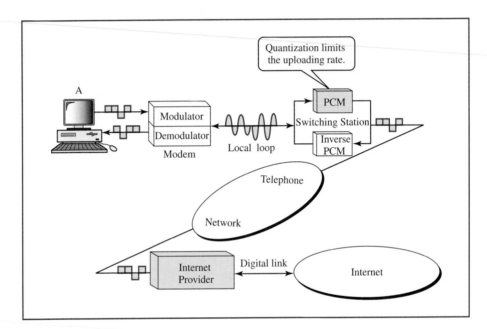

Figure 8.7   56K modems

Uploading
In the figure, transmission of data from the subscriber to the Internet provider (**uploading**) follows these steps:

1. Digital data are modulated by the modem at site A.
2. Analog data are sent from the modem to the switching station on the local loop.
3. At the switching station, data are converted to digital using PCM.
4. Digital data travel through the digital network of the telephone company and are received by the Internet provider computer.

The limiting factor in these steps is step 3. However, the user does not often need such a high data rate in this direction since only small blocks of data (such as email or a small file) are sent.

Downloading

Transmission of data from the Internet provider to the modem at site A (**downloading**) follows these steps:

1. Digital data are sent by the computer of the Internet provider through the digital telephone network.
2. At the switching station, digital data are converted to analog using inverse PCM.
3. Analog data are sent from the switching station at site A to the modem on the local loop.
4. Analog data are demodulated by the modem at site A.

Note that, in this direction, there is no quantization of data using PCM. The limitation when uploading is not an issue here; data can be sent at 56 kbps. This is what the user is looking for, since large files are typically downloaded from the Internet.

The maximum data rate in the uploading direction is 33.6 kbps, while the data rate in the downloading direction is 56 kbps.

DSL MODEMS

One example of multiplexing, demultiplexing, and modulation is a technology called **digital subscriber line** (DSL). DSL is a technology that uses the existing telecommunication networks such as the local loop telephone lines to accomplish high-speed delivery of data, voice, video, and multimedia.

DSL is a family of technologies; the most common one used for residential connection to the Internet is **asymmetrical DSL** (ADSL). Telephone companies have installed high-speed digital wide area networks to handle communication between their central offices. The link between the user (subscriber) and the network, however, is still an analog line (local loop). The challenge is to make these links digital—a digital subscriber line—without changing the existing local loops. The local loop is a twisted-pair cable with a potential bandwidth of 1 MHz or more.

ADSL is asymmetrical, which means it provides higher bit rates in the downstream direction (from the telephone central office to the subscriber's site) than the upstream direction (from the subscriber site to the telephone central office). This is what subscribers usually want. They want to receive high-volume files quickly from the Internet, but they usually have small files, such as a short email message, to send.

ADSL divides the bandwidth of a twisted-pair cable (one megahertz) into three bands. The first band, normally between 0 and 25 kHz, is used for regular telephone service (known as plain old telephone service or POTS). This service uses only 4 kHz of this band; the rest is used as the guard band to separate the voice channel from the data channels. The second band, usually between 25 and 200 kHz, is used for upstream communication. The third band, usually 250 kHz to 1 MHz, is used for downstream communication. Some implementations overlap the downstream and upstream band to provide more bandwidth in the downstream direction. Figure 8.8 shows the bands.

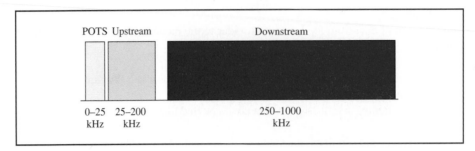

Figure 8.8 Bands for ADSL

Modulation Techniques

Most implementations of ADSL originally used a modulation technique similar to FM. The ANSI standard defines a rate of 60 kbps for each 4-kHz channel.

❏ The upstream channel usually occupies 25 channels, which means a bit rate of 25 × 60 kbps, or 1.5 Mbps. Normally, however, the bit rate in this direction ranges from 64 kbps to 1 Mbps due to noise.

❏ The downstream channel usually occupies 200 channels, which means a bit rate of 200 × 60 kbps, or 12 Mbps. Normally, however, the bit rate in this direction ranges from 500 kbps to 8 Mbps due to noise.

Figure 8.9 shows ADSL and the bit rates in each direction.

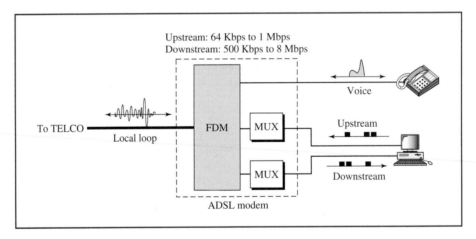

Figure 8.9 ADSL modem

8.3 CABLE TV NETWORK

The **cable TV** network was originally designed to use coaxial cable. The cable TV head end (office) was connected to the customer premises by coaxial cable with a bandwidth of 45 to 500 MHz. This bandwidth could accommodate up to 70 TV channels, with each channel requiring a 6-MHz bandwidth. The network used analog signals to modulate different carriers to spread the bandwidth. The connection used a treelike configuration of devices to amplify the weakened signals. The communication was one way, from the head end to the customer premises.

The cable TV network was originally designed for video propagation.

The situation is very different today. Most cable TV companies have changed their cable media to include both fiber-optic and coaxial cables. Due to these changes and other improvements, the bandwidth has increased. The bandwidth between 5 to 54 MHz is used for upstream communication, 54 to 550 MHz for downstream communication. The bandwidth between 550 to 750 MHz is used by some cable companies to deliver digital TV. Digital TV uses compression and this reduces the previous 6 MHz bandwidth requirement. One digital channel now needs less than 1 MHz. More than 200 TV channels can be accommodated. If there comes a time when the entire band is digital, cable TV could deliver more than 750 channels. Figure 8.10 illustrates a cable TV network.

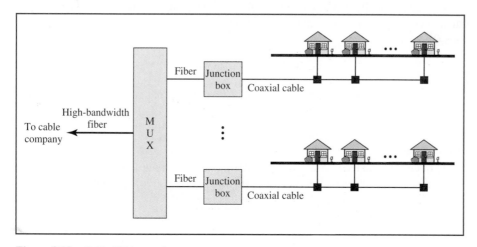

Figure 8.10   Cable TV network

INTERNET ACCESS VIA CABLE TV

The data rate limitation of traditional modems is mostly due to the narrow bandwidth of the local loop telephone line (up to 4 kHz). If higher bandwidths are available, one can design a modem that can handle much higher data rates.

Fortunately, cable TV provides residential premises with a coaxial cable that has a bandwidth up to 750 MHz and sometimes even more. This bandwidth is normally divided into 6 MHz bands using frequency division multiplexing (see Chapter 6). Each band can accommodate a TV channel. Two bands can be set aside to allow a user to download and upload information from the Internet.

Figure 8.11 shows the cable modem concept. Instead of the traditional cable box, we show a splitter. The splitter directs the TV bands to the TV set and the Internet access bands to the PC.

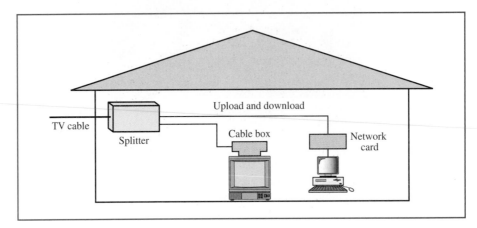

Figure 8.11 Cable modem

Downloading

Downloading usually requires a 6 MHz bandwidth in a range above 40 MHz. The demodulation technique uses 6 bits at a time. This means that a user can download information at a rate of

$$6 \text{ MHz} \times 6 = 36 \text{ Mbps}$$

However, PCs are not yet capable of receiving data at this rate. Presently, the rate is something between 3 and 10 Mbps.

Uploading

Uploading takes place at 5 MHz to 42 MHz, which is divided into 2 MHz bands for each customer. However, this band is very noisy because many types of household equipment create signals in this range. For this reason the rate is much lower, between 500 kbps and 2 Mbps.

SHARING

We must be aware that the DSL line is a dedicated line. When a subscriber uses a DSL modem and a DSL line, the entire capacity of the line belongs to the subscriber. In cable modem technology, however, the capacity is shared, in both directions, between several neighbors. This does not mean that the data rate is reduced, it means that there is contention for access to the line. Access is granted when the line is available. Ethernet LANs, discussed in Chapter 9, use the same principle.

BUSINESS FOCUS:
TELECOMMUNICATIONS REFORM ACT OF 1996

The Telecommunications Reform Act, passed on February 8, 1996, gave telephone and cable companies permission to provide both telephone services (local and long distance) and video services. The act specifies that any company can provide local telephone service, long-distance telephone service, video service, or any other services needed for telecommunication. Previous to this act, only cable companies could provide video services and only telephone companies could provide telephone services. In addition, telephone companies were restricted to provide either local or long-distance services, but not both. With the passage of the act, a telephone company or a cable company could now provide local and long-distance telephone services.

The purpose of the act was to allow competition between companies and thus lower the price and improve the quality of telecommunication services for consumers. The act is still relatively new and it is too soon to judge its effect on prices and quality of services.

A provision in the act provides low-cost access to the Internet for educational and nonprofit organizations.

CASE STUDY

NEW AGE HOME PHARMACY

For voice communication, NAHP uses telephone networks. The building is wired internally for 48 extensions. All lines use the same exchange digits (271); the remaining four digits are different for each line. In other words, each number has the form 271-XXXX. To carry voice out of the building, the company leases two T-1 lines (see Chapter 11). A T-1 line is capable of carrying 24 voice channels simultaneously.

Until recently, NAHP used DSL for its connection to the Internet. However, due to an increase in load, the Modern Networking consultants recommended leasing a T-3 line (see Chapter 11). When the chairperson heard that the company was moving to replace DSL with a T-3 line, she was concerned about the data rate of the T-3 line (close to 45 Mbps). She asked how a backbone of 100 Mbps can be connected to a line which can handle only 45 Mbps.

The consultant from Modern Networking assured the board that the backbone was not working at full capacity. In addition, some of the load imposed on the backbone is internal and for the moment, a data rate of 45 Mbps is more than the company needs.

Recently, one pharmacist heard about cable modem technology and its low cost. A letter was sent to Modern Networking about the possibility of moving from the T-3 line to a cable modem connection. Modern Networking responded that cable modem is a good choice for residential connections. However, for a business like NAHP, with its load, cable modem is not a good solution because the capacity is shared with neighbors and there is no guarantee of a specific data rate.

8.4   KEY TERMS

56K modem

asymmetrical DSL (ADSL)

cable modem

cable TV

carrier signal

common carrier

competitive local exchange
    carrier (CLEC)

demodulation

demodulator

digital subscriber line (DSL)

downloading

encoding

end office

frequency

incumbent local exchange
    carrier (ILEC)

interexchange carrier (IXC)

Internet service provider (ISP)

local access and transport
    area (LATA)

local exchange carrier (LEC)

local loop

modem

modulator

point of presence (POP)

switching office

touch-tone dialing

trunk

uploading

V.32bis

V.33

V.34

8.5   SUMMARY

❏   The telephone system has three major components: local loops, trunks, and
    switching offices.

❏   The United States is divided into more than 200 local access and transport areas
    (LATAs).

❏   Intra-LATA services are provided by incumbent local exchange carriers and
    competitive local exchange carriers. Inter-LATA services are handled by
    interexchange carriers.

❏   A home computer can access the Internet through the existing telephone system
    or through a cable TV system.

❏   Internet access through the telephone system requires a modem.

❏   56K modems are asymmetrical; they download at a rate of 56 kbps and send data
    at 33.6 kbps.

❏   ADSL technology allows a bit rate of up to 1 Mbps in the upstream direction
    and up to 8 Mbps in the downstream direction.

❏   The coaxial cable used for cable TV allows Internet access with a bit rate of up to
    2 Mbps in the upstream direction and up to 10 Mbps in the downstream direction.

 PRACTICE SET

Review Questions

1. What is the function of an ISP?
2. What are the three main components of a telephone system?
3. What is the local loop?

4. What is the bandwidth of a traditional telephone line?
5. What is the function of a trunk?
6. How is an ILEC different from a CLEC?
7. What is the function of a POP?
8. How are telephone services between LATAs handled?
9. Compare the signals used in rotary dialing with the signals used in touch-tone dialing.
10. What does the term *modem* stand for?
11. What is the function of a modulator? What is the function of a demodulator?
12. Explain the asymmetry of 56K modems.
13. How does a cable modem achieve such a high data rate?
14. Why are modems needed for telephone communications?

Multiple-Choice Questions

15. The local loop has _____ cable that connects the subscriber telephone to the nearest end office.
    a. twisted-pair
    b. coaxial
    c. fiber-optic
    d. b and c
16. Trunks are transmission media such as _____ that handle the telephone communication between offices.
    a. twisted-pair cable
    b. fiber-optic cable
    c. satellite links
    d. b and c
17. The established telephone company that provided services in a LATA before 1996 and owns the cabling system is called _____.
    a. an ILEC
    b. a CLEC
    c. an IXC
    d. a POP
18. A new telephone company that provides services in a LATA after 1996 is called _____.
    a. an ILEC
    b. a CLEC
    c. an IXC
    d. a POP
19. The telephone services between two LATAs is handled by _____.
    a. an ILEC
    b. a CLEC
    c. an IXC
    d. a POP

20. If the end office receives two bursts of analog signals with frequencies of 697 and 1477 Hz, then the number _____ has been punched.
    a. 1
    b. 2
    c. 3
    d. 4

21. Data from a computer is _____; the local loop handles _____ signals.
    a. analog; analog
    b. analog; digital
    c. digital; digital
    d. digital; analog

22. A traditional telephone line has a bandwidth of _____.
    a. 2000 Hz
    b. 4000 Hz
    c. 2000 MHz
    d. 4000 MHz

23. A demodulator takes _____ signal and turns it into _____ signal.
    a. an analog; an analog
    b. an analog; a digital
    c. a digital; a digital
    d. a digital; an analog

24. A 56K modem can download at a rate of _____ kbps and upload at a rate of _____ kbps.
    a. 33.6; 33.6
    b. 33.6; 56.6
    c. 56.6; 33.6
    d. 56.6; 56.6

25. The ADSL downstream bandwidth is _____ kHz.
    a. 25
    b. 175
    c. 750
    d. 1000

26. The ADSL bandwidth for POTS is _____ kHz.
    a. 25
    b. 175
    c. 750
    d. 1000

27. Which Internet access method provides the highest data rate?
    a. cable TV
    b. ADSL
    c. V.33 modem
    d. 56K modem

PART II

LAN and WAN Technology

CHAPTER 9

Local Area Networks
Part 1: Basic Concepts and
Wired Ethernet LANs

In Chapters 1 to 8, we discussed the layers of the data communications models, the transmission media that physically carry signals from one device to another, and the ways residential computers are connected to the Internet.

In Chapters 9 and 10, we discuss how the first two layers of the OSI model (physical and data link) are used to implement local area networks (LANs). In this chapter, we discuss the basics of LANs and Ethernet, the dominant LAN technology. In Chapter 10, we discuss wireless and virtual LANs.

OBJECTIVES

After reading this chapter, the reader should:

- ❏ Understand the use of LANs in an organization.
- ❏ List the components of a LAN.
- ❏ Be familiar with the IEEE standards.
- ❏ Be familiar with traditional Ethernet technology and its implementations.

- ❏ Be familiar with Fast Ethernet technology and its implementations.
- ❏ Be familiar with Gigabit Ethernet technology and its implementations.

9.1 BASIC CONCEPTS

A local area network (LAN) is a data communication system connecting a number of devices to each other. The size of a LAN is limited to a radius of a few miles. This means that a LAN cannot connect computers spread over a country or even over a city. Its physical size is usually limited to a building, campus, or site.

The data rate (the rate at which data is sent from one device to another) for LANs is ever increasing. In the last two decades, the data rate has gone from 10 Mbps to 100 Mbps, and then from 100 Mbps to 1 Gbps. The technology is moving towards 10 Gbps and beyond.

LAN COMPONENTS

A local area network or a LAN is a combination of hardware and software. The **hardware** is the part of the network that is tangible. The **software** is a collection of programs that allows the use of the physical components of the network.

Hardware

Let us first discuss the hardware. We can roughly divide the hardware used in a LAN into three categories: stations, transmission media, and connecting devices.

Stations   The purpose of a LAN is to connect **stations** such as computers, printers, and modems. These stations are sometimes referred to as nodes, but we prefer the term station.

Each station must be capable of being connected to the network to perform tasks such as sending and receiving data and monitoring the network. For this, a station needs extra hardware or software tools. The hardware usually comes in the form of a **network interface card** (NIC), which is commonly installed inside the station and contains the necessary circuitry (in the form of chips) to perform network functions.

Transmission Media   The **transmission medium** is the path that allows communication between stations. LANs today use either **guided** (cable) or **unguided** (air or vacuum) transmission media. A variety of transmission media are available. Wired LANs can use guided media such as twisted-pair cable, shielded twisted-pair cable, coaxial cable, and fiber-optic cable. Wireless LANs use air as the medium for transmitting data.

Connecting Devices   Two categories of **connecting devices** are used in LANs. One category consists of devices that connect transmission media to the stations; transceivers (devices that transmit and receive) and transceiver cables fall in this category. The second category consists of devices that connect segments of a network together; repeaters and bridges fall into this category.

Software

Software run on a LAN can be divided into two large groups: network operating system software and application programs.

Network Operating System   A **network operating system** (NOS) is a program that allows the logical connection of stations and devices to the network. It enables users to communicate and share resources. The most popular network operating systems for LANs are Novell Netware, Windows 2000, UNIX, and Linux.

Application Programs   **Application programs** allow users to solve special problems. Application programs are not specific to LANs; they are also used by stand-alone computers. An example of an application program is a program to calculate taxes.

LAN MODELS

From a user's point of view, a LAN can be configured either as a client-server LAN or a peer-to-peer LAN.

Client-Server Model

In a **client-server model,** one or more stations called **servers** gives services to other stations called **clients.** The server version of the network operating system is installed on the server or servers; the client version of the network operating system is installed on clients. A LAN may have several dedicated servers or one general server.

Dedicated Servers   A large network may have several servers, each dedicated to a particular task. For example, a network may have a mail server, a file server, and a print server. A mail server receives email for clients. This server must be running all the time so that no email is missed. The client can run its email software to access mail at any time. A file server allows the client to access shared data stored on the disk connected to the file server. When a user needs data, it accesses the server, which then sends a copy. A print server allows different clients to share a printer (probably high-speed). Each client can send data to be printed to the print server, which then spools (or prioritizes) and prints them. In this model, the file server station runs a file server program, a mail server station runs a mail server program, and a print server station runs a print server program. Depending on its need, a client runs a file client program, a mail client program, or a print client program. Figure 9.1 shows the idea of a client-server model with dedicated servers.

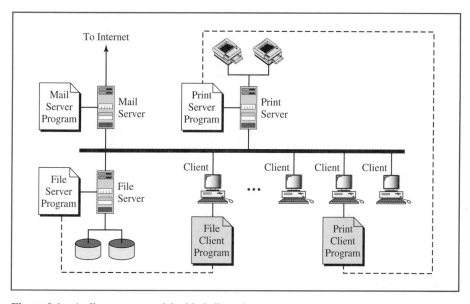

Figure 9.1   A client-server model with dedicated servers

In the figure, we show one client using the file client program to retrieve data from the file server. The second client uses a print client program to output a job on the shared printers.

One General Server   A small network may have only one **general server.** In this case, this one server is responsible for all services typically requested from a server. It can serve as a mail server, a file server, a print server, and so on. A general server runs all of the server programs all of the time. Figure 9.2 shows a client-server model with one general server.

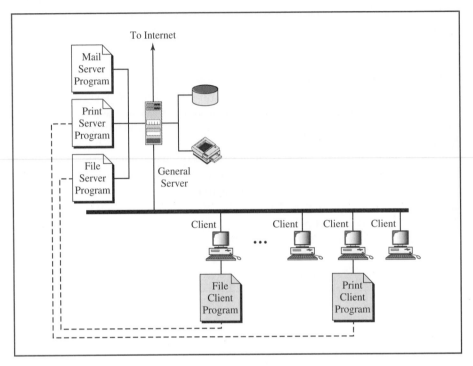

Figure 9.2   A client-server model with a general server

In this figure, two clients are accessing the general server. One client is requesting a service from the file server program. The other client is requesting a service from the print server program.

Peer-to-Peer Model
In a **peer-to-peer model,** a station can be both a client and a server. No stations are specifically designated as either a client or a server. If a station asks for a service from another station, the asking station is a client and the responding station is a server. In other words, if station A needs to copy a file from station B, station A runs a file client program and station B runs a file server program. Likewise, if station B wants to copy a file from station A, station B runs the client program and station A runs the server program. Each station must be running the server programs all the time, and the client programs only when needed (see Figure 9.3).

Comparison
From the above discussion, we conclude that the client-server model is preferable to the peer-to-peer model for an all-purpose network. The peer-to-peer model can be used for special purposes such as a small group of users working on a project that requires shared access to resources. For this reason, the peer-to-peer model is sometimes called the workgroup model.

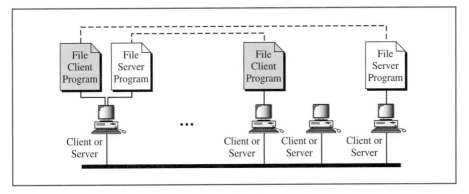

Figure 9.3 Peer-to-peer model

LAN APPLICATIONS

In this section, we briefly discuss some common applications of local area networks: office networks, industry networks, and backbone networks.

Office Networks

The most widely used application of a local area network is in the office environment. LANs are used in the office today for three purposes: sharing, interoffice communication, and Internet communication.

Sharing   A LAN in an office allows several users to share company resources such as hardware, software, and data.

❑   **Sharing Hardware.** Most companies use sophisticated and expensive hardware equipment such as fast, high-quality printers. However, the cost does not justify the installation of a printer for each individual user. Because a printer is not used all of the time, it can be shared. Users can be connected, through the local area network, to the shared printer. Jobs from each user are queued and printed on the same printer.

❑   **Sharing Software.** Large and sophisticated programs, such as accounting programs, can be stored on a machine and shared by all or some users. LANs can replace the time-sharing environment of the past in which the central processing was done by a mainframe computer with each user connected by a dumb terminal to the mainframe.

❑   **Sharing Data.** Sharing large files and databases between users is another advantage to having a local area network. In a typical company, different users may need to access a large file or database.

Interoffice Communication   Local area networks have created a new type of communication in an office environment. The employees of a company can communicate with each other using the network. They can send one-to-one, one-to-many, and one-to-all messages. This type of communication is sometimes more efficient than voice communication by phone.

External Communication   Another way that the LAN can be used in an office environment is external communication via the Internet. Each employee can use the LAN to connect to the Internet.

Industry Networks

Some LAN architectures are suitable for automated manufacturing and production. For example, a LAN can be used in the automobile industry to coordinate activities such as controlling robots, material handling, or warehouse inventory.

Backbone Networks

A high-speed LAN can be used as a backbone to connect several low-speed networks in an organization. For example, low-speed LANs in different buildings on a campus environment can be connected by a high-speed backbone LAN to allow different users in different buildings to be connected to each other. This scheme has many advantages. First of all, it would be too expensive to use one high-speed LAN to connect each individual user and it would be too slow to use one low-speed LAN to do so. In addition, using a backbone improves the reliability of the system; if one of the LANs fails, the rest will continue to function. The load is another issue; using a backbone, we can isolate the load on one network from others. We discuss backbone networks in more detail in Chapter 12 after we have discussed connecting devices.

TOPOLOGY

Topology defines how the devices (computers, printers, and so on) are connected together and how data flows from one device to another. The physical topology defines how the devices are physically connected together (wired); the logical topology defines how the data flows from one device to another.

The physical topology is often different from logical topology. As an analogy, two departments in an organization may be located physically next to each other (occupying adjacent rooms), but belong to different levels in the organization hierarchy and never interact with each other directly.

Physical Topology

The term physical topology defines how each device is connected to other devices in a LAN. It defines the physical relationship between devices. There are two dominant physical topologies: bus and star.

Physical Bus Topology   In a **physical bus topology,** all devices are connected to the transmission medium (bus) as shown in Figure 9.4.

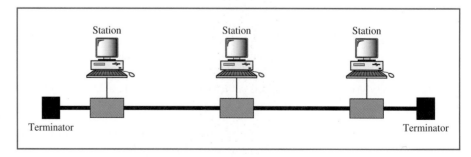

Figure 9.4   Physical bus topology

In a physical bus topology, the signals travel through the bus to both ends. There must be a **terminator** at each end of the bus to kill the signals. These terminators prevent the signals from reflecting back and being received by the devices over and over again.

One main problem with the physical bus topology is that the failure of the medium seriously affects the network. If the medium is damaged at any point, the signal will reflect back and cause errors. Any medium failure means that the whole network must be shut down and repaired.

Physical Star Topology In a **physical star topology,** each station is connected to a central node as shown in Figure 9.5.

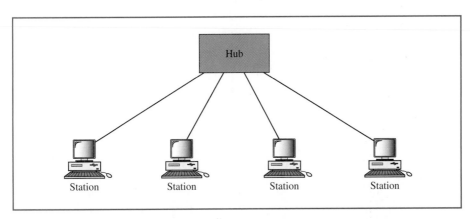

Figure 9.5 Physical star topology

The central node in a star topology can be either a hub or a switch. A **hub** is a device that only connects the branches of a star together. A **switch,** on the other hand, is more sophisticated and can check addresses. Address checking, as we will see shortly, can affect the logical topology of the network.

In a star topology, when a frame is received by a station, it is automatically removed from the system; the station drains the frame.

As you may have noticed, the star topology does not have the problem we saw in the bus topology; the failure of the medium between some station and the hub or switch does not seriously affect the rest of the network. Other stations can continue to operate until the damaged branch is repaired.

The star topology is the dominant physical topology today.

Logical Topology

The term *logical topology* defines how data flows in the network. Two logical topologies are common for LANs.

Logical Bus Topology In a **logical bus topology,** a frame sent by a station is received by every station in the network. However, only the true destination keeps the frame; the others drop it. A physical bus topology is logically a bus because every station receives a frame sent by another station. A physical star topology that uses a hub is also logically a bus because the hub just relays the frame to every other station.

Figure 9.6 shows a network that is physically and logically a bus and another network that is physically a star and logically a bus.

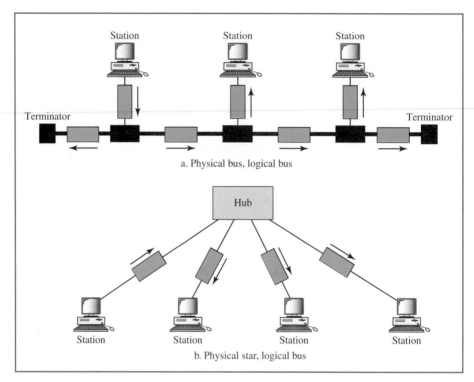

Figure 9.6   Logical bus topology

Logical Star Topology   In a **logical star topology,** a frame sent by a station is received only by the destination station; no other station is involved in the communication. The only physical topology that can support this logical flow of data is the star topology using a switch as the central node. The switch is able to check the physical (data link layer) address of the frame and route the frame to its true destination. Figure 9.7 shows a physical star topology with a logical star topology.

PROJECT 802

In 1985, the Computer Society of the IEEE started a project, called **Project 802,** to set standards to enable intercommunication between equipment from a variety of manufacturers. Project 802 does not seek to replace any part of the Internet model. Instead, it is a way of specifying functions of the physical layer and the data link layer.

In 1985, the Computer Society of the IEEE developed Project 802. It covers the first two layers of the Internet model.

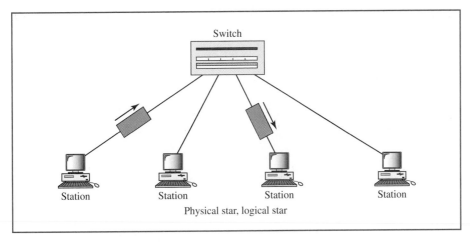

Physical star, logical star

Figure 9.7 Logical star topology

TECHNICAL FOCUS: RING TOPOLOGY

Another physical topology common at the beginning of the LAN era was the ring topology. In a ring topology, each station is connected to the next station as shown in the following figure:

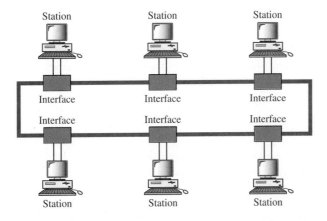

The relationship of IEEE Project 802 to the Internet model is shown in Figure 9.8. The IEEE has subdivided the data link layer into two sublayers: **logical link control** (LLC) and **medium access control** (MAC).

The LLC is nonarchitecture-specific; that is, it is the same for all IEEE-defined LANs. The MAC sublayer, on the other hand, contains a number of distinct modules; each carries proprietary information specific to the LAN product being used.

Project 802 has split the data link layer into two different sublayers: logical link control (LLC) and media access control (MAC).

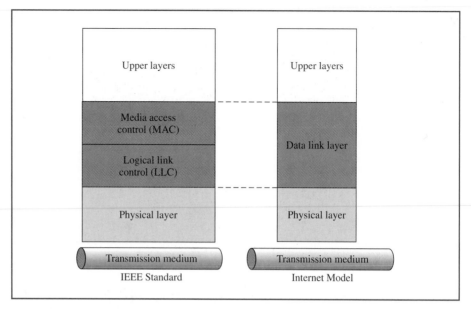

Figure 9.8 LAN compared with the Internet model

9.2 WIRED ETHERNET LANs

Most of today's LANs use guided transmission media and can be referred to as wired LANs. This is in contrast to wireless LANs, discussed in Chapter 10. In the last two decades several wired LAN technologies evolved, but only one has really survived; this is Ethernet. Ethernet technology itself has gone through many changes. In this section, we first discuss traditional Ethernet; we then discuss switched Ethernet, Fast Ethernet, and Gigabit Ethernet.

TRADITIONAL ETHERNET

Ethernet was originally developed by Xerox and later became a joint venture between Digital Equipment Corporation, Intel Corporation, and Xerox. Traditional Ethernet was one of the first LAN protocols standardized by IEEE; it is formally known as IEEE 802.3.

Access Method: CSMA/CD

We discussed access methods in Chapter 5. Traditional Ethernet uses carrier sense multiple access with collision detection or CSMA/CD. CSMA/CD is the result of an evolution from **multiple access** (MA) to **carrier sense multiple access** (CSMA), to **carrier sense multiple access with collision detection** (CSMA/CD). The original design was a multiple access method in which every workstation had equal access to a link. In MA, there was no provision for traffic coordination. Access to the line was open to any node at any time, with the assumption that the odds of two devices competing for access at the same time were small enough to be unimportant. Any station wishing to transmit did so, then relied on acknowledgments to verify that the transmitted frame had not been destroyed by other traffic on the line.

In a CSMA system, any workstation wishing to transmit must first listen for existing traffic on the line. A device listens by checking for a signal. If no signal is detected, the line is considered idle and transmission is initiated. CSMA cuts down on the number of collisions but does not eliminate them. Collisions can still occur. If another station has transmitted too recently for its signal to have reached the listening station, the listener assumes the line is idle and introduces its own signal onto the line.

The final step is the addition of collision detection (CD). In CSMA/CD the station wishing to transmit first listens to make certain the link is free, then transmits its data, then listens again. During the data transmission, the station checks the line for the extremely high signal level that indicates a collision. If a collision is detected, the station quits the current transmission, waits a predetermined amount of time for the line to clear, then sends its data again (see Figure 9.9).

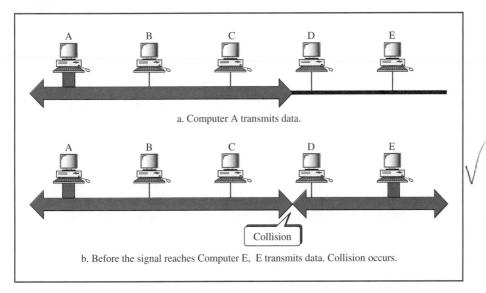

a. Computer A transmits data.

b. Before the signal reaches Computer E, E transmits data. Collision occurs.

Figure 9.9   Collision in CSMA/CD

TECHNICAL FOCUS: ETHERNET ADDRESSING

Each station on an Ethernet network (such as a PC, workstation, or printer) has its own **network interface card** (NIC). The NIC usually fits inside the station and provides the station with a 6-byte (48-bit) physical address.

TECHNICAL FOCUS: SIGNALING

Traditional Ethernet uses Manchester digital encoding (discussed in Chapter 6). In this type of signaling, the transition at the middle of each bit is used for synchronization between the sender and receiver.

Implementation

Although the bulk of the IEEE Project 802 standard focuses on the data link layer of the Internet model, the 802 model also defines some of the physical specifications for each of the protocols defined in the MAC layer. In the 802.3 standard, the IEEE defines the types of cable, connections, and signals that are to be used in each of four different

Ethernet implementations. All traditional Ethernet LANs are configured as logical buses, although they may be physically implemented in bus or star topologies. Each frame is transmitted to every station on the link but read only by the station to which it is addressed. Figure 9.10 shows the four implementations of traditional Ethernet.

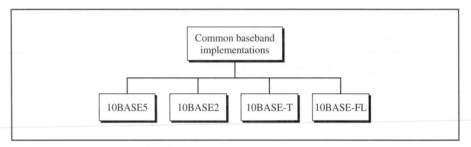

Figure 9.10 Implementations of Ethernet

Figure 9.11 shows the topology and physical connection of a station to the medium for each implementation.

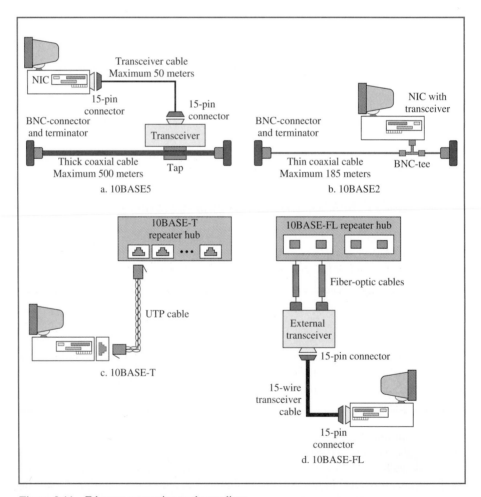

Figure 9.11 Ethernet connection to the medium

10BASE5: Thick Ethernet The first of the physical standards defined in the IEEE 802.3 standard is called **10BASE5, thick Ethernet,** or **Thicknet.** The nickname derives from the size of the cable, which is roughly the size of garden hose and too stiff to bend with your hands. 10BASE5 is a physical bus topology LAN that uses baseband signaling and has a maximum segment length of 500 meters.

10BASE2: Thin Ethernet The second Ethernet implementation defined by the IEEE 802 standard is called **10BASE2** or **thin Ethernet.** Thin Ethernet (also called **Thinnet, cheapnet, cheapernet,** and thin-wire Ethernet) provides an inexpensive alternative to 10BASE5 Ethernet, with the same data rate. Like 10BASE5, 10BASE2 is a physical bus topology LAN. The advantages of thin Ethernet include reduced cost and ease of installation (the cable is lighter weight and more flexible than that used in thick Ethernet). The disadvantages include a shorter range (185 meters as opposed to the 500 meters available with thick Ethernet) and smaller capacity (the thinner cable accommodates fewer stations). In many situations, these disadvantages are irrelevant, and the cost savings make 10BASE2 the better choice.

10BASE-T: Twisted-Pair Ethernet The most popular standard defined in the IEEE 802.3 series is **10BASE-T** (also called **twisted-pair Ethernet**), a physical star-topology LAN using unshielded twisted-pair (UTP) cable. It supports a data rate of 10 Mbps and has a maximum length (hub to station) of 100 meters.

10BASE-T Ethernet places all of its networking operations in an intelligent hub with a port for each station. Stations are linked into the hub by a four-pair cable (eight-wire UTP) terminated at each end by a male-type connector much like a telephone jack. The hub fans out any transmitted frame to all of its connected stations. Logic in the NIC assures that the only station to open and read a given frame is the station to which that frame is addressed.

10BASE-FL: Fiber Link Ethernet Although several types of fiber-optic 10-Mbps Ethernet are defined, the one implemented by most vendors is called **10BASE-FL** or **fiber link Ethernet.** 10BASE-FL uses a physical star topology to connect stations to a hub.

TECHNICAL FOCUS: ETHERNET FRAME

Traditional Ethernet has a frame with the following format:

Preamble 56 bits of alternating 1s and 0s.
SFD   Start field delimiter, flag (10101011)

Preamble	SFD	Destination address	Source address	Length PDU	Data and Padding	CRC
7 bytes	1 byte	6 bytes	6 bytes	2 bytes		4 bytes

SWITCHED ETHERNET

Traditional Ethernet uses a logical bus topology. The physical transmission media (physical bus or physical star) is shared between all stations. This means that if 10 stations have data to send at the same time, 9 stations must wait until that one station that has obtained access to the media is finished sending. This means that the data rate for traditional Ethernet is less than 10 Mbps if more than one station has data to send. The time used that is spent in waiting must also be considered. If a station has 10 Mbits of data to send, it can send it in one second if there is no waiting. However, if the station has to wait 4 seconds before sending its data, the total time spent is 5 seconds; the data rate has effectively been reduced to 10/5 or 2 Mbps. The 10 Mbps data rate in traditional Ethernet is shared between the number of stations that have data to send.

To improve the data rate, we move from a logical bus to a logical star topology. We use a physical star topology and replace the hub with a switch. A switch in this context is a device that opens the received frame and reads the physical address of the frame. It then directs the frame to the appropriate port. In this case, only the lengths of the medium that are connected to the true sender and the true receiver are occupied; the other stations can exchange data without interfering with each other. See Figure 9.12.

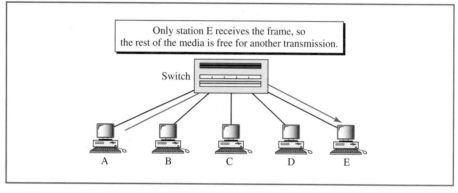

Figure 9.12   Switched Ethernet

If there are two links between a station and the switch (one for sending and one for receiving), each station becomes independent of any other station. Each station can send data to the switch and receive data from the switch. Of course, the switch must be sophisticated enough to store the data and distribute them accordingly.

No Need for CSMA/CD
In full-duplex switched Ethernet, there is no need for the CSMA/CD access method. In a switched full-duplex Ethernet, each station is connected to the switch via two separate links. Each station or switch can send and receive independently without worrying about collision. Each link is a point-to-point dedicated path between the station and the switch. There is no more need for carrier sensing, there is no more need for collision detection. The job of the MAC layer becomes much easier since the carrier sense and collision detection functionality of the MAC sublayer can be turned off.

FAST ETHERNET

The need for a higher data rate resulted in the design of the Fast Ethernet protocol (100 Mbps). Theoretically, Fast Ethernet is traditional Ethernet transmitting 10 times faster. The only thing that needs to be changed is the length of the network because sending data 10 times faster means collision must be detected 10 times earlier. This implies that with the same speed of propagation, the length of the network must be 10 times shorter. However, in practice, implementation of this approach required changes in other components such as the transmission media as we will see in the next section.

Fast Ethernet Implementation

Fast Ethernet can be categorized as either a two-wire or four-wire implementation. The two-wire implementation is called 100BASE-X, which can be either twisted-pair cable (100BASE-TX) or fiber-optic cable (100BASE-FX). The four-wire implementation is designed only for twisted-pair cable (100BASE-T4). In other words, we have three implementations: 100BASE-TX, 100BASE-FX, and 100BASE-T4 as shown in Figure 9.13.

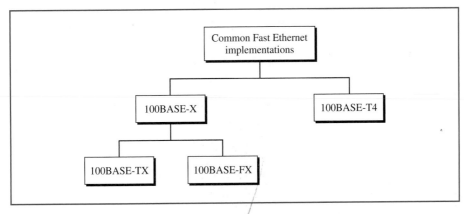

Figure 9.13 Fast Ethernet implementations

Figure 9.14 shows the topology and connection of the stations to the medium for each implementation of Fast Ethernet.

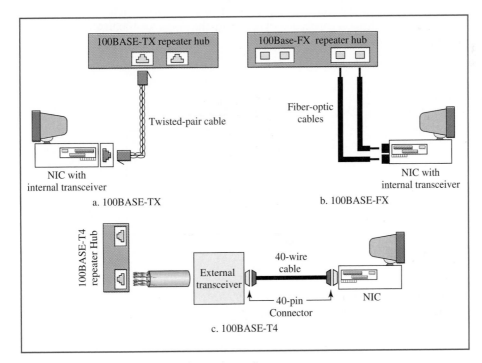

Figure 9.14 Fast Ethernet connection to the medium

100BASE-TX   **100BASE-TX** uses two pairs of twisted-pair cable (either category-5 UTP or STP) in a physical star topology. The logical topology is star for both half-duplex mode (CSMA/CD needed) and full-duplex mode (no need for CSMA/CD).

100BASE-FX   **100BASE-FX** uses two pairs of fiber-optic cable in a physical star topology. The logical topology is either a star or a bus as discussed in the 100BASE-TX implementation. Figure 9.14 shows the connection of a station to the medium and hub.

100BASE-T4   A 100BASE-TX network can provide a data rate of 100 Mbps, but it requires the use of category-5 UTP or STP cable. This is not cost efficient for buildings that already have been wired for voice grade twisted-pair (category 3). A new standard, called **100BASE-T4** was designed to use category 3 or higher UTP. The implementation uses 4 pairs of UTP for transmitting 100 Mbps. Figure 9.14 shows the connection of a station in a 100BASE-T4 network.

GIGABIT ETHERNET

The recent need for an even higher data rate resulted in the design of the Gigabit Ethernet protocol (1000 Mbps). Gigabit Ethernet uses a different approach from traditional Ethernet. This design uses a switched network with full-duplex transmission that totally eliminates the need for CSMA/CD.

Gigabit Ethernet Implementation

Gigabit Ethernet can be categorized as either a two-wire or four-wire implementation. The two-wire implementation is called 1000BASE-X, which can use short-wave optical fiber (1000BASE-SX), long-wave optical fiber (1000BASE-LX), or short copper jumpers (1000BASE-CX). The four-wire version uses twisted-pair cable (1000BASE-T). In other words, we have four implementations as shown in Figure 9.15. Figure 9.16 shows the topology and the physical connection of stations to the media for 1000BASE-SX/LX and 1000BASE-T.

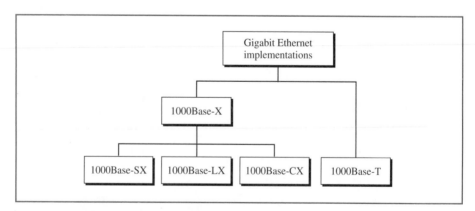

Figure 9.15   Gigabit Ethernet implementations

1000BASE-X   Both **1000BASE-SX** and **1000BASE-LX** use two pairs of fiber-optic media. The only difference between them is that the former uses a shortwave optical laser source and the latter uses a longwave optical laser source.

The **1000BASE-CX** implementation was designed to use STP cable, but it has yet to be implemented.

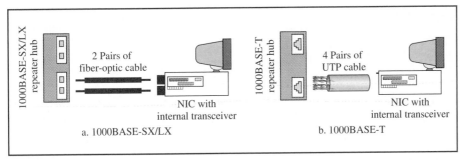

Figure 9.16   Gigabit Ethernet connection to the medium

1000BASE-T   To use category-5 UTP, **1000BASE-T** was designed. Four twisted pairs achieve a transmission rate of 1 Gbps.

TECHNICAL FOCUS: TOKEN RING NETWORKS

At the beginning of the LAN era, a LAN technology called Token Ring was developed by IBM and standardized under IEEE 802.5. It was designed to operate under two different data rates: 4 and 16 Mbps.

Token Ring was originally popular because, compared to traditional Ethernet, there is no collision on the network. However, with the advent of switched Ethernet, Fast Ethernet, and Gigabit Ethernet, Ethernet technology does not use CSMA/CD for medium access and there is no collision in modern Ethernet LANs. In addition, the data rate of Token Ring (4 or 16 Mbps) cannot compete with the 100 Mbps and 1 Gbps data rate of Ethernet.

Topology

The Token Ring network uses a ring topology as discussed in a previous Technical Focus box.

Access Method: Token Passing

Instead of CSMA/CD, Token Ring uses a token passing method. Whenever the network is unoccupied, a token circulates freely from one station to another. When a station has data to send, it captures the token and sends its frame. The sending station waits until it receives news about the frame (positive or negative). It then releases the token so that other stations have an opportunity to send data. The following figure shows the operation of the token passing method.

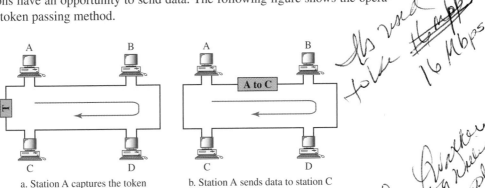

a. Station A captures the token   b. Station A sends data to station C

CASE STUDY

NEW AGE HOME PHARMACY

N AHP installed its LANs in 1998. Each floor has a full-duplex switched 10BASE-T network. Recall that such a network has no need for CSMA/CD. The access method is available, but not in use.

The following figure shows the layout of floors 2 and 3, occupied by the administrative assistants, accountants, and insurance clerks. The first floor (delivery room) and the top three floors, occupied by the pharmacists and technicians, have fewer computers, and thus a simpler configuration.

The 10BASE-T switch installed in the closet can support up to 24 devices. For floors 2 to 3, only

16 ports are in use, with the rest reserved for future additional devices. The closet is well ventilated and the temperature is set to the range recommended by the switch manufacturer.

Four pairs of category 5 unshielded twisted pair (UTP) cable connect each device to the switch. The UTP cables are bundled together and placed in conduits beneath the false floor. The cable connects to each station through an outlet installed under the desk of each user.

In future chapters we will see how NAHP's six LANs (one per floor) are connected to a backbone.

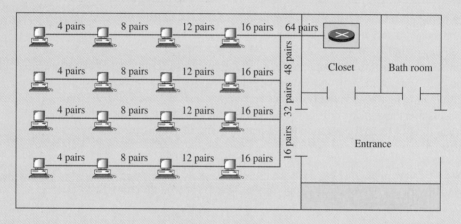

9.3 KEY TERMS

1000BASE-CX	carrier sense multiple access (CSMA)
1000BASE-LX	carrier sense multiple access with
1000BASE-SX	collision detection (CSMA/CD)
1000BASE-T	client-server model
100BASE-FX	connecting device
100BASE-T4	Fast Ethernet
100BASE-TX	full-duplex Ethernet
100BASE-X	general server
10BASE2	Gigabit Ethernet
10BASE5	half-duplex Ethernet
10BASE-FL	hub
10BASE-T	IEEE Project 802
application program	logical bus topology

logical link control (LLC)
logical star topology
logical topology
medium access control (MAC)
multiple access (MA)
network interface card (NIC)
network operating system (NOS)
peer-to-peer model
physical bus topology
physical star topology

physical topology
ring topology
star topology
station
switch
switched Ethernet
terminator
token passing
transmission media

9.4 SUMMARY

❏   Ethernet is the dominant LAN technology.
❏   The hardware components of a LAN include the stations, the transmission media, and connecting devices.
❏   The software components of a LAN include the network operating system and the application programs.
❏   A LAN can be configured either as a client-server LAN or a peer-to-peer LAN.
❏   LANs are commonly used as office networks, industry networks, and backbone networks.
❏   The two dominant physical LAN topologies are the bus and the star.
❏   The two dominant logical LAN topologies are the bus and the star.
❏   IEEE Project 802 set standards to enable intercommunication between equipment from a variety of manufacturers.
❏   Traditional Ethernet, with a data rate of 10 Mbps, uses CSMA/CD for its access method. The most popular implementation of traditional Ethernet is 10BASE-T.
❏   A switch allows each station on an Ethernet LAN to have the entire capacity of the network to itself. In full-duplex switched Ethernet, there is no need for the CSMA/CD access method.
❏   Fast Ethernet, with a data rate of 100 Mbps, has a maximum network length that is 10 percent that of traditional Ethernet.
❏   Gigabit Ethernet, with a data rate of 1000 Mbps, uses a switched network with full-duplex transmission that totally eliminates the need for CSMA/CD.
❏   Token Ring uses an access method that eliminates collision.

 PRACTICE SET

Review Questions

1. Discuss the size of a local area network.
2. What are the components of a LAN that can be classified as hardware?
3. What are the components of a LAN that can be classified as software?
4. What is a network interface card (NIC)?
5. What is a network operating system (NOS)?

6. What can be shared by users in a LAN office environment?
7. What is the difference between the terms *logical topology* and *physical topology?*
8. Compare a break in the medium of a LAN with a physical bus topology to a break in a LAN with a physical star topology.
9. What is the purpose of a terminator?
10. What is the purpose of IEEE Project 802?
11. Explain CSMA/CD and its use.
12. What is a collision?
13. Why should there be fewer collisions on a switched Ethernet network compared to a traditional Ethernet?
14. Compare the data transmission rates for traditional Ethernet, Fast Ethernet, and Gigabit Ethernet.

Multiple-Choice Questions

15. The size of a LAN is limited to a radius of a few _____.
    a. feet
    b. yards
    c. buildings
    d. miles
16. Traditional Ethernet has a data rate of _____ Mbps.
    a. 1
    b. 10
    c. 100
    d. 1000
17. _____ are considered a part of LAN hardware.
    a. Stations
    b. Transmission media
    c. Connecting devices
    d. All of the above
18. A _____ is software that allows the logical connection of stations and devices to the network.
    a. network interface card
    b. program application
    c. network operating system
    d. client-server program
19. If a network has a server that only handles email, this is called a _____ server.
    a. general
    b. dedicated
    c. client
    d. switch
20. In a _____ LAN, a station can be both a client and a server.
    a. peer-to-peer
    b. client-server
    c. dedicated
    d. general

21. A high-speed LAN can be used as a _____ to connect several low-speed networks.
    a. backbone
    b. switch
    c. terminator
    d. server

22. In a physical _____ topology, there must be a terminator at both ends.
    a. bus
    b. star
    c. ring
    d. all of the above

23. In a physical _____ topology, each station is connected to a central node.
    a. bus
    b. star
    c. ring
    d. all of the above

24. In a physical star topology, the _____ can check the address of a received frame.
    a. bus
    b. hub
    c. terminator
    d. switch

25. The physical _____ is the dominant topology today.
    a. bus
    b. star
    c. ring
    d. hub

26. IEEE Project 802 divides the data link layer into an upper _____ sublayer and a lower _____ sublayer.
    a. LLC, MAC
    b. MAC, LLC
    c. PDU, HDLC
    d. HDLC, PDU

27. In CSMA/CD, the number of collisions is probably _____ that in MA.
    a. greater than
    b. less than
    c. equal to
    d. twice

28. _____ uses a physical star topology.
    a. 10BASE5
    b. 10BASE2
    c. 10BASE-T
    d. none of the above

29. 10BASE2 uses _____ cable, while 10BASE5 uses _____.
   a. thick, thin
   b. twisted-pair, thick
   c. thin, thick
   d. fiber-optic, thin
30. 100BASE-X differs from 100BASE-T4 in _____.
   a. the data transmission rate
   b. topology
   c. the number of cables between the station and the hub
   d. all of the above

CHAPTER 10

Local Area Networks
Part 2: Wireless and Virtual LANs

Although the majority of LANs today are wired Ethernet LANs, wireless technology is finding its place in LAN architecture. Wireless LANs (WLANs) have specific applications, as we will see in this chapter. The need for these applications is becoming widespread, resulting in research and investment in wireless technology.

Wireless technology can be used for mid-size and small-size LANs. We discuss two standards that address these LAN categories: IEEE 802.11 and IEEE 802.15.

We also discuss virtual LANs in this chapter. A virtual LAN (VLAN) is not a new type of LAN; it is configuring an existing LAN to create several virtual segments. The technique allows an organization to divide a LAN into virtual (or logical) segments to provide efficiency and security.

OBJECTIVES

After reading this chapter, the reader should:

- Understand the different transmission techniques used in wireless LANs.
- Understand the main characteristics of IEEE 802.11 wireless LANs.
- Understand the applications of IEEE 802.11.
- Understand the characteristics of IEEE 802.15 LANs and the

Bluetooth technology that implements this standard.
- Understand the concept of virtual LANs.
- Understand the applications and rationale for VLANs.

10.1 WIRELESS LANs

Wireless communication is one of the fastest growing technologies. The demand for mobile devices has led to a need for wireless local area networks. Wireless LANs (WLANs) use radio or infrared waves to transmit data through the air. Wireless LANs provide mobility for users with usually a much lower data rate.

Applications for wireless LANs include the use of mobile stations in manufacturing or warehouse areas, construction sites, and medical and health care facilities.

Wireless technology is dominated today by two standards: IEEE 802.11 and IEEE 802.15. In this section, we first discuss transmission methods that are used by these standards before we discuss the standards themselves.

WIRELESS TRANSMISSION

Wireless LANs use two types of signals for transmission: radio frequency and infrared.

Radio Frequency Transmission

Radio frequency (RF) **signals,** having frequencies in the 1 to 20 GHz range, can be used to transmit data between stations in a wireless LAN. In 1985, the Federal Communications Commission (FCC) modified the radio spectrum regulations for unlicensed devices. The modification authorizes wireless LANs to operate in industrial, scientific, or medical (ISM) bands. The use of these bands does not require a license from the FCC if the equipment operates under 1 watt of power. Figure 10.1 shows the ISM bands.

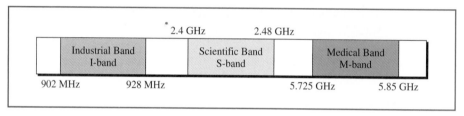

Figure 10.1   ISM bands

Note that the 902 MHz band and the 5.725 GHz band are available only in the United States; the 2.4 GHz band is available globally.

The RF signals are transmitted using one of two techniques: **frequency hopping spread spectrum** (FHSS) or **direct sequence spread spectrum** (DSSS).

FHSS   In this scheme, the sender sends on one carrier frequency for a short period of time, then hops to another carrier frequency for the same period of time, hops again to another frequency for the same period of time, and so on. After *N* hoppings, the cycle is repeated. The idea of FHSS is shown in Figure 10.2.

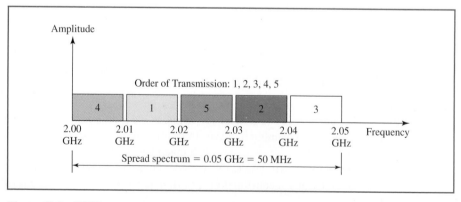

Figure 10.2   FHSS

Spreading prevents an intruder from gaining information. The sender and receiver agree on the sequence of the allocated bands. In the figure, the first bit (or group of bits) is sent in band 1, the second bit (or group of bits) is sent in band 2, and so on. An intruder who tunes his receiver to the frequencies in band 1 may receive the first bit, but receives nothing in this band during the second bit interval.

DSSS In this scheme, each bit to be sent by the sender is replaced by a sequence of bits called a **chip code.** The time needed to send one original bit should be the same as the time needed to send one chip code. This means that the data rate for sending chip codes must be N (N is the number of bits in each chip code) times the data rate of the original bit stream. For example, if the sender generates the original bit stream at 1 Mbps, and the chip code is 6 bits in length, the data rate for transferring chip codes must be $1 \times 6 = 6$ Mbps. Figure 10.3 shows the idea of DSSS.

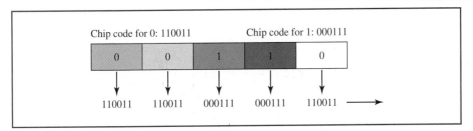

Figure 10.3 DSSS

Infrared Transmission
Another alternative for a wireless LAN is the use of **infrared waves.** Infrared transmission has some advantages over radio frequency transmission:

❏ Infrared is more secure because it cannot propagate through opaque objects such as walls.
❏ Infrared is immune to some types of electromagnetic interference such as radio transmission or microwave ovens.
❏ Infrared has a large bandwidth that allows higher data rates.

However, infrared transmission also has some disadvantages:

❏ Infrared is not suitable for mobile units because of its limited range.
❏ Infrared cannot propagate through opaque objects such as walls.
❏ Weather conditions (rain, fog, smog, and dust) severely affect the performance of infrared propagation.

10.2 IEEE 802.11: RF LANs

The IEEE 802.11 standard defines a mid-size LAN that can use either radio frequency or infrared transmission.

ARCHITECTURE

The standard defines two kinds of services: basic service set (BSS) and extended service set (ESS).

Basic Service Set

The IEEE 802.11 defines the **basic service set** (BSS) as the building block of a wireless LAN. A basic service set is made of stationary or mobile wireless stations and an optional central base station, known as the **access point** (AP). Figure 10.4 shows a set in this standard.

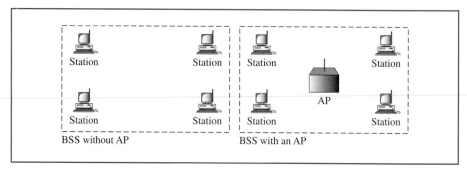

Figure 10.4   BSS

The BSS without an AP is a stand-alone network and cannot send data to other BSSs. It is called an *ad hoc architecture.*

Extended Service Set

An **extended service set** (ESS) is made up of two or more BSSs with APs. In this case, the BSSs are connected through a *distribution system,* which is usually a wired LAN. The distribution system connects the APs in the BSSs. The IEEE 802.11 does not restrict the distribution system; it can be any IEEE LAN such as an Ethernet or Token Ring. Note that the extended service set uses two types of stations: mobile and stationary. The mobile stations are normal stations inside a BSS. The stationary stations are AP stations that are part of a wired LAN. Figure 10.5 shows an ESS.

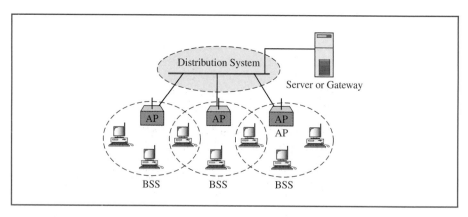

Figure 10.5   ESS

When BSSs are connected together, we have what is called an *infrastructure network*. In this network, the stations within reach of each other can communicate without the use of an AP. However, the communication between two stations in two different BSSs usually occurs via two APs. Note that a mobile station can belong to more than one BSS at the same time.

STATION TYPES

IEEE 802.11 defines three types of stations based on their mobility in a wireless LAN: no-transition, BSS-transition, and ESS-transition.

No-Transition Mobility

A station with **no-transition** mobility is either stationary (not moving) or moving only inside a BSS.

BSS-Transition Mobility

A station with **BSS-transition** mobility can move from one BSS to another, but the movement is confined inside one ESS.

ESS-Transition Mobility

A station with **ESS-transition** mobility can move from one ESS to another. However, IEEE 802.11 does not guarantee that communication is continuous when a station moves from one ESS to another.

TECHNICAL FOCUS: PORTABLE VERSUS MOBILE

In networking two terms are used to define nonstationary devices: portable and mobile. The term *portable* means that a device may move from one location to another, but it remains in a fixed place when in use. The term *mobile* means that the station can move during operation.

ACCESS METHOD

Wireless LANs use a contention method called **carrier sense multiple access with collision avoidance** (CSMA/CA), which is similar to the CSMA/CD used in Ethernet. Here, however, collision is avoided (instead of being allowed and detected). In this method when a station needs to send data, it senses the medium (air) and if there is no other station sending, the station sends a special packet to make a reservation for the time needed for its transmission. Other stations do not try to access the medium during this period.

TECHNICAL FOCUS: HIDDEN NODE PROBLEM

In a wired Ethernet, when a station sends a frame, every station connected to the shared medium senses (hears) the signal; stations are not hidden (electronically) from each other. On the other hand, in a wireless network, two stations may be separated from each other by a physical barrier (such as a wall). They are hidden (electronically) from each other.

In this case, both of these stations may start sending a frame at the same time without sensing the signal coming from the other station. In other words, a collision may occur without either station detecting it. This means that the CSMA/CD access method, which is based on the detection of a collision by the sender, does not work here.

The appropriate access method for wireless LANs is CSMA/CA, which does not depend on the detection of a collision. In this method the AP, which is supposed to be heard by every station, is the controller. When a station needs to send a frame to another station, it sends a request to send (RTS) message to the AP. The AP reserves the medium for this transmission by sending a clear to send (CTS) message to the requesting station.

IMPLEMENTATION

IEEE 802.11 defines three implementations: low-speed radio frequency LANs (802.11b), high-speed radio frequency LANs (802.11a), and infrared LANs.

IEEE 802.11a

Wireless LANs that operate under this standard use the 5.7-GHz ISM band with a data rate up to 54 Mbps. The ideal situation would be to increase the data rate to 100 Mbps to be compatible with Fast Ethernet.

IEEE 802.11b

Wireless LANs that operate under this standard use the 2.4-GHz ISM band with a data rate up to 11 Mbps (compatible with traditional Ethernet). The standard was designed for less expensive and less sophisticated equipment. The standard also allows the equipment to fall back to lower rates such as 5.5, 2, or 1 Mbps if the environment conditions do not support 11 Mbps.

TECHNICAL FOCUS: WIRELESS LAN ADDRESSING

The addressing mechanism in a wireless LAN is more complicated than in a wired LAN. In a wireless LAN a frame may travel:

1. from a station to another station in the same BSS.
2. from a station in one BSS to another station in another BSS.

In the second case, the frame journey is made of three trips:

a. from the source station to the AP of the source BSS.
b. from the AP of the source BSS to the AP of the destination BSS.
c. from the AP of the destination BSS to the destination station.

For this reason, a wireless frame has four address fields. The first address always defines the address of the next station (a station or an AP). The second address defines the address of the previous station (a station or an AP). In case 1, the third address defines the ID of the BSS and the fourth is ignored. In case 2, the third and the fourth addresses define the original source, the final destination, or the intermediate addresses.

10.3 IEEE 802.11: INFRARED LANs

LANs that use infrared operate under two different configurations: point-to-point and diffused.

POINT-TO-POINT

The point-to-point infrared LAN features point-to-point links between computers, bridges, or switches. The most common application is a wireless Token Ring network as shown in Figure 10.6.

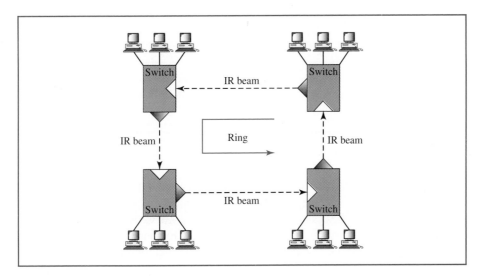

Figure 10.6   Infrared point-to-point LAN

In the figure, point-to-point infrared links create a Token Ring backbone between switches.

DIFFUSED

The diffused infrared LAN uses a reflecting object (a ceiling, for example). All of the transmitters at each station are focused to the ceiling. The ceiling reflects the infrared signals which can be received by all the stations in the network. Figure 10.7 shows one configuration.

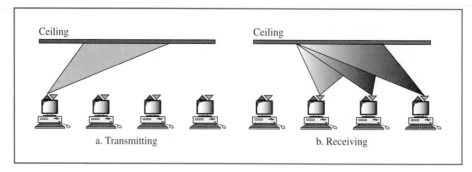

Figure 10.7   Infrared diffused LAN

10.4   IEEE 802.15 LANs: BLUETOOTH LANs

Bluetooth technology is the implementation of a protocol defined by the IEEE 802.15 standard. The standard defines a wireless personal area network (wireless PAN) operable in an area the size of a room or a hall. The standard specifies the use of short-range radio frequencies with a data rate from 1 to 20 Mbps. It is designed for small wireless LANs (8 to 16 stations) operating on battery power.

BUSINESS FOCUS: BLUETOOTH

Bluetooth was named after the king of Denmark, who tried to unite all of the Baltic Region countries (Denmark, Sweden, Norway, and Finland). He united Denmark and Norway, but was killed by his son in 986.

APPLICATIONS

Bluetooth technology has several applications. The peripheral devices of a computer can communicate with the computer through this technology (wireless mouse or keyboard). Monitoring devices can communicate with sensor devices in a small health care center. Home security devices can use this technology to connect different sensors to the main security controller. Conference attendees can synchronize their palmtop computers at a conference.

ARCHITECTURE

IEEE 802.15 defines two types of networks: piconets and scatternet.

Piconets

A Bluetooth network is called a **piconet,** a small net. A piconet can have up to eight stations, one of which is called the master; the rest are called slaves. All of the slave stations synchronize their clocks and hopping sequence with the master slave. Note that a piconet can have only one master station. The communication between the master and the slaves can be one-to-one or one-to-many. Figure 10.8 shows a piconet.

Although a piconet can have a maximum of seven slaves, an additional eight slaves can be in the *parked state*. A slave in a parked state is synchronized with the master, but

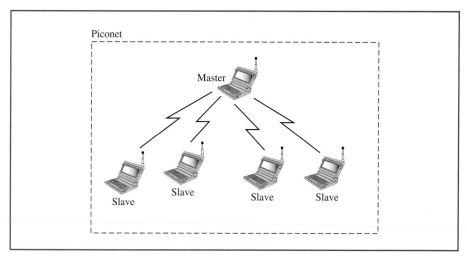

Figure 10.8   Piconet

cannot take part in communication until it is moved from the parked state. Because only eight stations can be active in a piconet, activating a station from the parked state means that an active station must go to the parked state.

Scatternet

Piconets can be combined to form what is called a **scatternet.** A slave station in one piconet can become the master in another piconet. This station can receive messages from the master in the first piconet (as a slave) and, acting as a master, deliver it to slaves in the second piconet. A station can be a member of two piconets. Figure 10.9 illustrates a scatternet.

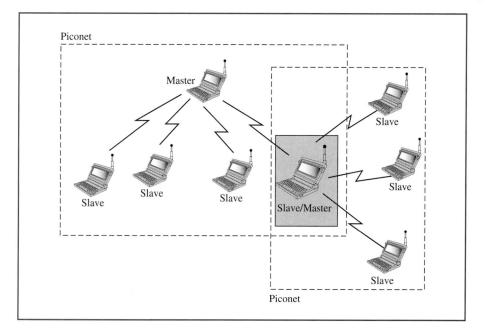

Figure 10.9   Scatternet

BLUETOOTH DEVICES

A Bluetooth device has a built-in short-range radio transmitter. The current data rate is 1 Mbps with a 2.4 GHz bandwidth. This means that there is a possibility of interference between the IEEE 11.b wireless LANs and Bluetooth LANs.

10.5 VIRTUAL LANs

We can roughly define a virtual local area network (VLAN) as a subnetwork or a segment of a local area network configured by software, not by physical wiring.

Let us use an example to elaborate on this definition. Figure 10.10 shows a switched LAN in an engineering firm in which 10 stations are grouped into three segments that are connected by a switch.

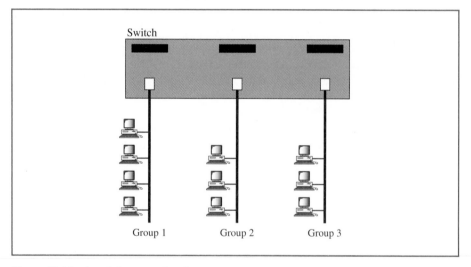

Figure 10.10 A switch connecting three segments

One reason for segmentation is to make broadcasting (sending a message to every station in the segment) possible at the data link layer. In other words, the stations in each segment form a group that can be the recipient of a broadcast message. The message can come from some station in the group or from another station outside of the group. In this configuration, people can work in a group. In our example, the first four engineers work together as the first group, the next three engineers work together as the second group, and the last two engineers work together as the third group. The LAN is configured to allow this arrangement.

But what happens if the managers need to move two engineers from the first group to the third group to speed up the project being done by the third group? The LAN configuration would need to be changed. The network technician must rewire. The problem reoccurs if in another week, the two engineers move back to their previous group. In a switched LAN, changes in the workgroup mean physical changes in the network configuration.

Figure 10.11 shows the same switched LAN divided into VLANs.

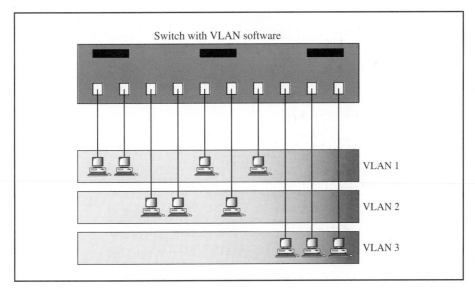

Figure 10.11　A switch using VLAN software

The whole idea of VLAN technology is to divide a LAN into logical, instead of physical, segments. A LAN can be divided into several logical LANs called VLANs. Each VLAN is a workgroup in the organization. If a person moves from one group to another, there is no need to change the physical configuration. The group membership in VLANs is defined by software, not hardware. Any station can be logically moved to another VLAN. All members belonging to a VLAN can receive broadcast messages sent to that particular VLAN. This means if a station moves from VLAN 1 to VLAN 2, it receives broadcast messages sent to VLAN 2, but no longer receives broadcast messages sent to VLAN 1.

It is obvious that the problem in our previous example can easily be solved using VLANs. Moving two engineers from one group to another using software is easier than changing the configuration of the physical network.

VLAN technology even allows the grouping of stations connected to different switches in a VLAN. Figure 10.12 shows a backbone local area network with two switches and three VLANs. Stations from switch A and B belong to each VLAN.

This is a good configuration for a company with two separate buildings. Each building can have its own switched LAN connected together by a backbone. People in the first building and people in the second building can be in the same workgroup even though they are connected to different physical LANs.

From these three examples, we can define a VLAN characteristic:

VLANs create broadcast domains.

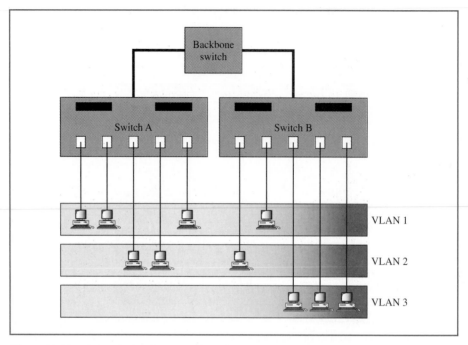

Figure 10.12 Two switches in a backbone using VLAN software

VLANs group stations belonging to one or more physical LANs into broadcast domains. The stations in a VLAN communicate with each other and with the stations outside the VLAN as though they belong to a physical segment.

MEMBERSHIP

What characteristic can be used to group stations in a VLAN? Vendors use a characteristic such as port number, MAC address, IP address, or a combination of two or more of the above.

Port Numbers

Some VLAN vendors use switch port numbers as a membership characteristic. For example, the administrator can group stations connecting to ports 1, 2, 3, and 7 into VLAN 1, stations connecting to ports 4, 10, and 12 into VLAN 2 and so on.

MAC Addresses

Some VLAN vendors use the 48-bit MAC address as a membership characteristic. For example, the administrator can group stations having MAC addresses E21342A12334 and F2A123BCD341 into VLAN 1.

IP Addresses

Some VLAN vendors use the 32-bit IP address as a membership characteristic. For example, the administrator can group stations with IP addresses 181.34.23.67, 181.34.23.72, 181.34.23.98, and 181.34.23.112 into VLAN 1.

Combination

Recently, the software available from some vendors allows all of these characteristics to be used in combination. The administrator can choose one or more characteristics when installing the software. In addition, the software can be reconfigured to change the settings.

CONFIGURATION

How are the stations grouped into different VLANs? Stations are configured in one of three ways: manual, semiautomatic, or automatic.

Manual Configuration

In a manual configuration, the network administrator uses the VLAN software to manually assign the stations into different VLANs at set up. Later migration from one VLAN to another is also done manually. Note that this is not a physical configuration; it is a logical configuration. The term *manually* here means the administrator types the port numbers, the IP addresses, or another characteristic using the VLAN software.

Automatic Configuration

In an automatic configuration, the stations are automatically connected or disconnected from a VLAN using criteria defined by the administrator. For example, the administrator can define the project number as the criteria for being a member of a group. When a user leaves the project, he or she automatically migrates to a new VLAN.

Semiautomatic Configuration

A semiautomatic configuration is something between a manual configuration and an automatic configuration. Usually, the initializing is done manually, with migrations done automatically.

COMMUNICATION BETWEEN SWITCHES

In a multiswitch backbone, each switch must know not only which station belongs to which VLAN, but also must know the membership of stations connected to other switches. For example, in Figure 10.12, switch A must know the membership status of stations connected to switch B, and switch B must know the same about switch A. Three methods have been devised for this purpose: table maintenance, frame tagging, and time-division multiplexing (TDM).

Table Maintenance

In this method, when a station sends a broadcast frame to its group members, the switch creates an entry in a table and records station membership. The switches send their tables to each other periodically for updating.

Frame Tagging

In this method, an extra header called a frame tag is added to the MAC frame traveling between switches to define the destination VLAN. The frame tag is used by the receiving switches to determine the VLANs to receive the broadcast message.

Time-Division Multiplexing (TDM)

In this method, the connection (trunk) between switches is divided into time-shared channels (see TDM in Chapter 3). For example, if the total number of VLANs in a backbone is 5, each trunk is divided into 5 channels. The traffic destined for VLAN 1 travels in channel 1, the traffic destined for VLAN 2 travels in channel 2, and so on. The receiving switch determines the destination VLAN by checking the channel from which the packet arrived.

IEEE STANDARD

In 1996, the IEEE 802.1 subcommittee passed a standard called 802.1Q that defines the format for frame tagging. The standard also defines the format to be used in multi-switched backbones and enables the use of multivendor equipment in VLANs. 802.1Q has opened the way for further standardization in other issues related to VLANs. Most vendors have already accepted the standard.

ADVANTAGES

There are several advantages to using VLANs.

Cost and Time Reduction

VLANs can reduce the migration cost of stations going from one group to another. Physical reconfiguration takes time and is costly. Instead of physically moving one station to another segment or even to another switch, it is much easier and quicker to move it using software.

Creating Virtual Workgroups

VLANs can be used to create virtual workgroups. For example, in a campus environment, professors working on the same project can send broadcast messages to each other without the necessity of belonging to the same department. This can reduce traffic if the multicasting capability of IP was previously used.

Security

VLANs provide an extra measure of security. People belonging to the same group can send broadcast messages with the guaranteed assurance that users in other groups will not receive these messages.

CASE STUDY

NEW AGE HOME PHARMACY

NAHP uses VLAN technology. The software was installed when a board member thought there should be better communication between employees who had similar tasks. She felt that the subnetworks should be configured according to task, not location. In other words, the employees involved in billing would comprise one network, the pharmacists and technicians another, and so on. Her request was sent to the consulting firm who recommended the use of VLAN technology to create the new logical subnetworks. There was no need to physically reconfigure the networks. The board members were delighted that this technology could achieve their goal quickly and significantly cheaper. A computer was installed in the basement (where the backbone switch is located) to reorganize the six LANs into five virtual LANs as shown in the following figure.

NAHP currently uses no types of wireless technology. However, management is negotiating to buy an eight-story building just across the street. One of the first questions raised in the board of directors' meeting concerned the connection method between the existing backbones in each of the two buildings. The network consultant proposed wireless technology. His idea is to install a microwave antenna on each roof to provide communication between the two buildings.

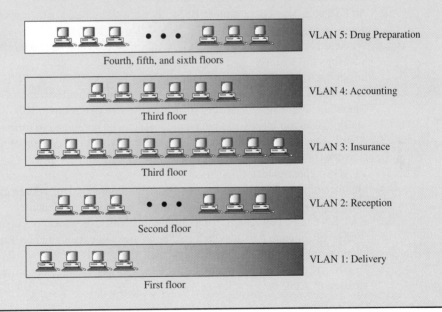

VLAN 5: Drug Preparation
Fourth, fifth, and sixth floors

VLAN 4: Accounting
Third floor

VLAN 3: Insurance
Third floor

VLAN 2: Reception
Second floor

VLAN 1: Delivery
First floor

10.6   KEY TERMS

access point
ad hoc architecture
basic service set (BSS)
Bluetooth technology
BSS-transition mobility station

carrier sense multiple access with
    collision avoidance (CSMA/CD)
chip code
diffused infrared LAN
diffused transmission

direct sequence spread spectrum (DSSS)
ESS-transition mobility station
extended service set (ESS)
frame tagging
frequency hopping spread
   spectrum (FHSS)
infrared transmission
infrared waves
infrastructure network
no-transition mobility station

parked state
piconet
point-to-point infrared LAN
point-to-point transmission
radio frequency (RF) signals
scatternet
spread spectrum
virtual LAN (VLAN)
wireless LAN
wireless transmission

10.7   SUMMARY

❑   Wireless LANs use radio or infrared waves to transmit data through the air.
❑   Radio frequency signals are usually transmitted using the frequency hopping spread spectrum technique or the direct sequence spread spectrum technique.
❑   The IEEE 802.11 standard for wireless LANs defines two services: basic service set (BSS) and extended service set (ESS).
❑   An ESS consists of two or more BSSs; they are connected via their access points (APs).
❑   Wireless LANs use the CSMA/CA contention method and have data rates of 5.5 Mbps to 11 Mbps.
❑   Infrared LANs are classified as either point-to-point or diffused.
❑   Bluetooth is an implementation of IEEE 802.15 that provides wireless communication between devices in an area the size of a room or hall.
❑   Multiple Bluetooth networks called piconets can be combined to form a scatternet.
❑   A virtual local area network (VLAN) is a subnetwork or a segment of a local area network configured by software, not by physical wiring.
❑   VLANs create broadcast domains.
❑   Membership in a VLAN can be based on port numbers, MAC addresses, IP addresses, IP multicast addresses, or a combination of these features.
❑   A VLAN can be configured manually, automatically, or semiautomatically.
❑   VLANs attached to a multiswitch backbone uses table maintenance, frame tagging, or TDM for communication.
❑   VLANs are cost and time efficient, can reduce network traffic, and provide an extra measure of security.

 PRACTICE SET

Review Questions

1. What is the transmission medium for wireless LANs?
2. What kind of electromagnetic waves transmit data in wireless LANs?
3. What are the three bands authorized by the FCC for use by wireless LANs?
4. What is the difference between FHSS and DSSS?

5. What is the purpose of an AP in a BSS?
6. How is an ESS different from a BSS?
7. What are the two types of infrared LANs?
8. What sorts of companies would use Bluetooth technology?
9. What is the relationship between a piconet and a scatternet?
10. How does a VLAN save a company time and money?
11. How does a VLAN reduce network traffic?
12. What is the basis for membership in a VLAN?
13. What is the difference between a VLAN that is configured automatically versus a VLAN that is configured manually?
14. What is frame tagging?

Multiple-Choice Questions

15. A wireless LAN using DSSS with an 8-bit chip code needs _____ MHz for sending data that originally required a 10 MHz bandwidth.
    a. 2
    b. 8
    c. 20
    d. 80
16. A wireless LAN using DSSS with _____-bit chip code needs 320 MHz for sending data that originally required a 20 MHz bandwidth.
    a. a 2
    b. an 8
    c. a 16
    d. a 32
17. In an ESS the _____ mobile.
    a. AP is
    b. distribution system is
    c. stations inside a BSS are
    d. all of the above
18. A station with _____ mobility can move from one BSS to another.
    a. no-transition
    b. BSS-transition
    c. ESS-transition
    d. b and c
19. A station with _____ mobility can move from one ESS to another.
    a. no-transition
    b. BSS-transition
    c. ESS-transition
    d. b and c
20. A station with _____ mobility is either stationary or moving only inside a BSS.
    a. no-transition
    b. BSS-transition
    c. ESS-transition
    d. b and c

21. Wireless LANs use a contention method called _____.
    a. token passing
    b. CSMA
    c. CSMA/CD
    d. CSMA/CA

22. A _____ infrared LAN uses a reflecting object.
    a. point-to-point
    b. diffused
    c. multipoint
    d. a and c

23. A scatternet is made of multiple _____.
    a. VLANs
    b. ESSs
    c. piconets
    d. Ethernets

24. VLAN technology divides a LAN into _____ segments.
    a. physical
    b. logical
    c. multiplexed
    d. framed

25. Which station characteristic can be used to group stations into a VLAN?
    a. port number
    b. MAC address
    c. IP address
    d. all of the above

26. In a VLAN, the stations are separated into groups by _____.
    a. physical methods
    b. software methods
    c. location
    d. switches

27. If an administrator has to type in the station port numbers to create VLANs, this is called _____ configuration.
    a. a manual
    b. a physical
    c. an automatic
    d. a characteristic

28. If stations are automatically connected and disconnected from a VLAN using criteria defined by an administrator, this is called _____ configuration.
    a. a manual
    b. a physical
    c. an automatic
    d. a characteristic

29. In a multiswitch backbone, the switches can communicate through the _____ method.
    a. table maintenance
    b. frame tagging
    c. TDM
    d. all of the above

30. In the _____ method for switch communication, the connection is divided into time-shared channels.
    a. table maintenance
    b. frame tagging
    c. TDM
    d. FDM
31. In the _____ method for switch communication, an extra header is added to the MAC frame to define the destination VLAN.
    a. table maintenance
    b. frame tagging
    c. TDM
    d. FDM
32. In the _____ method for switch communication, switches exchange their tables periodically.
    a. table maintenance
    b. frame tagging
    c. TDM
    d. FDM
33. IEEE 802.1Q defines a standard for _____.
    a. IPsec
    b. ESPs
    c. VPNs
    d. frame tagging

CHAPTER 11

Wide Area Networks

A wide area network (WAN) spans a larger area than a local area network. This factor makes a WAN very different from a LAN in many respects. First, a WAN is a network usually provided by a specialized company called a network provider. Individual organizations can use the services offered by these companies. Second, WANs have different topologies from LANs. A WAN often uses switches, as intermediate nodes, to create many-to-many connections between end devices. Third, LANs use connectionless delivery; each packet is an independent entity with no relationship, from the network point of view, to other packets belonging to the same message. WANs, on the other hand, use connection-oriented delivery; each message is seen by the network as a series of packets with an ordered relationship. There is a first packet, a second packet, and so on. To establish this relationship, a WAN normally establishes a virtual connection (a channel) that lasts until all packets belonging to the same message are delivered.

In this chapter, we first discuss point-to-point WANs, WANs that do not use switches. Then we discuss switched WANs. We focus especially on ATM, the dominant WAN technology. Finally, we discuss ATM LANs, LANs that use ATM WAN technology.

OBJECTIVES

After reading this chapter, the reader should be able to:

❑ Understand point-to-point WAN technologies: T-lines and SONET networks.

❑ Understand X.25 technology and why it is losing popularity.

❑ Understand Frame Relay technology and how it was designed to replace X.25.

❑ Understand ATM technology and its importance in today's WAN market.

❑ Understand ATM LANs.

11.1 POINT-TO-POINT WANs

A point-to-point WAN connects two distant devices using a line available from a public network provider such as a telephone network. We have already discussed several point-to-point WANs (telephone lines, DSL lines, and cable TV lines) in Chapter 8. In this chapter, we discuss two more types of point-to-point WANs: those used by organizations to connect themselves to the Internet and those used by switched WANs to connect switches.

T LINES

T lines are standard digital telephone carriers originally designed to transmit multi-plexed voice channels (after being digitized). Today, however, T lines are also used to carry data between a residence or an organization and the Internet. They provide a physical link between nodes in a switched wide area network. T lines are commercially available in two data rates: T-1 and T-3 (see Table 11.1).

Table 11.1 *T-line rates*

Line	Rate (Mbps)	Voice Channels
T-1	1.544	24
T-3	44.736	672

T-1 Line

The data rate of a T-1 line is 1.544 Mbps. Originally a T-1 line was used to multiplex 24 voice channels. Each voice channel is sampled and each sample digitized to 8 bits. An extra bit is added to provide synchronization. This makes the frame 193 bits in length. By sending 8000 frames per second, we get a data rate of 1.544 Mbps. When we use a T-1 line to connect to the Internet, we can use all or part of the capacity of the line to send digital data. Figure 11.1 shows a T-1 line.

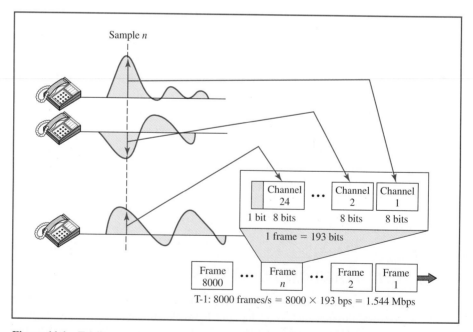

Figure 11.1 T-1 line

A T-1 line has a data rate of 1.544 Mbps.

T-3 Line

A T-3 line has a data rate of 44.736 Mbps. It is equivalent to 28 T-1 lines. In other words, 28 T-1 lines can be multiplexed to obtain a T-3 line.

A T-3 line has a data rate of 44.736 Mbps.

TECHNICAL FOCUS: FRACTIONAL T-LINES

Many subscribers may not need the entire capacity of a T line. To accommodate these customers, telephone companies offer fractional T-line services, which allow several subscribers to share one line by multiplexing their transmissions.

SONET

The high bandwidths of fiber-optic cable are suitable for today's highest data-rate technologies (such as video conferencing) and for carrying large numbers of lower-rate technologies at the same time. ANSI created a set of standards called **synchronous optical network (SONET)** for fiber-optic cables carrying high-speed data.

SONET first defines a set of electrical signals called synchronous transport signals (STSs). These signals are then converted to optical signals called optical carriers (OCs). The optical signals are transmitted at 8000 frames per second.

Table 11.2 shows the data rates for STSs and OCs. Note that the lowest level in this hierarchy has a data rate of 51.840 Mbps, which is greater than that of a T-3 line (44.736 Mbps).

Table 11.2 *SONET rates*

STS	OC	Rate (Mbps)
STS-1	OC-1	51.840
STS-3	OC-3	155.520
STS-9	OC-9	466.560
STS-12	OC-12	622.080
STS-18	OC-18	933.120
STS-24	OC-24	1244.160
STS-36	OC-36	1866.230
STS-48	OC-48	2488.320
STS-96	OC-96	4976.640
STS-192	OC-192	9953.280

Figure 11.2 shows a SONET network.

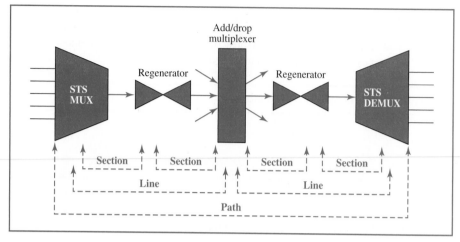

Figure 11.2 SONET

A SONET network is made of a **path** (end-to-end connection). A path connects an STS multiplexer to an STS demultiplexer. An STS multiplexer accepts data from different sources and multiplexes them to one optical channel. An STS demultiplexer does the reverse. A path is made of several **lines.** A line is the part of a path between two add/drop (internal) multiplexer/demultiplexers. A line in turn is divided into **sections,** which are separated by **regenerators** (or multiplexers).

11.2 SWITCHED WANs

Backbone networks in the Internet are usually switched WANs. A switched WAN is a wide area network that covers a large area (a state or a country) to provide access at several points to the user. Inside the network, there is a mesh of point-to-point networks that connect switches. The switches, multiple-port connectors, allow the connection of several inputs and outputs.

Switched WAN technology differs from LAN technology in many ways. First, instead of a bus or star topology, switches create multiple paths. LAN technology is considered a connectionless technology; there is no connection between packets sent by a sender to a receiver. Switched WAN technology, on the other hand, is a connection-oriented technology. Before a sender can send a packet, a connection must be established between the sender and the receiver. After the connection is established, it is assigned an identifier, which is used during the transmission. The connection is formally terminated when the transmission is over. The connection identifier is used instead of the source and destination addresses necessary in LAN technology.

We discuss three common switched WANs in this section. The first, X.25, is becoming obsolete. The second, Frame Relay, will still be in use for a few more years to come. The third, ATM, is the prevalent technology. Our discussion of the first two will be short; we focus on the third.

X.25

X.25, introduced in the 1970s, was the first switched WAN to become popular both in Europe and the United States. Although it is still used in Europe, it is disappearing from the United States. It was mostly used as a public network to connect individual computers or LANs. It provides an end-to-end service.

Although X.25 was (and still is, to some extent) used as the WAN to carry IP packets from one part of the world to another, there was always a conflict between IP and X.25. IP is a third- (network) layer protocol. An IP packet is supposed to be carried by a frame at the second (data link) layer. X.25, which was designed before the Internet, is a three-layer protocol; it has its own network layer. IP packets had to be encapsulated in the X.25 network-layer packet to be carried from one side of the network to the other. This is analogous to a person who has a car, but has to load it in a truck to go from one place to another.

Another problem with X.25 is that it was designed at a time when transmission media were not very reliable (pre-optical fiber era). For this reason, X.25 performs flow and error control at both the data link layer and the network layer. This makes transmission very slow and, given the ever increasing demand for speed, unpopular with customers.

For the above reasons, X.25 will most likely soon disappear from the Internet.

TECHNICAL FOCUS: TUNNELING

To use an X.25 network, an IP packet uses a technique called **tunneling.** Because X.25 does not allow IP packets to use their own network layer protocol, the IP packets are encapsulated in the network layer of the X.25 protocol. This can be compared to a car entering a tunnel. To an observer, the car disappears at one side of the tunnel and reappears at the other side. Likewise, an IP packet disappears at the entry point of an X.25 network and reappears at the exit point.

FRAME RELAY

Frame Relay, a switched technology that provides low-level (physical and data link layer) service, was designed to replace X.25. Frame Relay has some advantages over X.25:

1. **High Data Rate.** Although Frame Relay originally was designed to provide a 1.544-Mbps data rate (equivalent to a T-1 line), today most implementations can handle up to 44.736 Mbps (equivalent to a T-3 line).
2. **Bursty Data.** Some services offered by wide area network providers assume that the user has a fixed-rate need. For example, a T-1 line is designed for a user who wants to use the line at a consistent 1.544 Mbps. This type of service is not suitable for the many users today that need to send **bursty data** (non-fixed-rate data). For example, a user may want to send data at 6 Mbps for 2 s, 0 Mbps (nothing) for 7 s, and 3.44 Mbps for 1 s for a total of 15.44 Mbits during a period of 10 s. Although the average data rate is still 1.544 Mbps, the T-1 line cannot fulfill this type of demand because it is designed for fixed-rate data, not bursty data. Bursty data requires what is called **bandwidth on demand.** The user needs different bandwidth allocations at different times. Frame Relay accepts bursty data. A user is granted an average data rate that can be exceeded when needed.

3. **Less Overhead Due to Improved Transmission Media.** The quality of transmission media has improved tremendously in the last decade. They are more reliable and less error prone. There is no need to have a WAN that spends time and resources checking and double-checking potential errors. X.25 provides extensive error checking and flow control. Frame Relay does not provide error checking or require acknowledgment in the data link layer. Instead, all error checking is left to the protocols at the network and transport layer level that use the services of Frame Relay.

Frame Relay Architecture

The devices that connect users to the network are data terminal equipment (DTE). The switches that route the frames through the network are data circuit-terminating equipment (DCE) (see Figure 11.3). Frame Relay is normally used as a WAN to connect LANs or mainframe computers. In the first case, a router or a bridge can serve as the DTE and connects, through a leased line, the LAN to the Frame Relay switch, which is considered a DCE. In the second case, the mainframe itself can be used as a DTE with the installation of appropriate software.

© Corbis/Vol. 147

In some cases, the mainframe itself can be used as a DTE with the installation of appropriate software.

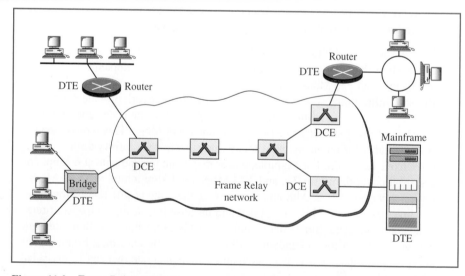

Figure 11.3 Frame Relay network

Virtual Circuits

Frame Relay, like other switched LANs, uses virtual circuits and virtual circuit identifiers called data link connection identifiers (DLCIs).

Frame Relay Layers

Frame Relay operates in only the physical and data link layers (see Figure 11.4). No specific protocol is defined for the physical layer in Frame Relay. Instead, it is left to the implementer to use whatever is available. Frame Relay supports any of the protocols recognized by ANSI.

At the data link layer, Frame Relay employs a simple protocol responsible for delivering data from one DTE to another.

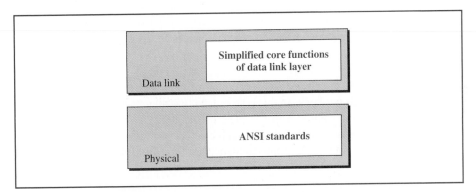

Figure 11.4   Frame Relay layers

TECHNICAL FOCUS: DLCIs

A Frame Relay network uses **data link connection identifiers (DLCIs)** which act as addresses. Each DLCI defines a channel between two adjacent devices (DTEs or DCEs). A path between a device at one end and another device at the other end is made of several DLCIs as shown in the following figure:

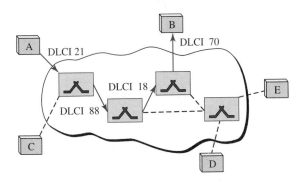

ATM

Asynchronous transfer mode (ATM) is the **cell relay** protocol designed by the ATM Forum and adopted by the ITU-T.

Design Goals

Among the challenges faced by the designers of ATM, six stand out. First and foremost is the need for a transmission system to optimize the use of high data-rate transmission media, in particular optical fiber. Second is the need for a system that can interface with existing systems, such as the various packet networks, and provide wide area inter-connectivity between them without lowering their effectiveness or requiring their replacement. Third is the need for a design that can be implemented inexpensively so that cost would not be a barrier to adoption. If ATM is to become the backbone of international communications, as intended, it must be available at low cost to every user who wants it. Fourth, the new system must be able to work with and support the existing telecommunications hierarchies (local loops, local providers, long-distance carriers, and so on). Fifth, the new system must be connection-oriented to ensure accurate and predictable delivery. And last but not least, one objective is to move as many of the functions to hardware as possible (for speed) and eliminate as many software functions as possible (again for speed).

Cell Networks

ATM is a cell network. A **cell** is a small data unit of fixed size that is the basic unit of data exchange in a **cell network.** In this type of network, all data are loaded into identical cells that can be transmitted with complete predictability and uniformity. Cells are multiplexed with other cells and routed through a cell network. Because each cell is the same size and all are small, any problems associated with multiplexing different-sized packets are avoided.

A cell network uses the cell as the basic unit of data exchange. A cell is defined as a small, fixed-sized block of information.

Asynchronous TDM

ATM uses asynchronous time-division multiplexing—that is why it is called asynchronous transfer mode—to multiplex cells coming from different channels. It uses fixed-size slots the size of a cell. ATM multiplexers fill a slot with a cell from any input channel that has a cell; the slot is empty if none of the channels has a cell to send.

Figure 11.5 shows how cells from three inputs are multiplexed. At the first tick of the clock, channel 2 has no cell (empty input slot), so the multiplexer fills the slot with a cell from the third channel. When all the cells from all the channels are multiplexed, the output slots are empty.

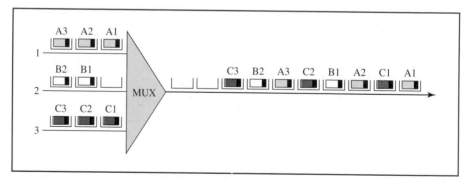

Figure 11.5 ATM multiplexing

ATM Architecture

ATM is a cell-switched network. The user access devices, called the end points, are connected through a **user-to-network interface** (UNI) to the switches inside the network. The switches are connected through **network-to-network interfaces** (NNIs). Figure 11.6 shows an example of an ATM network.

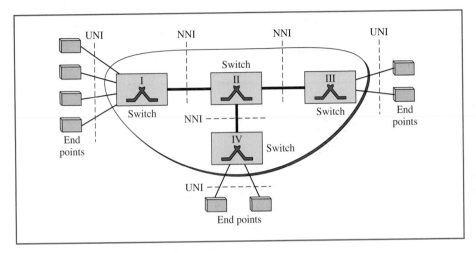

Figure 11.6   Architecture of an ATM network

TECHNICAL FOCUS: VPIs and VCIs

In an ATM network, connection between two end points is accomplished through transmission paths, virtual paths, and virtual circuits. A **transmission path** (TP) is the physical connection (wire, cable, satellite, and so on) between an end point and a switch or between two switches. Think of two switches as two cities. A transmission path is the set of all highways that directly connects the two cities.

A transmission path is divided into several virtual paths. A **virtual path** (VP) provides a connection or a set of connections between two switches. Think of a virtual path as a highway that connects two cities. Each highway is a virtual path; the set of all highways is the transmission path.

Cell networks are based on **virtual circuits** (VCs). All cells belonging to a single message follow the same virtual circuit and remain in their original order until they reach their destination. Think of a virtual circuit as the lanes of a highway (virtual path) as shown in the following figure:

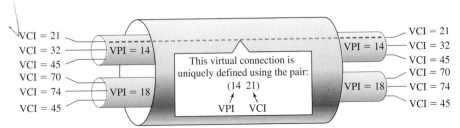

The figure also shows the relationship between a transmission path (a physical connection), virtual paths (a combination of virtual circuits that are bundled together because parts of their paths are the same), and virtual circuits that logically connect two points together.

In a virtual circuit network, to route data from one end point to another, the virtual connections need to be identified. For this purpose, the designers of ATM created a hierarchical identifier with two levels: a **virtual path identifier** (VPI) and a **virtual circuit identifier** (VCI). The VPI defines the specific VP and the VCI defines a particular VC inside the VP. The VPI is the same for all virtual connections that are bundled (logically) into one VP.

Cells   A cell is 53 bytes in length with 5 bytes allocated to header and 48 bytes carrying payload (user data may be less than 48 bytes). Most of the header is occupied by the VPI and VCI. Figure 11.7 shows the cell structure.

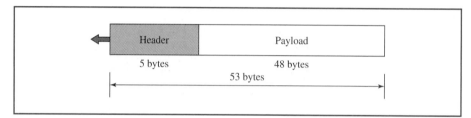

Figure 11.7   An ATM cell

ATM Layers

The ATM standard defines three layers. They are, from top to bottom, the application adaptation layer, the ATM layer, and the physical layer as shown in Figure 11.8.

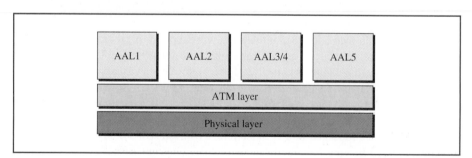

Figure 11.8   ATM layers

Application Adaptation Layer (AAL)   The **application adaptation layer** (AAL) allows existing networks (such as packet networks) to connect to ATM facilities. AAL protocols accept transmissions from upper-layer services (e.g., packet data) and map them into fixed-sized ATM cells. These transmissions can be of any type (voice, data, audio, or video) and can be of variable or fixed rate. At the receiver, this process is reversed—segments are reassembled into their original formats and passed to the receiving service.

❑ **AAL1.** AAL1 is designed for **constant-bit-rate** (CBR) data coming from applications that generate and consume bits at a constant rate. In this type of application, transmission delays must be minimal and transmission must simulate real time. Examples of constant-bit-rate applications include real-time voice (telephone calls) and real-time video (television).

❑ **AAL2.** AAL2 is designed for **variable-bit-rate** (VBR) data coming from applications that generate and consume bits at variable rates. In this type of application, the bit rate varies from section to section of the transmission, but within established parameters. Examples of variable-bit-rate applications include compressed voice, data, and video.

❑ **AAL3/4.** AAL3/4 is designed for connection-oriented packet protocols (such as X.25) that use virtual circuits.

❑ **AAL5.** AAL5 is designed for connectionless packet protocols that use a datagram approach to routing (such as the IP protocol in TCP/IP).

The IP protocol uses the AAL5 sublayer.

ATM Layer   The ATM layer provides routing, traffic management, switching, and multiplexing services. It processes outgoing traffic by accepting 48-byte segments from the AAL sublayers and transforming them into 53-byte cells by the addition of a 5-byte header.

Physical Layer   The physical layer defines the transmission medium, bit transmission, encoding, and electrical to optical transformation. It provides convergence with physical transport protocols, such as SONET and T-3, as well as the mechanisms for transforming the flow of cells into a flow of bits.

11.3   ATM LANs

ATM is mainly a wide area network (ATM WAN); however, the technology can be adopted to local area networks (ATM LAN). In this section we discuss the technology as applied to LANs.

The high data rate of the technology (155 and 622 Mbps) has attracted the attention of designers who are looking for increased data rates in LANs.

ATM LAN ARCHITECTURE

Today, we have three ways to incorporate ATM technology in a LAN architecture: creating a pure ATM LAN, making a legacy ATM LAN, or a mixture of both as shown in Figure 11.9.

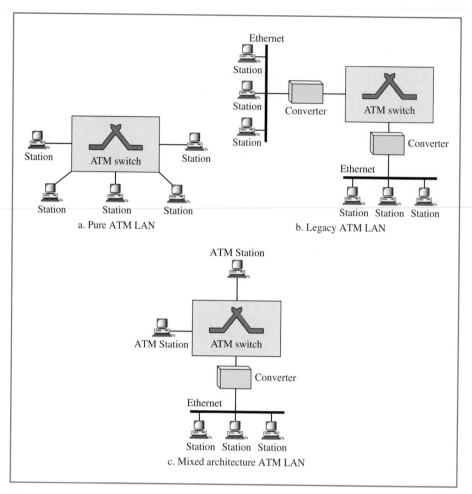

Figure 11.9   ATM LAN architectures

Pure ATM Architecture

In a pure ATM LAN, an ATM switch is used to connect the stations, in the same way stations are connected to an Ethernet switch. In this way, stations can exchange data at one of two standard rates of ATM technology (155 and 652 Mbps). However, the station uses a virtual path identifier (VPI) and a virtual connection identifier (VCI), instead of a source and destination address. This approach has a major drawback. The system needs to be built from the ground up; existing LANs cannot be upgraded into pure ATM LANs.

Legacy LAN Architecture

A second approach is to use ATM technology as a backbone to connect traditional LANs.

In this way, stations on the same LAN can exchange data at the rate and format of traditional LANs (Ethernet, Token Ring, etc.). But when two stations on two different

LANs need to exchange data, they can go through a converting device that changes the frame format. The advantage here is that output from several LANs can be multiplexed together to create a high data rate input to the ATM switch. We will see that there are several issues that must be resolved first.

Mixed Architecture

Probably the best solution is to mix the two previous architectures. This means keeping the existing LANs and, at the same time, allowing new stations to be directly connected to an ATM switch. This approach allows the gradual migration of legacy LANs into ATM LANs by adding more and more directly connected stations to the switch. Again, the stations in one specific LAN can exchange data using the format and data rate of that particular LAN. The stations directly connected to the ATM switch can use an ATM frame to exchange data. However, the problem is how a station in a traditional LAN can communicate with a station directly connected to the ATM switch and vice versa.

TECHNICAL FOCUS: LANE

At the surface level, the use of ATM technology in LANs seems plausible. However, on close inspection, we see that many issues need to be resolved, as summarized below:

❑ **Connectionless vs. Connection-oriented.** Traditional LANs, such as Ethernet, are connectionless protocols. On the other hand, ATM is a connection-oriented protocol; a station that wishes to send cells to another station first establishes a connection and, after all of the cells are sent, terminates the connection.

❑ **Physical Addresses vs. Virtual Connection Identifiers.** Closely related to the first issue is the addressing problem. A connectionless protocol, such as Ethernet, defines the route of a packet through source and destination addresses. However, a connection-oriented protocol, such as ATM, defines the route of a cell through virtual connection identifiers (VPIs and VCIs).

❑ **Multicasting and Broadcasting Delivery.** Traditional LANs, such as Ethernet, can both multicast and broadcast packets; a station can send packets to a group of stations or to all stations. There is no easy way to multicast or broadcast on an ATM network although point-to-multipoint connections are available.

❑ **Interpretability.** In a mixed architecture, a station connected to a legacy LAN must be able to communicate with a station directly connected to an ATM switch.

An approach called local area network emulation (LANE) solves the above-mentioned problems and allows stations in a mixed architecture to communicate with each other. The approach uses emulation. Stations can use a connectionless service that emulates a connection-oriented service. Stations use the source and destination addresses for initial connection and then use VPI and VCI addressing. The approach allows stations to use unicast, multicast, and broadcast addresses. Finally, LANE converts frames using a legacy format to ATM cells before being sent through the switch.

CASE STUDY

NEW AGE HOME PHARMACY

NAHP uses point-to-point WANs. As mentioned in Chapter 8, NAHP has two T-1 lines for voice communication to the outside world. A T-1 line (a digital point-to-point WAN) can sample and digitize 24 voice channels (telephone line). The capacity of the two T-lines is divided among the floors as shown in the figure at the bottom.

Each voice channel is sampled 8000 times per second; with 8 bits representing one sample, there are 256 levels available. So a T-1 line data unit is 8000 frames with each frame containing 193 bits (8 bits for each of the 24 channels, and 1 extra bit for synchronization). This means each T-1 line carries 8000 × 193 bits or 1,544,000 bits second (1.544 Mbps).

NAHP uses another T line, a T-3 line for connection to the Internet. However, since this line carries only digital data, no sampling is involved. The T-3 line has a capacity of 44.736 Mbps. The switch/router in the basement is connected to a device called a digital service unit/channel service unit (DSU/CSU) which prepares the data for transferal through the T-3 line as shown in the following figure:

Although Fast Ethernet has a capacity of 100 Mbps and packets are sent at this rate, this data rate is not continuous. Sometimes it is 100 Mbps and sometimes 0 Mbps (when there is no traffic). The switch/router in the basement buffers the data and sends them out at the rate designed for the T-3 line.

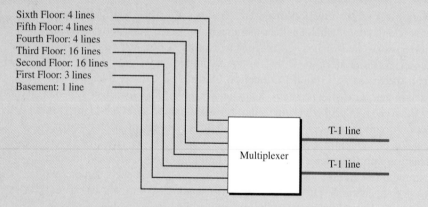

11.4 KEY TERMS

application adaptation layer (AAL)	bursty data
asynchronous transfer mode (ATM)	cell
ATM LAN	cell network
ATM switch	data link connection identifier (DLCI)
bandwidth on demand	fractional T line

Frame Relay
LAN emulation (LANE)
legacy LAN
mixed architecture LAN
point-to-point WAN
pure ATM LAN
switched WAN
synchronous optical network (SONET)
T line

T-1 line
T-3 line
tunneling
virtual circuit identifier (VCI)
virtual connection identifier
virtual path identifier (VPI)
wide area network (WAN)
X.25

11.5 SUMMARY

❏ A point-to-point WAN connects two distant devices using a line available from a public network provider.

❏ T lines carry data from a residence or organization to the Internet. T lines are commercially available in two data rates: T-1 and T-3.

❏ SONET is a high-speed network using fiber-optic cables.

❏ A switched WAN is a connection-oriented technology that uses switches to create multiple paths.

❏ X.25 is a switched WAN with its own network layer that is being replaced by other technologies.

❏ Frame Relay, a switched WAN that provides low-level service, eliminates the extensive error checking necessary in X.25 protocol.

❏ Asynchronous transfer mode (ATM) is a cell relay protocol designed to support the transmission of data, voice, and video through high data-rate transmission media such as fiber-optic cable.

❏ The ATM data packet is called a cell and is composed of 53 bytes (5 bytes of header and 48 bytes of payload).

❏ A cell network has small fixed-size data units.

❏ The ATM standard defines three layers: the application adaptation layer (AAL), the ATM layer, and the physical layer.

❏ There are four different AALs, each specific for a data type. IP uses AAL5, which converts data coming from a connectionless packet switching network.

❏ ATM technology can be adopted for use in a LAN (ATM LAN).

❏ In a pure ATM LAN, an ATM switch connects stations. In a legacy ATM LAN, the backbone that connects traditional LANs uses ATM technology. A mixed architecture ATM LAN combines features of a pure ATM LAN and a legacy ATM LAN.

❏ Local area network emulation (LANE) is a model that allows the use of ATM technology in LANs.

PRACTICE SET

Review Questions

1. Name three differences between a WAN and a LAN.
2. Name some types of point-to-point WANs.
3. How is the data rate of a T-1 line calculated?
4. What is the relationship between a T-1 line and a T-3 line?
5. What sort of transmission medium is used for SONET?
6. What are the factors contributing to the loss of popularity for X.25 as a switched WAN?
7. What is bursty data?
8. What is a DLCI?
9. What are some of the advantages of a cell network?
10. What is the difference between a VPI and a VCI?
11. Which AAL sublayer is used by IP?
12. What are the three ways to incorporate ATM technology in a LAN architecture?

Multiple-Choice Questions

13. A _____ can be considered a point-to-point WAN.
    a. T-1 line
    b. telephone line
    c. cable TV line
    d. all of the above
14. A T-3 line is equivalent to _____ T-1 lines.
    a. 3
    b. 8
    c. 28
    d. 8000
15. A SONET system uses _____ as a transmission medium.
    a. fiber-optic cable
    b. coaxial cable
    c. UTP
    d. fractional T lines
16. In a SONET system, a _____ connects an STS multiplexer to an STS demultiplexer.
    a. path
    b. line
    c. section
    d. regenerator
17. _____ is the dominant switched WAN technology.
    a. X.25
    b. Frame Relay
    c. ATM
    d. SONET

18. An IP packet has to be encapsulated in _____'s network-layer packet.
    a. X.25
    b. Frame Relay
    c. ATM
    d. SONET
19. Since _____ was designed when transmission media were not very reliable, flow and error control were necessary at both the data link and network layers.
    a. X.25
    b. Frame Relay
    c. ATM
    d. SONET
20. Frame Relay operates in the _____.
    a. physical layer
    b. data link layer
    c. physical and data link layers
    d. physical, data link, and network layers
21. _____ offers a service called bandwidth on demand.
    a. X.25
    b. Frame Relay
    c. ATM
    d. SONET
22. The _____ in a Frame Relay network connect to _____ outside the network.
    a. DTEs; DCEs
    b. DCEs; DTEs
    c. DTEs; DTEs
    d. DCEs; DCEs
23. Which ATM layer maps data into fixed-size cells?
    a. physical
    b. ATM
    c. application adaptation
    d. data adaptation
24. Which ATM layer has a 53-byte cell as an end product?
    a. physical
    b. ATM
    c. application adaptation
    d. cell transformation
25. Which application adaptation layer type can process a data stream having a non-constant-bit-rate?
    a. AAL1
    b. AAL2
    c. AAL3/4
    d. AAL5
26. Which AAL type is designed to support a data stream that has a constant-bit-rate?
    a. AAL1
    b. AAL2
    c. AAL3/4
    d. AAL5

27. IP uses the _____ sublayer.
   a. AAL1
   b. AAL2
   c. AAL3/4
   d. AAL5

28. In a _____ ATM LAN, all stations are connected to the ATM switch.
   a. pure
   b. legacy
   c. mixed architecture
   d. any of the above

29. A _____ ATM LAN could have Ethernet LANs and Token Ring LANs connected to an ATM switch.
   a. pure
   b. legacy
   c. mixed architecture
   d. b and c

30. _____ allows stations in a mixed architecture ATM to communicate with each other.
   a. Frame Relay
   b. X.25
   c. LANE
   d. SONET

PART III

Internetworking and Internet

CHAPTER 12

Connecting LANs and WANs: Making Backbone Networks

LANs and WANs are not found in isolation today; they are usually connected to one another. For example, a large company may consist of several LANs, each serving one part of the organization. There might be an engineering group with its own LAN, a human resources group with its own LAN and so on. To send a message from a station on one LAN to a station on another LAN requires that the LANs be connected.

In this chapter, we discuss devices that connect LANs and WANs and devices used for connection within a network. Backbone networks, networks that connect other networks, are also a topic of this chapter.

OBJECTIVES

After reading this chapter, the reader should be able to:

❏ Differentiate between the different connecting devices and the Internet layers each supports.

❏ Understand the functionality of a repeater and where it is used.

❏ Understand the functionality of a bridge and where it is used.

❏ Understand the functionality of a router and where it is used.

❏ Understand the difference between a two-layer and a three-layer switch.

❏ Understand the functionality of a backbone network and where it is used.

❏ Distinguish between a logical bus and a logical star backbone.

❏ Distinguished between a bridge-based network and a router-based backbone network.

12.1   CONNECTING DEVICES

In previous chapters we discussed LANs and WANs as the underlying technologies for the Internet and the TCP/IP protocol. However, the Internet is not made of a single LAN or a single WAN. The Internet is a combination of LANs and WANs. There must be a way to join these LANs and WANs together. We call these joining tools, connecting devices.

We discuss five such devices in this section: repeaters, hubs, bridges, routers, and switches. Repeaters and hubs operate in the first layer of the TCP/IP protocol suite. (This is comparable to the physical layer of the Internet model.) Bridges operate in the first two layers. Routers operate in the first three layers. We have two types of switches: the first type is a sophisticated bridge and the second is a sophisticated router. Figure 12.1 shows the layers in which each device operates.

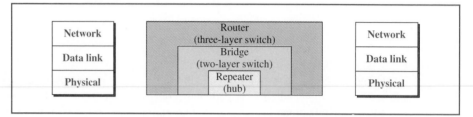

Figure 12.1   Connecting devices

REPEATERS

A repeater is a device that operates only in the physical layer. Signals that carry information within a network can travel a fixed distance before attenuation endangers the integrity of the data. A repeater receives a signal, and before it becomes too weak or corrupted, regenerates the original bit pattern. It then sends the refreshed signal. A repeater can extend the physical length of a network as shown in Figure 12.2.

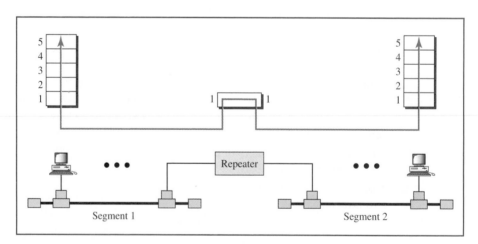

Figure 12.2   Repeater

A repeater connects segments of a LAN together.

A repeater can overcome the length restriction on a 10BASE5 Ethernet. In this standard, the length of the cable is limited to 500 meters. To extend this length, we divide the cable into segments and install repeaters between segments. Note that the whole network is still considered one LAN, but the portion of the networks separated by repeaters are called **segments.** The repeater acts as a two-interface node, but operates only in the physical layer. When it receives a packet from any of the interfaces, it regenerates and forwards it to the other interface.

A repeater forwards every packet; it has no filtering capability.

TECHNICAL FOCUS: REPEATERS AND AMPLIFIERS

It is tempting to compare a repeater to an amplifier, but the comparison is inaccurate. An amplifier cannot discriminate between the intended signal and noise; it amplifies equally everything fed into it. A repeater does not amplify the signal; it regenerates it. When it receives a weakened or corrupted signal, it creates a copy bit for bit, at the original strength. A repeater is a regenerator, not an amplifier.

Hubs

Although, in a general sense, the word hub can refer to any connecting device, it does have a specific meaning. A hub is actually a multiport repeater. It is normally used to create connections between stations in a physical star topology. We have seen examples of hubs in some Ethernet implementations (10BASE-T, for example). However, hubs can also be used to create multiple levels of hierarchy as shown in Figure 12.3.

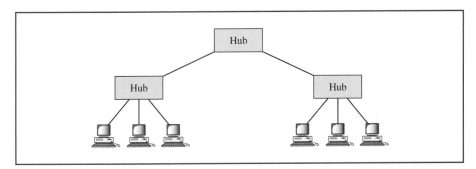

Figure 12.3   Hubs

Note that the whole network is still one single LAN. Note also that the network is considered a logical bus topology (if a station sends a packet, it is received by every other station. The hierarchical use of hubs removes the length limitation of 10BASE-T (100 meters).

TECHNICAL FOCUS: ACTIVE VERSUS PASSIVE HUB

A passive hub is a hub that is used to create a connection; it does not regenerate signals. An active hub, on the other hand, is a connector as well as a repeater. Today, most hubs are active hubs.

BRIDGES

A **bridge** operates in both the physical and the data link layers. As a physical layer device, it regenerates the signal it receives. As a data link layer device, the bridge can check the physical addresses (source and destination) contained in the packet. Note that a bridge, like a repeater, has no physical address. It acts only as a filter, not as an original sender to a final destination.

Filtering

One may ask what is the difference, in functionality, between a bridge and a repeater? A bridge has filtering capability. It can check the destination address of a packet and decide if the packet should be forwarded or dropped. If the packet is to be forwarded, the decision must specify the interface. A bridge has a table that maps addresses to interfaces.

A bridge has a table used in filtering decisions.

Let us give an example. In Figure 12.4, a LAN is divided into two segments separated by a bridge. If a packet destined for station 712B13456141 (or 712B13456142) arrives at interface 1, the bridge consults its table to find the departing interface. According to its table, packets for 712B13456141 leave through interface 1; therefore, there is no need for forwarding through interface 2; the packet is dropped. On the other hand, if a packet for 712B13456141 arrives at interface 2, the departing interface, again, is interface 1 and the packet is forwarded. In the first case, segment 2 remains free of traffic; in the second case, both segments have traffic. In our example, we show a two-interface bridge; in reality a bridge can have several interfaces. Note that all the segments connected to a bridge, are still part of one LAN.

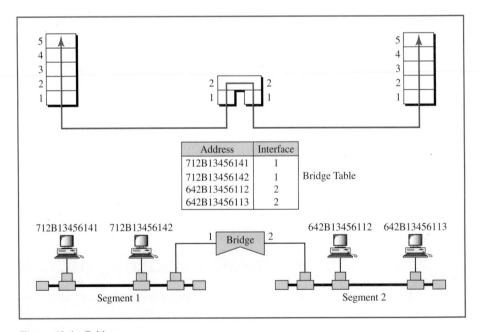

Figure 12.4 Bridge

Note also that a bridge does not change the physical addresses contained in the packet.

Transparent Bridges

Today's bridges are transparent (or learning) bridges; they can easily be installed between two segments of a LAN (plug and play). The bridge's table is originally empty, but as soon as a bridge receives and forwards a packet, it creates an entry in its table using the source address and the arriving interface. From then on, the bridge knows that every packet to that destination departs from that interface. The bridge also records information about the destination using the information contained in the packet. We do something similar when we reply to mail (or email).

ROUTERS

A **router** is a three-layer device; it operates in the physical, data link, and network layers. As a physical layer device, it regenerates the signal it receives. As a data link layer device, the router checks the physical addresses (source and destination) contained in the packet. As a network layer device, a router checks the network layer addresses (addresses in the IP layer).

A router is a three-layer (physical, data link, and network) device.

A router can connect LANs together; a router can connect WANs together; and a router can connect LANs and WANs together. In other words, a router is an internetworking device; it connects independent networks together to form an internetwork. According to this definition, two networks (LANs or WANs) connected by a router become an internetwork or an internet.

There are three major differences between a router and a repeater or a bridge.

1. A router has a physical and logical (IP) address for each of its interfaces.
2. A router acts only on those packets in which the destination address matches the address of the interface at which the packet arrives. This is true for unicast, multicast, or broadcast addresses.
3. A router changes the physical addresses of the packet (both source and destination) when it forwards the packet.

A repeater or a bridge connects segments of a LAN.

A router connects independent LANs or WANs to create an internetwork (internet).

Let us give an example. In Figure 12.5, we show two LANs separated by a router. The left LAN has two segments separated by a bridge. The router changes the physical source and destination addresses of the packet. When the packet travels in the left LAN, its source address is the address of the sending station; its destination address is the address of the router. When the same packet travels in the second LAN, its source address is the address of the router and its destination address is the address of the final destination.

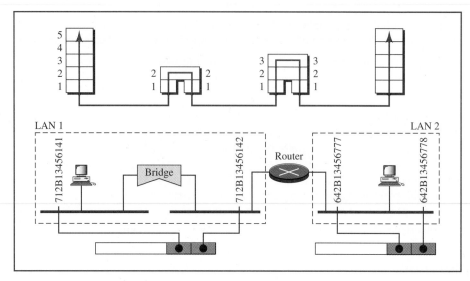

Figure 12.5 Routing example

Routers route packets among multiple interconnected networks. They route packets from one network to any of a number of potential destination networks on an internet. Routers act like stations on a network. But unlike most stations, which are members of only one network, routers have addresses on, and links to, two or more networks.

A router changes the physical addresses in a packet.

We will learn more about routers and routing in future chapters after we have discussed IP addressing.

TECHNICAL FOCUS: MULTIPROTOCOL ROUTER

At the network layer, a router by default is a single-protocol device. In other words, if two LANs are to be connected by a router, they must use the same protocol at the network layer. For example, both must use IP (the network layer protocol of the Internet) or IPX (the network layer protocol for Novell). The reason behind this is that the routing table must use one single addressing format.

However, **multiprotocol routers** have been designed to route packets belonging to two or more protocols. For example, a two-protocol router (for example, IP and IPX) can handle packets belonging to either of the two protocols. It can receive, process, and send a packet using the IP protocol or it can receive, process, and send a packet using the IPX protocol. In this case, the router has two routing tables: one for IP and one for IPX. Of course, the router cannot route a packet based on other protocols.

A **brouter (bridge/router)** is a single-protocol or multiprotocol router that sometimes acts as a router and sometimes as a bridge. When a single-protocol brouter receives a packet belonging to the protocol for which it is designed, it routes the packet based on the network layer address; otherwise, it acts as a bridge and passes the packet using the data link layer address.

Likewise, when a multiprotocol brouter receives a packet belonging to one of the protocols for which it is designed, it routes the packet based on the network layer address; otherwise, it acts as a bridge and passes the packet using the data link layer address.

SWITCHES

When we use the term switch, we must be careful because a switch can mean two different things. We clarify the term by adding the level at which the device operates. We can have a two-layer switch or a three-layer switch. Let us discuss each briefly.

Two-Layer Switch

A two-layer switch is a bridge, a bridge with many interfaces and a design that allows better (faster) performance. A bridge with a few interfaces can connect a few segments of a LAN together. A bridge with many interfaces may be able to allocate a unique interface to each station, with each station on its own independent segment. This means no competing traffic (no collision as we saw in Ethernet). In this book, to avoid confusion, we use the term *bridge* for a two-layer switch.

Three-Layer Switch

A three-layer switch is a router, a router with an improved design to allow better performance. A three-layer switch can receive, process, and dispatch a packet much faster than a traditional router even though the functionality is the same. In this book, to avoid confusion, we use the term *router* for a three-layer switch.

TECHNICAL FOCUS: GATEWAYS

Today, the term **gateway** is used mostly as a synonym for a router. However, in the past, the two terms had different meanings. A gateway defined a device that could potentially operate in all five layers of the Internet model. It was a protocol converter. A router was a device that could transfer, accept, and relay packets only across networks using similar protocols. A gateway, on the other hand, could accept a packet formatted for one protocol (e.g., AppleTalk) and convert it to a packet formatted for another protocol (e.g., TCP/IP) before forwarding it.

12.2 BACKBONE NETWORKS

The connecting devices discussed in this chapter can be used to connects LANs to a backbone network. A backbone network is one that allows several LANs to be connected together. In a backbone network, no station is directly connected to the backbone; the stations are part of a LAN and the backbone connects the LANs. The backbone is itself a LAN that uses a LAN protocol such as Ethernet; each connection to the backbone is itself another LAN.

Although, many different architectures can be used for a backbone, we discuss only the two most common: the logical bus and the logical star.

LOGICAL BUS BACKBONE

In a logical bus backbone, the logical topology of the backbone is a bus. The physical topology can be a bus or a star, but the backbone medium is shared between all LANs. The backbone itself can use one of the protocols that supports the logical bus such as 10BASE5, 10BASE2, 10BASE-T, or 100BASE-T (the most common one today).

In a logical bus backbone, the logical topology of the backbone is a bus; the physical topology can be a bus or a star.

Logical bus backbones are normally used as a distribution backbone to connect different buildings in an organization. Each building can be comprised of either a single

© Corbis/Vol. 11

One example of a logical bus backbone is one that
connects multifloor buildings. Each multistory
building has a backbone (usually a logical star)
that connects each LAN on a floor.

LAN or another backbone (normally a logical star backbone). A good example of a logical bus backbone is one that connects single- or multiple-floor buildings on a campus. Each single-floor building usually has a single LAN. Each multiple-floor building has a backbone (usually a logical star) that connects each LAN on a floor. A logical-bus backbone can connect these LANs and backbones together.

To connect LANs to the backbone, the logical bus backbone can use either bridges or routers. This means that we can have two types of logical bus backbones: bridge-based or router-based.

Bridge-Based Backbone

In a bridge-based backbone, the LANs are connected to the backbone through bridges. Figure 12.6 shows an example of a bridge-based backbone with four LANs. Note that although we show the backbone as a bus, the physical network can be a bus or a star as long as the media is shared between the bridges.

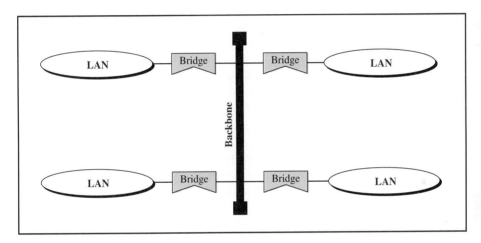

Figure 12.6 Bridge-based logical bus network

In a bridge-based backbone, the delivery of the frames uses the data link layer (MAC) address of the frame. This means that the whole system is viewed as one single network in which each station has a unique data link layer address.

In the above figure, if a station in a LAN needs to send a frame to another station in the same LAN, the corresponding bridge blocks the frame; the frame never reaches the backbone. However, if a station needs to send a frame to a station in another LAN, the bridge passes the frame to the backbone, which is received by the appropriate bridge and is delivered to the destination LAN. Each bridge connected to the backbone has a table that shows the stations on the LAN side of the bridge. The blocking or delivery of a frame is based on the contents of this table.

Router-Based Backbone

In a router-based backbone, the LANs are connected to the backbone through routers. Figure 12.7 shows an example of a router-based backbone with four LANs. Note that although we show the backbone as a bus, the physical network can be a bus or a star as long as the media is shared between the routers.

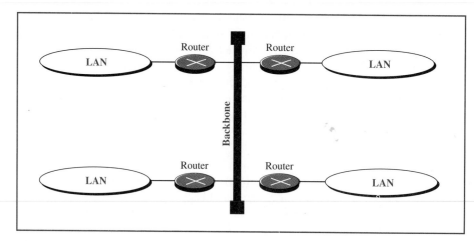

Figure 12.7   Router-base logical bus backbone

In a router-based backbone, the delivery of the frame uses the network layer (IP) address of the packet encapsulated inside the frame. This means that the system is viewed as several subnetworks with each LAN and the backbone each forming a subnet.

In the above figure, if a station in a LAN needs to send a frame to another station in the same LAN, the corresponding router blocks the frame; the frame never reaches the backbone. However, if a station needs to send a frame to a station in another LAN, the router passes the frame to the backbone, which is received by the appropriate router and is delivered to the destination LAN. Each router connected to the backbone has a routing table that shows how to route the frame to the appropriate router. The blocking or delivery of the frame is based on the contents of this table. Note that after a router finds the IP address of the destination router, it uses either static or dynamic mapping to find the data-link layer address of the destination router as discussed in Chapter 5.

LOGICAL STAR BACKBONE

In a logical star backbone, sometimes called a collapsed or switched backbone, the logical topology of the backbone is a star. In this configuration, the backbone is just one switch (that is why it is called, erroneously, a collapsed backbone) that connects the LANs together.

In a logical star backbone, the logical topology of the backbone is a star; the backbone is just one switch.

Figure 12.8 shows a logical star backbone. Note that, in this configuration, there is no need for bridges or routers to connect the LANs to the backbone (which is just one switch). The switch does the job of the backbone and, at the same, connects the LANs.

The delivery of frames in a logical star backbone can be based on the data link layer or network layer addresses. If the backbone switch is a two-layer switch, the delivery is based on the data link layer addresses, which means the whole system is still one single network. If the switch is a three-layer switch, acting a multiport router, the delivery is based on the network layer addresses. In this case, each LAN acts as a subnetwork (subnet).

Logical star backbones are mostly used as a distribution backbone inside a building. In a multifloor building, we usually find one LAN that serves each particular floor.

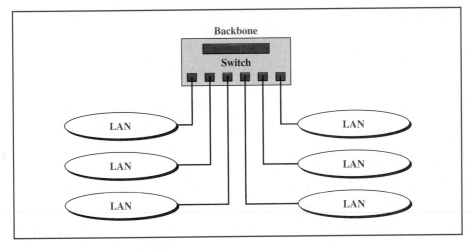

Figure 12.8   Logical star backbone

A logical star backbone connects these LANs together. The backbone network, which is just a switch, can be installed in the basement or the first floor and separate cables can run from the switch to each LAN. If the individual LANs have a physical star topology, the hubs (or switches) can be either installed in a closet on the corresponding floor or all can be installed close to the switch. We often find a rack or chassis in the basement where the backbone switch and all hubs or switches are installed.

TECHNICAL FOCUS: FDDI

Fiber distributed data interface (FDDI) is a local area network protocol standardized by ANSI and the ITU-T. It supports data rates of 100 Mbps. In the last two decades, FDDI was used as a backbone to connect LANs; today, other protocols such as Fast and Gigabit Ethernet are used for this purpose.

FDDI is implemented as a dual ring as shown below.

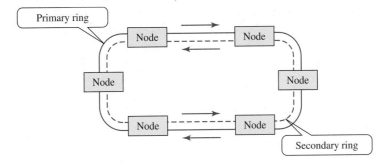

In most cases, data transmission is confined to the primary ring. The secondary ring is provided in case the primary fails. The secondary ring makes FDDI self-healing. When a problem occurs on the primary ring, the secondary can be activated to complete data circuits and maintain service.

CASE STUDY

NEW AGE HOME PHARMACY

N AHP uses three-layer switches. On each floor, a three-layer switch, which is actually a router, but faster, connects all computers on that floor to create a full-duplex switched Ethernet operating at 10 Mbps. Six switches are installed for this purpose, one on each floor. NAHP also uses a three-layer switch in the basement to connect all six switches together to form a backbone.

The NAHP backbone is a logical star configuration that connects six LANs, one on each floor. The protocol that controls the backbone is Fast Ethernet. The Fast Ethernet switch in the basement has one outside connection to the Internet, via a DSU/CSU and a T-3 line. The switch can be connected to 12 internal switches, of which only 7 are currently in use.

The following figure shows the connection of the backbone switch to the Internet and internal switches.

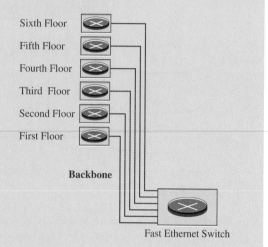

The transmission media is fiber optic cable. The implementation of this Fast Ethernet is called 100BASE-FX. Each connection to the Fast Ethernet switch is through a pair of fiber optic cables.

12.3   KEY TERMS

active hub
amplifier
bridge
bridge-based backbone
brouter (bridge/router)
connecting device
fiber distributed data
    interface (FDDI)
filtering
gateway
hub
internetworking devices
logical bus backbone
logical star backbone

multiport bridge
multiprotocol router
passive hub
repeater
router
router-based backbone
routing
routing switch
routing table
segment
simple bridge
three-layer switch
transparent bridge
two-layer switch

12.4 SUMMARY

❏ Internetworking devices connect LANs and WANs to create an internet.
❏ A repeater is a device that operates in the physical layer of the Internet model. Its purpose is regeneration of the signal.
❏ A hub is a multiport repeater that creates connections between stations in a physical star topology.
❏ Bridges operate in the physical and data link layers of the Internet model. They have access to station addresses and can forward or filter a packet in a network.
❏ Routers operate in the physical, data link, and network layers of the Internet model. They decide the path a packet must take.
❏ A bridge is a two-layer switch; a router is a three-layer switch.
❏ A backbone network, which is itself a LAN, connects several LANs together.
❏ A logical bus backbone can be bridge-based or router-based.
❏ A logical star backbone consists of just one switch.

 PRACTICE SET

Review Questions

1. What is the relationship between a repeater and a hub?
2. How can the length of a network be extended?
3. What is the difference between a bridge and a repeater?
4. What is the difference between a router and a bridge?
5. Rank the connecting devices (repeater, bridge, and router) according to their complexity and give the Internet layers in which they operate.
6. What is a two-layer switch? What is a three-layer switch?
7. What is a network?
8. What is an internetwork?
9. Name two types of logical bus backbones.
10. Describe the backbone of a logical star backbone.

Multiple-Choice Questions

11. Which of the following is a connecting device?
    a. bridge
    b. repeater
    c. router
    d. all of the above
12. Which of the following operates in the greatest number of layers of the Internet model?
    a. bridge
    b. repeater
    c. router
    d. two-layer switch

13. A bridge forwards or filters a packet by comparing the information in its address table to the packet's _____.
    a. layer 2 source address
    b. layer 2 destination address
    c. layer 3 source address
    d. layer 3 destination address
14. A simple bridge does which of the following?
    a. filters a data packet
    b. forwards a data packet
    c. extends a LAN
    d. all of the above
15. Repeaters function in the _____ layer(s).
    a. physical
    b. data link
    c. network
    d. a and b
16. Bridges function in the _____ layer(s).
    a. physical
    b. data link
    c. network
    d. a and b
17. A repeater takes a weakened or corrupted signal and _____ it.
    a. amplifies
    b. regenerates
    c. resamples
    d. reroutes
18. A bridge has access to the _____ address of a station on the same network.
    a. physical
    b. network
    c. service access point
    d. all of the above
19. Routers function in the _____ layers.
    a. physical and data link
    b. physical, data link, and network
    c. data link and network
    d. network and transport
20. A hub is a multiport _____.
    a. repeater
    b. bridge
    c. router
    d. gateway
21. A _____ connects LANs and WANs together.
    a. repeater
    b. bridge
    c. router
    d. hub

22. A _____ is a two-layer switch while a _____ is a three-layer switch.
    a. repeater; bridge
    b. bridge; router
    c. router; bridge
    d. bridge; hub

23. If a switch connects several LANs together, we have a _____ backbone.
    a. bridge-based
    b. router-based
    c. logical star
    d. logical bus

24. A logical bus backbone can be _____.
    a. bridge-based
    b. router-based
    c. switch-based
    d. a or b

25. In a bridge-based backbone, frame delivery involves the _____ address.
    a. data link layer
    b. network layer
    c. port
    d. source

26. In a router-based backbone, frame delivery involves the _____ address.
    a. data link layer
    b. network layer
    c. port
    d. source

CHAPTER 13

The Internet

The Internet has revolutionized many aspects of our daily lives. It has affected the way we do business as well as the way we spend our leisure time. Count the ways you've used the Internet recently. Perhaps you've sent electronic mail (email) to a business associate, paid a utility bill, read a newspaper from a distant city, or looked up a local movie schedule—all by using the Internet. Or, maybe you researched a medical topic, booked a hotel reservation, chatted with a fellow Trekkie, or comparison-shopped for a car. The Internet is a communication system that has brought a wealth of information to our fingertips and organized it for our use.

In this chapter we first give a brief history of the Internet. We formally introduce the TCP/IP protocol suite (Internet model) that we used as a networking model throughout the book. We then discuss briefly the next generation protocol. Access to the Internet, both residential and organizational, is also discussed. Finally we introduce private networks, intranets, and extranets.

OBJECTIVES

After reading this chapter, the reader should be able to:

- ❏ Know how the Internet began.
- ❏ Understand the architecture of today's Internet and its relationship with ISPs.
- ❏ Understand the importance of the TCP/IP protocol suite.
- ❏ Understand the role of IP, UDP, and TCP in the Internet.
- ❏ Understand the difference between the Internet, an intranet, and an extranet.

13.1 HISTORY AND ADMINISTRATION

A **network** is a group of connected, communicating devices such as computers and printers. An internet (note the lowercase *i*) is two or more networks that can communicate with each other. The most notable internet is the Internet (uppercase *I*), a collection of hundreds of thousands of interconnected networks. Private individuals as well as various organizations such as government agencies, schools, research facilities, corporations, and libraries in more than 100 countries use the Internet. Millions of people are users. Yet this extraordinary communication system only came into being in 1969.

ARPANET

In the mid-1960s mainframe computers in research organizations were stand-alone devices. Computers from different manufacturers were unable to communicate with one another. The Advanced Research Projects Agency (ARPA) in the Department of Defense (DOD) was interested in finding a way to connect computers together so that the researchers they funded could share their findings, thereby reducing costs and eliminating duplication of effort.

In 1967, at an Association for Computing Machinery (ACM) meeting, ARPA presented its ideas for **ARPANET,** a small network of connected computers. The idea was that each host computer (not necessarily from the same manufacturer) would be attached to a specialized computer, called an *interface message processor* (IMP). The IMPs, in turn, would be connected to each other. Each IMP had to be able to communicate with other IMPs as well as with its own attached host.

By 1969, ARPANET was a reality. Four nodes, at the University of California at Los Angeles (UCLA), the University of California at Santa Barbara (UCSB), Stanford Research Institute (SRI), and the University of Utah were connected via the IMPs to form a network. Software called the *Network Control Protocol* (NCP) provided communication between the hosts.

BIRTH OF THE INTERNET

In 1972, Vint Cerf and Bob Kahn, both of whom were part of the core ARPANET group, collaborated on what they called the *Internetting Project*. They wanted to link different networks together so that a host on one network could communicate with a host on a second, different network. There were many problems to overcome: diverse packet sizes, diverse interfaces, and diverse transmission rates, as well as differing reliability requirements. Cerf and Kahn devised the idea of a device called a *gateway* to serve as the intermediary hardware to transfer packets from one network to another.

TRANSMISSION CONTROL PROTOCOL/INTERNETWORKING PROTOCOL (TCP/IP)

Cerf and Kahn's landmark 1973 paper outlined the protocols to achieve end-to-end delivery of packets. This was a new version of NCP. This paper on transmission control protocol (TCP) included concepts such as encapsulation, the datagram, and the functions of a gateway. A radical idea was the transfer of responsibility for error correction from the IMP to the host machine. This ARPA Internet now became the focus of the communication effort. Around this time responsibility for the ARPANET was handed over to the Defense Communication Agency (DCA).

In October 1977 an internet consisting of three different networks (ARPANET, packet radio, and packet satellite) was successfully demonstrated. Communication between networks was now possible.

Shortly thereafter, authorities made a decision to split TCP into two protocols: Transmission Control Protocol (TCP) and Internetworking Protocol (IP). IP would handle datagram routing while TCP would be responsible for higher level functions such as segmentation, reassembly, and error detection. The internetworking protocol became known as TCP/IP.

In 1981, under a DARPA contract, UC Berkeley modified the UNIX operating system to include TCP/IP. This inclusion of network software along with a popular operating system did much to further the popularity of networking. The open (non-manufacturer-specific) implementation on Berkeley UNIX gave every manufacturer a working code base on which they could build their products.

In 1983 authorities abolished the original ARPANET protocols, and TCP/IP became the official protocol for the ARPANET. Those who wanted to use the Internet to access a computer on a different network had to be running TCP/IP.

THE INTERNET TODAY

The Internet has gone through many changes since 1983. The Internet today is not a simple hierarchical structure. It is made up of many wide and local area networks joined by connecting devices and switching stations. It is difficult to give an accurate representation of the Internet because it is continuously changing—new networks are being added, existing networks need more addresses, and networks of defunct companies need to be removed. Today most end users who want Internet connection use the services of Internet service providers (ISPs). There are international service providers, national service providers, regional service providers, and local service providers. The Internet today is run by private companies, not the government. Figure 13.1 shows a conceptual (not geographical) view of the Internet.

International Service Providers
At the top of the hierarchy are the international service providers that connect nations together.

National Service Providers (NSPs)
National service providers (NSPs) are backbone networks created and maintained by specialized companies. There are many NSPs operating in North America; some of the most well-known are SprintLink, PSINet, UUNet Technology, AGIS, and internet MCI. To provide connectivity between the end users, these backbone networks are connected by complex switching stations (normally run by a third party) called network access points (NAPs). Some NSP networks are also connected to each other by private switching stations called peering points. NSPs normally operate at a high data rate (up to 600 Mbps).

Regional Internet Service Providers
Regional Internet service providers or regional ISPs are small ISPs that are connected to one or more NSPs. They are at the third level of hierarchy with a lesser data rate.

Local Internet Service Providers
Local Internet service providers provide direct service to the end user. The local ISPs can be connected to regional ISPs or directly to NSPs. Most end users are connected

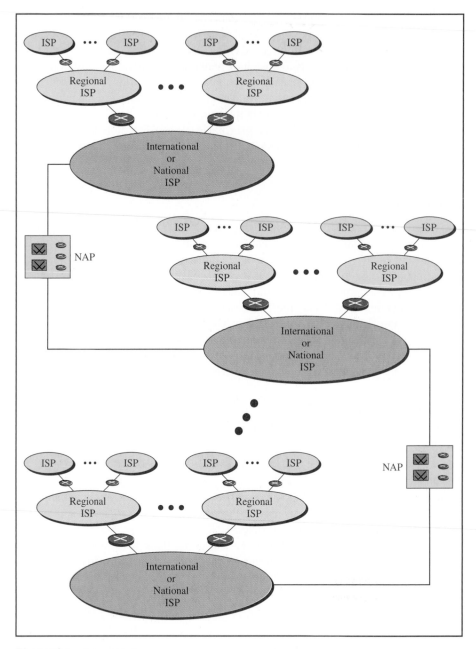

Figure 13.1 Internet today

to the local ISPs. Note that in this sense, a local ISP can be a company that just provides Internet services, a corporation with a network that supplies services to its own employees, or a nonprofit organization, such as a college or a university, that runs its own network. Each of these can be connected to a regional or national service provider.

© Corbis/Vol. 35

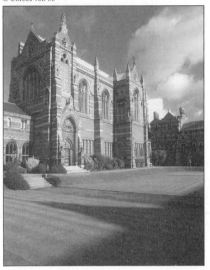

A local ISP can in some cases be a nonprofit
organization, such as a college or university that's
providing Internet service.

BUSINESS FOCUS: TIME LINE

The following is a list of important Internet events in chronological order:

❏ **1969.** Four-node ARPANET established.
❏ **1970.** ARPA hosts implement NCP.
❏ **1973.** Development of TCP/IP suite begins.
❏ **1977.** An internet tested using TCP/IP.
❏ **1978.** UNIX distributed to academic/research sites.
❏ **1981.** CSNET established.
❏ **1983.** TCP/IP becomes the official protocol for ARPANET.
❏ **1983.** MILNET born.
❏ **1986.** NSFNET established.
❏ **1990.** ARPANET decommissioned and replaced by NSFNET.
❏ **1995.** NSFNET goes back to being a research network.
❏ **1995.** Companies known as Internet service providers (ISPs) started.

GROWTH OF THE INTERNET

The Internet has grown tremendously. In just a few decades, the number of networks has
increased from tens to hundreds of thousands. Concurrently, the number of computers
connected to the networks has grown from hundreds to hundreds of millions. The Internet
is still growing. Factors that have an impact on this growth include the following:

❏ **New Protocols.** New protocols need to be added and obsolete ones need to be
removed. For example, a protocol superior in many respects to IPv4 has been
approved as a standard but not yet fully implemented.

❑ **New Technology.** New technologies are under development that will increase the capacity of networks and provide more bandwidth to the Internet's users.

❑ **Increasing Use of Multimedia.** It is predicted that the Internet, once just a vehicle to share data, will be used more and more for multimedia (audio and video).

INTERNET STANDARDS

An **Internet standard** is a thoroughly tested specification that is useful to and adhered to by those who work with the Internet. It is a formalized regulation that must be followed. There is a strict procedure by which a specification attains Internet standard status. A specification begins as an Internet draft. An **Internet draft** is a working document (a work in progress) with no official status and a six-month lifetime. Upon recommendation from the Internet authorities, a draft may be published as a **Request for Comment** (RFC). Each RFC is edited, assigned a number, and made available to all interested parties.

RFCs go through maturity levels and are categorized according to their requirement level.

TECHNICAL FOCUS: MATURITY LEVELS OF AN RFC

An RFC, during its lifetime, falls into one of six maturity levels: proposed standard, draft standard, Internet standard, historic, experimental, and informational (see Figure below).

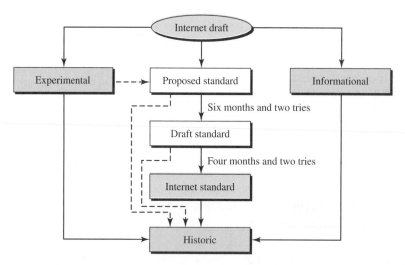

❑ A **proposed standard** is a specification that is stable, well understood, and of sufficient interest to the Internet community.

❑ A proposed standard is elevated to **draft standard** status after at least two successful independent and interoperable implementations.

❑ A draft standard reaches **Internet standard** status after demonstrations of successful implementation.

❑ A **historic RFC** is significant from a historical perspective. It either has been superseded by later specifications or has never passed the necessary maturity levels to become an Internet standard.

- ❏ An **experimental RFC** describes work related to an experimental situation that does not affect the operation of the Internet.
- ❏ An **informational RFC** contains general, historical, or tutorial information related to the Internet.

RFCs can be found at *http://www.rfc-editor.org*

INTERNET ADMINISTRATION

The Internet, with its roots primarily in the research domain, has evolved and gained a broader user base with significant commercial activity. Various groups that coordinate Internet issues have guided this growth and development. Appendix C gives the addresses, email addresses, and telephone numbers for some of these groups. Figure 13.2 shows the general organization of Internet administration.

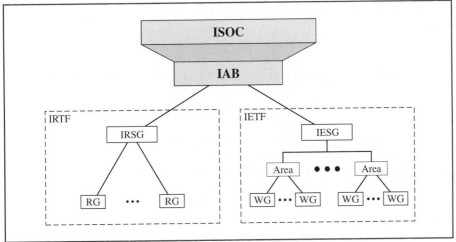

Figure 13.2   Internet administration

Internet Society (ISOC)

The **Internet Society** (ISOC) is an international, nonprofit organization formed in 1992 to provide support for the Internet standards process. ISOC accomplishes this through maintaining and supporting other Internet administrative bodies such as IAB, IETF, IRTF, and IANA (see the following sections). ISOC also promotes research and other scholarly activities relating to the Internet.

Internet Architecture Board (IAB)

The **Internet Architecture Board** (IAB) is the technical advisor to the ISOC. The main purposes of the IAB are to oversee the continuing development of the TCP/IP protocol suite and to serve in a technical advisory capacity to research members of the Internet community. IAB accomplishes this through its two primary components, the Internet Engineering Task Force (IETF) and the Internet Research Task Force (IRTF). Another responsibility of the IAB is the editorial management of the RFCs, described earlier in this chapter. IAB is also the external liaison between the Internet and other standards organizations and forums.

Internet Engineering Task Force (IETF)

The **Internet Engineering Task Force** (IETF) is a forum of working groups managed by the Internet Engineering Steering Group (IESG). IETF is responsible for identifying operational problems and proposing solutions to these problems. IETF also develops and reviews specifications intended as Internet standards. The working groups are collected into areas, and each area concentrates on a specific topic. Currently nine areas have been defined, although this is by no means a hard and fast number. The areas are:

❏ Applications
❏ Internet protocols
❏ Routing
❏ Operations
❏ User services
❏ Network management
❏ Transport
❏ Internet protocol next generation (IPng)
❏ Security

Internet Research Task Force (IRTF)

The **Internet Research Task Force** (IRTF) is a forum of working groups managed by the Internet Research Steering Group (IRSG). IRTF focuses on long-term research topics related to Internet protocols, applications, architecture, and technology.

Internet Assigned Numbers Authority (IANA) and Internet Corporation for Assigned Names and Numbers (ICANN)

The **Internet Assigned Numbers Authority** (IANA), supported by the U.S. government, was responsible for the management of Internet domain names and addresses until October 1998. At that time the **Internet Corporation for Assigned Names and Numbers** (ICANN), a private, nonprofit corporation managed by an international board, assumed IANA operations.

Network Information Center (NIC)

The **Network Information Center** (NIC) is responsible for collecting and distributing information about TCP/IP protocols.

13.2   TCP/IP PROTOCOL SUITE

The **Transmission Control Protocol/Internetworking Protocol** (TCP/IP) is a set of protocols, or a protocol suite, that defines how all transmissions are exchanged across the Internet. Named after its two most popular protocols, TCP/IP has been in active use for many years and has demonstrated its effectiveness on a worldwide scale.

The TCP/IP protocol suite is the Internet model we discussed in Chapter 1 and developed throughout the book. The suite is made of five layers. However, the Internet is only concerned with the top three layers. The TCP/IP protocol suite software, installed on any computer that uses this protocol, involves the network layer (IP and related protocols), the transport layer (UDP and TCP), and the application layer

(SMTP, TELNET, etc.). The lower two layers are the responsibility of the wide area and local area networks that form the physical Internet; they form the roads (a LAN can be viewed as a road) and highways (a WAN can be viewed as a highway) over which the Internet packets travel to reach their destinations.

In this section, we discuss the three upper layers of the Internet protocol (TCP/IP protocol suite). The layout of the TCP/IP protocol suite is repeated in Figure 13.3 for reference.

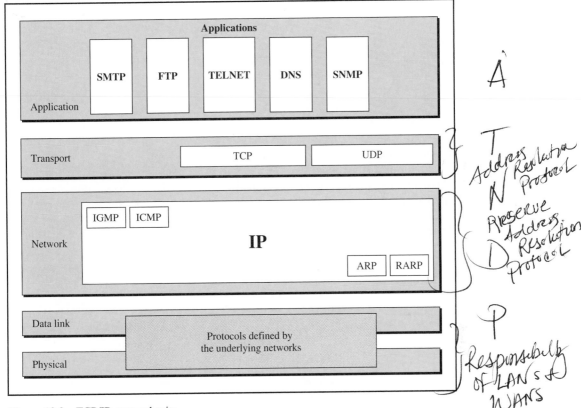

Figure 13.3 TCP/IP protocol suite

NETWORK LAYER

At the network layer (or, more accurately, the internetwork layer), TCP/IP supports the Internetwork Protocol (IP). IP, in turn, contains four supporting protocols: ARP, RARP, ICMP, and IGMP. Each of these protocols is described later in this chapter.

Internetwork Protocol (IP)

IP is the transmission mechanism used by TCP/IP. It is a best-effort delivery service. The term *best-effort* means that IP provides no error checking or tracking. IP assumes the unreliability of the underlying layers and does its best to get a transmission through to its destination, but with no guarantees. As we have seen in previous chapters, transmissions along physical networks can be destroyed for a number of reasons. Noise can cause bit errors during transmission across a medium; a congested router may discard a datagram if it is unable to relay it before a time limit runs out; routing quirks can end in looping and the ultimate destruction of a datagram; and disabled links may leave no usable path to the destination.

If reliability is important, IP must be paired with a reliable protocol such as TCP. An example of a more commonly understood best-effort delivery service is the post office. The post office does its best to deliver the mail but does not always succeed. If an unregistered letter is lost, it is up to the sender or would-be recipient to discover the loss and rectify the problem. The post office itself does not keep track of every letter and cannot notify a sender of loss or damage. An example of a situation similar to pairing IP with a protocol that contains reliability functions is a self-addressed, stamped postcard included in a letter mailed through the post office. When the letter is delivered, the receiver mails the postcard back to the sender to prove successful receipt of the letter. If the sender never receives the postcard, he or she assumes the letter was lost and sends out another copy.

IP transports data in packets called datagrams (described below), each of which is transported separately. Datagrams may travel along different routes and may arrive out of sequence or duplicated. IP does not keep track of the routes and has no facility for reordering datagrams once they arrive. Because it is a connectionless service, IP does not create virtual circuits for delivery. There is no call setup to alert the receiver to an incoming transmission.

The limited functionality of IP should not be considered a weakness, however. IP provides bare-bones transmission functions that free the user to add only those facilities necessary for a given application and thereby allows for maximum efficiency.

Datagram   Packets in the IP layer are called **datagrams.** Figure 13.4 shows the **IP datagram** format. A datagram is a variable-length packet consisting of two parts: header and data. The header can be from 20 to 60 bytes and contains information essential to routing and delivery.

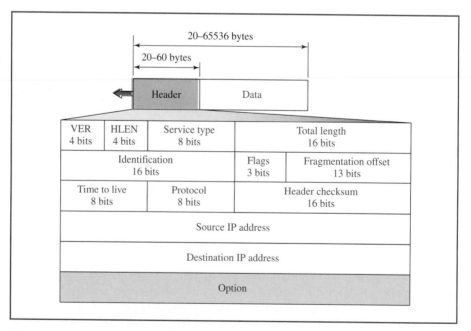

Figure 13.4   IP datagram

TECHNICAL FOCUS: INSIDE THE HEADER OF AN IP DATAGRAM

An IP datagram contains several fields. The most important are the source and destination addresses of the datagram (IP addresses). The header also contains fields related to fragmentation. The size of a datagram may be too large for some LAN or WAN protocols. In this case, the datagram is divided into fragments; each fragment carries the same identification number as well as other information to help the receiver assemble the datagram. The header also has two length fields; one defines the length of the header, the other defines the length of the entire packet. One field that can decrease traffic on the Internet holds the number of routers a packet can visit before it is discarded. The header also contains a checksum field to determine the validity of the packet.

Addressing   In addition to the physical addresses that identify individual devices, the Internet requires an additional addressing convention: an address that identifies the connection of a host to its network.

Each **Internet address** (IP address) consists of 32 bits, normally written as four decimal numbers separated by dots (called dotted-decimal notation). Figure 13.5 shows an IP address.

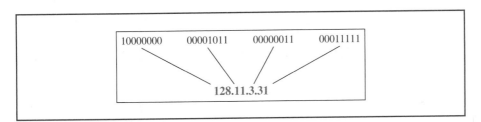

Figure 13.5   Internet address

TECHNICAL FOCUS: CLASSFUL VERSUS CLASSLESS ADDRESSING

With more and more organizations wanting to use the Internet, the Internet authorities are running out of IP addresses. Internet addresses were originally designed as classful addresses. By this, we mean that the total number of 32-bit addresses (2^{32} or almost four billion) was divided unevenly into five classes: A, B, C, D, and E. Classes A, B, and C are granted to organizations. Class A contains blocks of addresses with a very large range. Each block is granted to one organization, but most of these organizations never use their allotted number of addresses. This is a tremendous waste of addresses. Class B contains smaller blocks of addresses than Class A. Still, most organizations never use all the addresses that they are assigned. This is yet another waste of addresses. Class C contains smaller blocks of addresses (only 256 addresses per block). This range is so limited that even small organizations do not want a block of Class C addresses. Classes D and E are reserved, the first for multicasting and the second for future use. Many addresses in these classes are also unused.

Recently, a new design called classless addressing has been implemented. In this design, all available addresses are put into a big pool; each organization is granted a range of addresses according to its need. If all previously granted and reserved addresses can be recycled into this pool and new addresses assigned to each organization, the addressing problem of the Internet will be solved (at least for the next few decades).

A Sample Internet

Figure 13.6 shows a portion of the Internet made up of LANs and WANs. Each device (computer or router) connected to the Internet has one IP address for each connection. This means that if a router connects two LANs, it has two IP addresses, one for each connection. Hosts (computers) usually have only one address. A network is also defined by an address.

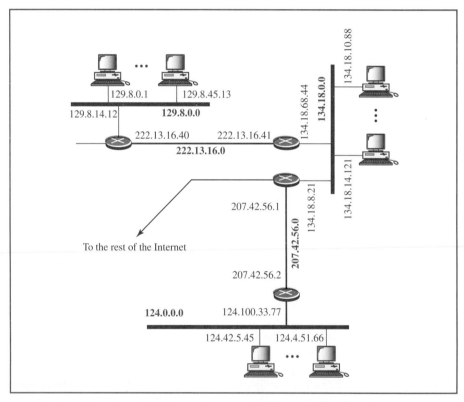

Figure 13.6   A part of the Internet

Other Protocols in the Network Layer

TCP/IP supports four other protocols in the network layer: ARP, RARP, ICMP, and IGMP.

Address Resolution Protocol (ARP)   The **Address Resolution Protocol** (ARP) associates an IP address with a physical address. On a typical physical network, such as a LAN, each device on a link is identified by a physical or station address usually imprinted on the network interface card (NIC).

Anytime a host, or a router, needs to find the physical address of another host on its network, it uses the services of ARP. It forms an ARP query packet that includes the known IP address and broadcasts the packet over the network. Every host on the network receives and processes the ARP packet, but only the intended recipient recognizes its internet address and sends back its physical address. With this new information, the requesting host or router can now send the datagram on its way.

Reverse Address Resolution Protocol (RARP)   The **Reverse Address Resolution Protocol** (RARP) allows a host to discover its internet address when it knows only its physical address. It was designed especially for diskless computers. Today, since a computer stores its IP address on its disk, RARP has little use.

Internet Control Message Protocol (ICMP)

The **Internet Control Message Protocol** (ICMP) is a mechanism used by hosts and routers to send notification of datagram problems back to the sender.

As we saw above, IP is essentially a best-effort delivery. ICMP, however, allows IP to inform a sender if a datagram is undeliverable. A datagram travels from router to router until it reaches one that can deliver it to its final destination. If a router is unable to route or deliver the datagram because of unusual conditions (disabled links, or the device has been removed) or because of network congestion, ICMP allows it to inform the original source.

ICMP can also be used to check the status of devices; it can check whether or not a device (computer or router) is functioning. This is done by sending a message to the device. A lack of response indicates that the device is down.

Internet Group Message Protocol (IGMP)

The IP protocol is involved in two types of communication: unicast and multicast. *Unicasting* is the communication between one sender and one receiver. It is a one-to-one communication. However, sometimes there is a need to send the same message to multiple numbers of receivers simultaneously. This is called *multicasting,* which is a one-to-many communication. Multicasting has many applications. For example, stockbrokers can be simultaneously informed of changes in a stock price, or travel agents can be informed of a trip cancellation. Some other applications include distance learning and video-on-demand.

The **Internet Group Message Protocol** (IGMP) helps a multicast router identify the hosts in a LAN that are members of a multicast group. It is a companion to the IP protocol.

TRANSPORT LAYER

The transport layer is represented in TCP/IP by two protocols: TCP and UDP. Of these, UDP is the simpler; it provides nonsequenced transport functionality when reliability and security are less important than size and speed. Most applications, however, require reliable end-to-end delivery and so use TCP.

The transport protocols of the TCP/IP suite define a set of connections to individual processes called protocol ports or, more simply, ports. A port is a source or destination point used by a particular process.

The IP is a host-to-host protocol, meaning that it can deliver a packet from one physical device to another. TCP/IP's transport level protocols are port-to-port protocols that work on top of the IP protocols to deliver the packet from the originating port to the IP services at the start of a transmission, and from the IP services to the destination port at the end.

Each port is defined by a positive integer address carried in the header of a transport layer packet. An IP datagram uses the host's 32-bit internet address. A packet at the transport level uses the process **port address** of 16 bits, enough to allow up to 65,536 (0 to 65,535) ports.

User Datagram Protocol (UDP)

The **User Datagram Protocol** (UDP) is the simpler of the two standard TCP/IP transport protocols. It is an end-to-end transport level protocol that adds only port addresses, checksum error control, and length information to the data from the upper layer. The packet produced by UDP is called a *user datagram* (see Figure 13.7).

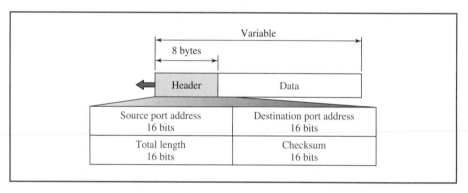

Figure 13.7   UDP user datagram format

UDP provides only the basic functions needed for end-to-end delivery of a transmission. It does not provide any sequencing or reordering functions and cannot specify the damaged packet when reporting an error (for which it must be paired with ICMP). UDP can discover that an error has occurred; ICMP can then inform the sender that a user datagram has been damaged and discarded. Neither, however, has the ability to specify which packet has been lost. UDP contains only a checksum; it does not contain an ID or sequencing number for a particular data segment.

The header of the UDP datagram is very simple: it contains only four fields. One field defines the application program that has sent the packet (the source), and another defines the application program that is to receive the packet (the destination). Another field defines the length of the entire packet. The last field carries a checksum for error detection.

Transmission Control Protocol (TCP)

The **Transmission Control Protocol** (TCP) provides full transport layer services to application programs. TCP is a reliable, stream-transport port-to-port protocol. The term *stream,* in this context, means connection-oriented: a connection must be established between both ends of a transmission before either may transmit data. By creating this connection, TCP generates a virtual circuit between sender and receiver that is active for the duration of a transmission. (Connections for the duration of an entire exchange are different, and are handled by session functions in individual applications.) TCP begins each transmission by alerting the receiver that datagrams are on their way (connection establishment) and ends each transmission with a connection termination. In this way, the receiver knows to expect an entire transmission rather than just a single packet.

The TCP Segment   The scope of the services provided by TCP requires that the segment header be extensive (see Figure 13.8). A comparison of the TCP segment format with that of the UDP user datagram shows the differences between the two protocols.

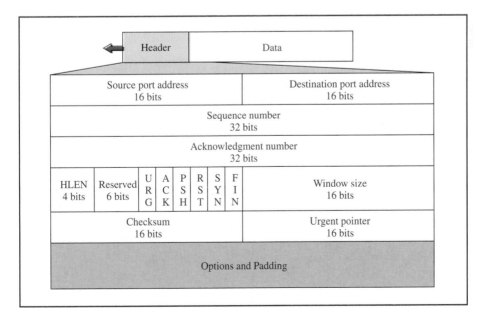

Figure 13.8 TCP segment format

TCP provides a comprehensive range of reliability functions, at the sacrifice of speed (connections must be established, acknowledgments waited for, etc.). Because of its smaller frame size, UDP is much faster than TCP, at the sacrifice of reliability.

TECHNICAL FOCUS: INSIDE A TCP SEGMENT HEADER

The header of a segment is very complicated and contains optional as well as mandatory fields. We briefly discuss just the required fields. One pair of fields defines the source and destination application programs. Another pair are used for error and flow control; one holds the unique sequence number, and the other holds the acknowledgment number. One field defines the size of the sliding window in the transport layer. The sliding window in the transport layer uses the same concept as the one in the data-link layer (see Chapter 5). There are also flags that define the purpose of the segment (for connection establishment, for termination, for acknowledgment, and so on). The last required field carries a checksum for error detection.

APPLICATION LAYER

The top layer in the TCP/IP protocol suite is the application layer. Several client-server programs are defined in this layer; these were discussed in Chapter 2. We will discuss one more application layer program in Chapter 16 when we talk about network management.

13.3   NEXT GENERATION

The network layer protocol in the TCP/IP protocol suite is currently IPv4 (Internetworking Protocol, version 4). IPv4 provides the host-to-host communication between systems in the Internet. Although IPv4 is well designed, data communication has evolved since the inception of IPv4 in the 1970s. IPv4 has some deficiencies that make it unsuitable for the fast-growing Internet, including the following:

❑   Although theoretically more than 4 billion addresses are available in IPv4, the addresses are used unwisely. Many organizations have received a multimillion-address block; many of the addresses are left unused.
❑   The Internet must accommodate real-time audio and video transmission. This type of transmission requires minimum delay strategies and reservation of resources not provided in the IPv4 design.
❑   The Internet must provide data security for some applications. No security is provided by IPv4.

To overcome these deficiencies, **Internetworking Protocol, version 6** (IPv6), also known as **Internetworking Protocol, next generation** (IPng) was designed and is now a standard. In IPv6, the protocol was extensively modified to accommodate the unforeseen growth of the Internet. The format and the length of the IP addresses were changed along with the packet format. Related protocols, such as ICMP, were also modified. Other protocols in the network layer, such as ARP, RARP, and IGMP, were either deleted or included in the ICMP protocol.

Communication experts predicted that IPv6 and its related protocols would soon replace the current IP version. However, some activities have delayed this change. The ISPs are using the IP addresses more wisely. Some of the unused addresses are being recycled. Security is now being implemented at the application and transport layer. The Internet authorities are hopeful that security will soon be implemented at the IP layer (see Chapter 14). For these reasons, the universal implementation of IPv6 has been delayed. There are some who predict that it may never happen.

13.4 ACCESS TO THE INTERNET

To use the Internet, one must access it. The technology used to access the Internet can be roughly divided into residential access and organizational access.

RESIDENTIAL ACCESS

We discussed residential access to the Internet in Chapter 8. Access can be either through a modem (and telephone line), through a DSL line, or through a cable-TV line.

ORGANIZATIONAL ACCESS

An organization usually needs a higher bandwidth than that offered to the residential user. The solution can be a high-speed point-to-point WAN connection such as a T-1 or T-3 line connected to an ISP. An organization can also use the services of a SONET line that is connected to the Internet. Another solution is connection to a switched wide area network that already has a connection to the Internet. In all of these cases, the organization gains access to the Internet and becomes part of it. The Internet grows every time a new user is connected.

13.5 PRIVATE NETWORKS: INTRANET AND EXTRANET

A private network is designed primarily for use inside an organization. It allows access to shared resources and, at the same time, provides privacy. Before we discuss some aspects of these networks, let us define two commonly used terms: intranet and extranet.

INTRANET

An **intranet** is a private network (LAN) that uses the TCP/IP protocol suite. However, access to the network is limited only to the users inside the organization. The network uses application programs defined for the global Internet, such as HTTP and may have web servers, print servers, and file servers, and so on.

EXTRANET

An **extranet** is the same as an intranet with one major difference. Some resources may be accessed by specific groups of users outside the organization under the control of the network administrator. For example, an organization may allow authorized customers access to product specifications, availability, and online ordering. A university or a college can allow distance learning students access to the computer lab after passwords have been checked.

TECHNICAL FOCUS: NETWORK ADDRESS TRANSLATION (NAT)

A technology that is related to private networks is **network address translation** (NAT). The technology allows a site to use a set of private addresses for internal communication and a set of (at least one) global Internet addresses for communication with other sites. The site must have only one single connection to the global Internet through a router that runs the NAT software. The following figure shows a simple implementation of NAT.

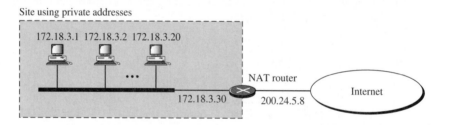

As the figure shows, the private network uses private addresses. The router that connects the network to the global address uses one private address and one global address. The private network is transparent to the rest of the Internet; the rest of the Internet sees only the NAT router with the address 200.24.5.8.

All of the outgoing packets go through the NAT router, which replaces the *source address* in the packet with the global NAT address. All incoming packets also pass through the NAT router, which replaces the *destination address* in the packet (the NAT router global address) with the appropriate private address.

An ISP that serves dial-up customers can use NAT technology to conserve addresses. For example, imagine an ISP is granted 1000 addresses, but has 100,000 customers. The ISP can divide the customers into 1000 groups, with each group covering 100 customers. Each of the customers in a group is assigned a private network address. The customers in each group form an imaginary private network. The ISP translates each of the 100 source addresses in outgoing packets to one global address; it translates the global destination address in incoming packets to the corresponding private address.

N AHP depends heavily on the Internet and therefore the TCP/IP protocol for its business. First, it has a website that enables physicians and home care centers to learn about the available services. Second, it uses the World Wide Web and email to receive orders from patients, physicians, and home care centers. The Internet is also used to communicate with the vendors and raw materials providers.

NAHP is connected via a T-3 line to a local ISP. As we saw in Chapter 4, the company has 256 IP addresses (from 201.14.56.0 to 201.14.56.255). Every IP packet with one of these addresses as the destination is routed to the company. As a matter of fact, the company is known to the rest of the Internet as site address 201.14.56.0.

When a router anywhere in the world receives a packet with 201.14.56 as the first three numbers of the destination address, the packet is routed to the router (switch) in the basement. This router is known, by the rest of the Internet, as the destination for the above 256 addresses. The rest of the Internet has no idea how the 256 addresses are distributed inside NAHP, but they know that the packet must be sent to the router in the basement. The following figure shows the situation.

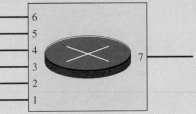

Fast Ethernet Switch

The router uses the following routing table:

Address	Interface
201.14.56.0 to 201.14.56.31	6
201.14.56.32 to 201.14.56.63	5
201.14.56.64 to 201.14.56.95	4
201.14.56.96 to 201.14.56.127	3
201.14.56.128 to 201.14.56.159	2
201.14.56.160 to 201.14.56.191	1

13.6   KEY TERMS

address resolution protocol (ARP)
Advanced Research Project
    Agency (ARPA)
Advanced Research Project Agency
    Network (ARPANET)
datagram
dotted-decimal notation
Internet address
Internet Architecture Board (IAB)
Internet Assigned Numbers
    Authority (IANA)
Internet Control Message
    Protocol (ICMP)
Internet Corporation for Assigned
    Names and Numbers (ICANN)

Internet draft
Internet Engineering Task Force (IETF)
Internet Group Message Protocol
    (IGMP)
Internet service provider (ISP)
Internet Society (ISOC)
Internet standard
Internetworking Protocol (IP)
Internetworking Protocol, next
    generation (IPng)
Internetworking Protocol,
    version 6 (IPv6)
Internet Research Task Force (IRTF)
intranet
IP address

IP datagram
IPv4
local ISP
maturity level
multicasting
national service provider (NSP)
network access point (NAP)
network address translation (NAT)
Network Information Center (NIC)
port address
private network

regional ISP
Request for Comment (RFC)
Reverse Address Resolution
    Protocol (RARP)
segment
Transmission Control Protocol (TCP)
Transmission Control Protocol/
    Internetworking Protocol (TCP/IP)
unicasting
user datagram
User Datagram Protocol (UDP)

13.7 SUMMARY

❏ A network is a group of connected, communicating devices. An internet is two or more connected networks.

❏ The Internet is a collection of hundreds of thousands of networks.

❏ ARPANET began as a network with four nodes.

❏ Local Internet service providers (ISPs) connect individual users to the Internet.

❏ Regional Internet service providers connect local Internet service providers.

❏ National service providers (NSPs) are backbone networks created and maintained by specialized companies.

❏ An RFC goes through the proposed standard level and then the draft standard level before it becomes an Internet standard.

❏ The Internet Society (ISOC) promotes research and other scholarly activities relating to the Internet.

❏ The Internet Architecture Board (IAB) is the technical advisor to the ISOC.

❏ The Internet Engineering Task Force (IETF) is a forum of working groups responsible for identifying operational problems and proposing solutions to these problems.

❏ The Internet Research Task Force (IRTF) is a forum of working groups focusing on long-term research topics related to Internet protocols, applications, architecture, and technology.

❏ The Internet Corporation for Assigned Names and Numbers (ICANN), formerly known as IANA, is responsible for the management of Internet domain names and addresses.

❏ The Network Information Center (NIC) is responsible for collecting and distributing information about TCP/IP protocols.

❏ Transmission Control Protocol/Internetworking Protocol (TCP/IP) is a set of rules and procedures that govern the exchange of messages in an internetwork. TCP/IP is the protocol suite for the Internet.

❏ The Internetwork Protocol (IP) defines operations at the network layer. IP is a best-effort delivery protocol.

❏ The IP packet, called the datagram, consists of a variable-length header and a variable-length data field.

❏ An internet address (better known as the IP address) uniquely defines the connection of a host to its network.

❑ The 32-bit IP address is usually written in dotted-decimal notation.
❑ The address resolution protocol (ARP) finds the physical address of a device given the IP address.
❑ The reverse address resolution protocol (RARP) will find a host's IP address from its physical address.
❑ The internet control message protocol (ICMP) handles control and error messages in the IP layer.
❑ There are two protocols at the transport level: User Datagram Protocol (UDP) and Transmission Control Protocol (TCP).
❑ A protocol port is a source or destination point of an executing program in the application layer.
❑ UDP is unreliable and connectionless. The UDP packet is called a user datagram.
❑ TCP is reliable and connection-oriented. The packet is called a segment.
❑ IPv6 is the latest version of the Internet Protocol.
❑ A private network is solely for the internal use of an organization.
❑ An intranet is a private network that uses the TCP/IP protocol suite.
❑ An extranet is an intranet that allows authorized access from outside users.
❑ Network address translation allows a private network to use a set of private addresses for internal communication and a set of global Internet addresses for external communication.

 PRACTICE SET

Review Questions

1. What is the difference between an internet and the Internet?
2. What is the significance of ARPANET in Internet history?
3. How did the TCP/IP protocol suite come into being?
4. Name the different types of service providers and show their hierarchy.
5. What is an RFC?
6. Which Internet group is responsible for the management of Internet domain names and addresses?
7. Name the five layers of the TCP/IP protocol suite. Which layers concern the Internet?
8. What is the purpose of ICMP?
9. What is the packet produced by UDP called? What is the packet produced by TCP called?
10. Name some differences between IPv4 and IPv6.
11. How does an intranet differ from an extranet?

Multiple-Choice Questions

12. Three computers and one printer all connected together can be called _____.
    a. an internet
    b. an Internet
    c. a network
    d. an internetwork

13. The first network was called _____.
    a. ARPANET
    b. Internet
    c. ISP
    d. TCP/IP

14. A residential customer probably uses the services of _____ service provider for Internet access.
    a. an international
    b. a national
    c. a regional
    d. a local

15. _____ is a thoroughly tested specification that is useful to and adhered to by those who work with the Internet.
    a. An Internet draft
    b. An RFC
    c. An Internet standard
    d. A draft standard

16. Which group oversees all other Internet administration groups?
    a. ICANN
    b. ISOC
    c. ISO
    d. IETF

17. Packets in the IP layer are called _____.
    a. headers
    b. datagrams
    c. segments
    d. user segments

18. Packets in the transport layer produced by TCP are called _____.
    a. headers
    b. datagrams
    c. segments
    d. user segments

19. An Internet address is _____ numbers separated by dots.
    a. 3
    b. 4
    c. 5
    d. any of the above

20. The purpose of ARP on a network is to find the _____ given the _____.
    a. Internet address, domain name
    b. Internet address, netid
    c. Internet address, station address
    d. station address, Internet address

21. Which of the following apply to UDP?
    a. unreliable
    b. contains destination and source port addresses
    c. connectionless
    d. all of the above

22. Which of the following applies to both UDP and TCP?
    a. transport layer protocols
    b. port-to-port communication
    c. services of IP layer used
    d. all of the above
23. When a host knows its physical address but not its IP address, it can use _____.
    a. ICMP
    b. IGMP
    c. ARP
    d. RARP
24. This transport layer protocol requires acknowledgment.
    a. UDP
    b. TCP
    c. FTP
    d. NVT
25. IPv6 is also known as _____.
    a. TCPv6
    b. IPnew
    c. IPnext
    d. IPng
26. An _____ is a private network with no external access that uses the TCP/IP protocol suite.
    a. Internet
    b. internet
    c. intranet
    d. extranet
27. An _____ is a private network with limited external access that uses the TCP/IP protocol suite.
    a. Internet
    b. internet
    c. intranet
    d. extranet

PART IV

Security and Management

CHAPTER 14

Network Security:
Firewalls and VPNs

Today, few networks exist in isolation. The LANs and backbone networks of an organization are often connected to the backbones and LANs of other organizations. This is done either through the Internet or some other wide area network and allows the quick access and rapid exchange of information between organizations.

However, because information is an asset and because of the way the Internet has been set up, criminals and other evil-doers have the opportunity to engage in illegal activities. The integrity of an organization may be in danger if appropriate security precautions are not implemented to protect the assets.

In this chapter, we look at four issues of security: privacy, authentication, integrity, and nonrepudiation. We show how the first can be achieved through secret-key or private-key encryption. We discuss a concept called digital signature that satisfies the three other conditions. We talk about how security is implemented in the Internet. One way is to lock out intruders through the use of firewalls. We also discuss virtual private networks, a technology that allows private communication between geographically-separate sections of an organization via the public Internet. And finally, we briefly consider the topic of access control methods.

OBJECTIVES

After reading this chapter, the reader should be able to:

❏ List and distinguish between the four conditions of security.

❏ Understand how privacy can be achieved through encryption/decryption.

❏ Understand the digital signature concept and how it can be used to provide authentication, integrity, and nonrepudiation.

❏ Understand firewalls and their use in isolating an organization from intruders.

❏ Be familiar with VPN technology and how it provides privacy.

❏ Understand the different access control methods.

14.1 INTRODUCTION

Security is becoming more and more crucial as the volume of data being exchanged on the Internet increases. When people use the Internet, they have certain expectations. They expect confidentiality and data integrity. They want to be able to identify the sender of a message. They want to be able to prove that a message has in fact been sent by a certain sender even if the sender denies it.

© Corbis/Vol. 13

As the electronic process is increasingly a part of the way money is transferred and tracked, keeping the integrity of the data is vital.

Based on the above expectations, we can say that network security involves four conditions: privacy (confidentiality), message authentication, message integrity and nonrepudiation (see Figure 14.1).

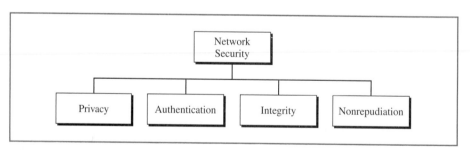

Figure 14.1 Aspects of security

PRIVACY

Privacy means that the sender and the receiver expect confidentiality. The transmitted message must make sense to only the intended receiver. To all others, the message must be unintelligible.

AUTHENTICATION

Authentication means that the receiver is sure of the sender's identity and that an imposter has not sent the message.

INTEGRITY

Integrity means that the data must arrive at the receiver exactly as it was sent. There must be no changes during the transmission, either accidental or malicious. As more and more monetary exchanges occur over the Internet, integrity is crucial. For example, it would be disastrous if a request for transferring $100 changes to a request for $10,000 or $100,000. The integrity of the message must be preserved in a secure communication.

NONREPUDIATION

Nonrepudiation means that a receiver must be able to prove that a received message came from a specific sender. The sender must not be able to deny sending a message that he, in fact, did send. The burden of proof falls on the receiver. For example, when a customer sends a message to transfer money from one account to another, the bank must have proof that the customer actually requested this transaction.

© Corbis/Vol. 253

When a customer sends a message to transfer money from one account to another, the bank must have proof that the customer actually requested this transaction.

14.2 PRIVACY

The concept of how to achieve privacy has not changed for thousands of years: The message must be encrypted. That is, the message must be rendered unintelligible to unauthorized parties. A good privacy technique guarantees to some extent that a potential intruder (eavesdropper) cannot understand the contents of the message.

The data to be encrypted at the sender site is called plaintext. The encrypted data is called ciphertext and is decrypted at the receiver. There are two categories of encryption/decryption methods: secret-key methods and public-key methods.

SECRET-KEY ENCRYPTION/DECRYPTION

In secret-key encryption/decryption, the same key is used by both parties. The sender uses this key and an encryption algorithm (program) to encrypt data; the receiver uses the same key and the corresponding decryption algorithm to decrypt the data (see Figure 14.2).

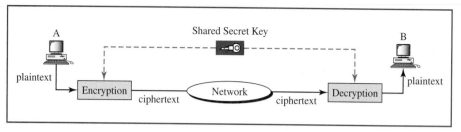

Figure 14.2   Secret-key encryption

In secret-key encryption, the same key is used by the sender (for encryption) and the receiver (for decryption). The key is shared.

BUSINESS FOCUS: DES

One common method of secret-key encryption is the data encryption standard (DES). DES was designed by IBM and adopted by the U.S. government as the standard encryption method for nonmilitary and nonclassified use. The algorithm manipulates a 64-bit plaintext with a 56-bit key. The text is put through 19 different and very complex procedures to create a 64-bit ciphertext.

PUBLIC-KEY ENCRYPTION

In public-key encryption, there are two keys: a private key and a public key. The private key is kept by the receiver. The public key is announced to the public.

Suppose user A as shown in Figure 14.3 wants to send a message to user B. A uses the public key to encrypt the message. When the message is received by B, the private key is used to decrypt the message.

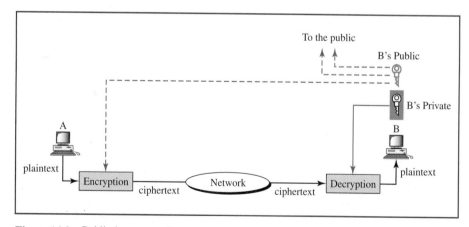

Figure 14.3   Public-key encryption

In public-key encryption/decryption, the public key that is used to encrypt the algorithm is different from the private key that is used to decrypt the algorithm. The public key is available to the public; the private key is kept by each individual.

TECHNICAL FOCUS: RSA

One popular public-key encryption technique is called RSA (for Rivest, Shamir, and Adleman). The technique uses number theory and the fact that it is easy to create two large numbers and multiply them, but difficult to find the original numbers when the product is given. The public key is made of two large numbers (n and e). The private key is made of two large numbers (n and d). The first number is the same for both keys, while the second number is different. To encrypt, the sender first transforms the plaintext character to a number using any method. The encryption algorithm then calculates:

$$C = P^e \bmod n$$

where P is the number representing the plaintext and C is the number representing the ciphertext to be sent. The mod operation means C is the remainder when P^e is divided by n.

The receiver uses the same procedure but with the private key numbers as shown:

$$C = P^d \bmod n$$

If the numbers d and e are very large, it is very difficult to guess the value of d (which is private) given the value of e (which is public).

14.3 DIGITAL SIGNATURE

We said that security has four conditions: privacy, authentication, integrity, and non-repudiation. We have already discussed privacy. The other three can be achieved using what is called **digital signature.**

The idea is similar to the signing of a document. When we send a document electronically, we can also sign it through encryption. We have two choices: we can sign the entire document or we can sign a digest (condensed version) of the document.

SIGNING THE WHOLE DOCUMENT

Public-key encryption can be used to sign a document. However, the roles of the public and private key are different here. The sender uses her private key to encrypt (sign) the message just as a person uses her signature (which is private in the sense that it is difficult to forge) to sign a paper document. The receiver, on the other hand, uses the public key of the sender to decrypt the message just as a person can verify another person's signature.

In digital signature the private key is used for encryption and the public key for decryption. This is possible because the encryption and decryption algorithms used today are mathematical formulas and their structures are similar. Figure 14.4 shows how this is done. Digital signature can provide integrity, authentication, and nonrepudiation.

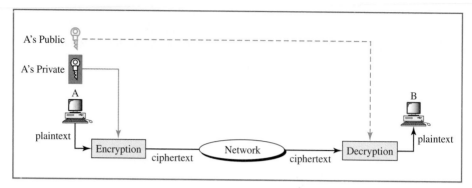

Figure 14.4   Signing the whole document

Digital signature cannot be achieved using secret-key encryption.

Integrity   The integrity of a message is preserved because, if an intruder intercepts the message and partially or totally changes it, the decrypted message would be (with a high probability) unreadable.

Authentication   We can use the following reasoning to show how a message can be authenticated. If an intruder (user X) sends a message pretending that it is coming from someone else (user G), she must use her own private key (private X) for encryption. The message is then decrypted with the public key of user G and will therefore be nonreadable. Encryption with X's private key and decryption with G's public key results in garbage.

Nonrepudiation   Digital signature also provides nonrepudiation. If the sender denies sending the message, her private key corresponding to her public key can be tested on the original plaintext. If the result of decryption matches the original message then we know the sender sent the message.

Digital signature does not provide privacy. If there is a need for privacy, another layer of encryption/decryption must be applied.

SIGNING THE DIGEST

Using a public key to sign the entire message is very inefficient if the message is very long. The solution is to let the sender sign a digest of the document instead of the whole document. The sender creates a miniature version of the document and signs it; the receiver then checks the signature on the miniature.

To create a digest of the message, we use a function (called hash function). The hash function creates a fixed-size digest from a variable-length message as shown in Figure 14.5.

Note that a hash function must have two properties to guarantee its success. First, hashing is one-way; the digest can only be created from the message, but not vice versa. Second, hashing is a one-to-one function; there is little probability that two messages will create the same digest.

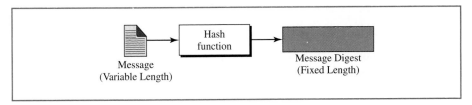

Figure 14.5   Signing the digest

After the digest has been created, it is encrypted (signed) using the sender's private key. The encrypted digest is attached to the original message and sent to the receiver. Figure 14.6 shows the sender site.

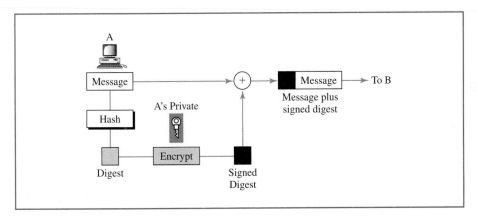

Figure 14.6   Sender site

The receiver receives the original message and the encrypted digest. She separates the two. She applies the same hash function to the message to create a second digest. She also decrypts the received digest using the public key of the sender. If the two digests are the same, all three aspects of security are preserved. Figure 14.7 shows the receiver site.

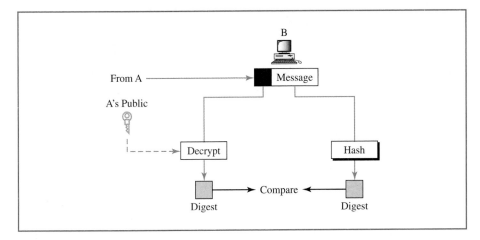

Figure 14.7   Receiver site

14.4   SECURITY IN THE INTERNET

All of the principles and concepts discussed can be used in the Internet to provide security. In particular, security measures can be applied to the application layer, transport layer, and the IP layer.

APPLICATION LAYER SECURITY

At the application layer, each application is responsible for providing security. The implementation of security at this level is the simplest. It concerns two entities: the client and the server.

The implementation of security at the application layer is more feasible and simpler particularly when the Internet communication involves only two parties, as in the case of email. The sender and the receiver can agree to use the same protocol and to use any type of security services they desire.

TECHNICAL FOCUS: PRETTY GOOD PRIVACY

Pretty Good Privacy (PGP), invented by Phil Zimmermann, is an example of a security scheme designed to provide all four aspects of security (privacy, integrity, authentication, and nonrepudiation) in the sending of email.

PGP uses digital signature to provide integrity, authentication, and nonrepudiation. It uses a combination of secret-key and public-key encryption to provide privacy. Specifically, it uses one hash function, one secret key, and two private-public key pairs.

TRANSPORT LAYER SECURITY

At the transport layer, security is more complicated. One example of a security method at this layer is **Transport Layer Security** (TLS). TLS was derived from a security protocol developed by Netscape to provide security on the WWW. For transactions on the Internet, the following are needed:

1. The customer needs to be sure that the server belongs to the actual vendor, not an imposter. For example, a customer does not want an imposter to make charges on her credit card. In other words, the server must be authenticated.

2. The customer needs to be sure that the contents of the message are not modified during transition. A bill for $100 must not be changed to $1000. The integrity of the message must be preserved.

3. The customer needs to be sure that an imposter does not intercept sensitive information such as a credit card number. There is a need for privacy.

There are other optional security aspects that can be added to the above list. For example, the vendor may also need to authenticate the customer. TLS can provide additional features to cover these aspects of security.

At the IP layer, implementation of security features is very complicated since every device must be able to handle it. IP provides services for user applications, as well as services for other protocols such as OSPF, ICMP, and IGMP. This means that implementation of security at this level is not very effective until all devices are ready to use it.

Security at the IP level is implemented using IP Security (IPSec). IPSec is a collection of protocols designed by the IETF (Internet Engineering Task Force) to provide security for a packet carried on the Internet. IPSec does not define the use of any specific encryption or authentication method. Instead, it provides a framework and a mechanism; it leaves the selection of the encryption/authentication and hashing methods to the user.

TECHNICAL FOCUS: AH AND ESP

IPSec uses two protocols: authentication header (AH) and encapsulating security payload (ESP) to achieve security. The authentication header (AH) protocol is designed to provide integrity. The method involves a digital signature using a hashing function. The message digest created by applying the hashing function is included in a header (AH header), and inserted between the IP header and transport-layer data and header.

The AH protocol does not provide privacy, only integrity and message authentication (digital signature). IPSec defines another protocol that provides privacy as well as a combination of integrity and message authentication. This protocol is called encapsulating security payload (ESP).

14.5   FIREWALLS

One way an organization can protect itself from the outside world is through a firewall. A firewall is a router installed between the internal network of an organization and the rest of the Internet. It is designed to forward some packets and filter (not forward) others. Figure 14.8 shows a firewall.

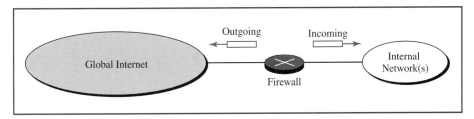

Figure 14.8   Firewall

For example, a firewall may filter all incoming packets destined for a specific host or a specific server such as TELNET (port 23). A firewall is used to deny access to a specific host or a specific service in the organization.

Firewalls are classified as a packet-filter firewall or as a proxy-based firewall.

PACKET-FILTER FIREWALL

A firewall can be used as a packet filter. It can forward or block packets based on the information in the network-layer and transport-layer headers: source and destination IP addresses, source and destination port addresses, and type of protocol (TCP or UDP). A packet-filter firewall is a router that uses a filtering table to decide which packet must be discarded (not forwarded).

PROXY FIREWALL

The packet-filter firewall is based on the information available in the network layer and transport layer headers (IP and TCP/UDP). However, sometimes we need to filter a message based on the information available in the message itself (at the application layer). As an example, assume that an organization wants to implement the following policies regarding its Web pages: Only those Internet users who have previously established business relations with the company can have access; access to other users must be blocked. In this case, a packet-filter firewall is not feasible because the router cannot distinguish between the packets arriving at TCP port 80 (HTTP). Testing must be done at the application level (using URLs).

One solution is to install a proxy computer (sometimes called an application gateway), which stands between the customer (user client) computer and the corporation computer. When the user client process sends a message, the proxy computer runs a server process to receive the request. The server opens the packet at the application level and finds out if the request is legitimate. If it is, the server acts as a client process and sends the message to the real server in the corporation. If it is not, the message is dropped and an error message is sent to the external user. In this way, the requests of the external users are filtered based on the contents at the application layer.

A proxy firewall filters at the application layer.

14.6   VIRTUAL PRIVATE NETWORKS (VPN)

One way a company can provide inside privacy is through **Virtual Private Network (VPN)** technology. VPN is a technology that is gaining popularity among large organizations that use the global Internet for both intra- and inter-organization communication, but require privacy in their intra-organization communication.

ACHIEVING PRIVACY

To achieve privacy, organizations can use one of three strategies: private networks, hybrid networks, or virtual private networks.

Private Networks

An organization that needs privacy when routing information inside the organization can use a private network as discussed previously. A small organization with one single site can use an isolated LAN. People inside the organization can send data to one another that totally remain inside the organization, secure from outsiders. A larger organization with several sites can create a private internet. The LANs at different sites can be connected to each other using routers and leased lines. In other words, an internet can be made out of private LANs and private WANs. Figure 14.9 shows such a situation for an organization with two sites. The LANs are connected to each other using routers and one leased line.

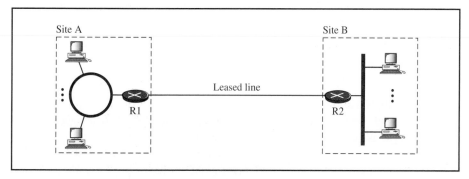

Figure 14.9   Private network

In this situation, the organization has created a private internet that is totally isolated from the global Internet. For end-to-end communication between stations at different sites, the organization can use the TCP/IP protocol suite. However, there is no need for the organization to apply for IP addresses with the Internet Authority. It can use private IP addresses. The organization can use any IP class and assign network and host addresses internally. Because the internet is private, duplication of addresses by another organization in the global network is not a problem.

Hybrid Networks

Today, most organizations need to have privacy in intra-organization data exchange, but, at the same time, they need to be connected to the global Internet for data exchange with other organizations. One solution is the use of a hybrid network. A hybrid network allows an organization to have its own private internet and, at the same time, access to the global Internet. Intra-organization data is routed through the private internet; inter-organization data is routed through the global Internet. Figure 14.10 shows an example of this situation.

An organization with two sites uses routers 1 and 2 to connect the two sites privately through a leased line; it uses routers 3 and 4 to connect the two sites to the rest of the world. The organization uses global IP addresses for both types of communication. However, packets destined for internal recipients are routed only through routers 1 and 2. Routers 3 and 4 route the packets destined for outsiders.

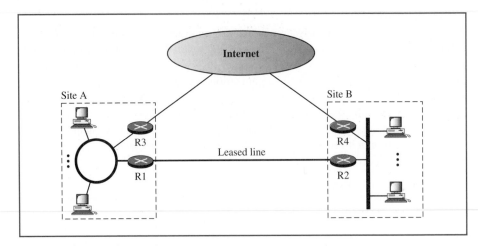

Figure 14.10   Hybrid network

Virtual Private Networks

Both private and hybrid networks have a major drawback: cost. Private wide area networks are expensive. To connect several sites, an organization needs several leased lines, which means a high monthly cost. One solution is to use the global Internet for both private and public communication. A technology called Virtual Private Networks (VPN), allows organizations to use the global Internet for both purposes.

VPN creates a network which is private, but virtual. It is private because it guarantees privacy inside the organization. It is virtual because it does not use real private WANs; the network is physically public, but virtually private.

Figure 14.11 shows the idea of a virtual private network. Routers 1 and 2 use VPN technology to guarantee privacy for the organization.

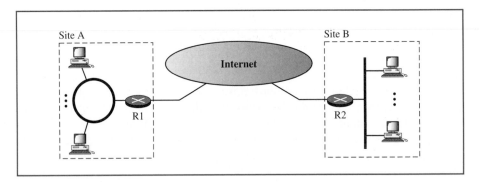

Figure 14.11   Virtual private network

VPN TECHNOLOGY

VPN technology uses two simultaneous techniques to guarantee privacy for an organization: IPSec and tunneling.

IPSec

We discussed IPSec earlier in this chapter. A virtual private network can use IPSec to provide authentication and privacy.

Tunneling

To guarantee privacy for an organization, VPN specifies that each IP datagram destined for private use in the organization must be encapsulated in another datagram. This is called tunneling because the original datagram is hidden inside an outer datagram.

14.7   ACCESS CONTROL

A preventative action that can provide security for an organization is access control. An organization needs to have an access control policy to prevent unauthorized users from accessing its resources. Three methods are commonly used for access control: passwords, tokens, and biometrics. (See Figure 14.12.) A password is something a user *knows;* a token is something a user *has;* a biometric characteristic is something a user *is*.

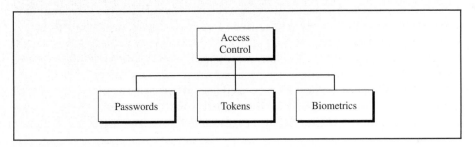

Figure 14.12   Access control methods

PASSWORDS

A common technique for authorization is the use of a password. Each user is assigned a password. When the user needs to access the system, she needs to use her password. To be effective, a password must have several characteristics:

❏   A password should be long (at least 6 characters).
❏   A password should be assigned by the administrator, not the user. Users often choose easily-guessed passwords.
❏   The password should be changed frequently (by the administrator, not the user). Ideally a password should be used only once, but this is impossible in many cases.

TOKENS

A token is a small device (in the form of a card, key, etc.) that can fit in a wallet or pocket. It contains electronic circuitry for security control.

BIOMETRICS

Biometrics is the use of some characteristic of the user to gain access to a system. It could be the user's voice, patterns on the palms, pattern of the retina, or facial configuration.

CASE STUDY

New Age Home Pharmacy

N AHP is not a fully secured network. One reason some aspects of security are not needed is that the NAHP operation is confined to one building; there is no need for technologies such as VPN. The future expansion of NAHP to other cities and states may require the use of VPN to provide privacy in interoffice communication.

Last year, there was a suggestion for security at the application layer. Pretty Good Privacy (PGP) was recommended. However, the recommendation was not approved because the pharmacists believe that most physicians and patients have not installed this software.

NAHP does have security at the transport layer. TLS is in place when patients, physicians, and home care centers access the NAHP site and order services or drugs. The information sent is secured to protect the privacy of the patient.

NAHP has both packet-filter and proxy firewalls. A packet-filter firewall confines FTP packets to inside the company and prevents the entry of FTP packets from the outside. The firewall does not allow an FTP client to request the services of an FTP server exterior to NAHP. This reduces the load; downloading huge files may create congestion on the T-3 line that connects the company to the Internet. Also, the firewall does not allow an exterior FTP client to access the FTP server installed on the server computer in the basement. This prevents outsiders from accessing the private files of NAHP.

NAHP also has a proxy firewall. This firewall limits access to the website for those patients, physicians, and home care centers that already have an established relationship with the company. The proxy firewall filters out HTTP messages received from those customers unknown to the company.

The SMTP server is open to the public. Anybody can send an email to the company and any company employee can send email to whomever. Email is often used to create a new contact between a customer and NAHP.

14.8   KEY TERMS

access control	password
authentication	plaintext
authentication header protocol	Pretty Good Privacy (PGP)
biometric	privacy
ciphertext	private key
data encryption standard (DES)	private network
decryption	proxy firewall
digest	public key
digital signature	public-key encryption
encapsulating security payload (ESP)	RSA encryption
encryption	secret key
firewall	secret-key encryption
hash function	security
hybrid network	token
integrity	Transport Layer Security (TLS)
IP Security (IPSec)	tunneling
nonrepudiation	virtual private network (VPN)
packet-filter firewall	

14.9 SUMMARY

❏ The issues involved in security are privacy, authentication, integrity, and nonrepudiation.

❏ Privacy is achieved through encryption of the plaintext and decryption of the ciphertext.

❏ In secret-key encryption, the sender and the receiver share a secret key.

❏ In public-key encryption, the public key is known to everyone but the private key is known only to the receiver.

❏ Authentication, integrity, and nonrepudiation are achieved through a method called digital signature.

❏ We can use digital signature on the entire message or on a digest of the message. A hash function creates the digest from the original document.

❏ Security methods can be applied in the application layer, transport layer, and IP layer.

❏ Transport Layer Security (TLS) provides security at the transport layer.

❏ Security at the IP layer is implemented using IPSec.

❏ A firewall is a router installed between the internal network of an organization and the rest of the Internet.

❏ A packet-filter firewall blocks or forwards packets based on information in the network and transport layers.

❏ A proxy firewall blocks or forwards packets based on information in the application layer.

❏ A virtual private network (VPN) provides privacy for LANs that must communicate through the global Internet.

❏ VPN technology involves the simultaneous use of encryption/authentication and tunneling to guarantee privacy.

❏ Passwords, tokens, and biometric characteristics are methods of access control.

PRACTICE SET

Review Questions

1. What are the four aspects of security?
2. Why is nonrepudiation necessary?
3. Discuss the key in secret-key encryption.
4. Discuss the keys in public-key encryption.
5. What is a digest and how is it formed?
6. Name a security method used for a specific application in the application layer.
7. Name a security method used in the transport layer.
8. Name a security method used in the IP layer.
9. How is a packet-filter firewall different from a proxy firewall?
10. What are two techniques used in VPN to guarantee privacy?
11. What are three methods of access control?

Multiple-Choice Questions

12. Encryption/decryption provides a network with _____.
    a. privacy
    b. authentication
    c. integrity
    d. nonrepudiation

13. Secret-key encryption involves the use of _____.
    a. one key
    b. two keys
    c. hash functions
    d. all of the above

14. Public-key encryption involves the use of _____.
    a. one key
    b. two keys
    c. hash functions
    d. all of the above

15. In secret-key encryption, the secret key is used for _____.
    a. encryption
    b. decryption
    c. hashing
    d. a and b

16. In public-key encryption, the public key is used for _____.
    a. encryption
    b. decryption
    c. hashing
    d. a and b

17. In public-key encryption, the private key is used for _____.
    a. encryption
    b. decryption
    c. hashing
    d. a and b

18. If user A wants to send an encrypted message to user B, the plaintext is encrypted with the public key of _____.
    a. user A
    b. user B
    c. the network
    d. a or b

19. Digital signature can provide _____ for a network.
    a. authentication
    b. integrity
    c. nonrepudiation
    d. all of the above

20. In the digital signature technique, the sender of the message uses _____ to create ciphertext.
    a. her own secret key
    b. her own private key
    c. her own public key
    d. the receiver's private key

21. In the digital signature technique, the receiver of the message uses _____ to create plaintext.
    a. her own secret key
    b. her own private key
    c. her own public key
    d. the sender's public key
22. A method to provide for the secure transmission of email is called _____.
    a. RSA
    b. DES
    c. BVD
    d. PGP
23. _____ is a protocol that provides security at the transport-layer level.
    a. PGP
    b. AH
    c. TLS
    d. ESP
24. _____ is a collection of protocols that provide security at the IP layer level.
    a. TLS
    b. VPN
    c. PGP
    d. IPSec
25. A _____ network can use a leased line for intra-organization communication and the Internet for inter-organization communication.
    a. private
    b. hybrid
    c. virtual private
    d. any of the above
26. A VPN uses _____ to guarantee privacy.
    a. IPSec
    b. tunneling
    c. both a and b
    d. none of the above
27. A firewall is usually _____ installed between the internal network of an organization and the rest of the Internet.
    a. a bridge
    b. a router
    c. software
    d. tunnel
28. _____ is a biometric characteristic that can be used for access control.
    a. A palm print
    b. A secret key
    c. A password
    d. A token

CHAPTER 15

Network Analysis, Design, and Implementation

Every system has a life cycle. At one time the system is new, in its infancy, and has all the latest technologies. Eventually, as time progresses, the system ages; it might lose efficiency and become a drain on financial resources. The system is past its prime and needs to be replaced. A network system is no exception. In fact, due to the constant advances in networking technologies, network systems become obsolete very quickly.

In this chapter, we discuss the network development life cycle (NDLC) which consists of three phases: analysis, design, and implementation. We first discuss the cycle itself. We then discuss the steps in the analysis phase, the steps in the design phase, and finally the steps in the implementation phase. Business students will find NDLC to be less complicated than the traditional system development life cycle (SDLC) used in business systems.

OBJECTIVES

After reading this chapter, the reader should be able to:

❑ Understand NDLC and the difference between NDLC and SDLC.

❑ Understand the analysis phase and its steps.

❑ Understand the design phase and its steps.

❑ Understand the implementation phase and its steps.

15.1 NETWORK DEVELOPMENT LIFE CYCLE

Most organizations today have a network system. By *network system,* we mean a collection of physical networks (LANs, backbone, and WANs), network protocols, client and server programs, application programs, files and databases, procedures, documentation, maintenance contracts, and even staff organization. In other words, everything that gives users (both external and internal) access to the organization's resources.

A network development life cycle (NDLC) is a set of strategies for upgrading (or totally replacing) an organization's network system. NDLC is derived from a well-established system, the system development life cycle (SDLC), which is a generic methodology for developing any system.

Although some organizations (and some network designers) believe that NDLC should closely follow the established principles of SDLC, others argue that a network system is by nature different from other systems. The differences can be summarized as follows:

1. A network system needs to be replaced more frequently than other system types because network technology is itself changing rapidly. For example, many traditional 10 Mbps Ethernets have been successively replaced by 100 Mbps Ethernets and then by 1000 Mbps Ethernets, all in the past decade. As another example, CDs are replacing the traditional floppy disks. The development of new technologies has been propelled by the use of the Internet by network systems.

2. A network system expands more rapidly. The number of network users grows each year with increased demands for more bandwidth and more access to network resources.

3. The cost of network installation is decreasing continuously.

The above differences have convinced many network designers that the generic SDLC should be replaced by NDLC. These points are basic to NDLC:

❑ The development process must take less time.
❑ The cost of the process must be less to justify the frequency.

There is not yet a standard NDLC that is universally agreed upon. We use an approach with elements common to SDLC that meets the above two criteria. SDLC, familiar to most business students, has five phases:

❑ Planning
❑ Analysis
❑ Design
❑ Implementation
❑ Maintenance

Our NDLC has three of these phases:

❑ Analysis
❑ Design
❑ Implementation

We remove *planning* from the list because it is usually a long and expensive process; this goes against the first and second criteria. We exclude the last phase, *maintenance,* because it is usually a task for the network manager and not the network designer. We discuss an NDLC that covers the remaining three phases. In addition, we include steps in each phase that match the nature of network system development. Figure 15.1 shows the phases in our NDLC. The process is cyclic; after the implementation phase, a new cycle starts.

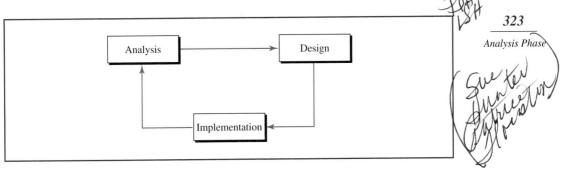

Figure 15.1   NDLC cycle

15.2   ANALYSIS PHASE

The analysis phase in our NDLC is made of two major steps: analysis of the existing system (called baselining) and analysis of the needs for the new network as shown in Figure 15.2.

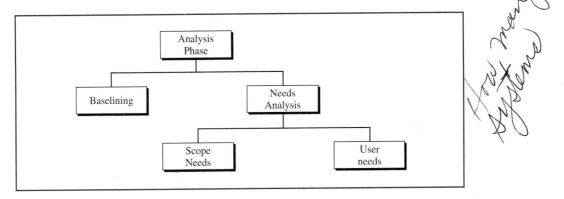

Figure 15.2   Analysis phase

BASELINING

Baselining is the measurement and recording of characteristics and features of the existing network system over a specific period of time. The analyst must do a careful study of system users, system nodes, protocols, application programs, and network traffic.

System Users
Baselining is usually the measurement of system users (average, peak, and maximum). Other measures of system users include the types of applications used, the number of hours a system is used, and the level of utilization.

System Nodes
The information collected about system nodes can include the number of nodes, type of node (computer, router, bridge, switch, hub, etc.), logical location of the node on the network, the model number, serial number, and vendor name/address/telephone number.

Protocols

The information collected about protocols can contain the type of the protocol (for example, TCP/IP), the version, the computer on which it is installed, and the level of utilization.

Application Programs

The information collected about application programs can contain the type of application, the computer on which it is installed, and the frequency of utilization.

Network Traffic

The most important measurement in baselining is the collection of network traffic information. The analyst needs to carefully measure and record the following:

- ❑ Throughput (average and peak)
- ❑ Frame size (average and maximum)
- ❑ Number of frames per second (average and peak)
- ❑ Number of collisions (average and peak)
- ❑ Number of dropped frames due to error detection (average and peak)
- ❑ Number of dropped frames due to congestion (average and peak)

NEEDS ANALYSIS

Baselining defines the characteristics of the existing network system; needs analysis defines the characteristics of the new proposed network system. Needs analysis is usually two separate activities: scope needs analysis and user needs analysis.

Scope Needs Analysis

Scope needs analysis defines the logical layout of the new network system. It shows all the proposed networks that will make up the physical network system. The analysis is composed of three parts: local networks, backbones, and global access.

Local Networks   These are the networks that will connect internal users (desktop computers inside a building or on a floor) to the network system.

The report must include the existing network configuration as well as the need for any changes in layout. The type of existing physical network, the capacity of the network, and the types and models of the connecting devices are also part of the local network analysis. The report can also include disadvantages of the network and problems encountered in the past.

Since local networks are usually owned by the organization, the report should include the maintenance costs for each network, which can be a factor in the upgrading or renovation of each network in the next (design) phase.

Backbone Network   The backbone connects local networks to create a network system for the organization. Analyzing the backbone includes creating a drawing that shows the connection of the backbone to the local networks. Each local network analyzed in the previous step must have a connection to the backbone. The drawing must show the percentage of the backbone used for each local network. The report at this step must also include the total capacity of the backbone, the type of backbone (router-based or switched-based), the type of transmission media used, and the protocol. The report should also include any problems, if any. If there is a need for change or extension in the layout, this should also be mentioned.

Since a backbone is usually owned by the organization, the analysis must cover the monthly and yearly maintenance cost, which can be a factor in the upgrading or renovation of the backbone in the next (design) phase.

Global Connection The analysis of a network system does not end with the backbone; an organization normally uses wide area networks or the Internet to either connect different sites of the organization or connect to other organizations. Global connection is also part of the network system and is part of the baseline analysis.

An organization may have created private wide area networks to connect different sites (using leased lines). Or perhaps an organization may be using the services of a commercial wide area network and paying a service provider. A diagram must show these private or public wide area networks. A report must detail the monthly and yearly costs of access to the global network; this is used in the decision making process of the design phase.

User Needs Analysis

User needs must be carefully evaluated during the analysis phase. A user needs hardware resources, software resources, and bandwidth. The software (application programs and data) performs a task, the hardware runs an application program, and the bandwidth (network capacity) downloads the application program and data.

Hardware Resources The hardware resources needed by a typical internal user may include a desktop computer, a dedicated or general-purpose printer, a dedicated storage device (hard drive), and the storage capacity of a server or general purpose computer.

The hardware needs of each user must be defined and documented during the analysis phase. The analyst must determine the type of desktop or laptop computer best suited for each user (or category of users). For example, a high-level manager may need a computer with a high-resolution monitor and lots of memory (for teleconferencing, or demonstrations, for example), but may not need a large capacity hard drive. Conversely, a large capacity hard drive might be needed for an engineer dealing with huge image files.

© Corbis/Vol. 15 © Corbis/Vol. 147

The hardware needs of each user must be defined. Considerations such as desktop or laptop should be determined based on job needs.

Software Resources   A typical user needs software resources. The internal user may use application programs (such as a spreadsheet), a client or server program (such as SMTP or TELNET), or data resources (such as an employee database). A typical external user needs to access server programs and, occasionally, data resources. Each application or data resource requires regulation for each user (or group of users). This analysis can later be used to define the installation site of each application and security measures needed for the data resources. Data access must be restricted for both external and internal users.

Bandwidth   The number of users (present and future) and their need for the organization networks and/or backbone are important factors in bandwidth design. Today, an organization does not operate in complete isolation. A typical user not only accesses the resources on the organization network, but also the resources available on the Internet. The world wide web is a valuable source of information. A user also corresponds via email with others both internal and external to the organization. All of this data transmission generates traffic and consumes bandwidth.

It is difficult to estimate the average bandwidth required by each user. It all depends on the organization type and the position of the user in the organization. For example, in a college or university environment, a professor may interact with a large number of students every day. A professor may also use the Internet for research, which can involve the downloading of large files. Students may access the university resources using TELNET. They may also be able to register on-line.

Determination of the bandwidth requirements for a network system requires careful study. The capacity of the bandwidth must be determined for each network and for the entire backbone. Peak hours must be determined and documented.

BUSINESS FOCUS:
METHODS FOR COLLECTING DATA FOR USER NEEDS

An analyst must gather information about user needs before designing a new network system or upgrading an existing one. Information can be collected using one or a combination of the following methods:

❑ **Sampling.** In this method, the analyst takes samples that represent the needs of a typical user. The samples are then applied to the whole population.

❑ **Interviewing.** In this method, the analyst interviews each user to determine the hardware, software, and bandwidth requirements. Unfortunately, most typical users are not aware of what they need or the number of hours spent on individual tasks, such as answering email.

❑ **Questionnaire.** Very close to the interviewing method is the use of questionnaires. These are sometimes less effective than interviewing, as people are sometimes reluctant to answer a long list of questions.

❑ **Observation.** The analyst can observe how the network resources are used and how bandwidth is consumed. This method can be supported by software analyzers that find, for example, how much data is downloaded by a typical user (to define the bandwidth requirement).

❑ **Prototyping.** In prototyping, an analyst uses available published information. For example, there may be a statistic defining the bandwidth needed at a university for a typical instructor or student. Or, even more specifically, the bandwidth for a student in a particular department.

15.3   DESIGN PHASE

The design phase uses the information collected during the analysis phase to create specifications for the new network system. The design phase looks at the baseline and needs analysis reports to determine what the new network should be.

We can divide the design phase into four major activities: upper-layer protocol decision, lower-layer protocol decision, hardware decision, and global connection decision as shown in Figure 15.3.

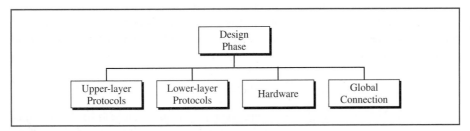

Figure 15.3   Design phase

UPPER-LAYER PROTOCOLS

Most designers find it easier to first define the upper-layer (layers 4 and above) protocols to be run on the network system. This decision involves two steps.

Defining the Protocol Suite

The designer first selects the protocol suite, the protocols that are run in the upper layers. There are many choices: the TCP/IP protocol suite, Windows 2000, Novell, and so on. The decision is usually based on factors such as the applications to be used, the type of equipment needed, and the type of interaction between the nodes.

Defining the Type and Location of Servers

A second decision is the selection of the application layer protocols and deciding where they should be installed. For example, if the TCP/IP protocol suite is chosen in the previous step, the designer may choose to use SMTP and POP to handle the email, TELNET to handle login, and FTP to handle file transfer. The designer may choose to install all of these application layer protocols on one computer or distribute them over several.

LOWER-LAYER PROTOCOLS

After the decision of the upper-layer protocols has been made, the designer needs to focus on the lower-layer protocols for each network or subnetwork. The decision at this step depends on the capacity needs of each network. The capacity of a network is the number of bits per second each network can handle. The information collected during baselining and user needs analysis can determine the capacity of the network. Although this seems difficult at first glance, it really is not because the choices are limited, usually 10, 100, or 1000 Mbps. The choice of capacity automatically defines the protocol to be used at the lower layers. For example, a capacity of 100 Mbps means the choice is 100BASE-T.

Note that the decision about each local network and the backbone need not be the same. For example, if the backbone connects five networks, each using 10BASE-T, 100BASE-T can be selected for the backbone.

HARDWARE

After selection of the lower-layer protocols for each network and the backbone is accomplished, hardware decisions are made. The information collected during baselining and the user needs report can define the type and number of computers needed for each user. The information obtained from the scope needs report and the lower-layer protocol decisions define the types and number of hardware pieces required to create a network. For example, if the designer has selected 10BASE-T for a network with 20 users, a 10BASE-T hub with at least 20 ports is needed. It is also clear that the type of transmission medium is UTP; scope needs analysis defines the length of the cable needed for this network.

GLOBAL CONNECTION

The network designer also needs to define how the organization is to be connected to other organizations or to other sites of the same organization. The decision depends on many factors including the needs for security, the total capacity and bandwidth of the backbone, and so on. For example, if the capacity of the proposed backbone is 100 Mbps and 20 percent of the capacity is being used by data flow from the outside, it is clear that the organization needs to be connected to the outside world with a bandwidth of at least 20 Mbps. This means the organization needs, for example, a T-1 line.

15.4 IMPLEMENTATION PHASE

After the design phase is completed, the implementation phase starts. The implementation phase usually includes several steps: purchasing or renting new hardware and software, installation of new hardware and software, training of users, testing of the system, and documentation. Figure 15.4 shows the steps.

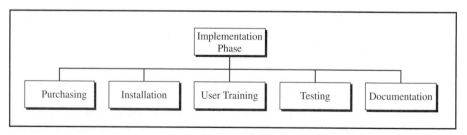

Figure 15.4 Implementation phase

PURCHASING

In this stage the new hardware or software is purchased or leased. This phase can vary time wise, depending on the type and size of the organization. For example, in a small, private organization, hardware and software are normally bought off the shelf. For a medium-sized or large organization, a *request for proposal* (RFP) is needed. The vendors respond to the request by proposing their best price. The proposals are evaluated based on the specifications defined during the design phase. The best proposal (not necessarily the least expensive) is selected and the hardware or software is purchased or leased.

INSTALLATION

The installation of the new hardware or software can either be done by the internal staff, the vendor specialists, or a third party. Normally the vendor is asked to either do the installation or supervise the installation unless the hardware or software is purchased off the shelf.

USER TRAINING

Although the upper-layer and lower-layer protocols are transparent to the users, the users do need training in accessing the system and the use of the new hardware. Also, users need to know the benefits of the upgrade. Users can be trained individually or, more commonly, in groups, based on the level of use.

TESTING

After the users are trained, the system is tested. Testing can be done by monitoring the system while the users are using the system. Although some people believe that testing should be done before the users use the system, this is an artificial situation.

DOCUMENTATION

For a system to be used properly and to be maintained efficiently documentation is needed. Usually two separate sets of documentation are prepared: user documentation and system documentation.

User Documentation
To use the network properly, the user needs documentation. The user needs to know the commands, the potential problems, the person to call in case of malfunction.

System Documentation
System documentation defines the network itself. It must be written so that the network can be maintained and modified by people other than the original developers. There must be system documentation for all three phases of system development.

CASE STUDY

NEW AGE HOME PHARMACY

The network system in NAHP was designed two years ago. However, Modern Networking, which is responsible for maintaining and updating the network, is constantly monitoring it. After the implementation of the new network system materialized last year, Modern Networking started a new analysis phase.

Modern Networking created several criteria for baselining. Network traffic is randomly being monitored. The throughput is measured three times a month; once in the morning, once in the afternoon (when traffic is at its peak), and once in the evening. The measurement is made during different days of the week, including the weekends as well as the weekdays.

Modern Networking also monitors the use of application programs. Three months ago, NAHP received a memo from Modern Networking regarding the need for installation of a new version of Eudora, the software that creates an interface between the user and SMTP. A 50-user license was procured and a new version was installed by the Modern Networking technician. Each user participated in a one-hour training session to learn the new features of the new version.

Traffic on the switches is also constantly monitored. There was just one occasion in which an Ethernet switch, on the first floor, dropped several packets. The switch was replaced and the monitoring of the new switch intensified. It was proven that the packet dropping was due to the faulty switch and not the traffic.

Modern Networking has also distributed forms to the users to record any observed problems. The forms are to be sent to the receptionist, who then forwards them at the end of the day to the Modern Networking office.

Modern Networking has informed the NAHP management that a new design phase will start at the beginning of the year 2003. This decision is based on NAHP's plan for adding a second building to expand its business.

15.5   KEY TERMS

analysis phase

baselining

design phase

implementation phase

needs analysis

network development life cycle (NDLC)

network system

network traffic

scope needs

system development life cycle (SDLC)

system documentation

testing phase

user documentation

user needs

15.6   SUMMARY

❏   A network development life cycle (NDLC) is a set of strategies for upgrading or replacing an organization's network system.

❏   An NDLC consists of an analysis phase, a design phase, and an implementation phase.

❏   The analysis phase requires a procedure called baselining and a needs analysis.

❏   Baselining is the measuring and recording of existing network characteristics and features.

❏ Needs analysis consists of two areas. One is finding the needs of the networks, backbone, and global access (scope needs). The other is finding the hardware, software, and bandwidth needs of the user (user needs).

❏ The design phase requires decisions on the upper-layer protocols, lower-layer protocols, hardware, and global connection method.

❏ The implementation phase requires the purchasing or leasing of hardware and software, installation of hardware and software, the training of users, system tests, and user and system documentation.

 PRACTICE SET

Review Questions

1. What is the difference between SDLC and NDLC?
2. What comprises a network system?
3. Why is a network system's life cycle so short?
4. Name the three phases in a network development life cycle.
5. What are the two steps in NDLC's analysis phase?
6. What are the most important measurements in baselining?
7. Name the three areas that must be investigated for a scope needs analysis.
8. What factors need to be included in a user needs analysis?
9. What are the four major decisions that need to be made in the design phase of the NDLC?
10. Name the five steps of the implementation phase of the NDLC.

Multiple-Choice Questions

11. The _____ phase is a phase in the network development life cycle.
    a. analysis
    b. design
    c. implementation
    d. all of the above
12. _____ is the first phase in the network development life cycle.
    a. Planning
    b. Analysis
    c. Design
    d. Implementation
13. The measuring and recording of a network's throughput and frame size is part of _____.
    a. needs analysis
    b. the design phase
    c. baselining
    d. scope analysis
14. Network traffic can be measured by the number of _____ per second.
    a. dropped frames
    b. collisions
    c. frames
    d. all of the above

15. The recording of information about existing networks and planned new networks is a part of _____ analysis.
    a. scope needs
    b. user needs
    c. baselining
    d. resource

16. The hardware, software, and bandwidth needs of users are part of the _____ analysis.
    a. scope needs
    b. user needs
    c. baselining
    d. resource

17. Deciding what upper-layer protocols and lower-layer protocols to use is part of the _____ phase.
    a. planning
    b. design
    c. implementation
    d. analysis

18. Specifications for a new network system are created in the _____ phase.
    a. planning
    b. design
    c. implementation
    d. analysis

19. The first step in the implementation phase of the network development life cycle is _____.
    a. testing
    b. installation
    c. purchasing
    d. designing

20. What kind of documentation is necessary in the implementation phase of the network development life cycle?
    a. user
    b. system
    c. global
    d. a and b

21. The _____ connects local networks to create a network system.
    a. server
    b. protocol
    c. baseline
    d. backbone

22. SMTP, TELNET, spreadsheets, and word processing programs can be considered part of _____ resources.
    a. hardware
    b. software
    c. baseline
    d. backbone

CHAPTER 16

Network Management

We can define **network management** as the monitoring, testing, configuring, and troubleshooting of network components to meet a set of requirements defined by an organization. These requirements include the smooth efficient operation of the network to provide a predefined quality of service for users. To accomplish this task, a network management system involves hardware, software, and human users.

In this chapter we first define and explain the five aspects of network management: configuration management, fault management, performance management, accounting management, and security management. Management tools, both hardware and software, are used to manage networks. We discuss the most common software tools and two general groups of hardware tools: line monitors and protocol analyzers.

OBJECTIVES

After reading this chapter, the reader should be able to:

❏ Understand the importance of configuration management and its two components: reconfiguration and documentation.

❏ Understand the importance of fault management and its two components: reactive and proactive management.

❏ Understand the importance of performance management and its four measurements: capacity, traffic, throughput, and response time.

❏ Understand the importance of accounting management and the reasons for using it.

❏ Be familiar with the SNMP protocol as a software management tool.

❏ Be familiar with hardware management tools such as line monitors and protocol analyzers.

The International Organization for Standardization (ISO) defines five areas of network management: configuration management, fault management, performance management, accounting management, and security management as shown in Figure 16.1.

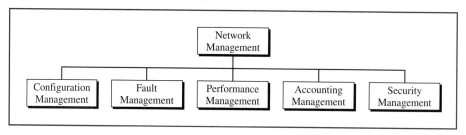

Figure 16.1   Areas of network management

BUSINESS FOCUS: NETWORK MANAGER FUNCTIONS

The following are some of the functions expected from a network manager:

❏   Monitor daily network operation.
❏   Support network users.
❏   Manage budgetary issues.
❏   Keep abreast of the latest networking technologies.
❏   Apply the general networking policy of the organization.

16.1   CONFIGURATION MANAGEMENT

A large network is usually made up of hundreds of entities that are physically or logically connected to each other. These entities have an initial configuration when the network is set up, but can change with time. Desktop computers may be replaced with newer models; application software may be updated to newer versions; and users may move from one group to another. The **configuration management** system must know, at any time, the status of each entity and its relation to other entities. Configuration management can be divided into two subsystems: reconfiguration and documentation as shown in Figure 16.2.

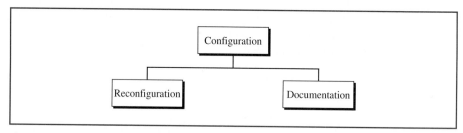

Figure 16.2   Configuration management

RECONFIGURATION

Reconfiguration can be a daily occurrence in a large network. There are three types of reconfiguration: hardware reconfiguration, software reconfiguration, and user-account reconfiguration.

Hardware Reconfiguration

Hardware reconfiguration covers all changes to the hardware. For example, a desktop computer may need to be replaced. A router may need to be moved to another part of the network. A subnetwork may be added or removed from the network. All of these need the time and attention of network management. In a large network, there must be specialized personnel trained for quick and efficient hardware reconfiguration. Unfortunately, this type of reconfiguration cannot be automated and must be manually handled case by case.

Software Reconfiguration

Software reconfiguration covers all changes to the software. For example, new software may need to be installed on servers or clients. An operating system may need updating. Fortunately, most software reconfiguration can be automated. For example, updating an application on some or all clients often requires just downloading electronically from the server.

User-Account Reconfiguration

User-account reconfiguration is not simply adding or deleting users on a system. You must also consider user privileges of the individual and the group member. For example, a user may have read and write permissions with regard to some files, but only read permission with regard to other files. User-account reconfiguration can be, to some extent, automated. For example, in a college or university, at the beginning of each quarter or semester, new students are added to the system. The students are normally grouped according to the courses they take or the majors they pursue. The members of each group have specific privileges; computer science students may need to access a server providing different computer language facilities, while engineering students may need to access servers that provide computer assisted design (CAD) software.

DOCUMENTATION

The original network configuration and each subsequent change must be recorded meticulously. This means that there must be documentation for hardware, software, and user accounts.

Hardware Documentation

Hardware documentation normally involves two sets of documents: maps and specifications.

Maps **Maps** track each piece of hardware and its connection to the network. There can be one general map that shows the logical relationship between each subnetwork. There can also be a second general map that shows the physical location of each subnetwork. For each subnetwork, then, there is one or more maps that show all pieces of equipment. The maps use some kind of standardization so that they can be easily read and understood by current and future personnel.

Specifications Maps are not enough per se. Each piece of hardware also needs to be documented. There must be a set of **specifications** for each piece of hardware connected to the network. These specifications must include information such as hardware type, serial number, vendor (address and phone number), time of purchase, and warranty information.

Software Documentation

All software must also be documented. **Software documentation** includes information such as the software type, the version, the time installed, and the license agreement.

User-Account Documentation

Most operating systems have a utility that allows the documentation of user accounts and their privileges. The management must make sure that the files with this information are updated and secured. Some operating systems record access privileges in two documents; one shows all files and access types for each user; the other is a list of users who have a particular access to a file.

16.2 FAULT MANAGEMENT

Complex networks today are made up of hundreds of components. Proper operation of the network depends on the proper operation of each component individually and in relation to each other. **Fault management** is the area of network management that handles this issue.

An effective fault management system has two subsystems: reactive fault management and proactive fault management as shown in Figure 16.3.

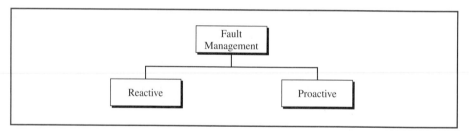

Figure 16.3 Fault management

REACTIVE FAULT MANAGEMENT

A **reactive fault management** system is responsible for detecting, isolating, correcting, and recording faults. It handles short-term solutions to faults.

Detecting

The first step taken by a reactive fault management system is to find the exact location of the fault. A fault is defined as an abnormal condition in the system. When a fault occurs, either the system stops working properly or the system creates excessive errors. A good example of a fault is a damaged communication medium. This fault may interrupt communication or produce excessive errors.

Isolating

The next step taken by a reactive fault management system is isolating the fault. A fault, if isolated, usually affects only a few users. After isolation, the affected users are immediately notified and given an estimated time of correction.

Correcting

The next step is correcting the fault. This may involve replacing or repairing the faulty component(s).

Recording

After the fault is corrected, it must be documented. The record must show the exact location of the fault, the possible cause, the action or actions taken to correct the fault, the cost, and time it took for each step. Documentation is extremely important for several reasons:

❏ The problem may reoccur. Documentation can help the present or future administrator or technician solve a similar problem.

❏ The frequency of the same kind of failure is an indication of a major problem in the system. If a fault happens frequently in one component, it must be replaced with a similar one or the whole system should be changed to avoid the use of that type of component.

❏ The statistics are helpful to performance management, another component of network management.

PROACTIVE FAULT MANAGEMENT

Proactive fault management tries to prevent faults from occurring. Although this is not always possible, some types of failures can be predicted and prevented. For example, if a manufacturer specifies a lifetime for a component or a part of a component, it is a good strategy to replace it before that time. As another example, if a fault happens frequently at one particular point of a network, it is wise to carefully reconfigure the network to prevent the fault from happening again.

16.3 PERFORMANCE MANAGEMENT

Performance management, which is closely related to fault management, tries to monitor and control the network to ensure that it is running as efficiently as possible. Performance management tries to quantify performance using some measurable quantity such as capacity, traffic, throughput, or response time as shown in Figure 16.4. Some protocols such as SNMP, which is discussed later in this chapter, can be used in performance management.

CAPACITY

One factor that must be monitored by a performance management system is the **capacity** of the network. Every network has a limited capacity and the performance management system must ensure that it is not used above this capacity. For example, if a LAN is designed for 100 stations at an average data rate of 2 Mbps, it will not operate properly

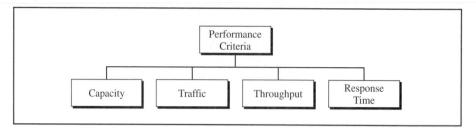

Figure 16.4   Performance criteria

if 200 stations are connected to the network. The data rate will decrease and blocking (stopping of data transmission) may occur.

TRAFFIC

Traffic can be measured in two ways: internally and externally. Internal traffic is measured by the number of packets (or bytes) traveling inside the network. External traffic is measured by the exchange of packets (or bytes) outside the network. During peak hours, when the system is heavily used, blocking may occur if there is excessive traffic.

© Corbis/Vol. 62

Traffic buildup on the network can block the transfer of data in much the same way that traffic on the freeway can cause a roadblock.

THROUGHPUT

We can measure the **throughput** of an individual device (such as a router) or a part of the network. Performance management monitors the throughput to make sure that it is not reduced to unacceptable levels.

RESPONSE TIME

Response time is normally measured from the time a user requests a service to the time the service is granted. Other factors such as capacity and traffic can affect the response time. Performance management monitors the average response time and the peak-hour response time. Any increase in response time is a very serious condition as it is an indication that the network is working above its capacity.

16.4 ACCOUNTING MANAGEMENT

Accounting management is the controlling of users' access to network resources through charges. Under accounting management, individual users, departments, divisions, or even projects are charged for the services they receive from the network. Charging does not necessary mean cash transfer; it may mean debiting the departments or divisions. Today, organizations use an accounting management system for the following reasons:

❏ It prevents users from monopolizing limited network resources.
❏ It prevents users from using the system inefficiently.
❏ Network managers can do short- and long-term planning based on the demand for network use.

16.5 SECURITY MANAGEMENT

Security management is responsible for controlling access to the network based on the pre-defined policy. We discussed network security in Chapter 14.

16.6 NETWORK MANAGEMENT TOOLS

Network managers need tools to do their jobs. We can roughly divide network tools into two broad categories: software tools and hardware tools.

SOFTWARE TOOLS

A software tool is designed to support the management of network components, usually from a central point. During the last two decades, several software tools have emerged, but by far the most popular is **Simple Network Management Protocol** (SNMP). SNMP is a very complex protocol that includes several other protocols. In this section, we briefly discuss those aspects of SNMP protocol that are useful to a network manager.

SNMP
SNMP is a framework for managing devices in an internet using the TCP/IP protocol suite. It provides a set of fundamental operations for monitoring and maintaining an internet.

TECHNICAL FOCUS: SNMP VERSIONS

SNMP has gone through three versions. SNMPv1 was based on the network management principles defined by the OSI model. SNMPv2 was designed to be totally dependent on the Internet model instead of the OSI model. SNMPv3 is the latest version and adds security management to SNMPv2.

Concept SNMP uses the concept of manager and agent. That is, a manager, usually a host, controls and monitors a set of agents, usually routers (see Figure 16.5).

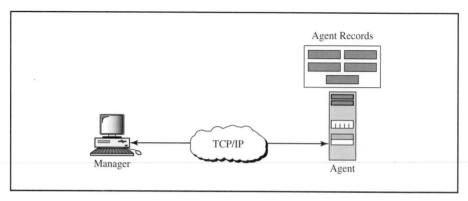

Figure 16.5 SNMP concept

SNMP is an application-level protocol in which a few manager stations control a set of agents. The protocol is designed at the application level so that it can monitor devices made by different manufacturers and installed on different physical networks. In other words, SNMP frees management tasks from both the physical characteristics of the managed devices and the underlying networking technology. It can be used in a heterogeneous internet made of different LANs and WANs connected by routers or made by different manufacturers.

Managers and Agents A management station, called a **manager,** is a host that runs the SNMP client program. A managed station, called an **agent,** is a router (or a host) that runs the SNMP server program. Management is achieved through simple interactions between a manager and an agent.

The agent keeps performance information in a database (a series of related files). The manager has access to the values in the database. For example, a router can store the number of packets received and forwarded in appropriate records. The manager can then fetch and compare the values of these two pieces of information to see whether or not the router is congested.

The manager can also make the router perform certain actions. For example, a router periodically checks the value of a reboot counter to see when it should reboot itself. It reboots itself, for example, if the value of the counter is 0. The manager can use this feature to reboot the agent remotely at any time. It simply sends a packet to force a 0 value in the counter.

Agents can also contribute to the management process. The server program running on the agent can check the environment and, if it notices something unusual, it can send a warning message (called a *trap*) to the manager.

In summary, management with SNMP is based on three basic ideas:

1. A manager checks an agent by requesting information that reflects the behavior of the agent.
2. A manager forces an agent to perform a task by resetting values in the agent database.
3. An agent contributes to the management process by warning the manager of an unusual situation.

To perform its job, SNMP uses other protocols. One of these protocols is called **Structure of Management Information** (SMI). SMI is used to do the following:

1. Universally and uniquely name objects to be managed.
2. Define the type of data that can be stored in an object.
3. Show how to encode data for transmission over the network.

TECHNICAL FOCUS: MIB

SNMP uses another important protocol called **Management Information Base** (MIB). SMI defines how a universal collection of objects should be universally named and managed. MIB, on the other hand, defines which of these objects should be included in a particular agent. In other words, whereas SMI defines a big pool, MIB defines a subset (small pond) with only some of the universal objects.

HARDWARE TOOLS

Hardware tools are the second category of tools available to network managers. Although there are many hardware tools that can be used by a manager, they can be divided into two large groups: line monitors and protocol analyzers.

Line Monitors

A line monitor detects the signal flowing between a host (end-user computer) and the network. A line monitor can be analog, digital, or analog/digital.

Analog Line Monitor   An analog line monitor can be used if data are transmitted using analog signals (for example, through a modem). An analog line monitor can be used as a debugging tool by measuring the three characteristics of an analog signal (amplitude, frequency, and phase). It is particularly useful in measuring the level of noise that may have caused distortion in a signal.

Digital Line Monitor   A digital line monitor displays the data and control characters being transmitted. Some digital line monitors even allow the manager to poll the system by sending some data and checking the response of the system.

Analog/Digital Line Monitor   Some manufacturers make line monitors that can act both as an analog and a digital monitor.

Protocol Analyzer

A protocol analyzer is a sophisticated line monitor with extra capabilities. A protocol analyzer can simulate the behavior of a network component (such as a modem or a router). It can also check the behavior of some network protocols (such as IP or TCP). It is a particularly useful tool for a network manager.

Network management at NAHP is the responsibility of Modern Networking Corporation. When NAHP first moved to the six-floor building, one pharmacist insisted on creating a networking department with a network manager and network technicians to take care of the new network designed and implemented by Modern Networking. After an investigation, it was apparent that, for a company the size of NAHP, it was less expensive to contract with an outside company for management instead of having a full time on-site crew.

Modern Networking is located three blocks from NAHP and provides network management for several companies like NAHP. The company has network engineers and technicians trained especially to handle Ethernet, Fast Ethernet, and Gigabit Ethernet.

Modern Networking has done an excellent job in configuration management. Every piece of installed or reconfigured hardware or software is meticulously documented. Hard and soft copies are kept both at NAHP and the Modern Networking office.

In the area of fault management, Modern Networking has detected 18 small-scale faults that have been corrected in less than one hour (on average). Proactive fault management has also been taken into consideration. The 12 devices that created the 18 faults are constantly being tested and observed. A fault has occurred once in seven devices, twice in four devices, and three times in one device. The device with three faults (one of the switches) was replaced with a new one.

Performance management is also a consideration. However, because the system is new, there are no concerns regarding this issue as yet. The system is functioning well under the designed capacity.

Modern Networking uses SNMP to control the behavior of the switches and computers. The manager station is a computer at the Modern Networking office. Management is done remotely via the Internet. The traffic on each switch, in particular, the number of packets received from each port, the number of packets sent through each port, and the number of packets dropped are recorded. Daily and weekly reports are prepared by the manager station. The daily report is kept at Modern Networking; a copy of the weekly report is sent to NAHP.

16.7   KEY TERMS

accounting management

agent

capacity

configuration management

fault management

hardware documentation

hardware reconfiguration

line monitor

Management Information Base (MIB)

manager

network management

performance management

proactive fault management

protocol analyzer

reactive fault management

response time

security management

Simple Network Management
   Protocol (SNMP)

software documentation

software reconfiguration

specification

Structure of Management
   Information (SMI)

throughput

traffic

user-account documentation

user-account reconfiguration

16.8   SUMMARY

- ❏ The five areas comprising network management are configuration management, fault management, performance management, accounting management, and security management.
- ❏ Configuration management is concerned with the physical or logical changes of network entities.
- ❏ Configuration management includes the reconfiguration and documentation of hardware, software, and user accounts.
- ❏ Fault management is concerned with the proper operation of each network component.
- ❏ Fault management can be reactive or proactive.
- ❏ Performance management is concerned with the monitoring and controlling of the network to ensure the network runs as efficiently as possible.
- ❏ Performance is quantified by measuring capacity, traffic, throughput, and response time.
- ❏ Security management is concerned with controlling access to the network.
- ❏ Accounting management is concerned with the controlling of user access to network resources through charges.
- ❏ Simple Network Management Protocol (SNMP) is a framework for managing devices in an internet using the TCP/IP protocol suite.
- ❏ In SNMP, a manager, usually a host, controls and monitors a set of agents, usually routers.
- ❏ The manager is a host that runs the SNMP client program.
- ❏ The agent is a router or host that runs the SNMP server program.
- ❏ Line monitors and protocol analyzers are hardware tools for network management.

 PRACTICE SET

Review Questions

1. Name the five types of management needed to properly administer a network.
2. Give an example of hardware, software, and user-account reconfiguration.
3. What kinds of documents are needed for hardware documentation?
4. What is the difference between reactive fault management and proactive fault management?
5. What are the four steps in reactive fault management?
6. By what criteria can we measure the performance of a network?
7. What is accounting management?
8. What does SNMP define as a manager? What does SNMP define as a client?
9. What two protocols does SNMP need to manage a network?
10. What is the difference between a line monitor and a protocol analyzer?

11. _____ is a subsystem of configuration management.
    a. Documentation
    b. Traffic management
    c. Cost management
    d. Proactive management

12. Controlling access to the network is a function of _____ management.
    a. configuration
    b. fault
    c. performance
    d. security

13. _____ management is concerned with controlling access to network resources by charging for services.
    a. Configuration
    b. Performance
    c. Accounting
    d. Security

14. _____ management is concerned with the reconfiguration of hardware, software, and user accounts and with the documentation of this reconfiguration.
    a. Configuration
    b. Performance
    c. Accounting
    d. Security

15. When a server fails, the _____ management system is responsible for detecting, isolating, correcting, and recording the failure.
    a. fault
    b. performance
    c. accounting
    d. security

16. A _____ management system tries to quantify criteria such as capacity and throughput to measure how efficiently a network is running.
    a. configuration
    b. fault
    c. performance
    d. accounting

17. _____ is a performance criterion.
    a. Traffic
    b. Throughput
    c. Response time
    d. All of the above

18. The idea of _____ fault management is to replace a network component prior to the end of its lifetime as defined by the manufacturer.
    a. performance
    b. reactive
    c. proactive
    d. active

19. Configuration, fault, performance, accounting, and security management are all areas of _____ management.

   a. OSI
   b. network
   c. proactive
   d. business

20. Hardware documentation involves _____.
   a. maps
   b. specifications
   c. agents
   d. a and b

21. When a fault is detected, the last step in reactive fault management is _____ the fault.
   a. isolating
   b. correcting
   c. recording
   d. measuring

22. The _____ on a network can be measured by the number of packets traveling inside the network or the exchange of packets outside the network.
   a. capacity
   b. traffic
   c. throughput
   d. response time

23. _____ runs the SNMP client program; _____ runs the SNMP server program.
   a. A manager; a manager
   b. An agent; an agent
   c. A manager; an agent
   d. An agent; a manager

24. SNMP uses _____ to monitor a network.
   a. SMI
   b. MIB
   c. BVD
   d. a and b

25. A _____ detects the signal flowing between a host and the network.
   a. line monitor
   b. class monitor
   c. protocol analyzer
   d. bridge

26. A _____ can simulate the behavior of a modem.
   a. router
   b. bridge
   c. protocol analyzer
   d. gateway

ASCII Code

The American Standard Code for Information Interchange (ASCII) is the most commonly used code for encoding printable and nonprintable (control) characters.

ASCII uses seven bits to encode each character. It can therefore represent up to 128 characters. Table A.1 lists the ASCII characters and their codes in both binary and hexadecimal form.

Table A.1 *ASCII table*

Decimal	Hexadecimal	Binary	Character	Description
0	00	0000000	NUL	Null
1	01	0000001	SOH	Start of header
2	02	0000010	STX	Start of text
3	03	0000011	ETX	End of text
4	04	0000100	EOT	End of transmission
5	05	0000101	ENQ	Enquiry
6	06	0000110	ACK	Acknowledgment
7	07	0000111	BEL	Bell
8	08	0001000	BS	Backspace
9	09	0001001	HT	Horizontal tab
10	0A	0001010	LF	Line feed
11	0B	0001011	VT	Vertical tab
12	0C	0001100	FF	Form feed
13	0D	0001101	CR	Carriage return
14	0E	0001110	SO	Shift out
15	0F	0001111	SI	Shift in
16	10	0010000	DLE	Data link escape
17	11	0010001	DC1	Device control 1
18	12	0010010	DC2	Device control 2
19	13	0010011	DC3	Device control 3
20	14	0010100	DC4	Device control 4

(continued)

Table A.1   *ASCII table* *(continued)*

Decimal	Hexadecimal	Binary	Character	Description
21	15	0010101	NAK	Negative acknowledgment
22	16	0010110	SYN	Synchronous idle
23	17	0010111	ETB	End of transmission block
24	18	0011000	CAN	Cancel
25	19	0011001	EM	End of medium
26	1A	0011010	SUB	Substitute
27	1B	0011011	ESC	Escape
28	1C	0011100	FS	File separator
29	1D	0011101	GS	Group separator
30	1E	0011110	RS	Record separator
31	1F	0011111	US	Unit separator
32	20	0100000	SP	Space
33	21	0100001	!	Exclamation mark
34	22	0100010	"	Double quote
35	23	0100011	#	Pound sign
36	24	0100100	$	Dollar sign
37	25	0100101	%	Percent sign
38	26	0100110	&	Ampersand
39	27	0100111	'	Apostrophe
40	28	0101000	(	Open parenthesis
41	29	0101001	)	Close parenthesis
42	2A	0101010	*	Asterisk
43	2B	0101011	+	Plus sign
44	2C	0101100	,	Comma
45	2D	0101101	-	Hyphen
46	2E	0101110	.	Period
47	2F	0101111	/	Slash
48	30	0110000	0	
49	31	0110001	1	
50	32	0110010	2	
51	33	0110011	3	
52	34	0110100	4	
53	35	0110101	5	
54	36	0110110	6	
55	37	0110111	7	
56	38	0111000	8	

Decimal	Hexadecimal	Binary	Character	Description
57	39	0111001	9	
58	3A	0111010	:	Colon
59	3B	0111011	;	Semicolon
60	3C	0111100	<	Less than sign
61	3D	0111101	=	Equal sign
62	3E	0111110	>	Greater than sign
63	3F	0111111	?	Question mark
64	40	1000000	@	At sign
65	41	1000001	A	
66	42	1000010	B	
67	43	1000011	C	
68	44	1000100	D	
69	45	1000101	E	
70	46	1000110	F	
71	47	1000111	G	
72	48	1001000	H	
73	49	1001001	I	
74	4A	1001010	J	
75	4B	1001011	K	
76	4C	1001100	L	
77	4D	1001101	M	
78	4E	1001110	N	
79	4F	1001111	O	
80	50	1010000	P	
81	51	1010001	Q	
82	52	1010010	R	
83	53	1010011	S	
84	54	1010100	T	
85	55	1010101	U	
86	56	1010110	V	
87	57	1010111	W	
88	58	1011000	X	
89	59	1011001	Y	
90	5A	1011010	Z	
91	5B	1011011	[	Open bracket
92	5C	1011100	\	Backslash

(continued)

Table A.1 *ASCII table (continued)*

Decimal	Hexadecimal	Binary	Character	Description
93	5D	1011101	]	Close bracket
94	5E	1011110	^	Caret
95	5F	1011111	_	Underscore
96	60	1100000	`	Grave accent
97	61	1100001	a	
98	62	1100010	b	
99	63	1100011	c	
100	64	1100100	d	
101	65	1100101	e	
102	66	1100110	f	
103	67	1100111	g	
104	68	1101000	h	
105	69	1101001	i	
106	6A	1101010	j	
107	6B	1101011	k	
108	6C	1101100	l	
109	6D	1101101	m	
110	6E	1101110	n	
111	6F	1101111	o	
112	70	1110000	p	
113	71	1110001	q	
114	72	1110010	r	
115	73	1110011	s	
116	74	1110100	t	
117	75	1110101	u	
118	76	1110110	v	
119	77	1110111	w	
120	78	1111000	x	
121	79	1111001	y	
122	7A	1111010	z	
123	7B	1111011	{	Open brace
124	7C	1111100	|	Bar
125	7D	1111101	}	Close brace
126	7E	1111110	~	Tilde
127	7F	1111111	DEL	Delete

Numbering Systems and Transformation

Today's computers make use of four numbering systems: decimal, binary, octal, and hexadecimal. Each has advantages for different levels of digital processing. In the first section of this appendix, we describe each of the four systems. In the second section, we show how a number in one system can be transformed into a number in another system.

B.1 NUMBERING SYSTEMS

All of the numbering systems examined here are positional, meaning that the position of a symbol in relation to other symbols determines its value. Within a number, each symbol is called a digit (decimal digit, binary digit, octal digit, or hexadecimal digit). For example, the decimal number 798 has three decimal digits. Digits are arranged in order of ascending value, moving from the lowest value on the right to the highest on the left. For this reason, the leftmost digit is referred to as the most significant and the rightmost as the least significant digit (see Figure B.1). For example, in the decimal number 1,234, the most significant digit is the 1 and the least significant is the 4.

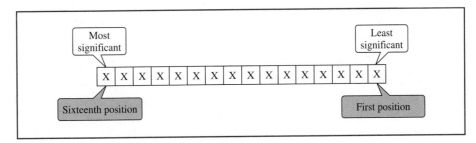

Figure B.1 Digit positions and their significance

DECIMAL NUMBERS

The decimal system is the one most familiar to us in everyday life. All of our terms for indicating countable quantities are based on it, and, in fact, when we speak of other numbering systems, we tend to refer to their quantities by their decimal equivalents. Also called base 10, the name *decimal* is derived from the Latin stem *deci,* meaning ten. The decimal system uses 10 symbols to represent quantitative values: 0, 1, 2, 3, 4, 5, 6, 7, 8, and 9.

Decimal numbers use 10 symbols: 0, 1, 2, 3, 4, 5, 6, 7, 8, and 9.

Weight and Value

In the decimal system, each weight equals 10 raised to the power of its position. The weight of the first position, therefore, is 10^0, which equals 1. So the value of a digit in the first position is equal to the value of the digit times 1. The weight of the second position is 10^1, which equals 10. The value of a digit in the second position, therefore, is equal to the value of the digit times 10. The weight of the third position is 10^2. The value of a digit in the third position is equal to the value of the digit times 100 (see Table B.1).

Table B.1 *Decimal weights*

Position	Fifth	Fourth	Third	Second	First
Weight	10^4 (10,000)	10^3 (1,000)	10^2 (100)	10^1 (10)	10^0 (1)

The value of the number as a whole is the sum of each digit times its weight. Figure B.2 shows the weightings of the decimal number 4,567.

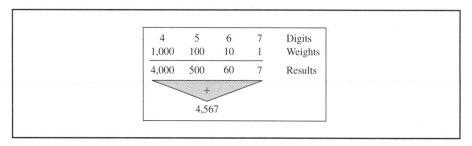

Figure B.2   Example of a decimal number

BINARY NUMBERS

The binary number system provides the basis for all computer operations. Computers work by manipulating electrical current on and off. The binary system uses two symbols, *0* and *1*, so it corresponds naturally to a two-state device, such as a switch, with 0 to represent the off state and 1 to represent the on state. Also called base 2, the word *binary* derives from the Latin stem *bi,* meaning two.

Binary numbers use two symbols: 0 and 1.

Weight and Value

The binary system is also a weighted system. Each digit has a weight based on its position in the number. Weight in the binary system is two raised to the power represented by a position, as shown in Table B.2. Note that the value of the weightings is shown in decimal terms next to the weight itself. The value of a specific digit is equal to its face value times the weight of its position.

Table B.2 *Binary weights*

Position	Fifth	Fourth	Third	Second	First
Weight	2^4 (16)	2^3 (8)	2^2 (4)	2^1 (2)	2^0 (1)

To calculate the value of a number, multiply each digit by the weight of its position, and then add together the results. Figure B.3 demonstrates the weighting of the binary number 1101. As you can see, 1101 is the binary equivalent of decimal 13.

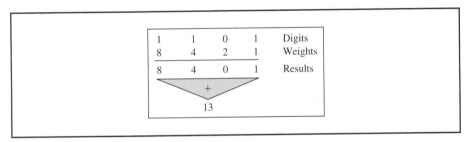

Figure B.3 Example of a binary number

OCTAL NUMBERS

The octal number system is used by computer programmers to represent binary numbers in a compact form. Also called base 8, the term *octal* derives from the Greek stem *octa*, meaning eight. Eight is a power of two (2^3) and therefore can be used to model binary concepts. The octal system uses eight symbols to represent quantitative values: 0, 1, 2, 3, 4, 5, 6, and 7.

Octal numbers use eight symbols: 0, 1, 2, 3, 4, 5, 6, and 7.

Weight and Value

The octal system is also a weighted system. Each digit has a weight based on its position in the number. Weight in octal is eight raised to the power represented by a position, as shown in Table B.3. Once again, the value represented by each weighting is given in decimal terms next to the weight itself. The value of a specific digit is equal to its face value times the weight of its position. For example, a 4 in the third position has the equivalent decimal value 4×64, or 256.

Table B.3 *Octal weights*

Position	Fifth	Fourth	Third	Second	First
Weight	8^4 (4,096)	8^3 (512)	8^2 (64)	8^1 (8)	8^0 (1)

To calculate the value of an octal number, multiply the value of each digit by the weight of its position, then add together the results. Figure B.4 shows the weighting for the octal number 3471. As you can see, 3471 is the octal equivalent of decimal 1,849.

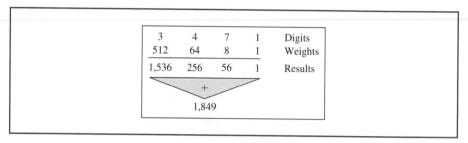

Figure B.4   Example of an octal number

HEXADECIMAL NUMBERS

The term *hexadecimal* is derived from the Greek stem *hexadeca,* meaning 16 (*hex* means 6, and *deca* means 10). So the hexadecimal number system is base 16. Sixteen is also a power of 2 (2^4). Like octal, therefore, the hexadecimal system is used by programmers to represent binary numbers in a compact form. Hexadecimal uses 16 symbols to represent data: 0, 1, 2, 3, 4, 5, 6, 7, 8, 9, A, B, C, D, E, and F.

Hexadecimal numbers use 16 symbols: 0, 1, 2, 3, 4, 5, 6, 7, 8, 9, A, B, C, D, E, and F.

Weight and Value

Like the others, the hexadecimal system is a weighted system. Each digit has a weight based on its position in the number. The weight is used to calculate the value represented by the digit. Weight in hexadecimal is 16 raised to the power represented by a position, as shown in Table B.4. Once again, the value represented by each weighting is given in decimal terms next to the weight itself. The value of a specific digit is equal to its face value times the weight of its position. For example, a 4 in the third position has the equivalent decimal value 4×256, or 1,024. To calculate the value of a hexadecimal number, multiply the value of each digit by the weight of its position, then add together the results. Figure B.5 shows the weighting for the hexadecimal number 3471. As you can see, 3471 is the hexadecimal equivalent of decimal 13,425.

Table B.4 *Hexadecimal weights*

Position	Fifth	Fourth	Third	Second	First
Weight	16^4 (65,536)	16^3 (4,096)	16^2 (256)	16^1 (16)	16^0 (1)

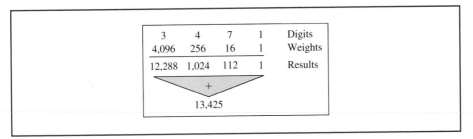

Figure B.5 Example of a hexadecimal number

B.2 TRANSFORMATION

The different numbering systems provide different ways of thinking about a common subject: quantities of single units. A number from any given system can be transformed into its equivalent in any other system. For example, a binary number can be converted to a decimal number, and vice versa, without altering its value. Table B.5 shows how each system represents the decimal numbers 0 through 15. As you can see, decimal 13 is equivalent to binary 1101, which is equivalent to octal 15, which is equivalent to hexadecimal D.

Table B.5 *Comparison of four systems*

Decimal	Binary	Octal	Hexadecimal
0	0	0	0
1	1	1	1
2	10	2	2
3	11	3	3
4	100	4	4
5	101	5	5
6	110	6	6
7	111	7	7
8	1000	10	8
9	1001	11	9
10	1010	12	A

(continued)

Table B.5 *Comparison of four systems (continued)*

Decimal	Binary	Octal	Hexadecimal
11	1011	13	B
12	1100	14	C
13	1101	15	D
14	1110	16	E
15	1111	17	F

FROM OTHER SYSTEMS TO DECIMAL

As we saw in the discussions above, binary, octal, and hexadecimal numbers can be transformed easily to their decimal equivalents by using the weights of the digits. Figure B.6 shows the decimal value 78 represented in each of the other three systems.

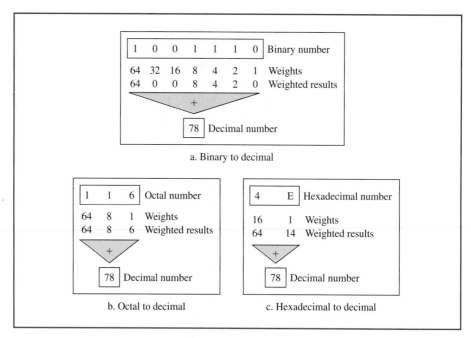

Figure B.6 Transformation from other systems to decimal

FROM DECIMAL TO OTHER SYSTEMS

A simple division trick gives us a convenient way to convert a decimal number to its binary, octal, or hexadecimal equivalent (see Figure B.7).

To convert a number from decimal to binary, divide the number by 2 and write down the resulting remainder (1 or 0). That remainder is the least significant binary digit. Now, divide the result of that division by 2 and write down the new remainder in the second position. Repeat this process until the quotient becomes zero.

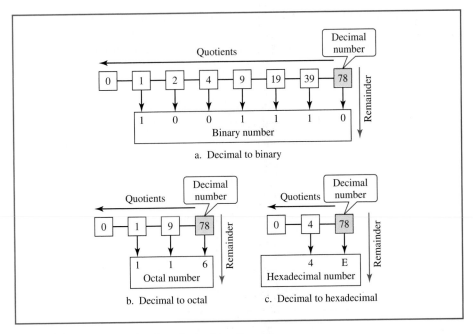

Figure B.7 Transformation from decimal to other systems

In Figure B.7, we convert the decimal number 78 to its binary equivalent. To check the validity of this method, we convert 1001110 to decimal using the weights of each position.

$$2^6 + 2^3 + 2^2 + 2^1 \rightarrow 64 + 8 + 4 + 2 \rightarrow 78$$

To convert a number from decimal to octal, the procedure is the same but the divisor is 8 instead of 2. To convert from decimal to hexadecimal, the divisor is 16.

FROM BINARY TO OCTAL OR HEXADECIMAL

To change a number from binary to octal, we first group the binary digits from right to left by threes. Then we convert each tribit to its octal equivalent and write the result under the tribit. These equivalents, taken in order (not added), are the octal equivalent of the original number. In Figure B.8, we convert binary 1001110.

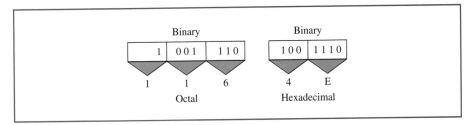

Figure B.8 Transformation from binary to octal or hexadecimal

To change a number from binary to hexadecimal, we follow the same procedure but group the digits from right to left by fours. This time we convert each quadbit to its hexadecimal equivalent (use Table B.5). In Figure B.8, we convert binary 1001110 to hexadecimal.

FROM OCTAL OR HEXADECIMAL TO BINARY

To convert from octal to binary, we reverse the procedure above. Starting with the least significant digit, we convert each octal digit into its equivalent three binary digits. In Figure B.9, we convert octal 116 to binary.

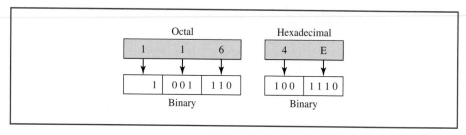

Figure B.9   Transformation from octal or hexadecimal to binary

To convert a number from hexadecimal to binary, we convert each hexadecimal digit to its equivalent four binary digits, again starting with the least significant digit. In Figure B.9, we convert hexadecimal 4E to binary.

Contact Addresses

The following is a list of contact addresses for various organizations mentioned in the text.

ATM FORUM

Presidio of San Francisco
P.O. Box 29920 (mail)
572B Ruger Street (surface)
San Francisco, CA 94129-0920
Telephone: 415.561-6275
Email: info@atmforum.com
http://www.atmforum.com

FEDERAL COMMUNICATIONS COMMISSION (FCC)

445 12th Street S.W.
Washington, DC 20554
Telephone: 1-888-225-5322
Email: fccinfo@fcc.gov
http://www.fcc.gov

INSTITUTE OF ELECTRICAL AND ELECTRONICS ENGINEERS (IEEE)

Operations Center
445 Hoes Lane
Piscataway, NJ 08855-1331
Telephone: 732.981-0060
http://www.ieee.gov

INTERNATIONAL ORGANIZATION FOR STANDARDIZATION (ISO)

1, rue de Varembe
Case postale 56
CH-1211 Geneve 20
Switzerland

Telephone: 41 22 749 0111
Email: central@iso.ch
http://www.iso.org

International Telecommunication Union (ITU)

Place des Nations
CH-1211 Geneva 20
Switzerland
Telephone: 41 22 730 5852
Email: tsbmail@itu.int
http://www.itu.int/ITU-T

Internet Architecture Board (IAB)

Email: IAB@isi.edu
http://www.iab.org

Internet Corporation for Assigned Names and Numbers (ICANN)

4676 Admiralty Way, Suite 330
Marina del Rey, CA 90292-6601
Telephone: 310.823-9358
Email: icann@icann.org
http://www.icann.org

Internet Engineering Steering Group (IESG)

Email: iesg@ietf.org
http://www.ietf.org/iesg.html

Internet Engineering Task Force (IETF)

Email: ietf-infor@ietf.org
http://www.ietf.org

Internet Research Task Force (IRTF)

Email: irtf-chair@ietf.org
http://www.irtf.org

Internet Society (ISOC)

775 Weihle Avenue, Suite 102
Reston, VA 20190-5108
Telephone: 703.326-9880
Email: info@isoc.org
http://www.isoc.org

GLOSSARY

1000Base-CX   A two-wire implementation of Gigabit Ethernet using shielded twisted pair cables.

1000Base-LX   A two-wire implementation of Gigabit Ethernet using optical fibers transmitting long-wave laser signals.

1000Base-SX   A two-wire implementation of Gigabit Ethernet using optical fibers transmitting short-wave laser signals.

1000Base-T   A four-wire implementation of Gigabit Ethernet using twisted-pair cables.

100Base-FX   A two-wire implementation of Fast Ethernet using fiber-optic cable.

100Base-T4   A four-wire implementation of Fast Ethernet using twisted-pair cable.

100Base-TX   A two-wire implementation of Fast Ethernet using twisted-pair cable.

100Base-X   A two-wire implementation of Fast Ethernet.

10Base-FL   The IEEE 802.3 standard for twisted-pair Ethernet. The standard specifies a star topology with stations connected by a pair of fiber-optic cables to a hub. The data rate is defined to be 10 Mbps.

10Base-T   The IEEE 802.3 standard for twisted-pair Ethernet. The standard specifies a star topology using twisted-pair cable. The data rate is defined to be 10 Mbps.

10Base2   The IEEE 802.3 standard for Thin Ethernet. The standard specifies a bus topology using thin coaxial cable with a maximum segment length of 185 meters. The data rate is defined to be 10 Mbps. (Also called cheapernet or cheapnet.)

10Base5   The IEEE 802.3 standard for Thick Ethernet. The standard specifies a bus topology using thick coaxial cable with a maximum segment length of 500 meters. The data rate is defined to be 10 Mbps.

56K modem   A modem with a downloading bit rate of 56,000 bps.

A

AAL   See *application adaptation layer.*

ACK   See *acknowledgment.*

access control   Management to determine which device has control over a link.

access point (AP)   A central station in a BSS.

accounting management   A branch of network management responsible for charging users access to network resources.

acknowledgment (ACK)   A response sent by the receiver to indicate the successful receipt and acceptance of data.

active hub   A hub that repeats or regenerates a signal.

ad hoc architecture   A BSS without an AP. This is a stand-alone network that cannot send data to other BSSs.

Address Resolution Protocol (ARP) In TCP/IP a protocol for obtaining the physical address of a station when the Internet address is known.

addressing A mechanism that identifies a computer.

ADSL See *asymmetrical digital subscriber line.*

Advanced Research Project Agency (ARPA) The government agency that funded ARPANET.

Advanced Research Project Agency Network (ARPANET) The packet switching network that was funded by ARPA.

agent A router or a host that runs the SNMP server program.

American National Standards Institute (ANSI) A national standards organization that defines standards in the United States.

amplifier A device that amplifies signals.

amplitude The strength of a signal, usually measured in volts, amperes, or watts.

amplitude shift keying (ASK) A digital-to-analog conversion method in which the amplitude of the carrier is varied to represent binary 0 or 1.

analog data Data that are continuous and smooth and not limited to a specific number of values.

analog signal A continuous waveform that changes continuously over time.

analog-to-digital conversion The representation of analog information by a digital signal.

analysis phase In the NDLC, the analysis of the existing system (called baselining), and the analysis of the needs for the new network.

anonymous FTP A protocol in which a remote user can access another machine without an account or password.

ANSI See *American National Standards Institute.*

AP See *access point.*

application adaptation layer (AAL) A layer in ATM protocol that breaks user data into 48-byte payloads.

application layer The seventh layer in the OSI model; provides access to network resources.

application program Application layer software that accomplishes a specific task.

application-to-application delivery Delivery of a packet from the application on the source host to the application on the destination host.

ARP See *address resolution protocol.*

ARPA See *Advanced Research Project Agency.*

ARPANET See *Advanced Research Project Agency Network.*

ASK See *amplitude shift keying.*

asymmetrical DSL (ADSL) A communication technology in which the downstream data rate is higher than the upstream rate.

asynchronous protocol A set of rules for asynchronous transmission.

asynchronous TDM Time-division multiplexing in which link time is allocated dynamically according to the activity of the links.

asynchronous transfer mode (ATM) A wide area network protocol featuring high data rates and equal-sized packets called cells.

asynchronous transmission Transfer of data with start and stop bit(s) and a variable time interval between data units.

ATM See *asynchronous transfer mode.*

ATM forum A group of parties interested in the promotion and rapid development of ATM.

ATM LAN   A LAN using ATM technology.

ATM switch   An ATM device providing both switching and multiplexing functions.

attenuation   The loss of a signal's energy due to the resistance of the medium.

authentication   Verification of the sender of a message.

Authentication Header protocol   A protocol defined by IPSec at the network layer that provides integrity to a message through the creation of a digital signature by a hashing function.

B

bandwidth   The difference between the highest and the lowest frequencies of a composite signal. It also measures the information-carrying capacity of a line or a network.

bandwidth on demand   A digital service that allows subscribers higher speeds through the use of multiple lines.

baselining   In the NDLC, the analysis of the existing system.

basic service set (BSS)   The building block of a wireless LAN as defined by the IEEE 802.11standard.

baud rate   The number of signal elements transmitted per second. A signal element consists of 1 or more bits.

BGP   See *Border Gateway Protocol.*

biometric   The use of some characteristic of the user to gain access to a system.

bipolar encoding   A digital-to-digital encoding method in which binary 0 is represented by 0 amplitude and binary 1 is represented by alternating positive and negative amplitudes.

bit   A binary digit; the smallest unit of information; 1 or 0.

bit interval   The time required to send 1 bit.

bit rate   The number of bits transmitted per second.

bit-oriented protocol   A protocol in which a frame is seen as a bit stream.

bits per second (bps)   A measurement of data speed; bits transmitted per second.

Bluetooth technology   The implementation of a protocol defined by the IEEE 802.15 standard. The standard defines a wireless personal area network (wireless PAN) operable in an area the size of a room or a hall.

Border Gateway Protocol (BGP)   An inter-autonomous system routing protocol based on path vector routing.

bps   See *bits per second.*

bridge   A network device operating at the first two layers of the OSI model with filtering and forwarding capabilities.

bridge-based backbone   A backbone in which the LANs are connected through bridges.

brouter (bridge/router)   A device that functions as both a bridge and a router.

browser   An application program that displays a WWW document. A browser usually uses other Internet services to access the document.

BSS   See *basic service set.*

BSS-transition mobility station   A station that can move from one BSS to another, with the movement confined inside one ESS.

buffer   Memory set aside for temporary storage.

burst error   Error in a data unit in which 2 or more bits have been altered.

bursty data   Data with varying instantaneous transmission rates.

C

cable modem   A technology in which the TV cable provides Internet access.

cable TV   A communication system using coaxial cable that brings multiple channels of programs into homes.

capacity   In a LAN, the number of bits a station can transmit per second.

carrier sense multiple access (CSMA)   A contention access method in which each station listens to the line before transmitting data.

carrier sense multiple access with collision avoidance (CSMA/CA)   A CSMA access method in which collision is avoided.

carrier sense multiple access with collision detection (CSMA/CD)   CSMA with retransmission when collision is detected.

carrier signal   A high frequency signal used in digital-to-analog and analog-to-analog modulation. A carrier characteristic is changed according to the modulating data.

cell   A small, fixed-size data unit; also, in cellular telephony, a geographical area served by a cell office.

cell network   A network using the cell as its basic data unit.

channel   A communications pathway.

character-oriented protocol   A protocol in which the frame or packet is interpreted as a series of characters.

chatting   An application in which two parties are involved in a real-time exchange of text, audio, and video.

chip code   A sequence of bits that replaces one bit in the DSSS technique.

ciphertext   The encrypted data.

CLEC   See *competitive local exchange carrier.*

client   See *client process.*

client process   A running application program on a local site that requests service from a running application program on a remote site.

client-server model   The model of interaction between two application programs in which a program at one end (client) requests a service from a program at the other end (server).

coaxial cable   A transmission medium consisting of a conducting core, insulating material, and a second conducting sheath.

common carrier   A transmission facility available to the public and subject to public utility regulation.

competitive local exchange carrier (CLEC)   A telephone company that cannot provide main telephone services; instead, other services such as mobile telephone service, and toll calls inside a LATA are provided.

complex signal   A signal composed of more than 1 sine wave.

compression   The reduction of a message without significant loss of information.

configuration management   The branch of network management that deals with the status of each entity in relation to other entities.

congestion   Excessive network or internetwork traffic causing a general degradation of service.

connecting device   A tool that connects computers or networks.

connection establishment   The preliminary setup necessary for a logical connection prior to actual data transfer.

connection termination   A message sent to end a connection.

connectionless delivery   Data delivery without the establishment and termination of a connection.

connection-oriented delivery   Data delivery involving establishment and termination of a connection.

contention   An access method in which two or more devices try to transmit at the same time on the same channel.

controlled access   A medium access method in which a permit is needed before a frame can be sent.

critical angle   In refraction, the value of the angle of incidence that produces a 90-degree angle of refraction.

CRC   See *cyclic redundancy check.*

crosstalk   Noise on a line caused by signals traveling on another line.

CSMA   See *carrier sense multiple access.*

CMSA/CA   See *carrier sense multiple access with collision avoidance.*

CSMA/CD   See *carrier sense multiple access with collision detection.*

cyclic redundancy check (CRC)   A highly accurate error detection method based on interpreting a pattern of bits as a polynomial.

D

damage control   The management of errors to ensure reliable service.

data   Information in a specific form such as numbers, text, images, and audio.

data encryption standard (DES)   The U.S. government standard encryption method for nonmilitary and nonclassified use.

data link connection identifier (DLCI)   A number that identifies a virtual circuit.

data link layer   The second layer in the OSI model. It is responsible for node-to-node delivery.

datagram   In packet-switching, an independent data unit.

decryption   Recovery of the original message from the encrypted data.

de facto standard   A protocol that has not been approved by an organized body but adopted as a standard through widespread use.

de jure standard   A protocol that has been legislated by an officially recognized body.

demodulation   The process of separating the carrier signal from the information bearing signal.

demodulator   A device that performs demodulation.

DES   See *data encryption standard.*

design phase   In the NDLC, creation of specifications for the new network system.

destination address   The address of the receiver of the data unit.

diffused infrared LAN   A wireless LAN that uses a reflecting object for transmission.

diffused transmission   A transmission technique in infrared wireless LANs in which a reflecting object (such as a ceiling) is used to guide the signals.

digest   A condensed version of a document.

digital data   Data represented by discrete values or conditions.

digital signal   A discrete signal with a limited number of values.

digital signature   A method to authenticate the sender of a message.

digital subscriber line (DSL)   A technology using existing telecommunication networks to accomplish high-speed delivery of data, voice, video, and multimedia.

digital-to-analog modulation   The representation of digital information by an analog signal.

digital-to-digital encoding   The representation of digital information by a digital signal.

direct sequence spread spectrum (DSSS)   A wireless transmission method in which each bit to be sent by the sender is replaced by a sequence of bits called a chip code.

distance vector routing   A routing method in which each router sends its neighbors a list of networks it can reach and the distance to that network.

distortion   Any change in a signal due to noise, attenuation, or other influences.

distributed database   Information stored in many locations.

distributed processing   Division of a task among multiple computers.

DLCI   See *data link connection identifier.*

DNS   See *domain name system.*

Domain Name System (DNS)   A TCP/IP application service that converts user-friendly names to IP addresses.

dotted-decimal notation   A notation devised to make the IP address easier to read; each byte is converted to its decimal equivalent and then set off from its neighbor by a decimal.

downloading   Retrieving a file or data from a remote site.

DSL   See *digital subscriber line.*

DSSS   See *direct sequence spread spectrum.*

duplicate control   The management of duplicate packets to ensure reliable service.

dynamic routing table   A routing table which has its entries updated automatically by the routing protocol.

E

echo   An error that occurs when a sending device receives some of the energy it has sent.

EHF   See *extremely high frequency.*

EIA   See *Electronics Industries Association.*

electromagnetic interference (EMI)   A noise on the data transmission line that can corrupt the data. It can be created by motors, generators, and so on.

electromagnetic spectrum   The frequency range occupied by electromagnetic energy.

electronic mail (email)   A method of sending messages electronically based on mailbox addresses rather than a direct host-to-host exchange.

Electronics Industries Association (EIA)   An organization that promotes electronics manufacturing concerns. It has developed interface standards such as EIA-232, EIA-449, and EIA-530.

email   See *electronic mail.*

EMI   See *electromagnetic interference.*

Encapsulating Security Payload (ESP)   A protocol defined by IPSec that provides privacy as well as a combination of integrity and message authentication.

encoding   Transforming information into signals.

encryption   Converting a message into an unintelligible form that is unreadable unless decrypted.

end office   A switching office that is the terminus for the local loops.

error   A mistake.

error control   The detection and handling of errors in data transmission.

error correction   The process of correcting bits that have been changed during transmission.

error detection   The process of determining whether or not some bits have been changed during transmission.

ESP   See *Encapsulating Security Payload.*

ESS   See *extended service set.*

ESS-transition mobility station   A station that can move from one ESS to another.

Ethernet   A local area network using CSMA/CD access method. See *IEEE Project 802.3.*

Extended Service Set (ESS)   A wireless LAN service composed of two or more BSSs with APs as defined by the IEEE 802.11 standard.

exterior routing   Routing between autonomous systems.

extremely high frequency (EHF)   Radio waves in the 30-GHz to 300-GHz range using space propagation.

F

Fast Ethernet   See *100Base-T.*

fault management   An area of network management responsible for the proper operation of each component individually and in relation to each other.

FCC   See *Federal Communications Commission.*

FDDI   See *fiber distributed data interface.*

FDM   See *frequency division multiplexing.*

Federal Communications Commission (FCC)   A government agency that regulates radio, television, and telecommunications.

FHSS   See *frequency hopping spread spectrum.*

fiber distributed data interface (FDDI)   A high speed (100-Mbps) LAN, defined by ANSI, using optical fiber, dual ring topology, and a token passing access method.

File Transfer Protocol (FTP)   In TCP/IP, an application layer protocol that transfers files between two sites.

filtering   The capability of a bridge to check the destination address of a packet and decide if the packet should be forwarded or dropped.

firewall   A device (usually a router) installed between the internal network of an organization and the rest of the Internet to provide security.

flooding   Saturation of a network with a message.

flow control   A technique to control the rate of flow of frames (packets or messages).

FM   See *frequency modulation.*

forum   An organization that tests, evaluates, and standardizes a specific new technology.

forward error correction   Correction of errors without retransmission.

fractional T line   A service which allows several subscribers to share one line by multiplexing their transmissions.

fragmentation   The division of a packet into smaller units to accommodate a protocol's MTU.

frame   A group of bits representing a block of data.

Frame Relay   A packet-switching specification defined for the first two layers of the OSI model. There is no network layer. Error checking is done on end-to-end basis instead of on each link.

Frame Relay Forum   A group formed by Digital Equipment Corporation, Northern Telecom, Cisco, and StrataCom to promote the acceptance and implementation of Frame Relay.

frame tagging   In a VLAN, a method that adds a tag to a frame as it travels between switches.

framing Insertion of a packet from the network layer into a data link layer frame and adding a header and a trailer.

frequency The number of cycles per second in a periodic signal.

frequency division multiplexing (FDM) The combining of analog signals into a signal.

frequency hopping spread spectrum (FHSS) A wireless transmission method in which the sender transmits at one carrier frequency for a short period of time, then hops to another carrier frequency for the same amount of time, hops again for the same amount of time, and so on. After N hops, the cycle is repeated.

frequency modulation (FM) An analog-to-analog modulation method in which the carrier signal's frequency varies with the amplitude of the modulating signal.

frequency shift keying (FSK) A digital-to-analog conversion method in which the frequency of the carrier is varied to represent binary 0 or 1.

FSK See *frequency shift keying.*

FTP See *file transfer protocol.*

full duplex transmission A transmission mode in which communication can be two way simultaneously

full-duplex Ethernet An Ethernet implementation in which every station is connected by two separate paths to the central hub.

G

gateway A device used to connect two separate networks that use different communication protocols.

general server A server that is responsible for all services on a network.

geosynchronous orbit An orbit that allows a satellite to remain fixed above a certain spot on earth.

Gigabit Ethernet Ethernet with a 1000 Mbps data rate.

H

half-duplex Ethernet An Ethernet in which 2 stations or a station and a switch can send frames to each other only one at a time (not simultaneously).

half duplex transmission A transmission mode in which communication is two way, but not at the same time.

hardware documentation A part of configuration management that records all changes in hardware.

hardware reconfiguration A part of configuration management that is responsible for changes in the hardware.

hash function An algorithm that creates a fixed-size digest from a variable-length message.

HDLC See *high-level data link control.*

header Control information added to the beginning of a data packet. Also, in an email, the part of the message that defines the sender, the receiver, the subject of the message, and other information.

hierarchical routing A routing technique in which the entire address space is divided into levels based on specific criteria.

high-level data link control (HDLC) A bit-oriented data link protocol defined by the ISO. It is used by the X.25 protocol and is the basis for many data link protocols.

hop-to-hop delivery The delivery of a packet from one connecting device to another.

hostid   The part of an IP address that identifies a host.

host-to-host delivery   The delivery of a packet from the source host to the destination host.

HTML   See *hypertext markup language.*

HTTP   See *hypertext transfer protocol.*

hub   A central device in a star topology that provides a common connection among the nodes.

hybrid network   A network with a private internet and access to the global Internet.

Hypertext Markup Language (HTML)   The computer language for specifying the contents and format of a Web document. It allows additional text to include codes that define fonts, layouts, embedded graphics, and hypertext links.

Hypertext Transfer Protocol (HTTP)   An application service for retrieving a Web document.

I

IAB   See *Internet Architecture Board.*

IANA   See *Internet Assigned Numbers Authority.*

ICANN   See *Internet Corporation for Assigned Names and Numbers.*

ICMP   See *Internet Control Message Protocol.*

ICMPv6   See *Internet Control Message Protocol, version 6.*

IEEE   See *Institute of Electrical and Electronics Engineers.*

IEEE Project 802   A project by IEEE to define LAN standards for the physical and data link layers of the OSI model.

IETF   See *Internet Engineering Task Force.*

IGMP   See *Internet Group Management Protocol.*

ILEC   See *incumbent local exchange carrier.*

IMAP   See *Internet Mail Access Protocol.*

implementation phase   In the NDLC, purchasing or renting new hardware and software, installation of new hardware and software, training of users, testing of the system, and documentation.

impulse noise   Spike noise that suddenly affects the medium.

incumbent local exchange carrier (ILEC)   A telephone company that provided services before 1996 and is the owner of the cabling system.

infrared transmission   Transmission of infrared waves.

infrared waves   Electromagnetic waves with frequencies just below the visible spectrum.

infrastructure network   A connection of BSSs; stations within reach of each other can communicate without the use of an AP.

Institute of Electrical and Electronics Engineers (IEEE)   A group consisting of professional engineers which has specialized societies whose committees prepare standards in members' areas of specialty.

integrity   A data quality of being noncorrupted.

interexchange carrier (IXC)   A long-distance company that, prior to the Act of 1996, provided communication services between two customers in different LATAs.

interior routing   Routing inside an autonomous system.

International Organization for Standardization (ISO)   A worldwide organization that defines and develops standards on a variety of topics.

International Telecommunications Union–Telecommunication Standardization Sector (ITU–T)   A standards organization formerly known as the CCITT.

internet   A collection of networks connected by internetworking devices such as routers or gateways.

Internet   A global internet that uses the TCP/IP protocol suite.

Internet address   A 32-bit or 128-bit network-layer address used to uniquely define a host on an internet using the TCP/IP protocol.

Internet Architecture Board (IAB)   The technical adviser to the ISOC; oversees the continuing development of the TCP/IP protocol suite.

Internet Assigned Numbers Authority (IANA)   A group supported by the U.S. government that was responsible for the management of Internet domain names and addresses until October 1998.

Internet Control Message Protocol (ICMP)   A protocol in the TCP/IP protocol suite that handles error and control messages.

Internet Corporation for Assigned Names and Numbers (ICANN)   A private, nonprofit corporation managed by an international board that assumed IANA operations.

Internet draft   A working Internet document (a work in progress) with no official status and a six-month lifetime.

Internet Engineering Task Force (IETF)   A group working on the design and development of the TCP/IP protocol suite and the Internet.

Internet Group Management Protocol (IGMP)   A protocol in the TCP/IP protocol suite that handles multicasting.

Internet Mail Access Protocol (IMAP)   A complex and powerful protocol to handle the transmission of electronic mail.

Internet model   A five-layer de facto model for data communications on the Internet based on TCP/IP.

Internet Network Information Center (INTERNIC)   An agency responsible for collecting and distributing information about TCP/IP protocols.

Internet Protocol   See *Internetworking Protocol.*

Internet Research Task Force (IRTF)   A forum of working groups focusing on long-term research topics related to the Internet.

Internet service provider (ISP)   Usually, a company that provides Internet services.

Internet Society (ISOC)   The nonprofit organization established to publicize the Internet.

Internet standard   A thoroughly tested specification that is useful to and adhered to by those who work with the Internet. It is a formalized regulation that must be followed.

internetworking devices   Electronic devices such as routers and gateways that connect networks together to form an internet.

Internetworking Protocol (IP)   The network-layer protocol in the TCP/IP protocol suite governing connectionless transmission across packet-switching networks.

Internetworking Protocol, next generation (IPng)   Another term for the sixth version of the Internetworking Protocol.

Internetworking Protocol, version 6 (IPv6)   The sixth version of the Internetworking Protocol; it features major IP addressing changes.

INTERNIC   See *Internet Network Information Center.*

intranet   A private network that uses the TCP/IP protocol suite.

inverse multiplexing   Taking data from one source and breaking it into portions that can be sent across lower-speed lines.

IP   See *Internetworking Protocol.*

IP address   See *Internet address.*

IP datagram   The Internetworking Protocol data unit.

IP Security (IPSec)   A collection of protocols designed by the IETF (Internet Engineering Task Force) to provide security for a packet carried on the Internet.

IPng (IP next generation)   See *IPv6.*

IPSec   See *IP Security.*

IPv4   The Internetworking Protocol, version 4. It is the current version.

IPv6   See *Internetworking Protocol, version 6.*

IR   See *infrared.*

IRTF   See *Internet Research Task Force.*

ISO   See *International Organization of Standardization.*

ISOC   See *Internet Society.*

ISP   See *Internet service provider.*

ITU–T   See *International Telecommunications Union–Telecommunication Standardization Sector.*

IXC   See *interexchange carrier.*

J

jitter   A phenomenon in real-time traffic caused by gaps between consecutive packets at the receiver.

L

LAN   See *local area network.*

LAN emulation (LANE)   A client-server model that allows the use of ATM technology in LANs.

LANE   See *LAN emulation.*

LATA   See *Local Access and Transport Area.*

LEC   See *local exchange carrier.*

legacy LAN   A LAN in which ATM technology is used as a backbone to connect traditional LANs.

LF   See *low frequency.*

line configuration   The relationship between communication devices and their pathway.

line monitor   A device that detects the signal flowing between a host (end-user computer) and the network.

line-of-sight propagation   The transmission of very high frequency signals in straight lines directly from antenna to antenna.

link   The physical communication pathway that transfers data from one device to another.

link state routing   A routing method in which each router shares its knowledge of changes in its neighborhood with all other routers.

listserv   An application which allows a group of users to discuss a common topic of interest.

LLC   See *logical link control.*

Local Access and Transport Area (LATA)   An area covered by one or more telephone companies.

local area network (LAN)   A network connecting devices inside a single building or inside buildings close to each other.

local exchange carrier (LEC)   A telephone company that handles services inside a LATA.

local ISP   An Internet service provider that provides direct service to the end user.

local login   Using a terminal directly connected to the computer.

local loop   The link that connects a subscriber to the telephone central office.

logical bus backbone   A backbone in which the logical topology is a bus.

logical bus topology   A logical topology in which a frame sent by a station is received by every station in the network.

logical link control (LLC)   The upper sublayer of the data link layer as defined by IEEE Project 802.2.

logical star backbone   A backbone in which the logical topology is a star.

logical star topology   A logical topology in which a frame sent by a station is received only by the destination station.

logical topology   The arrangement of nodes in a network that defines how data flows.

longitudinal redundancy check (LRC)   An error-detection method dividing a data unit into rows and columns and performing parity checks on corresponding bits of each column.

loss control   The management of missing packets to ensure reliable service.

low frequency (LF)   Radio waves in the 30-KHz to 300-KHz range.

LRC   See *longitudinal redundancy check.*

M

MA   See *multiple access.*

MAC   See *medium access control.*

mail transfer agent (MTA)   An SMTP component that transfers email across the Internet.

MAN   See *metropolitan area network.*

management information base (MIB)   The database used by SNMP that holds the information necessary for management of a network.

manager   The host that runs the SNMP client program.

maturity level   The phases through which an RFC goes.

maximum transfer unit (MTU)   The largest size data unit a specific network can handle.

medium access control (MAC)   Methods (controlled or random) to determine a computer's access to the medium.

message   Data sent from source to destination. Or, in SMTP, the headers and the body portion of email.

metric   A cost assigned for passing through a network.

metropolitan area network (MAN)   A network that can span a geographical area the size of a city.

MF   See *middle frequency.*

MIB   See *management information base.*

microwave   Electromagnetic waves ranging from 2 GHz to 40 GHz.

microwave transmission   Communication using microwaves.

middle frequency (MF)   Radio waves in the 300-KHz to 3-MHz range.

MIME   See *Multipurpose Internet Mail Extension.*

mixed architecture LAN An ATM LAN which combines the features of a pure ATM LAN and a legacy ATM LAN.

modem A device consisting of a modulator and a demodulator. It converts a digital signal into an analog signal (modulator) and vice versa (demodulator).

modulation Modification of one or more characteristics of a carrier wave by the information-bearing signal.

modulator A device that converts a digital signal into an analog signal.

MTA See *mail transfer agent.*

MTU See *maximum transfer unit.*

multicasting A transmission method that allows copies of a single packet to be sent to a selected group of receivers.

multimode graded-index fiber An optical fiber having a core with a graded index of refraction.

multimode step-index fiber An optical fiber having a core with a uniform index of refraction.

multiple access (MA) A line access method in which every station can access the line freely.

multipoint configuration A line configuration in which 3 or more devices share a common transmission line.

multiport bridge A bridge that connects more than 2 LANs.

multiprotocol router A router that can handle packets from different protocols.

Multipurpose Internet Mail Extension (MIME) A supplement to SMTP that allows non-ASCII data to be sent through SMTP.

N

NAK See *negative acknowledgment.*

NAP See *Network Access Point.*

NAT See *network address translation.*

national service provider (NSP) A backbone network created and maintained by a specialized company.

NDLC See *network development life cycle.*

needs analysis In the NDLC, finding the needs of the networks, backbone, and global access (scope needs) and finding the hardware, software, and bandwidth needs of the user (user needs).

negative acknowledgment (NAK) A message sent to indicate the rejection of received data.

netid The part of an IP address that identifies the network.

network A system consisting of connected nodes made to share data, hardware, and software.

Network Access Point (NAP) A complex switching station that connects backbone networks.

network address An address that identifies a network to the rest of the Internet; it is the first address in a block.

network address translation (NAT) A technology that allows a private network to use a set of private addresses for internal communication and a set of global Internet addresses for external communication.

network development life cycle (NDLC) A set of strategies for upgrading or replacing an organization's network system.

Network Information Center (NIC)   An agency responsible for collecting and distributing information about TCP/IP protocols.

network interface card (NIC)   An electronic device, internal or external to a station, that contains circuitry to enable the station to be connected to the network.

network layer   The third layer in the OSI model, responsible for the delivery of a packet to the final destination.

network management   Monitoring, testing, configuring, and troubleshooting network components to meet a set of requirements defined by the organization.

network operating system (NOS)   A program that allows the logical connection of stations and devices to the network. It enables users to communicate and share resources.

network-specific routing   Routing in which all hosts on a network share one entry in the routing table.

network system   A collection of physical networks (LANs, backbone, and WANs), network protocols, client and server programs, application programs, files and databases, procedures, documentation, maintenance contracts, and even staff organization.

network traffic   The number of packets on a network as measured by throughput, frame size, frames per second, collisions, and dropped frames.

network virtual terminal (NVT)   A TCP/IP application protocol that allows remote login.

next-hop routing   A routing method in which only the address of the next hop is listed in the routing table instead of a complete list of the stops the packet must make.

NIC   See *network interface card* or *Network Information Center.*

node-to-node delivery   Transfer of a data unit from one node to the next.

nonrepudiation   A security aspect in which a receiver must be able to prove that a received message came from a specific sender.

NOS   See *network operating system.*

no-transition mobility station   A station that is either stationary (not moving) or moving only inside a BSS.

NSP   See *national service provider.*

NVT   See *network virtual terminal.*

O

Open Shortest Path First (OSPF)   An interior routing protocol based on link state routing.

Open Systems Interconnection (OSI) model   A seven-layer model for data communications defined by ISO.

optical fiber   A high-bandwidth transmission medium that carries signals in the form of light pulses. It consists of a glass or plastic core surrounded by glass or plastic cladding.

order control   The management of correct packet sequencing to ensure reliable service.

OSI   See *Open Systems Interconnection.*

OSPF   See *Open Shortest Path First.*

P

packetizing   Encapsulation of data from an upper layer into the data field and adding a header and possibly a trailer.

packet-filter firewall   A firewall that forwards or blocks packets based on the information in the network-layer and transport-layer headers.

parallel transmission   Transmission in which bits in a group are sent simultaneously, each using a separate link.

parity check   An error detection method using a redundant bit added to a data unit.

parked state   A state in which a slave is synchronized with the master, but cannot take part in communication.

passive hub   A hub used only for connection; there is no signal regeneration.

password   An authorization technique in which the user logs on with a word known only to the user.

path   The channel through which a signal travels.

PCM   See *pulse code modulation.*

peer-to-peer model   A LAN model in which a station can be both a client and a server.

performance management   A branch of network management responsible for monitoring and controlling the network to ensure that it is running as efficiently as possible.

period   The amount of time required to complete one full cycle.

PGP   See *Pretty Good Privacy.*

phase   The relative position of a signal in time.

phase shift   The phase change of a signal.

phase shift keying (PSK)   A digital-to-analog conversion method in which the phase of the carrier is varied to represent binary 0 or 1.

physical address   The address of a device used at the data link layer (MAC address).

physical bus topology   A physical topology in which all devices are connected to the transmission medium (bus).

physical layer   The first layer of the OSI model, responsible for the mechanical and electrical specifications of the medium.

physical star topology   A physical topology in which each station is connected to a central node.

physical topology   The manner in which devices are connected in a network.

piconet   A Bluetooth network.

plaintext   In encryption/decryption, the original message.

point of presence (POP)   A switching office where carriers can interact with each other.

point-to-point configuration   A line configuration in which 2 devices share a common transmission line.

point-to-point infrared LAN   An infrared LAN that features point-to-point links between computers, bridges, or switches.

point-to-point transmission   Communication between two devices sharing a common transmission line.

point-to-point WAN   A WAN that connects two distant devices using a line available from a public network provider such as a telephone network.

polar encoding   A digital-to-digital encoding method that has two levels (one positive and one negative).

poll   In the primary/secondary access method, a procedure in which the primary station asks a secondary station if it has any data to send.

poll/select   An access method protocol using poll and select procedures.

POP   See *point of presence.*

POP3   See *Post Office Protocol, version 3.*

port address   In TCP/IP protocol an integer identifying a process.

port number   An integer that defines a process running on a host.

Post Office Protocol, version 3 (POP3)   A popular but simple SMTP mail access protocol.

prefix   For a network, another name for the common part of the address range (similar to the netid).

presentation layer   The sixth layer of the OSI model responsible for translation, encryption, authentication, and data compression.

Pretty Good Privacy (PGP)   A protocol that provides all four aspects of security in the sending of email.

primary computer   In the primary/secondary access method, a station that issues commands to the secondary stations.

privacy   A security aspect in which the message makes sense only to the intended receiver.

private key   In conventional encryption, a key shared by only one pair of devices, a sender and a receiver. In public-key encryption, the private key is known only to the receiver.

private network   A network that is isolated from the Internet.

proactive fault management   A part of fault management that tries to prevent faults.

protocol   Rules for communication.

protocol analyzer   A sophisticated line monitor that can simulate the behavior of a network component (such as a modem or a router) and can check the behavior of some network protocols

proxy firewall   A firewall that filters a message based on the information available in the message itself (at the application layer).

PSK   See *phase shift keying.*

public key   In public-key encryption, a key known to everyone.

public-key encryption   A method of encryption based on a nonreversible encryption algorithm. The method uses two types of keys: The public key is known to the public; the private key (secret key) is known only to the receiver.

pulse code modulation (PCM)   A technique that modifies PAM pulses to create a digital signal.

pure ATM LAN   A LAN in which an ATM switch is used to connect the stations in a LAN, in the same way stations are connected to an Ethernet switch.

Q

quantization   Assigning a specific number of bits to a sample of an analog signal.

R

radio frequency (RF) signal   A signal with frequencies in the 1 to 20 GHz range that can be used to transmit data between stations in a wireless LAN.

radio frequency wave   Electromagnetic energy in the 3-KHz to 300-GHz range.

random access   A medium access method in which each computer contends for access to the medium.

RARP   See *reverse address resolution protocol.*

reactive fault management   A part of fault management that deals with the fault after it has happened.

receiver   The target point of a transmission.

redundancy   The addition of bits to a message for error control.

reflection   The phenomenon related to the bouncing back of light at the boundary of two substances of different densities.

refraction   The phenomenon related to the bending back of light at the boundary of two substances of different densities.

regional ISP   A small ISP that is connected to one or more NSPs.

reliability   A network criterion that can be measured by frequency of failure, recovery time after a failure, and a network's robustness in a catastrophe.

reliable service   A service that guarantees damage control, loss control, order control, and duplicate control.

remote login (rlogin)   The process of logging on to a remote computer from a terminal connected to a local computer.

repeater   A device that extends the distance a signal can travel by regenerating the signal.

Request for Comment (RFC)   A formal Internet document concerning an Internet issue.

response time   The amount of time from the user request to the time the service is granted.

Reverse Address Resolution Protocol (RARP)   A TCP/IP protocol that allows a host to find its Internet address given its physical address.

RF   See *radio frequency.*

RFC   See *Request for Comment.*

ring topology   A topology in which the devices are connected in a ring. Each device on the ring receives the data unit from the previous device, regenerates it, and forwards it to the next device.

RIP   See *routing information protocol.*

rlogin   A remote login application designed by BSD UNIX.

router   An internetworking device operating at the first three OSI layers. A router is attached to two or more networks and forwards packets from one network to another.

router-based backbone   A backbone in which the LANs are connected through routers.

routing   The process performed by a router; finding the next hop for a datagram.

Routing Information Protocol (RIP)   A routing protocol based on the distance vector routing algorithm.

routing switch   A switch that combines the functions of a bridge and a router using the network layer destination address.

routing table   A table containing information a router needs to route packets. The information may include the network address, the cost, the address of the next hop, and so on.

RSA encryption   A popular public-key encryption method developed by Rivest, Shamir, and Adleman.

S

sampling   The process of obtaining amplitudes of a signal at regular intervals.

scatternet   A combination of piconets.

scope needs   In the NDLC, finding the needs of the networks, backbone, and global access.

SDLC   See *system development life cycle.*

secondary computer   In the primary/secondary access method, a station that sends a response in answer to a command from a primary computer.

secret key   The key used by both sender and receiver in secret-key encryption.

secret-key encryption   A security method in which the key for encryption is the same as the key for decryption; both sender and receiver have the same key.

security   The protection of a network from unauthorized access, viruses, and catastrophe.

security management   A branch of network management dealing with the security and integrity of a network.

segment   The packet at the TCP layer.

select   In the primary/secondary access method, a procedure in which the primary computer asks a secondary if it is ready to receive data.

semantics   The meaning of each section of bits.

sender   The originator of a message.

sequence number   The number that denotes the location of a frame or packet in a message.

serial transmission   Transmission of data one bit at a time using only one single link.

server   A program that can provide services to other programs called clients.

session layer   The fifth layer of the OSI model, responsible for the establishment, management, and termination of logical connections between two end users.

SHF   See *superhigh frequency.*

shielded twisted-pair (STP)   Twisted pair cable enclosed in a foil or mesh shield that protects against electromagnetic interference.

shortest path   The optimal path from the source to the destination.

signal   Electromagnetic waves propagated along a transmission medium.

simple bridge   A networking device that links two segments; requires manual maintenance and updating.

Simple Mail Transfer Protocol (SMTP)   The TCP/IP protocol defining electronic mail service on the Internet.

Simple Network Management Protocol (SNMP)   The TCP/IP protocol that specifies the process of management in the Internet.

sine wave   An amplitude-versus-time representation of a rotating vector.

single-bit error   Error in a data unit in which only one bit has been altered.

single-mode fiber   An optical fiber with an extremely small diameter that limits beams to a few angles, resulting in an almost horizontal beam.

sliding window ARQ   An error control method that allows multiple data units to be in transition before receiving an acknowledgment.

SMI   See *Structure of Management Information.*

SMTP   See *Simple Mail Transfer Protocol.*

SNMP   See *Simple Network Management Protocol.*

software documentation   Part of configuration management that records all software changes.

software reconfiguration   A part of configuration management that governs all changes to the software.

SONET   See *synchronous optical network.*

source address   The address of the sender of the message.

source-to-destination delivery   The transmission of a message from the original sender to the intended recipient.

space propagation   A type of propagation that can penetrate the ionosphere.

specification Hardware information such as hardware type, serial number, vendor (address and phone number), time of purchase, and warranty information.

spread spectrum A wireless transmission technique that requires a bandwidth several times the original bandwidth.

standard A basis or model to which everyone has agreed.

star topology A topology in which all stations are attached to a central device (hub).

static routing table A routing table used in static routing; usually manually updated.

station A device such as a computer, printer, or modem on a LAN; sometimes called a node.

stop-and-wait ARQ An error control method that allows only one data unit to be in transition before receiving an acknowledgment.

Structure of Management Information (SMI) In SNMP, a component used in network management.

subnet See *subnetwork*.

subnet address The network address of a subnet.

subnetid The part of an IP address common to all computers connected to the same subnet.

subnetwork A part of a network.

suffix For a network, the varying part (similar to the hostid) of the address. In DNS, a string used by an organization to define its host or resources.

superhigh frequency (SHF) Radio waves in the 3-GHz to 30-GHz range using line-of-sight and space propagation.

switch A device connecting multiple communication lines together.

switched Ethernet An Ethernet in which a switch, replacing the hub, can direct a transmission to its destination.

switched WAN A connection-oriented wide area network that covers a large area (a state or a country) to provide access at several points to the user. Frame Relay and ATM are switched WANs.

switching office The place where telephone switches are located.

synchronization points Reference points introduced into the data by the session layer for the purpose of flow and error control.

synchronous optical network (SONET) A standard developed by ANSI for fiber-optic technology that can transmit high-speed data. It can be used to deliver text, audio, and video.

synchronous TDM A multiplexing technique in which each frame contains at least one time slot for each device.

synchronous transmission A transmission method that requires a constant timing relationship between the sender and the receiver.

syntax The structure or format of data, meaning the order in which they are presented.

system development life cycle (SDLC) A generic methodology for developing any system.

system documentation Documentation for the maintenance and future modification of a network.

T

T-1 line A 1.544-Mbps digital transmission line.

T-3 line A 44.736-Mbps digital transmission line.

T-lines   A hierarchy of digital lines designed to carry speech and other signals in digital forms. The hierarchy defines T-1, T-2, T-3, and T-4 lines.

TCP   See *Transmission Control Protocol.*

TCP/IP   See *Transmission Control Protocol/Internetworking Protocol.*

TCP/IP protocol suite   A group of hierarchical protocols used in an internet.

TDM   See *time-division multiplexing.*

Telcordia   A company (formerly Bellcore) involved in the research and development of telecommunications technology.

telecommunication   Exchange of information over distance using electronic equipment.

TELNET   See *Terminal Network.*

Terminal Network (TELNET)   A general purpose client-server program that allows remote login.

terminator   An electronic device that prevents signal reflections at the end of a cable.

testing phase   In the NDLC, monitoring the system while the users are using the system.

TFTP   See *Trivial File Transfer Protocol.*

three-layer switch   A router that can receive, process, and dispatch a packet much faster than a traditional router even though the functionality is the same.

three-way handshake   A sequence of events for connection establishment or termination consisting of the request, then the acknowledgment of the request, and then confirmation of the acknowledgment.

throughput   The number of bits that can pass through a point in 1 second.

time division multiplexing (TDM)   The technique of combining signals from low-speed channels to share time on a high-speed path.

timing   Referring to when data must be sent and how fast it can be sent.

TLS   See *Transport Layer Security.*

token   A small packet used in token-passing access method.

token passing   An access method in which a token is circulated in the network. The station that captures the token can send data.

TOS   See *type of service.*

touch-tone dialing   A telephone dialing method in which each key is represented by 2 small bursts of analog signals.

traffic   The number of packets (or bytes) traveling inside or outside the network.

trailer   Control information appended to a data unit.

translation   Changing from one code or protocol to another.

Transmission Control Protocol (TCP)   A transport protocol in the TCP/IP protocol suite.

Transmission Control Protocol /Internetworking Protocol (TCP/IP)   A five-layer protocol suite that defines the exchange of transmissions across the Internet.

transmission medium   The physical path linking two communication devices.

transparent bridge   Another name for a learning bridge.

transport layer   The fourth layer in the OSI model; responsible for reliable end-to-end delivery and error recovery.

Transport Layer Security (TLS)   A security protocol at the transport level designed to provide security on the WWW.

Trivial File Transfer Protocol (TFTP)   An unreliable TCP/IP protocol for file transfer that does not require complex interaction between client and server.

trunk   Transmission media that handle the communication between offices.

tunneling   In multicasting, a process in which the multicast packet is encapsulated in a unicast packet and then sent through the network. In VPN, the encapsulation of an encrypted IP datagram in a second outer datagram. For IPv6, a strategy used when two computers using IPv6 want to communicate with each other when the packet must pass through a region that uses IPv4.

twisted-pair cable   A transmission medium consisting of 2 insulated conductors in a twisted configuration.

two-layer switch   A bridge with many interfaces and a design that allows better (faster) performance.

type of service (TOS)   A criteria or value that specifies the handling of the datagram.

U

UA   See *user agent.*

UDP   See *user datagram protocol.*

UHF   See *ultrahigh frequency.*

ultrahigh frequency (UHF)   Radio waves in the 300-MHz to 3-GHz range using line-of-sight propagation.

unguided medium   A transmission medium with no physical boundaries.

unicasting   The sending of a packet to just one destination.

uniform resource locator (URL)   A string of characters (address) that identifies a page on the World Wide Web.

unipolar encoding   A digital-to-digital encoding method in which one nonzero value represents either 1 or 0; the other bit is represented by a zero value.

unreliable service   A service that cannot guarantee damage control, loss control, order control, and duplicate control.

unshielded twisted-pair (UTP)   A cable with wires that are twisted together to reduce noise and crosstalk.

uploading   Sending a local file or data to a remote site.

URL   See *uniform resource locator.*

user agent (UA)   An SMTP component that prepares the message, creates the envelope, and puts the message in the envelope.

user datagram   The name of the packet in the UDP protocol.

User Datagram Protocol (UDP)   A connectionless TCP/IP transport layer protocol.

user documentation   Documentation for the user such as commands, potential problems, and the person to call in case of malfunction.

user needs   In the NDLC, finding the hardware, software, and bandwidth needs of the user.

user-account documentation   A part of configuration management that records changes in user accounts.

user-account reconfiguration   A part of configuration management responsible for changes in the user accounts.

UTP   See *unshielded twisted-pair.*

V

V.32bis   An ITU-T modem that is an enhanced version of V.32; it features an automatic fall-back and fall-forward mechanism.

V.33   An ITU-T 2400-baud modem that is an enhanced version of V.32; it uses trellis-coded modulation based on 128-QAM.

V.34   An ITU-T 2400-baud modem that provides data compression.

VCI   See *virtual connection identifier.*

vertical redundancy check (VRC)   An error-detection method based on per-character parity check.

videoconferencing   A service that allows a group of users to exchange real-time video and audio data over a network.

virtual circuit identifier (VCI)   A field in an ATM cell that identifies a circuit.

virtual connection identifier   A VPI or VCI.

virtual LAN (VLAN)   A technology that divides a LAN into virtual workgroups.

virtual path identifier (VPI)   A field in an ATM cell header that identifies a path.

virtual private network (VPN)   A technology which creates a network which is physically public, but virtually private.

VLAN   See *virtual LAN.*

VPI   See *virtual path identifier.*

VPI/VCI   See *virtual path identifier/virtual channel identifier.*

VPN   See *virtual private network.*

VRC   See *vertical redundancy check.*

W

WAN   See *wide area network.*

wave division multiplexing (WDM)   The combining of modulated light signals into one signal.

WDM   See *wave division multiplexing.*

Web   Synonym for World Wide Web (WWW).

well-known port number   A port number that identifies a process on the server.

white noise   An unwanted signal due to the heat created by the movement of electrons.

wide area network (WAN)   A network that uses a technology that can span a large geographical distance.

wireless communication   Communication using unguided media.

wireless LAN   A LAN using unguided medium for data transmission.

wireless transmission   Data transmission using unguided medium.

World Wide Web (WWW)   A multimedia Internet service that allows users to traverse the Internet by moving from one document to another via links that connect them together.

WWW   See *World Wide Web.*

X

X.25   An ITU-T standard that defines the interface between a data terminal device and a packet-switching network.

INDEX